POPULAR
LITURGI-
CAL
LIBRARY

The Church's

YEAR OF GRACE

by

DR. PIUS PARSCH

revised according to the directives for the Simplification
of the Rubrics and the Restored Holy Week Liturgy

TRANSLATED BY
Reverend William G. Heidt, O.S.B.

Volume 4
June, July, August

THE LITURGICAL PRESS
ST. JOHN'S ABBEY   COLLEGEVILLE, MINNESOTA

Nihil obstat: John Eidenschink, O.S.B., J.C.D., *Censor deputatus. Imprimi potest*: ✠ Baldwin Dworschak, O.S.B., Abbot of St. John's Abbey. *Imprimatur*: ✠ Peter W. Bartholome, D.D., Bishop of St. Cloud, August 1, 1959. Copyright 1959 by The Order of St. Benedict, Inc., Collegeville, Minnesota.

Printed by The North Central Publishing Company, St. Paul.

February 1962

The Proper of the Season

THE SEASON AFTER PENTECOST

1. The Sundays after Pentecost. Both the octave of Pentecost and the Easter season come to an end on the Saturday after Pentecost (at None, the afternoon prayer of the Church). Thereupon the Church continues with another phase of the year of grace, one that may be called the Season after Pentecost; it is not, however, a distinct cycle in the sense formerly understood and taught. For Pentecost belongs to the Easter cycle, it is its denouement, or prolongation. The Sundays after Pentecost are the echo of the Easter solemnities.

Nevertheless, one may say that these twenty-four or more weeks do form a special group differentiated from Eastertide, for instance, by a limitation in the use of *Alleluia*. As to content, there is only a loose connection with Easter. The Christian who at Easter received divine life through baptism or through its sacramental renewal should during the course of the year, especially on Sundays, nurture and bring it to maturity by means of the Eucharist; he should again and again reject all that is unholy or worldly while awaiting the Lord with readiness and sincere yearning. Sunday, the "Lord's Day," should, as a little Easter feast, refresh in Christian souls the whole good fortune of Easter (baptism, confirmation, Eucharist) and should equip them against the world, lower self, and hell. Such was the import of the olden Sunday liturgy, and such also is the significance of the current series of Sundays.

The liturgy for these Sundays originated in the earliest centuries of the Church, but its present form and arrangement date to the pontificate of Pope St. Gregory the Great. Modifications, of course, and rearrangements which did not always add to the

3

perfection of the text were made during the Middle Ages; it would be a task for liturgical scholars to publish anew the original form and arrangement of the various Mass formularies.

As children of a streamlined age, we would love to find in the current array of twenty-four Sundays a progression of thought, a system, a unifying principle; and therefore the attempt has often been made to inject into them some schematic development or idea evolution. This was not the mentality of ancient times. In the early centuries Mother Church merely wished to give her children little Easter feasts, little parousia feasts. Sunday after Sunday in colorful array she presented the mysteries of redemption, usually with reference to baptism or as a preparation for Christ's Second Coming. Much less than in the Masses of the previous cycle of Lent and Easter are we to seek a unifying theme, since even the Lessons (i.e., Epistle and Gospel), which in other Masses are often related, now are seldom of like or complementary mold.

Furthermore, the ancient arrangement of pericopes for successive Sundays has been lost. It happened this way. For centuries there were no missals containing the complete text for a given Mass; the various parts were scattered about in several books, e.g., the chants in the antiphonary, the Epistles in the lectionary, the Gospels in the Gospel-book, the Orations in the sacramentary. Then, for example, if a change was made in the order of Lessons taken from the lectionary by adding or omitting a reading (which actually happened), the readings on all the following Sundays would be affected. As a matter of fact, it is difficult today to tell which chants, which Orations, which Epistles and which Gospels belonged originally to a given date. With regard to the coming Sundays, however, this displacement is of no great significance because the separate formularies have no specific thought unity and because the various Sundays are quite similar to each other in general theological content.

Surveying these Sundays as a whole, we quickly note three motifs, of which one is now dominant, now the other. The first concerns the past, the Easter motif. It is anchored in the Easter

solemnity and seeks to renew the Easter mysteries every Sunday;
here we see Christ as the Giver of life, as Physician, as Savior.
The second scans the future, the parousia motif; it emphasizes
the *majestas Domini* and prepares us for Christ's Second Coming.
The ancient Church journeyed through this world in pilgrim's
garb, homesick at heart. The *Maranatha* — "Come, Lord, come!"
— of the first Christians has left its impress upon the sacred
text of the liturgy. This motif bestows a peculiar beauty upon the
final Sundays of the season (18th to 24th). The third motif, that
of suffering and conflict, touches the present; its spirit is strongest
in the middle group of Pentecost Sundays; the inroad of night
upon day in nature is symbolic of this conflict as the year
approaches its end.

From the viewpoint of content, the Sunday Masses of the
Pentecost cycle could well be divided into three groups. The
first emphasizes miracle-cures. Accounts of Christ's miracles are
related, yet these narratives are not intended for instruction primarily, but rather as indications of the operations of God's grace
in the Mass. Such, too, was the ultimate aim and end of our Lord
when He worked wonders. In the days of His earthly life He
healed bodily infirmities, now during His mystical life in the
Church He wills to be the "Savior" of the soul's infirmities; this
He accomplishes primarily through baptism and through the
holy Eucharist. The miracle-cures of the Gospel are used to
present pictorially the inner, sanctifying action of Sunday Mass.
This is what is meant by the term *mysterium*.

A second group tends to employ contrast pictures — the kingdom of God versus the kingdom of the world. These contrast
pictures are found principally in the Masses from the seventh to
the fourteenth Sunday after Pentecost. It is not implied that the
Church leaves us free to choose between the two kingdoms; but
she would have us realize that we ought more diligently "seek
the kingdom of God" and banish from the soul the latest and
least advance of Satan's kingdom. Ancient piety often employed
this pedagogical method (e.g., the Didache; Psalm 1).

The third class, which concentrates on the parousia, is proper to the Sundays from the fifteenth to the end of the year. These Masses are exceptional for variety of mood and depth of doctrine.

Other approaches to and evaluations of the Pentecost Mass formularies have been made. Some authors give as thematic the three theological virtues, with love dominant during the first six Sundays; faith, or more correctly, life flowing from faith during a middle group; and hope, in the ancient Christian sense of yearning for the Second Advent, from the eighteenth Sunday to the end. As a matter of fact, the first Sundays do treat of love, e.g., the Epistle on the first Sunday, the Collect and Epistle on the second Sunday, the Collect, Epistle, and Gospel on the fifth Sunday, the Collect on the sixth Sunday. Neither can it be disputed that hope dominates the final Sundays. Therefore the most that can be doubted is the faith-motif for the middle group. Had this classification been intended, it no doubt would have been an application of the Collect on the thirteenth Sunday after Pentecost: "Almighty and eternal God, grant unto us an increase of faith, hope, and love. . . ."

At some occasion the Masses of the Pentecost season were subjected to a full-scale editing, as is evident from the numerical order in the sequence of the chants. Such sequence, however, is not alien to liturgical method.

Sunday	Intr.	Allel.	Off.	Comm.
1	Ps. 12	Ps. 5	Ps. 5	Ps. 9
2	17	7	6	12
3	24	7	9	—
4	26	9	12	17
5	26	20	15	26
6	27	30	16	26
7	46	46	—	30
8	47	47	17	33
9	53	58	18	—
10	54	64	24	50
11	67	80	29	—
12	69	87	—	103

Sunday	Intr.	Allel.	Off.	Comm
13	73	89	30	-
14	83	94	33	-
15	85	94	39	-
16	85	97	39	-
17	118	101	—	-
18	—	101	—	-
19	—	104	—	-
20	—	107	—	-
21	—	113	—	-
22	—	113	—	-
23	—	129	—	—

The Readings, too, betray a systematizing. For instance, the Epistles consist of selections from Scripture, yet they follow the Bible order from the sixth Sunday to the twenty-fourth; the one exception occurs on the eighteenth Sunday, a sign indicating insertion at a later date.

Whether the frequency of St. Luke's Gospel until the sixteenth Sunday and St. Matthew's on the last Sundays indicates editing or an ancient *lectio continua* remains open to investigation.

During medieval times the Sundays after Pentecost were grouped about and named after the feasts of certain saints. Thus the Sundays preceding and following the feast of Sts. Peter and Paul were so designated, likewise the Sundays after the feast of St. Lawrence (11th to 15th Sundays), the Sundays after the feast of St. Cyprian (16th to 19th), and the Sundays after Michaelmas (20th to 24th). The superficial character of such grouping would not be difficult to establish.

From the above remarks on structure and sequence it is legitimate to infer the venerable antiquity of the Pentecost Mass formularies. Nevertheless, an air of mystery will always becloud their origin. The sphinx does not guard its secrets more cautiously.

A final, brief observation, for we must not overlook the literary beauty of the coming Masses. "It is exactly in their unassuming, modest dress that they conceal an unusual wealth of sprightliness and life, of mood and spirit. To the sensitive soul they reveal the loving, longing spirit of Mother Church, and do much to spread that spirit" (*Die betende Kirche*, 2. Auflage, Augustinus-Verlag, Berlin, p. 357).

2. **Scripture Reading during the Time after Pentecost.** A liturgically-minded Christian will discipline himself to regular, daily reading of the Bible. For the relations between Bible and liturgy are most important. To the question: Has the Church, in reading the books of the Old Testament, a deeper, more profound purpose than that of moral instruction and edification?, Abbot Herwegen has given this reply: In the course of the ecclesiastical year from Advent until Pentecost, the liturgy treats the historical life of Jesus and bestows its concomitant graces. In the time after Pentecost, however, it borrows typical scenes from the annals of the Old Testament for presenting Christ's kingdom. The story of the kingdom of God, the *civitas Dei*, as unfolded by the liturgy is therefore sacred prophecy which through the centuries becomes actual in the Church of Christ.

Three major periods can be discerned in the development of the kingdom-mystery during the Pentecost season. The first period treats the establishment and spread of Christ's kingdom. Samuel, who gave unity to his people, prepares the kingdom (1st to 3rd Sunday); David (4th to 7th) and Solomon (8th), the bearers of royalty during its finest era, are types of rulers pleasing to God. But also during days of spiritual decline does God's powerful arm rule over king and people; for He acts through His chosen ones, Elias (8th to 10th Sunday) and Isaias (11th Sunday).

With the first Sunday in August, the second phase in the history of Christ's kingdom begins. Attention is no longer directed to historical episodes but rather is centered upon interior edification, principally by the Books of Wisdom. The Parables of Solomon (1st Sun.), Ecclesiastes (2nd Sun.), the Book of Wisdom (3rd Sun.), and Ecclesiasticus (4th and 5th Sun.) deepen our knowledge of God and of the requirements of moral living.

Instruction in biographical dress is the burden of the two books, Job (1st and 2nd Sun. of September), and Tobit (3rd Sun.). These readings form a transition from the theology of the Sapiential books to the concrete, ideal personalities of Judith (4th Sun.) and Esther (5th Sun.), whose hero-love toward the true God and toward their people is so much more impressive because it is embodied in women. The protection of God's kingdom and the defense of His spiritual possessions gave rise to the Hasmonean heroes, the story of whose exploits forms the burden of the two Books of the Machabees (October).

The prophet Ezechiel introduces the third phase, the consummation of Christ's kingdom, and stamps it with an eschatological seal (November). Ezechiel's visions and the oracles of the remaining prophets down to Malachias, who closes the series, tell of the last times, of the transition of the earthly *civitas Dei* into the heavenly, and of God's eternal rule (see *Alte Quellen neuer Kraft*, p. 109 ff.).

FIRST SUNDAY AFTER PENTECOST

On the first Sunday after Pentecost there begins the *tempus per annum*, a time marked by no special mysteries in the Proper of the Season. Immediately, however, some Sundays are supplanted or overshadowed by feasts. Thus the first Sunday after Pentecost yields its place to the feast of the Most Holy Trinity. The Sunday liturgy, commemorated in the Orations, may, of course, be resumed on the ferial days of the ensuing week.

FEAST OF THE
MOST HOLY TRINITY

Glory be to the Father, and to the Son, and to the Holy Spirit

The feasts and seasons that have occurred thus far during the ecclesiastical year were closely linked to sacred history, especially to the Gospel narratives of Christ's life. From Christmas to Pentecost we observed in mystery the earthly activity of our holy Redeemer. The Sacrifice of Mass offered on various feasts and ferials actualized the sacred event commemorated, making present its peculiar graces. Now we meet certain feasts that are oriented quite differently, "faith-feasts" in which a mystery of our religion is made the object of liturgical worship. In these faith-feasts, the bond with the Sacrifice itself is no longer so intimate; for the Church celebrates holy Mass on the occasion simply in honor of a given dogma. The first of these, the feast of the Most Holy Trinity, has as object the greatest, the most profound and incomprehensible truth of our holy faith. The feast was introduced into the Roman Church by Pope John XXII in 1334.

1. **The dogma of faith** which forms the object of today's feast is this: There is one God and in this one God there are three divine Persons; the Father is God, the Son is God, the Holy Spirit is God. Yet there are not three Gods, but one, eternal, incomprehensible God! The Father is not more God than the Son, neither is the Son more God than the Holy Spirit. The Father is the first divine Person; the Son is the second divine Person, begotten from the nature of the Father from eternity; the Holy Spirit is the third divine Person, proceeding from the Father and the Son. No mortal can fully fathom this sublime

truth. But I submit humbly and say: Lord, I believe, help my weak faith.

Why is this feast celebrated at this particular time? It may be interpreted as a finale to all the preceding feasts. All three Persons contributed to and shared in the work of redemption. The Father sent His Son to earth, for "God so loved the world as to give His only-begotten Son." The Father called us to the faith. The Son, our Savior Jesus Christ, became man and died for us. He redeemed us and made us children of God. He ever remains the liturgist *par excellence* to whom we are united in all sacred functions. After Christ's ascension the Holy Spirit, however, became our Teacher, our Leader, our Guide, our Consoler. On solemn occasions a thanksgiving *Te Deum* rises spontaneously from Christian hearts.

The feast of the Most Holy Trinity may well be regarded as the Church's *Te Deum* of gratitude over all the blessings of the Christmas and Easter seasons; for today's mystery is a synthesis of Christmas, Epiphany, Easter, Ascension and Pentecost. This feast, which falls on the first Sunday after Pentecost, should make us mindful that actually every Sunday is devoted to the honor of the Most Holy Trinity, that every Sunday is sanctified and consecrated to the triune God. Sunday after Sunday we should recall in a spirit of gratitude the gifts which the Blessed Trinity is bestowing upon us. The Father created and predestined us; on the first day of the week He began the work of creation. The Son redeemed us; Sunday is the "Day of the Lord," the day of His resurrection. The Holy Spirit sanctified us, made us His temple; on Sunday the Holy Spirit descended upon the infant Church. Sunday, therefore, is *the* day of the Most Holy Trinity.

Meditation. Try to realize how your whole life begins and ends by virtue of the Holy Trinity. Recall how the sacraments or how the blessings are administered in the Name of the Father, Son, and Holy Spirit. Take, for instance, the sacrament of baptism, "I baptize you in the Name of the Father, and of the Son, and of the Holy Spirit." Or the sacrament of penance, "I absolve you from your sins in the Name of the Father, and of the Son, and of the

Holy Spirit." At your deathbed the priest will say: "Go forth from this world, O Christian soul, in the Name of God the Father almighty who created you; in the Name of Jesus Christ, the Son of the living God, who suffered for you; in the Name of the Holy Spirit who has been poured forth upon you." The life of a Christian begins and ends in the Name of the Blessed Trinity. Therefore, begin and close each day, each week, each prayer with the words: "In the Name of the Father, and of the Son, and of the Holy Spirit."

One could also meditate upon the many prayers that are directed to the Blessed Trinity. First of all, the "Glory be to the Father, and to the Son, and to the Holy Spirit, as it was in the beginning, is now, and ever shall be, world without end. Amen." Surely no prayer is said more often. It forms the conclusion to every psalm, and every Hour of the Divine Office is begun with it. Truly the "Glory be" is like a chime in the church tower that is ever ringing. Every priest prays this acclamation of praise to the Blessed Trinity more than fifty times each day. The "Glory be" is called the lesser doxology, while the greater doxology is the *Gloria in excelsis* of the Mass. The soul-stirring *Te Deum*, a praise and thanksgiving chant to the triune God, is prayed very frequently at the end of Matins.

A splendid array of prayers in honor of the Blessed Trinity has developed to form the Ordinary of the Mass. One immediately sees how the Mass of the Catechumens is Trinitarian throughout; the *Kyrie* — petition to the Blessed Trinity; the *Gloria* — praise to the triune God; the Oration — directed to the three divine Persons by its conclusion. The three messages — Epistle, Gospel, Sermon — are linked very closely to the three divine Persons, while the *Credo* is a joyous acknowledgment of our faith in the Father, Son, and Holy Spirit. A special profession of faith in the Trinity is made today at Prime, the Athanasian Creed. The finest prayer to the Blessed Trinity is holy Mass itself, for it is the supreme expression of praise, thanksgiving, and petition to the triune God.

2. **Holy Mass (Benedicta sit).** The Mass formulary is not

difficult to understand. The *Introit* voices the spirit of the celebrant upon approaching the altar and of the people upon coming to church. As we enter God's house today, the Blessed Trinity appears before us in might, in goodness, in beauty; and our hearts burst forth in song: "Blessed be the holy Trinity, because He has shown us mercy." The Introit psalm is a nature-hymn which praises the triune God for having "shown Himself wonderful in the world, in the lips of children, and in the stars of heaven."

The *Collect* speaks of a twofold divine greatness, the mighty *unity* and the harmonious *plurality* in the Godhead. We acclaim the majesty of the Trinity and adore the inherent oneness of nature; with unflinching faith in this mystery we plead for protection in all the vicissitudes of life. The mystery also affords a model for action, because our lives and personalities should reflect our origin; may our thought and conduct show holy unity and a beautiful, lovable harmony.

In the *Epistle* Paul is filled with amazement when, with the eyes of faith, he scans the unfathomable mystery: "Oh, the depths of the riches. . . ." He scarcely finds words to express his awe in the presence of the infinite, impenetrable dogma of the triune God. "Of Him (the Father), and by Him (the Son), and in Him (the Holy Spirit) are all things." In the *Gradual-Alleluia* we respond with a threefold *Blessed!* as in spirit we scan a tremendous field; we watch God surveying the depths as He sits enthroned over all the cherubim; to our fathers, in the fortunes of mankind, in the ways of men, the Blessed Trinity manifests Its glory.

In the *Gospel* we meet the principal Scripture passage which mentions the three divine Persons. Christ gives His apostles the command: "Go . . . baptize in the Name of the Father and of the Son and of the Holy Spirit." Our own selves should be the gift dedicated to the Blessed Trinity at the *Offertory*. During the distribution of holy Communion the Church says to us: This Bread from heaven is a love-token from the triune God. Christ effected your salvation, the Father preordained your redemption by calling you, the Holy Spirit is infusing grace after grace to insure your perseverance. The *Secret* prays for the sanctification of the offered gifts; by holiness of life you may make yourself an abiding oblation to the holy Trinity. For a third time at the *Communion* we praise the holy Trinity "because He has shown His mercy to us." *Postcommunion*: the holy Sacrifice should confirm our faith in the sublime mystery and provide protection against the dangers besetting body and soul.

In ancient times this Sunday was aliturgical because the Mass of Ember Saturday was celebrated toward Sunday morning. Later the formulary of the first Sunday after Pentecost was introduced, then the feast of All Saints from the Orient. Only in the fourteenth century did the feast of the Blessed Trinity supplant the Sunday liturgy; since then the latter is resumed on the ferial days preceding Corpus Christi.

FIRST SUNDAY AFTER PENTECOST

Mercy Sunday

As we celebrate this Mass, we immediately sense the change in mood and spirit — no longer are we in the festive Easter season. During Eastertide every chant ended with an *alleluia*, not so now. And the Gradual occurs again. There are, as a rule, two chants between the Readings — the Gradual, an echo of the Epistle, and the Alleluia, a prelude to the Gospel. In liturgical symbolism the Gradual is, by nature, a chant of petition and of penance. Therefore it is omitted during Eastertide and in its place a double Alleluia is sung. Now the two usual chants appear again, and thereby we wish to indicate that ordinarily joy is mixed with sober reserve, and penance with praise.

1. **Text Analysis.** It is a long time since the priest came to the altar clothed in green vestments. This color, it is true, was

foreign to ancient liturgy; neither does liturgical history provide an explanation for its symbolism. Nevertheless, it is not forbidden to attach symbolic meanings to a custom once it has been introduced. Green is the color of the olive or the olive tree, which reminds us of Christ, the Anointed. Green, too, is the color of the sprouting seed; the time after Pentecost is the period of growth in God's kingdom upon earth, the time between the Lord's ascension into heaven and His Second Coming, the time of joyous hope in the approaching end.

During antiquity this Sunday was called "Mercy Sunday," for its many beautiful texts are charged with "mercy and love." I have received the mercy of God in plentiful measure through the graces of redemption: "By this has the love of God been proven to us — He has sent His only-begotten Son into the world that we may live through Him" (*Epist.*). I have experienced His mercy in forgiveness (*Intr.*). And I should return that love to my brothers through love, sympathy, and pardon: "Therefore be merciful as your Father also is merciful. Do not judge, and you will not be judged. Forgive and you will be forgiven" (*Gosp.*). "If God so loved us, we too ought love one another" (*Epist.*). The nexus between the love of God and the love of neighbor is arrestingly stated: "If any man says, 'I love God,' but hates his brother, he is a liar. For he who does not love his brother whom he sees, how can he love God whom he does not see? This commandment we have from God: he who loves God must also love his brother."

In today's formulary the noblest commandment of Christianity is enjoined, and that in a clear and appealing manner. Today's Mass "is, as it were, a sublime and sacred inscription upon the archway leading into the Sundays after Pentecost" (Schott, *Messbuch*).

2. **Holy Mass (Domine in tua).** Depressed by the burdens of life, the soul appears before the face of God (*Intr.* — such is the case at most Sunday Masses during the Pentecostal cycle), but not in a spirit of despair, "I trust in Your kindness," i.e., in the saving graces which now in the holy Sacrifice will be given out abundantly. Psalm 12 covers the whole scale of emotions from

utter dejection to grateful joy. The *Collect* continues the theme; God is the strength of those who hope in Him; without Him human efforts are vain. With His aid we can observe the commandments. It is a terse, thought-crammed prayer that could well be made the object of a lengthy meditation.

A precious *Epistle*, from the pen of the beloved Apostle, treats of love, that all-embracing love which goes out from God, returns to Him, embraces all. The *Gradual* is antiphonal in structure, that is, the first verse is the antiphon and the second verse is the first verse of the psalm (that could be said *in toto*). This chant links God's mercy with man's mercy, the principal object of the Mass. Mercy is the keyword of the entire formulary (*Intr., Grad., Gosp.*). The *Alleluia* verse is not true to type; it should voice praise, not a heavy-hearted petition. In the *Gospel* Jesus opens His heart on the subject of love of neighbor and its reward; He condemns the pharisee who sees the faults of others but is blind to his own shortcomings.

At the *Offertory* I approach the altar imploring help, for "my King and my God" is there enthroned. The *Secret* requests a gracious acceptance of the gifts we offer because they can be "a source of constant help." At the *Communion* our voices ring out in a joyful hymn over the wonders of grace that have been our portion. Such, indeed, is the mood of most Sundays — earnest petition at the beginning, joyous thanksgiving at the end. The *Postcommunion* implies gratitude for the princely gifts we have received, gifts that are the seed from which good fruit unto eternal life ought grow. May our life be a continual Eucharist, i.e., a continual thanksgiving.

3. Divine Office. "Speak, Lord, for Your servant is listening." These words form the text for the first Magnificat antiphon in the Pentecost season. How well they give the program for the entire period. God will speak to the soul repeatedly, every Sunday, daily, in fact. Oh, would that each divine word, like so many kernels of seed wheat, fell upon receptive, fertile ground! Let us "be swift to hear, slow to speak" (James 1:19).

Do not overlook the wholesome comment St. Augustine makes

upon the Gospel. "There are two works of mercy that secure our salvation, and our Blessed Lord describes them briefly in the Gospel: *Forgive, and you will be forgiven; give, and it will be given to you.* The first has reference to a ready spirit of overlooking and pardoning faults, the second to the practice of almsgiving. What does He say about pardoning? If you want your own sins to be pardoned, there are others which you must pardon. As regards almsgiving, a beggar asks of you and you are God's beggar. For whenever we pray we are beggars before God. We come to the door of the Father's house, we prostrate ourselves, groaning and begging to receive something; and this something is God Himself. What does the beggar ask of you? Bread. And what do you ask of God? Christ, who says: I am the living Bread that came down from heaven. Do you want forgiveness? Then forgive! Do you want to receive something? Give, and it will be given to you!"

THE FEAST OF CORPUS CHRISTI

Living Bread and Bread Life-bringing

1. **Introduction.** What is it that the Church is celebrating today? The feast is entitled, *Festum Sanctissimi Corporis Christi* — the feast of the most holy Body of Christ. Corpus Christi, then, is a Eucharistic solemnity, or better, the solemn commemoration of the institution of that sacrament. It is, moreover, the Church's official act of homage and gratitude to Christ, who by instituting the holy Eucharist gave to her her greatest treasure. Holy Thursday, assuredly, marks the anniversary of the institution, but the commemoration of the Lord's passion that very night suppresses the rejoicing proper to the occasion. Today's observance, therefore, accents the joyous aspect of Holy Thursday. The first

Thursday after the close of the Easter season was chosen for the feast.

The liturgy for the feast was edited or composed by St. Thomas Aquinas upon the request of Pope Urban IV in the year 1264. It is unquestionably a classic piece of liturgical work, wholly in accord with the best liturgical traditions. Yet a difference may be noted between the Corpus Christi liturgy and the liturgies of older feasts. The latter resemble a virgin-forest, while the Office of Corpus Christi is like an artistically kept flower garden. The older formularies, cast in the mighty mold of the age of martyrs, are generally not too finely or artistically arranged; the newer compositions are distinguished by systematic sequences and by specific art forms. In this latter class Corpus Christi takes a first place. It is a perfect work of art; both in the Mass and in the Office we constantly uncover new evidences of structural grandeur. Let us consider this masterpiece in detail.

Matins begin with an act of royal homage: "Let us adore Christ the King, the Lord of nations." Since the institution of the feast of Christ the King, Christian piety has become more alert to kingship texts in the Bible and liturgy. Readily we see how Corpus Christi is a royalty-feast, an occasion to pay homage to the King who in the Eucharist reigns over the nations.

The hymn follows. The hymns of Corpus Christi taken collectively give proof of the high poetic endowments of their author. In spirit, in rhyme and rhythm they resemble Adam of St. Victor's (1192) much extolled lyrical poetry. Reference need only be made to the monumental verse in the hymn for Lauds (*Verbum Supernum*):

> By birth, our fellow man was He,
> Our Food, while sitting at the board:
> He died, our Ransomer to be,
> He ever reigns, our great reward.

The poet Santolius said he would gladly have given all his works to become the author of these four lines.

Ordinarily the three nocturns of Matins show a development

of the mystery; the first presents the Old Covenant as a foretype, the second is devoted to the feast; while the third brings the Hour to a climax in the Gospel. In Matins today, however, the Lessons of the first nocturn are not taken from the Old Testament but from the New, while the responsories put before us three of the finest figures of the holy Eucharist, the paschal lamb, the manna, and Elias' hearth-cake. St. Thomas shows himself a master in choosing psalms and in adorning them with appropriate antiphons, keys to the psalm's bearing on the Eucharist. The Lessons of the second nocturn, composed by the saint himself, are taken from those writings about which Christ said to him: "Thomas, you have written well of Me!" The responsories of Corpus Christi betray special artistry, for in all of them (excepting one) we find one part taken from the writings of the Old Law and the other from the New; furthermore, in those of the first nocturn the first part presents the type and the versicle its fulfillment.

2. **Divine Office.** With a joyous ring the feast is ushered in by first Vespers, a mosaic of types and their fulfillment. We see "the priest forever after the order of Melchisedech offering bread and wine" (Ps. 109). We see the divine Moses, Christ, on the desert journey of life, "giving food to them that fear Him" (Ps. 110). After the Babylonian exile of unredemption, gratitude is in place: "What shall I render to the Lord for all He has granted me? I will take the chalice of salvation" (Ps. 115). Then a lovely family scene. About a table we see Christ as the Father who earned the family Bread by hardest toil; the Church as the Mother, a fruitful vine; and her children, sprouts on the olive tree (Ps. 127). Psalm 147 shows Jerusalem finally at peace, while her Lord is nourishing all guests with the fat of wheat. "Oh, how loving is Your spirit, Lord! To show sweet kindness to Your children You provide the most delicious, heavenly Bread. You fill the hungry with good things, and send the haughty rich away empty!" (*Magn. Ant.*).

It is night; the Church is praying Matins. How beautifully the Hour flows on, with its crystal-like antiphons interpreting the psalms, with its spirited responsories, with its profoundly theological Lessons! St. Thomas himself composed those of the second nocturn:

"How inestimable a dignity, beloved brethren, divine bounty has bestowed upon us Christians from the treasury of its infinite goodness! For there neither is nor ever has been a people to whom the gods were so nigh as our Lord and God is nigh unto us.

"Desirous that we be made partakers of His divinity, the only-begotten Son of God has taken to Himself our nature so that having become man, He would be enabled to make men gods. Whatever He assumed of our nature He wrought unto our salvation. For on the altar of the Cross He immolated to the Father His own Body as victim for our reconciliation and shed His blood both for our ransom and for our regeneration. Moreover, in order that a remembrance of so great benefits may always be with us, He has left us His Body as food and His Blood as drink under appearances of bread and wine.

"O banquet most precious! O banquet most admirable! O banquet overflowing with every spiritual delicacy! Can anything be more excellent than this repast, in which not the flesh of goats and heifers, as of old, but Christ the true God is given us for nourishment? What more wondrous than this holy sacrament! In it bread and wine are changed substantially, and under the appearance of a little bread and wine is had Christ Jesus, God and perfect Man. In this sacrament sins are purged away, virtues are increased, the soul is satiated with an abundance of every spiritual gift. No other sacrament is so beneficial. Since it was instituted unto the salvation of all, it is offered by Holy Church for the living and for the dead, that all may share in its treasures.

"My dearly beloved, is it not beyond human power to express the ineffable delicacy of this sacrament in which spiritual sweetness is tasted in its very source? in which is brought to mind the remembrance of that all-excelling charity which Christ showed in His sacred passion? Surely it was to impress more profoundly upon the hearts of the faithful the immensity of this charity that our loving Savior instituted this sacrament at the last supper when, having celebrated the Pasch with His disciples, He was about to leave the world and return to the Father. It was to serve as an unending remembrance of His passion, as the fulfillment of ancient types —this the greatest of His miracles. To those who sorrow over His departure He has given a unique solace."

Early in the morning we pray Lauds, creation's morning prayer of praise. Today creation has special reason for praising God, for nature was supremely privileged when Christ made its products, bread and wine, the mantle for His sacramental presence. If men feel honored because of the incarnation of the Son of God, inanimate creation may glory because of the institution of the holy Eucharist.

By way of exception the antiphons at Lauds are not the same as at Vespers and have no direct bearing to their respective psalms. Unlike those of Matins and Vespers, these antiphons do not give the key to the psalms but unravel directly the significance of the Eucharist. Today's five antiphons merit special study.

1) Christ, the divine Wisdom, the wise Architect, has built a house, the Church; here He ministers as the good Host, mingling wine for His guests and preparing the table — the Eucharistic banquet!

2) With the food of angels God nourishes His people; Bread from heaven He offers them!

3) In Psalm 62 we pray: "Let my soul be filled as with marrow and fatness." This verse occasioned the third antiphon: "The Bread of Christ is nourishing; it is a delicacy for kings." We Christians are kings, not slaves to sin.

4) The fourth antiphon culls words from the *Benedicite*, "O ye priests of the Lord, bless the Lord," and points out that the priest can give to the Lord the greatest praise through the incense of liturgical prayer and through the Bread of the Eucharist. This is also true of the lay priesthood.

5) It is characteristic of the liturgy to point to the future toward the end of a sequence of prayers. The Apocalypse promises: "To him who overcomes I will give the hidden manna and a new name." The "hidden manna" foreshadows everlasting

beatitude, the heavenly counterpart to Communion. For the Eucharist typifies the eternal enjoyment of the Godhead. So we have five antiphons that illumine our concept of the Eucharist as food, as power unto holiness, as sacrifice, and as pledge. Practically the same points are brought out in the Magnificat antiphon of second Vespers, which summarizes so well the whole theology of the Eucharist:

O Holy Banquet (*1. Ant. at Lauds*)
in which Christ is received, (*2. Ant.*)
in which the memory of His passion is renewed, (*4. Ant.*)
in which the soul is filled with grace, (*3. Ant.*)
and a pledge of future glory is given us. (*5. Ant.*)

3. **Holy Mass (Cibavit eos).** Terce has been said and it is time now for the feast's magnificent Mass. Its every prayer rings true, and carries a full message. The *Entrance Chant* is a genuine introit, a festal ringing of bells, an invitation to the Sacrifice. The holy Eucharist is the fat of wheat, the nourishment of the life of grace, honey and spiritual sweetness from out the rock, Christ. The whole psalm (fresh in our minds from Pentecost Monday) belongs here.

The *Collect*, a classic in theological content and in liturgical form, blends art and liturgy as it sums up our knowledge of the Eucharist in concise and simple phrases. *The preamble*: in the Eucharist Christ has left a memorial of His passion, the Mass; for the Mass is the re-actualization of the Sacrifice of the Cross, a physical memorial, not merely a mental recollection. *The petition*: we ought adore the mystery of the Flesh and Blood in such a way as to carry within us always the fruits of redemption. The word *venerari*, to venerate, does not imply some mere pious action but the proper disposition of will and heart and an active, personal offering of the Mass; the "veneration of the sacred mystery of Christ's Flesh and Blood" consists in an active participation in the holy Sacrifice, in the fitting use of It as food, and in living virtuously as the consequence.

The *Epistle* (the same as on Holy Thursday) gives the oldest account of the institution of the Eucharist; it too contains an admonition unto worthy "veneration." The momentous words, "You will show the death of the Lord," signify a showing in act or a re-actual-ization of Calvary at the present time. The intermediary chants are structurally excellent — the *Gradual*, a text from the Old Testament, the *Alleluia*, a verse from the New. The first takes its setting in the plane of nature; God, the nourisher, furnishes the table for all creation and creation says its table prayer. This, however, symbolizes the table of God; of this the Alleluia treats as a prelude to the Gospel (from which its principal verse is taken). The *Sequence*, true to type, consists in a meditation upon and a development of the Alleluia verse. It is one of the feast's finest texts, a dogmatic poem reviewing the whole doctrine of the Eucharist.

The *Gospel* gives the principal portion of Christ's great Eucharistic discourse; the Eucharist, the fulfillment of the manna, is the Bread of life, the Bread from heaven. We find these truths beautifully synthesized in a single phrase of the Sequence, *Panis vivus et vitalis*, "Living Bread and Bread Life-bringing." The *Offertory*: all of us are "royal priests" and offer bread (work) and incense (prayer); therefore we ought be holy and ought never defile the Name of God. Take the admonition seriously. The *Secret*, too, is a theological gem; it explains the symbolism of the offered gifts. Bread and wine are symbols of peace and unity. Many kernels, many grapes must be made *one* to obtain flour or wine; and fields and vineyards flourish best in times of peace. The Eucharist is the sacrament of unity and of peace with Christ. The *Communion* repeats the principal verse of the Epistle. The *Postcommunion* directs our thoughts to that blessed state of which the Eucharist is the figure and pledge.

After the Mass follows the Corpus Christi procession. This, however, is not the essential thing; it was not included when the feast was instituted nor was it prescribed until the fifteenth century. Therefore the method of holding the procession lacks uniformity; the Roman Ritual simply provides for one and suggests certain chants. In various dioceses in Germany four altars are erected along the way, one toward each of the cardinal points; at each there is given the blessing with the monstrance after the beginning lines of one of the four Gospels are read. The initial verses are regarded, as often is the case in the liturgy, as the whole; the content of the first verses makes no difference because of the symbolism: Christ should reign as King throughout the world. Frequently the procession takes the character of a sacramental invoking the blessing of good weather during the coming summer.

In the afternoon second Vespers are chanted, the feast's solemn finale. The Hour is a thanksgiving prayer for all the day's graces. The *Magnificat* antiphon summarizes the whole Eucharistic mystery in words which beautifully betray the genius of St. Thomas Aquinas. This prayer deserves our further attention.

4. **The Office of Corpus Christi** sheds revealing light upon the mystery of the Eucharist to illumine its every aspect, its Old Testament types, its power to sanctify, its meaning for the Church and for souls. When the day reaches its finale at second Vespers, the whole beautiful ensemble is given an incomparably beautiful synthesis in the *Magnificat* antiphon:

O holy Banquet, in which Christ is received, in which the memory of His passion is renewed, in which the soul is filled with grace and a pledge of future glory is given us, alleluia.

O holy Banquet, in which Christ is received. . . . The first thing St. Thomas tells us is this: a holy banquet is prepared for us. Our thoughts go back into Biblical history and we see the children of Israel traveling through the wilderness with God their leader and nourisher. "He made a remembrance of His wonderful works, being a merciful and gracious Lord. He has given food to them that fear Him." The manna in the wilderness was an incontestable proof of divine Providence. And it foreshadowed a future reality, since Jesus said: "Moses did not give you bread from heaven. . . . This is the Bread that has come down from heaven — not as your fathers ate manna and are dead. He who eats this Bread will live forever."

We Christians are more fortunate than the children of Israel;

a table is made ready for us, too, in the wilderness of this life. Daily we are nourished with Manna, a Manna that surpasses the manna of Moses in a twofold way: it is a living Bread and it gives Life. The Sequence of the Mass phrases it very beautifully: "Living Bread and Bread Life-bringing" — *Panis vivus et vitalis!* O holy Banquet, in which Christ is received! The Fathers of the Church say that as the Lord went about to select a food for the soul, all creation passed in review before Him. Nothing was satisfactory, and therefore He decided upon His own Body and Blood. Yes, it is Christ Himself who is the food at this sacred Banquet.

> O wondrous gift indeed!
> The poor and lowly may
> Upon their Lord and Master feed!

The memory of His passion is renewed. . . . The opening acclamation of our antiphon implied peace and plenty. But now our thoughts are turned to Calvary and suffering: "in which the memory of His passion is renewed." In these few, common words lies imbedded the whole story of redemption. We see the tree of knowledge in paradise, the first sin, all the sorrow of unredeemed mankind. And then we see the "Servant of God" coming to earth, Christ Jesus. The crib is His cradle, the Cross, His deathbed. With royal dignity, though not without bitterest suffering, He takes upon Himself the punishment of death. After three days He rises again and soon ascends triumphantly into heaven. He died that we need not remain dead forever. He rose as the first-born from the dead so that we may rise. He ascended into heaven, blazing the way for our entrance. All this — life, death, resurrection, ascension — is comprehended by the liturgy in the words, "the passion of Christ."

Now we should be mindful of these acts of redemption not merely as historical data but as actualities mystically real and effective here and now — the *mysterium* of our religion. For in the holy Sacrifice Christ re-enacts His death, His resurrection, His ascension, His whole work of redemption. This too is included

in the phrase, "in which the memory of His passion is renewed."
With this background, how much more intelligible the prayer
immediately after the consecration becomes: "Therefore are we
mindful of the blessed passion, the resurrection from the dead
and glorious ascension of Christ. . . ."

More meaningful, too, are St. Paul's fearsome words (sung at
the Communion today): "As often as you eat this bread and
drink the chalice, you proclaim the death of the Lord until He
comes." By the Mass we show the death of the Lord, not in
words, but in holy action; through the *mysterium* the death,
resurrection, and ascension are made present in themselves and
their effects. Try to realize the greatness of this mystery. In it see
accomplished the whole work of redemption, from it receive
strength and perseverance.

The soul is filled with grace. . . . What does this Banquet "in
which Christ is received," this Banquet "in which the memory
of His passion is renewed" do for the soul? The answer is given
here — the "soul is filled with grace." Again we must go back
to the cradle of humanity. Man is in paradise. God most lovingly
provides for him in all respects. He places in paradise two trees,
the tree of knowledge and the tree of life. The latter could preserve man's earthly life; for he was to be immortal by eating the
fruit of this tree. But when Adam and Eve sinned, God drove
them out of paradise and placed cherubim and a flaming sword
at the gate; for now they were not to eat of the tree of life and
live. Through sin came physical death, the sign and symbol of
eternal death.

Yet God sent a Redeemer who willed to take sin away and
restore life to man. "Eternal life" is a favorite theme of the
evangelist John. Christ came upon earth that we might have
eternal life, that we might live as children of God forever. It is
through the waters of baptism that we are born unto life everlasting. Yet as our first parents in paradise needed the tree of
life to preserve their preternatural gifts, so we need the New
Covenant's tree of life to remain spiritually alive, to grow and to
be healthy. Does someone ask where this tree is standing? Surely

everyone knows that the tree of the Cross is our tree of life, and its branches hang heavily laden with fruit. That fruit is holy Communion, the means to retain the divine life received in baptism. But not only to retain that life but to make it grow and develop, to preserve it from disease and death — such is the purpose of the tree of the Cross and the Eucharist.

The pledge of eternal glory. . . . We have considered the holy Eucharist from various viewpoints. Is there still another? St. Thomas directs our gaze toward the endless future. Will there be a Eucharist, a Bread of angels, a Bread from heaven in eternity? No, the holy Eucharist is only for earthly pilgrims. St. Paul stated this very clearly: "As often as you eat this Bread and drink the chalice, you show the death of the Lord, until He comes." Therefore, with the Lord's Second Advent, the sacrament of the holy Eucharist will cease. Nevertheless, it has a most direct bearing upon heaven because the holy Eucharist typifies the heavenly banquet; it is the seal and pledge of eternal glory.

What is a type? In the strict sense a type is a person or thing which according to God's designs prefigured a future person or thing. The Old Covenant contained many types for the New. Christ Himself referred to several; for instance, He expressly related the manna in the Sinai desert to the Eucharist. In an extended sense the Church as such also bears the character of a type, i.e., she foreshadows the kingdom of God perfected in heaven. The authority for these statements is St. John's Apocalypse. The Church upon earth is a type of the heavenly Jerusalem. Yes, in heaven there will be magnificent liturgy, to which our liturgy bears a faint resemblance. And the Eucharist, too, is a faint foretaste and type of the coming heavenly banquet.

How this can be or will be is still, of course, a mystery. But today's Postcommunion clearly says: "May we some day be satiated with the enjoyment of Your divinity, which already now is prefigured through the reception of Your precious Body and Blood." Here we meet Christ in a transient, temporary manner, there eternally; here we possess Him through faith, there by vision; here the Mass is a *transitus Domini*, Christ passing by;

but there we shall see Him face to face and enjoy His presence forever.

Of this everlasting blessedness the Eucharist is also the pledge or seal. It is the right to, yes, the *seed* of eternal glory. Christ could not have put it more precisely: "He who eats My flesh and drinks My blood has everlasting life; and I will raise him up in the last day." Whoever eats the Body of the Lord bears within him the seed of immortality, he will not die!

SECOND SUNDAY AFTER PENTECOST
SUNDAY AFTER THE FEAST OF CORPUS CHRISTI

Say to them who were invited that they should come, for now all things are ready

According to the 1955 calendar reform, the formulary for today's Mass is that of the second Sunday after Pentecost, while the text for the Divine Office continues to be that for the Sunday within the octave of Corpus Christi. It would almost seem that the Sunday Gospel recounting the parable of the great supper was chosen with a view to the current Eucharistic feast, yet this was not the case because the Sunday liturgy took form centuries before the institution of Corpus Christi.

1. **Divine Office.** Throughout the day our thoughts are directed to the sublime mystery of the holy Eucharist. It is the theme of all the Hours, especially of Matins, at which the Church's "golden-mouthed" orator, St. John Chrysostom, addresses us with profound and moving words (a good sample of his oratorical ability):

"Because the Word of God has said, *This is My Body*, we ought give our assent, and believe, and look upon Him with spiritualized vision. For Christ did not bequeath to us material memorials of His presence but by means of tangible things blessed us with the sublimest spiritual realities. Take baptism, for instance. By means of the visible sign, water, is the gift conferred; the marvel that is wrought is spiritual, our rebirth, our restoration to divine favor. If you were a spirit-creature without flesh and blood, the Lord would communicate these gifts of grace directly and without the use of matter; but because the soul is inextricably united to a body, He conveys to you the things of the spirit through a visible veil. Some indeed will say: I want to see how He looks, what clothes He wears, what shoes! Yes, you do see Him, you may touch Him, you may even take Him as food. You wish to see what clothes He wears, and He responds by granting you the privilege not only of seeing, but of eating, of holding and consuming Him.

"Approach the altar, then, not halfheartedly or with a spirit of disdain; rather, with hearts on fire, fervent, enthusiastic. Remember, the Jews ate the lamb in haste, standing, with their shoes on and with traveling staffs in their hands; and you ought be much more alert and ready. For they were planning a journey to Palestine and were acting accordingly; while you should be planning your trip to heaven.

"Therefore you must be on guard at all times; the punishment in store for those who eat unworthily at the Lord's table is no small matter. Think how incensed you become against him who betrayed Jesus and against those who crucified Him; and be concerned that you yourself do not become guilty of Christ's Body and Blood. They put to death that most holy Body, but you bring Him into a defiled soul — and that after so many blessings! The Lord did not consider it enough simply to become man, to be struck with blows, to be crucified; He willed to identify Himself with us, and that not by faith alone but in very deed and reality by making us His Body.

"How pure must one be who partakes of such a sacrificial Banquet! The hand that distributes this Flesh, must it not be more radiantly clean than even a ray from the sun? Or the mouth filled with that spiritual Fire, or the tongue reddened by the Blood of God? Try to realize the incomparable honor that has accrued to you, the unique Banquet to which you are invited. That upon which the angels look with fear and trembling, that which they find difficult to behold because of the intense splendor radiating therefrom, that do we eat, to that we are united; we are made into one Body with Christ, into one Flesh.

"Who can proclaim the marvels wrought by the Lord, or herald His praises perfectly? Where is the shepherd who pastures his sheep on his own blood? I need not speak of shepherds. There are mothers enough who, after the pains of childbirth, hand their infants over to nurses. Christ could never have done this; with His own Blood He Himself would nourish us, would unite and identify Himself with us in the most intimate manner imaginable."

For comment on the first nocturn Lessons, see p. 153.

2. **Love of Neighbor.** The two Readings of the Sunday Mass will easily occasion profitable reflections and aspirations. St. John continues last Sunday's Epistle on the love of neighbor, words that could well echo in our ears throughout the coming week: "If anyone hates his brother, he is a murderer. From this we have come to know the meaning of love, namely, that He laid down His life for us. . . . Little children, let us not love in word or in speech, but in deed and in truth." Love is the proof of the grace within.

3. **The Great Supper.** What was our Lord's purpose in telling today's Gospel parable? He wanted to sum up in a single picture God's work of redemption in man's behalf. The various means of grace, the sacraments, holy Mass, all that the Church has and gives, in short, the kingdom of God, may be likened to a heavily laden table to which mankind has been invited. Among those asked to come, three groups may be distinguished — the city's citizens, the city's poor, and strangers outside the city.

To be more specific. The city's citizens were the Jews. Christ first preached in Israel and invited His own kinsmen to acknowledge Him as the Messiah; the pharisees, the scribes, the priests in particular should have led the way into the kingdom. Nevertheless, they did not. So poor a Messiah, one who would only

bring them spiritual benefits, they refused to accept. So Jesus set His face toward the poor, the outcasts of Jewry, and went to Galilee, there to herald the joyous news; and indeed, the poor fishermen, the despised tax-gatherer, the sin-laden Magdalen accepted His invitation, became His followers. In the parable these are the lame and the crippled.

Yet the spacious banquet halls of the kingdom could hold many more. Therefore Jesus sent the apostles and their successors to those outside the city, that is, to the Gentiles, to invite them to attend the banquet. Joyfully they responded, becoming Christians, zealous children of God. So by this parable Jesus indicated the rejection of the Jews, the calling of the humble in Israel, but especially the inclusion of non-Jews in the kingdom of God.

What, however, are the lessons that the Church wishes to teach us today by the parable? First, we should remember in a spirit of sincerest gratitude that we belong to the third group. We have been called from paganism to the banquet table of the Church; we are most fortunate to be sharers in the many means unto

sanctification. Regard yourself a guest of God; never consider it
"a matter of course" that you have been baptized a Christian.

Not without purpose did our Savior emphasize the "great supper" in His parable. By it He may have understood the whole
work of sanctification and the many spiritual treasures of the
Church, but His thoughts must have tarried on the holy Eucharist — no greater Banquet could He have prepared for us, His
own Flesh and Blood. For this reason our Gospel is ideal for the
Sunday after the feast of Corpus Christi. The parable's message
becomes actuality in the Mass. We are in church, our heavenly
Father's home, His banquet hall. Here we truly are guests of
God. A table is set for us; Christ Himself is our Host, and the
victuals are His own Body sacrificed in death. See, the whole
work of redemption is synthesized at the altar table of sacrifice!

These various Readings afford choice material for our Sunday
meditation. The first nocturn gives the serious, sobering side of
the picture, one that appears again in the parable, i.e., the misuse
of the gifts of grace. The other three Lessons treat of the gifts
themselves: Eucharist (second nocturn), love (Epistle), and
God's kingdom (Gospel).

4. **Holy Mass (Factus est).** The *Entrance Chant* is a thanksgiving song to God, our Protector and Savior. Who is voicing
thanks? Christ and His Body, the Church, are grateful for the
blessing of redemption, for divine Love. God has adopted me as
His child, He has freed me from spiritual death because He loves
me, and for that reason I sing a song of praise to Him: "I love
You, Lord. You are my strength." King David sang this hymn
at the end of his life, one so full of work and suffering.

The *Epistle* and *Introit* treat of love, and the *Collect* too; we
should both love and fear the holy Name of God. A most important combination. It is not sufficient to love God without
fearing Him. What does it mean to love God, to fear God? The
love of God must be identified with the observance of the commandments. This prayer also teaches us our relation to God; it
is a union of love and fear, let us say, of holy fear and reverential love. It is, moreover, a union in love that must be lasting,

steadfast, constant. Nor can we develop this love by ourselves; it is a grace given by God to those who pray for it. Note, too, the conclusion. God does not abandon anyone whom He has established steadfastly in His love. Therefore we can be confident. God wills to lead us closer to Himself if we only cooperate.

Glance now at the *Secret* and note what the Mass should accomplish: "May this offering purify us and lead us day by day to a more heavenly way of life." Two effects are mentioned: the Sacrifice should cleanse us from the dross of sin, and it should make us constantly more holy, more virtuous. The Masses we offer should be as rungs upon which we ascend from the depths of sin and approach ever closer to heaven. Thus they would serve as a wonderful Jacob's ladder to God on High.

The *Gradual* and *Offertory* are prayers of complaint and petition. What reason do we have to murmur, to complain? Perhaps it is because God's command to love our brother is not perfectly observed; perhaps we still esteem too little the fortune of having been invited into God's kingdom. And if we think about the many millions of our fellow men who do not respond to God's invitation, it is easy to see how fitting Psalm 6 is for the Offertory. When the moment for *Communion* arrives, we again are flooded by a spirit of grateful joy over the holy Meal prepared for us. May our repeated presence at this holy table assure our salvation (*Postc.*).

FEAST OF
THE MOST SACRED HEART

One of the soldiers opened His side
and there flowed out blood and water

1. **Historical Sketch.** Matins of our feast contain a history of the devotion to the Sacred Heart and of the feast's origin.

Already in ancient times, the opened side of Jesus was given mystical connotations by the Fathers and Doctors of the Church; the blood and water were interpreted as symbolizing the Church, existing by virtue of the waters of baptism and the Blood of the Eucharist. The cult of the wound in the sacred side received notable impetus during the Middle Ages through devotion to the Heart of Christ as the fount of divine-human love, a devotion fostered and furthered by St. Bernard, St. Gertrude, and St. Mechtilde.

Modern devotion to the Heart of Jesus dates from the time of St. John Eudes, who is usually considered its originator (d. 1680), and to the revelations granted to St. Margaret Mary Alacoque (d. 1690). In three wondrous revelations the significance of devotion to the Sacred Heart was communicated to this humble virgin. As a result of her spiritual experiences a new feast was instituted on the Friday after the octave of Corpus Christi, with emphasis on atonement. The feast was approved for specified dioceses by Clement XIII in 1765, and extended to the whole Church by Pius IX in 1856. In 1889 Pope Leo XIII elevated it to the rank of first class, and through an encyclical letter in 1899 dedicated the whole Catholic world to the Sacred Heart of Jesus.

In 1928 the feast was favored with an octave of the third order by Pope Pius XI, and thereby it enjoyed a rank equal to Christmas and Ascension. At the same time its Office was completely recast. The previous Sacred Heart Office lacked unity, being a synthesis of ready texts; in part it was Eucharistic and in part an Office on the passion. Wishing an original, unified Office, Pius XI appointed a commission of theologians and himself supervised their work. As a theme for the Office, Christ's words to St. Margaret Mary were chosen: "Behold the Heart which has loved men so greatly but which has been given so little love in return." It became a feast of atonement for human ingratitude toward God, a feast in praise of the peaceful triumph of Christ's boundless love. A final modification in the status of the feast occurred in 1955, when as part of the calendar reform, the octave was abolished. But the Office of the Sacred Heart is still said on the Sunday after the feast. ✓

2. Holy Mass (Cogitationes). As we begin the Mass, the Church wants us to think of our Lord and Redeemer. His Name need not be mentioned; we know He is present, close to us. "The thoughts of His Heart. . . . " His thoughts, His designs are totally devoted to mankind's redemption. He wills to restore life to the spiritually dead, to nourish the hungry. About the altar those participating answer the words of the Church with a jubilant song of praise, Psalm 32. This psalm brings our Lord before us as the divine Shepherd in the planes of nature and of grace; in the skies above He shepherds the stars in their orbits while here below He leads His sheep into heavenly pastures and foils the ambitions of evildoers. Thus the *Introit* sketches a picture of the Sacred Heart along ancient Christian lines.

The *Collect* touches upon the two objectives of the feast, viz., sincere devotedness to Christ, from whose Heart flow "boundless treasures of love," and a willingness to make "worthy amends and expiation" for sinners. Aided by the apostle Paul we are given a profound and comprehensive view of that "boundless treasury of love" in the *Epistle*. Paul, or rather the Church, was chosen to unlock the treasury of the divine Heart to men, and that in a twofold way, viz., through faith (Mass of the Catechumens) and through grace (Mass of the Faithful). The Sacred Heart feast, in fact the whole liturgy, is dedicated to this objective.

All the liturgical observances of the Church year "herald the unfathomable riches of Christ"; but to a still greater extent do the channels of the divine blood-stream flowing from the fountain of Christ's pierced Heart open themselves in the holy Eucharist. The *Epistle* that Mother Church pours forth today is a most fitting and practical prayer; kneeling before the "Father of our Lord Jesus Christ," she petitions (a) that we be strengthened in regard to the inward man; (b) that Christ should dwell by faith (and grace) in our hearts; (c) that we become firmly rooted and established in charity. In the Introit the Church enlightened us on the aims and spirit of our Redeemer, in the Epistle on the human implications of redemption.

The *Gradual* voices the reflections of the congregation, while with the *Alleluia* our Redeemer stands vividly before us again in the supreme work and example of His earthly life. It is as if now at the *Gospel* our Cross-laden Savior enters, turns to us and says: "Take My yoke upon you." The Gospel transports us to Mount Calvary and makes us witness the piercing of the divine Heart. We know the symbolism of the act; the opening of Christ's sacred side connotes the creation of the Church; for as a second Eve, the Church arose from the side of the second Adam, His "helper" and bride. Her continued existence is due to the water (baptism) and the Blood (Eucharist) that flow from the side of her divine Bridegroom.

In the *Offertory* the Church seeks to become identified with the great offering of Christ and therefore makes His lament her own. Her heart melts and becomes indiscernibly one with the Heart of her Savior; participation in the sufferings of Christ brings glorification to the Mystical Body. The *Secret* returns to the two principal points inculcated by the feast, the ineffable love manifested by the Sacred Heart of God's beloved Son and atonement for sin. Then the liturgy does full justice to the day's mystery in the *Preface*, a new composition:

It was Your will
that Your only-begotten Son,
while hanging on the Cross,
should be pierced by a soldier's spear,
so that when His Heart,
the sanctuary of divine bounty, was opened,
the torrents of mercy and of grace
could flood in upon us;
for this Heart
which never ceases to burn with love for us
should be a place of rest to the devout,
and should open a haven of salvation
to the repentant.

may the grace of the holy spirit

so lavishly poured out upon us

vitalize our failing faith and

confirm our hope in eternal life ✝

Now in the holy Sacrifice the Bridegroom, red with blood, shares with His bride the treasures of His Heart that she might become His "fullness." We are on Golgotha near the Cross once more at the *Communion*. The Church wishes to say that the holy Eucharist which we are receiving has its origin in the opened Heart. And at the very end we turn again to Christ, imploring that the holy Banquet perfect the work of redemption within us, that "we may learn to despise what is earthly and love what is heavenly."

3. **Divine Office.** As an Office composed and added to the liturgy in recent decades, it deserves our special study. First a few general observations. First and second Vespers are completely different, both as to psalms and as to antiphons. The psalms of Matins were chosen with reference to content, follow numerical order, and are adorned with verses from the psalms themselves as antiphons. A portion of the encyclical of Pius XI serves as reading for the second nocturn; and in the third St. Bonaventure unravels the mystery of divine love.

First Vespers accents the meekness and mercy of our Lord Jesus: "Rule, O Lord, with Your sweet yoke in the midst of Your enemies."

"A gracious and merciful Lord gives food to them that fear Him."

"For the upright in heart a light has risen in the darkness: a merciful and gracious Lord."

"With the Lord there is mercy and plentiful redemption."

The Chapter reminds us of the "unfathomable riches" which should be proclaimed throughout the world by means of devotion to the Sacred Heart. The Gospel scene of Calvary, the soldier piercing Christ's sacred side, is the theme of the hymn; from the wounded Heart of Jesus "sprang the Church, the Savior's bride," from it "issues a perennial stream of grace in wondrous sevenfold flood."

Matins contains psalms which are seldom used, e.g., Psalms 40, 93, and 107. The Invitatory heralds the feast's theme: "The Heart of Jesus wounded for love of us. . . ." The psalms fall into two classes; either they concern Christ and come from His mouth

(Pss. 32, 40, 60, 93, 107), or they are hymns of praise from our lips. The first nocturn Lessons are taken from the prophet Jeremias. In them the Sacred Heart reveals His love toward men: "I have loved you with an everlasting love; therefore I have drawn you, taking pity on you." It is readily apparent why every Lesson makes allusion to the heart.

The second nocturn Lessons give the historical background of the feast. St. Bonaventure, called the "Seraphic Doctor" because of his profound insights into divine love, explains the Gospel in the third nocturn. The responsories follow the pattern set by the psalms; in some the wounded Heart of our Savior laments over the ingratitude of men or reveals the immensity of His mercy; in others we are the speakers and praise the mercy of the divine Heart.

Lauds has proper antiphons, with no direct bearing on the psalms; beginning with the account of the piercing of the sacred side, they tell of Christ's boundless love toward men. The psalms of second Vespers are identical with those of Corpus Christi.

4. The Sacred Heart Mysticism of St. Bonaventure. "Beloved brethren, since it had been ordained by a merciful Providence that the Church should be formed from the side of the crucified Christ and that the words of the Scriptures be fulfilled: *They shall look upon Him whom they have pierced* — a soldier armed with a lance opened the sacred Breast. The Blood mingled with water, which was shed from that pierced side, was the price of our salvation. Flowing from the hidden fount of the Sacred Heart, it gave to the sacraments their power of conferring the life of grace, and to those already living in Christ a draught of the living fount, gushing forth unto life eternal.

"Arise, therefore, O soul friendly to Christ! Cease not your vigil; bring close your lips, that you may draw waters from out the Savior's fountain. Oh, how good and how pleasant it is to dwell in this most Sacred Heart. Your Heart, dearest Jesus, is the great treasure, the precious jewel which we will find in the dug field of Your sacred Body. Who is there who would throw away this jewel? Rather would I throw away all my own jewels, my thoughts and my affections, and cast my cares upon Your Sacred Heart, which will nourish me without fail. I beg of You, sweet Jesus my God, place my prayer among those that You will answer. Draw me wholly into Your Heart. For unto this end Your side was pierced, that an entrance would lie open to us. Unto this end Your Heart was wounded, that detached from worldly tumult, we would be able to dwell in it.

"But above all, Your Heart was wounded so that a visible scar would enable us to see the invisible wound of Your love. For how could the ardor of Your love be better shown than by this, that not only Your Body but even Your very Heart was pierced with a lance? Truly the wounds of the flesh showed forth the wounds of the spirit. Who is there who would not love One so loving? My dearly beloved, let us pray that the Sacred Heart may deign to wound our heart still so hard, still so impenitent, and bind it with the sweet bonds of His love."

THIRD SUNDAY AFTER PENTECOST
SUNDAY AFTER THE FEAST OF THE SACRED HEART

The Sacred Heart in ancient Christian piety

During this week the Church employs two parables to show God's love for sinners, that of the lost sheep and of the lost coin (*Gosp.*). The touching picture of the Good Shepherd with a lamb upon His shoulders should continue in our minds throughout the week; do not miss its beautiful bearing on the Sacred Heart feast, for how could the love of Jesus be better portrayed than by the picture of the Good Shepherd with the found sheep in His arms! The Epistle brings home the moral in the story — we must be obedient and alert. Man can give his allegiance to either of two leaders, the Good Shepherd (*Gosp.*) or the howling lion, the devil (*Epist.*).

1. **Holy Mass (Respice).** Seeking aid we approach the Good Shepherd: "Look upon me and have mercy upon me, O Lord" (*Intr.*). The altar to which we come is Christ. The principal trait of the Good Shepherd is mercy, and the word will occur often during today's Mass. "So forsaken and poor am I! See my abjection and my labor and forgive me all my sins." Psalm 24, a prayer full of trust and humility, expresses well our spiritual condition.

The *Collect* covers an unusually large number of truths; a good meditation could be made upon it. First, it pinpoints our true citadel of strength, namely, God the Protector (let us call Him the Good Shepherd) of those who trust in Him. Willingly we admit that without God we have no virtue, no security, no sanctity. Such acknowledgment of our own helplessness is the best disposition for the reception of grace. Our petition rests upon the Good Shepherd's peculiar trait, mercy; we ask that through the guidance and rule of God, or better, of Christ the Good Shepherd, we may so pass through temporal blessings as not to lose eternal beatitude.

The two Readings will receive special consideration later. Even though the devil goes about like a roaring lion, cast your cares upon the Lord; He will sustain you (*Grad.*). The *Alleluia* verse asks: Will God be a strict, angry Judge? The *Gospel* answers in the negative with two parables: No, as Good Shepherd He will carry the sheep upon His shoulders into the heavenly meadows. Gladdened by the Gospel, the *Offertory* radiates confidence; God does not abandon those who search for Him, since He Himself seeks out the lost. The *Secret*: Look, Lord, upon the gifts of Your suppliant Church, and may the faithful who receive them be sanctified by them. A terse and concisely worded *Postcommunion* pleads for the two fruits of sacrifice; negative, purification from sin (which implies God's mercy); positive, an increase in divine life. *Sancta* was an ancient word for the holy Eucharist.

2. **Text Analysis.** Today's formulary is a good example of spiritual ascent from conflict and suffering to victory and joy. In this ascent every prayer, chant, and reading contributes. It is a holy drama, and the Good Shepherd takes the leading role. The

Mass-action opens as we, straying sheep, cry out to our divine Shepherd and acknowledge our utter helplessness. We continue our plea in the Collect, beseeching God's protection, mercy, and guidance. There is a "bad shepherd" too, the "roaring lion" heard in the Epistle. The Gradual, true to its nature, echoes the message of the Reading it follows (which is not too often the case). The question asked in fear and awe in the Alleluia verse receives a kindly response in the Gospel; for God is not only a Judge, He is a merciful Shepherd, too. Which brings us to a climax — the lost has been found.

The Offertory, accordingly, is a prayer of gratitude to the Good Shepherd: "Sing praise to the Lord . . . for He did not disregard the cry of those in trouble." Even in the high heavens there is response to the mystery of mercy and love on earth, "joy among the angels of God when a single sinner does penance" (*Comm.*). A final statement of the theme occurs in the Postcommunion; the Eucharist means life and atonement. Thus the movement of the drama runs parallel to the Mass-action; the liturgy of the Word, excluding the Gospel, voices the spirit of

fear and anxious petition; the Gospel and the Sacrifice proper
come from hearts joyfully grateful.

3. **Divine Office.** The Gospel affords Pope St. Gregory the
Great an occasion to give one of his excellent homilies (34); it
would serve as good spiritual reading:

"You have heard in the Gospel account, my brothers, how
sinners and publicans approached our Redeemer; and they were
welcomed not only to listen, but even to eat with Him. The
pharisees, however, became indignant upon observing such
familiarity. You may deduce from the Gospel story, then, that
true holiness includes sympathy, while mock piety easily becomes
indignant. Of course, the just man may rightly take a stand
against sinners; but that which has its roots in pride is quite
different from that which arises from zeal and discipline.

"The good man may become indignant in the presence of evil
but will not act in an offensive manner; he may doubt about the
conversion of the evildoer, but will not despair; and it is through
love that the just will withstand the unjust. For even when they
devise multiple forms of external restraints against the wicked,
interiorly they retain the spirit of kindness because of their virtue
of love. For in spirit they often place those whom they are cor-
recting before themselves, and consider those whom they judge
as better than themselves. Thus by discipline they preserve their
subjects and by humility they safeguard themselves. On the other
hand, those who act proudly through a sense of false piety despise
everybody else; never do they condescend to show mercy to the
weak, and to the degree they believe they are saints, to that
degree have they become worse sinners.

"To this latter group did the pharisees assuredly belong. They
criticized the Lord because He treated sinners kindly, they were
unwilling to allow the fountain of divine mercy to empty itself
upon desolate hearts. It was because they were sick and did not
realize it that the heavenly Physician sought to heal them with
suitable medicine and to bring them to realize their sorry state.
He gave them a lovely parable to digest and thereby endeavored
to soften the hard, tumorous growth over their hearts."

4. Meditation upon the Sunday. A. *The Lessons of the Mass.* Today's Gospel is taken from St. Luke's collection of parables. In chapter 15 of the third Gospel we find three parables that evidently have the same purpose, three parables treating of the lost and the found, namely, the parables of the lost sheep, of the lost drachma, of the lost son. The first two are used as today's Gospel. What did Christ wish to teach by these three parables? An exceptionally beautiful lesson, a truly joyous message on the mercy of God! After each parable our Savior therefore added: "I say to you, there shall be JOY before the angels of God upon one sinner doing penance."

That the Church wishes to emphasize this truth we see from the Communion; for while the faithful are partaking of the Body of their Lord, the choir sings: "I say to you, there is joy before the angels of God upon one sinner doing penance." Whenever the Church wishes to give special stress to a point in the Gospel, she takes the passage and repeats it in a chant, e.g., as the Alleluia verse or the Communion. If in the latter, there is usually another implication, viz., the Church wishes to imply that the passage in question is being fulfilled in the Eucharistic banquet. As "lost sheep" we came to Mass, but the Good Shepherd "found us" in the holy Sacrifice; He placed us on His shoulders and now at the Communion, with gleaming joy in His eyes, He carries us home.

Yes, the heavens, one might say, are opened before us and we see the angels exulting, rejoicing over our conversion. Of course, this conversion has already taken place long ago at baptism; then did the heavens actually open for us; then did the angels rejoice over heaven's new citizen. But at present each Mass is a renewal and a perfecting of baptism, especially each Sunday Mass. And holy Communion is security and pledge to the fact that the Good Shepherd is carrying us home on His shoulders.

The second parable is less well known. What is its meaning? The woman in search of a lost coin represents Mother Church, whose principal task upon earth is to search and seek after that which is lost, to find sinful men and to ready them for heaven. She goes out into wretched, dirty hovels (i.e., the earth with all its enticement to sin) and there kindles a light, Christ. Isn't this a heartening comparison — the Church carrying in her hands the Light of the world, Christ, Christ in the holy Eucharist? And this Light she shines upon the darkness of earthly life and into the black recesses of the soul. There she finds the lost groat —the human soul fallen through sin. Another fine analogy, the soul a coin. As a coin bears a stamp which often is the image of the ruler, so also there is impressed upon your soul the image of your heavenly King. The soul the image of God! Yes, Christ should constantly become more clearly etched upon your soul. Let yourself "be found" by Mother Church and be put away as a precious gem in the heavenly treasury.

The Epistle is quite unlike the Gospel. The Gospel treats of the Good Shepherd, who, full of love, places the lost sheep upon His shoulders; but in the Epistle we hear the "roaring lion going about seeking whom he may devour." Man stands at the crossroads; he may choose between two leaders, either the Good Shepherd, Christ, or the roaring lion, Satan. The One wills to heal, the other to lacerate; the One wishes to direct His flock into heavenly fields, the other to strangle victims in his fiendish jaws. Surely it should not be difficult to make a choice. Have we not already renounced the devil and all his works and promptings at baptism? And yet time and time again do we permit ourselves to be deceived.

Now what is the practical lesson flowing from these two Readings? To your "Good Shepherd" you must be an obedient, docile lamb and place your entire trust in His guidance. And you must likewise be a spirited, energetic fighter against the roaring lion. As the shepherd boy David fell upon the lion which sought to rob him of his sheep, so must you resist the devil for your soul's sake. Something strikes us in this Mass that is different — during Eastertide we heard no such things; there was no mention of the devil or of sin. Mother Church restricted herself to joyful messages, and there seemed to be no end to happy *alleluias*. We then were in the blessed time of childhood. At Easter we all were reborn. But Pentecost came and we were declared of age, we were given confirmation, the sacrament of manly courage. Now Mother Church is sending us into areas of battle, of work, of temptation.

Today's liturgy, wholly concerned with the present, readies us for the needs of life. The only disturber of peace, an enemy wholly disregarded during Eastertime, now makes its appearance, sin. Today's Mass proves that such a kill-joy exists in God's kingdom. Nevertheless, the Church does not wish to discourage us; she does, however, wish to prepare us. So she announces the glad tidings: "Cast your care upon the Lord, and He will sustain you" (*Grad.*). Sin for Him is no insurmountable obstacle to the work of sanctification; with persevering love He goes after each soul in sin. He Himself engaged the roaring lion in battle upon the Cross; to save the sheep He fell victim to the sting of death. Now He has given to us a Mother, the Church, who seeks and who finds us. Such is the message of today's liturgy. So let us joyously continue in God's service, aided by the conviction that we have over us the best Good Shepherd.

B. *The Good Shepherd.* Modern piety spontaneously portrays Christ's boundless love in terms of His Sacred Heart. Not so the ancient Church. In the early centuries it was Christ as the Good Shepherd. Upon the walls of the catacombs, in ancient basilicas, upon tombs, everywhere one may find this lovely picture. The liturgical texts, too, often treated of the Good Shepherd, and that frequently at the beginning of a new phase in the ecclesiastical year. Certainly the ancient Sacred Heart representation is as meaningful and as lovable as the present-day one. Let us consider the Good Shepherd approach of the early Christians.

1) What does the picture of a

shepherd with a lamb upon his shoulders symbolize? Christ as the Redeemer. A lamb has strayed from the flocks of God, has lost itself, has fallen among thorns. That was mankind, which through sin lost paradise and grace. Christ was sent into the world to fetch that lamb home. He sought it, called it, yes, He placed Himself in the lion's path to rescue it; He even was clawed to death. But now with great love He is carrying it upon His shoulders into the heavenly corrals. Thus the picture summarizes the work of Christ as the Redeemer of men.

2) The picture also expresses the spiritual odyssey of each Christian. St. Paul told us during the Lenten season: "You were heretofore darkness, but now light in the Lord." After Easter St. Peter, the first vicar of the Good Shepherd, reminded us: "You were as sheep going astray, but you are now converted to the Shepherd and Bishop of your souls." That great event was holy baptism. In baptism the Good Shepherd found you and placed you upon His shoulders. Baptism also was the occasion of which the Redeemer speaks in today's Gospel, the great moment when the angels of God rejoiced upon one sinner doing penance. So in the second place the picture reminds us of our baptism.

3) And further — the Good Shepherd does not remove the sheep from His shoulders; His will is to remain intimately united with it. Now what is most important in the Christian religion? It is divine life, the grace of being a child of God. This most intimate union of Christ with the Church, with the individual Christian, is the greatest of all blessings. "Abide in My love" was the legacy of our departing Master. Our greatest ambition must be to retain this divine life, to cherish it, to bring it to maturity, ever to perfect this vital union with Christ. How marvelously, then, does the Good Shepherd picture portray our oneness with God.

4) What means must we employ to retain this divine union? The sufferings of Christ earned divine life for us; the memorial of His passion and death can preserve it, i.e., the Sacrifice of Mass, the holy Eucharist. For in no other way does the Lord show Himself the Good Shepherd more wondrously than in the Eucharist. In no other way can we obtain or maintain a more intimate union

with Him. In baptism we received divine life, but the Eucharist
preserves, develops it. Recall the Lord's own words: "He who
eats My Flesh and drinks My Blood *abides* in Me and I in him."

5) Thus the Good Shepherd picture summarizes and reveals
the fundamentals of Christianity concerning Christ the Redeemer — baptism, mystical union with God, the holy Eucharist.
And lastly, it tells of our blessed return home to heaven. For the
Good Shepherd carries the found sheep into the heavenly pastures. This is the real reason why the picture was repeated so
often in the catacombs, the burial places of the first Christians. For
it proclaimed to the faithful the glad tidings that after the afflictions of earthly life the Good Shepherd will carry the Christian
soul into the great sheepfold of eternal beatitude. This hope was
so strong among the early Christians that they considered the
sufferings of life, even the bloody death of martyrdom as trifling;
they lived not only in faith and in love toward Christ Jesus, but
with a glowing hope in eternal glory. We modern Christians live
all too much in the present and are too strongly attracted to things
earthly. May the Good Shepherd picture help develop in us something of the spirit of His primitive flock.

FOURTH SUNDAY AFTER PENTECOST

Jesus, the Fisher of men

On the second and third Sundays after Pentecost we were
shown God's love and providence toward us, a love inviting us
(the parable of the supper) and a love seeking us (the parable of
the lost sheep). Today we see how our divine Savior in His love
establishes a spiritual home, the Church, and appoints its care-
takers — fishermen. Thus the liturgy continues to present Christ
to us in very appealing pictures; last Sunday it was as the Good
Shepherd, this Sunday as the Fisher of men.

About this time there occurs the feast of Sts. Peter and Paul, a feast with which today's liturgy has definite relationships; at one period the Sundays following this feast were designated according to their order after it. Peter receives the high call as fisher of men. His little ship, from which the Savior preaches, is a symbol of the Catholic Church. At this time of the year Holy Orders are also conferred in many countries.

1. **Text Analysis.** Suffering and anxiety of soul oppress the community assembled about the altar, while the day's liturgy seeks to instill confidence and spiritual strength. God is the true Light in the darkness of earthly life, and our trust is in Him (*Intr.*); we ask for peace and order among nations (*Coll.*); suffering keeps us mindful of our pilgrim status and makes us long for heaven (*Epist.*). Suffering too comes as punishment for sin (*Grad.*), and our physical and spiritual needs occasion trust and

48

prayerful petition (*Off., Comm.*). Thus throughout the Mass formulary the pangs and pains of human life are put in balance by the mightier realities of trust and confidence in a God who aids.

2. Holy Mass (Dominus illuminatio.) Christ's faithful are entering the house of God. The *Introit* voices the spirit with which that entrance is made. On many Sundays and feasts the Introit sets the tone for the entire day. The Christian comes out of a world of battle, a world of suffering and persecution; accordingly the entrance hymn is usually a call for assistance, yet a call stemming from fullest confidence. It would be to our advantage to reflect upon and to live into the spirit of the Introit psalm already on Saturday evening; when entering the church the following morning we would then more easily realize the beauty of the text and taste its sweetness.

The various emotions expressed by the psalm are, one may say, concentrated in the antiphon. Therefore it would be best to pray the Introit in the manner in which it was formerly sung, i.e., with the antiphon repeated between each verse of the psalm. The antiphon may be compared to the bed of a river upon which the waves of the psalm flow serenely along. Psalm 26, today's Entrance Chant, is a song of heartfelt confidence and expresses genuine trust in God. I must expect persecution and suffering; accordingly I will rely upon Christ my Light, my Protector, my Conqueror. This initial prayer also provides a good picture of the Church. Persecuted from without, and within loaded down by the Cross, she is strong and invincible through Christ. Christ in Sunday Mass stands as a lighthouse amidst the darkness of the week.

In the *Collect* we pray for peace on earth "in order that the Church may rejoice in undisturbed worship of God." We have just left a world hostile to the supernatural. By the *Epistle* we are taught that earthly sufferings are necessary for the child of God; they are the birth pains of beatitude. A most consoling passage: "The sufferings of this time are not worthy to be compared with the glory to come, the glory that will be revealed in us." The Epistle is a profound meditation upon nature, upon nature that longs for stability, for redemption; upon nature that is endeavor-

ing to instill in our hearts a lively desire for the Second Advent of
Christ our Lord.

The *Gradual* continues the general theme. We storm heaven
for mercy and help on the plea that otherwise non-Christians
would ridicule God's impotence. The *Alleluia*, too, implores our
enthroned King for aid. Almost every part of the Mass contains
a petition for help, because holy Church and the individual soul
are in interior and exterior straits today. The *Gospel* alone seems
to reflect a different hue. Nevertheless not wholly, because the
purpose of the Gospel is not only to instruct but to provide
the *mysterium* for the Mass-action. Therefore it shows us how the
Church is, above all, an institution for the care of souls, how it is
Peter's ship and at the same time the net in which the "little fishes
of Christ" are caught.

Moreover, we hear that Christ is the great Fisher of men. His
helpers are the apostles, the bishops, and the priests. Their greatest
task is to be successful fishermen. See how the Gospel is pastoral
instruction! But the account likewise takes actual form in today's
holy Mass. For we are the crowds Jesus teaches from Peter's boat,
yes, we are the fish drawn out from the sea of the world as it
becomes "day," as Christ becomes our "light" (*Intr., Off.*). All
this happened to us for the first time at baptism, and it is re-hap-
pening now in the presence of the altar. We should resemble
Peter who, full of humility, cried out: "Depart from me, for I
am a sinful man," and who obediently followed the call of the
Master as he "left all things."

The hymn at the *Offertory* procession resumes the theme of
suffering in harmony with the Introit. In the latter Christ was
the Light and the Conqueror, while at the Offertory, among the
gifts we carry to the altar is a petition for spiritual enlightenment
and for victory over the enemy. In the minds of early Christians
light and enlightenment were proper to baptism and to the graces
of baptism that abound so profusely at Easter. Now each Sunday
is Easter, because each Sunday the mystery of baptism is repeated.
At the Offertory we therefore ask for the flowering of baptism's
blessings.

Enemies have often been spoken of, and toward one such enemy we must ever remain fully alert. This enemy, our perverse will, is continually seeking to topple us out of the bark of Peter. There is only one Person able to tame a stubborn will — it is He who calmed the stormy sea, Christ — Christ in the holy Sacrifice. This is the burden of the *Secret*. The *Communion*, too, contains sentiments in accord with the Introit, even though the psalm has the ring of triumph. Psalm 17, a hymn composed by David as an old man in thanksgiving for many victories, wonderfully portrays the storms and battles of an exciting life. Also for us in the holy Eucharist, Christ is "a firmament, a refuge, a deliverer." The fruits of the Sacrifice-banquet are purification and protection. May we be purified and preserved from further defilement. To state in resumé the Mass's unifying mystery: *in conflict and in suffering the Christian finds strength and comfort in Christ, if he only stays in the boat that is His holy Church.*

3. Divine Office. The Biblical narrative of the encounter between David and Goliath and the Sunday Gospel are the features special to today's Office. Both afford interesting reading material. From St. Ambrose's allegorical exposition of the Gospel may be seen how the Fathers often extended their commentary on a Scripture passage:

"The Lord healed many and from the most diverse kinds of sicknesses. Neither did considerations of time or place keep the multitudes from asking for cures. Night was approaching, still the crowds surged about Him. The sea lay before them, and they continued to press on. Jesus stepped into Peter's boat. That boat, according to Matthew, was being tossed to and fro; that boat, according to Luke, became filled with fish. Thereby one may perceive a picture of the Church beginning her journey on stormy seas but later carrying a full load of passengers. Those still in the sea of this earthly life are the fish.

"In Matthew, Christ remains asleep among His disciples; in Luke, He is giving them directions. Among those who fear, He sleeps; but He watches with the vigilant. That ship does not roll about in which prudence holds the helm, from which unbelief is absent, for which faith fills the sails. Indeed, how could that ship have foundered under the captaincy of Him who is the Church's sure foundation? Where there was little faith, therefore, there was alarm, but here in the presence of perfect Love there is full security.

"If others were told to lower their nets, it was to Peter alone that it was said: Launch out into the deep, that is, into the depths of the divine mysteries. For what is more profound than to look into the depths of the heavenly treasury, to know the Son of God and to proclaim His divine generation? Even though the human mind is not able to comprehend this truth fully through the searchings of reason, it is nevertheless grasped by the fullness of faith. Indeed, it is not granted to me to understand how He was begotten, but neither is it granted to me to remain ignorant that He was begotten. I do not know the manner in which He was begotten, but I do know the source of His generation. We were not present when the Son of God was born of the Father, but men were present when He was proclaimed by the Father to be the Son of God. If we do not believe God, whom shall we believe? Everything that we do believe, we believe either because we have seen it or heard it. Now one cannot always trust his eyes; but we do have faith in our hearing."

For the Lessons of the second and third nocturns, see p. 156.

4. **Meditation upon the Sunday Liturgy. A.** The Symbol of the Fish and of the Fisherman. Last Sunday the Church presented our Redeemer as the Good Shepherd in the act of taking His little lambs upon His shoulders. Without doubt this was the symbol most frequently used by the first Christians. Today another very appealing picture is put before us, that of the good Fisherman and His catch. It is another lovely and meaningful symbol. Let us consider it in detail.

a) *The Fisher of men.* First look at the picture on page 57. Modeled upon an extremely old design found in catacombs dating to the earliest centuries of Christianity, it visualizes the words of our Savior, "From now on you will catch men." Nevertheless, the fisher of men here presented is Christ Himself. The fish He has just caught is another Christian. Do you know when it was that He landed you? At baptism. As He drew you out of the water of baptism, you became, symbolically speaking, Christ's little fish. A vessel and a net are given in the same picture. In the vessel are other fishes. This symbolizes the Church, which the Savior Himself compared to a fisherman's net. See what love, what care and zeal our Lord devotes to His work. Now every Sunday is Easter in miniature, every Sunday brings a renewal of your baptism. This is what holy Church wishes to say in the Gospel: You are one of Christ's little fishes; you were caught through the waters of baptism. Allow yourself to be caught again and again by the good Fisher of men, Christ, through the Eucharistic mystery.

Into the whole world Christ has sent His fishers of men. They are easily recognizable, because they are the priests of the Catholic Church. They are His helpers. In His stead and at His command and with His grace they cast out the Gospel net into the sea of the world. In priests, therefore, let us see the divine Fisherman Himself. For just as Peter without Christ fished in vain through-

out the entire night, so all the priestly work of caring for souls would be futile if the commission and the grace did not come from Jesus. And contrariwise, how joyous and blessed is the work of the priestly ministry, founded not upon human motives but upon the grace that comes from above. Whomsoever the Father has given Him, he shall come into the net; but Christ's priests take that fish, protect and guard it.

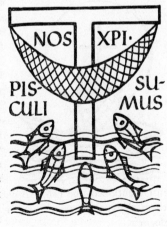

b) *The little fishes*. Now let

us examine the design on page 53. There we see little fishes swimming toward a net; the net is suspended from a T-shaped beam. The significance is clear. Again the fishes are men, the water is the world; the net is the Church, and the T-shaped beam is the Cross of salvation. The net is hanging from this beam because the Church derives all her power from the Cross of Christ. Without the Cross the Church would be a mere society seeking to proffer mankind some advice. From the Cross she secures all graces, all blessings, all strength. And from the Cross divine life flows into the souls of men through baptism, through the holy Eucharist. With the same single intent as the fishes in the picture, so should we on Sundays hasten to holy Mass, to the net that hangs from the Cross. Translated, the Latin inscription reads: "We are the little fishes of Christ!" This beautiful phrase, written by a Father of the ancient Church named Tertullian, fits nicely with the words of our Savior in today's holy Gospel.

c) *The great Fish.* If Christians are the little fishes, then Christ is the great Fish. In her discipline of the secret the ancient Church spoke with predilection of her Lord as the "Fish." The Greek

word for fish is ἰχθύς, in our script ICHTHYS. These five letters are the initial letters of our divine Savior's full title: I(esus) Ch(ristus) Th(eou) Y(ios) S(oter). The words in English mean: Jesus Christ, Son of God, Savior. Under certain circumstances the early Christians kept their faith hidden from the pagans. When speaking to one another they would use signs or symbols, as, for instance, that just mentioned, the fish. No one knew what it meant but they themselves; they spoke about a fish but would mean their Redeemer.

It was also very common to represent the fish with a basket of bread. The basket with five loaves and a fish would remind them of the miraculous multiplication of the loaves and fishes, a type of the holy Eucharist. The water in which the fish swim signifies the waters of baptism. Here again are represented the two principal sacraments, baptism and the Eucharist. These two sacraments were esteemed most highly by the first Christians; they ought also be most dear to us. Through holy baptism we received divine life; through the holy Eucharist this divine life is nourished and strengthened.

d) *The ship*. Now a bit of explanation about the picture on this page. The boat into which the Messiah stepped belonged to Peter. Peter's boat is a symbol of the Church. From it the Savior preached, from it the great catch was made. All this is significant. In the Church Christ is still teaching today, and from out the sea of the world men are still being gathered into the Church, to become Christ's little fishes. (Because the parish church represents the whole Church in miniature, it too stands as a symbol of Christ's Mystical Body.) So here we have another picture illustrating the Sunday liturgy. The faithful assembled together at Mass are Christ's fish in Peter's boat.

Let us examine this picture more minutely. The ship is the Church. Its sails bear the word *Ecclesia*. At the helm St. Peter is sitting, representing the Pope, who guides and governs the Church. Toward the front stands St. Paul, representative of the Church's office of teacher. The ship has the structure of a fish, and accordingly there is printed on its side the Greek word *Ichthys*, fish. The implications of the word we already know. But can a ship constructed like a fish represent both Christ and the Church? Certainly. Because the Church is the Body of Christ. St. Paul loved to speak of the Church in these terms. Christ is the Head, we the members. The Church is His Body. This is a deep, a wonderful, a glorious truth! We all are members of Christ, divine life is flowing into us from Christ. Oh, what important personages we really are! How we should love and honor holy Church, the Body of the Lord!

e) *The anchor.* The early Christians were expert in the art of devising symbols and in using them extensively. Even in the implements on board ship they saw spiritual content. Especially the anchor. The anchor, a very important and useful adjunct to the ship, secures it, particularly when storms would toss it to and fro. So there arose the expression, "the anchor of hope." Now as the anchor bears a certain resemblance to the Cross and the Cross is the great source of supernatural hope, the early Christians spontaneously employed the anchor as the symbol of the Cross, of redemption, of salvation. As a result we often find the anchor in some form or other upon graves in the catacombs. Fellow Christians, let us make the Cross of Christ the anchor of our lives. Christ the Crucified must be our all. In the Cross is salvation!

B. The Pilgrimage. Again and again Mother Church reminds us that we have no lasting cities here on earth. We are foreigners on earth, pilgrims on their way to a heavenly fatherland. Sunday, in particular, Sunday, the day of God, the Lord's day, is the day upon which we are to remind ourselves that we are wanderers, pilgrims. It is the day when, with compass in hand, we are to determine our goal, the day when we are to receive the strength and courage needed to continue our pilgrimage. Today's holy Mass very beautifully shows the way and notes the stages. Listen as Mother Church explains these various stages to us.

First stage. We began the journey heavenward on the day of baptism. Prior to baptism we were swimming in the turgid waters of earthly life. Then came the moment when the divine Fisherman cast His net and landed us in the ship of the Church. From then on we have been Christ's little fishes. In a spirit of gratitude let us recall that day of our baptism, because every Sunday is ordained unto the renewal of baptism; every Sunday centers upon baptism and perfects it. Every Sunday the graces of baptism are unfolded further and enhanced through the Eucharistic Sacrifice.

Second stage. For some time now we have been on our journey. What kind of trip has it been? Already on the third Sunday after Easter, Mother Church showed us that life on earth is no paradise: "You shall be made sorrowful, but the world shall rejoice; you shall lament and weep." Yes, this certainly is the case; and today she paints this rugged pilgrimage in starkest colors.

She shows us the enemy, or better, three of them: (1) the visible world. Non-Christians are never kindly disposed toward Christians. They regard Christians as foreigners — and rightly so. Therefore we need not expect anything good from the world, from men. In the Collect we pray that the course of secular events may be peacefully ordered so that the Church may worship unmolested. We should be happy if the world leaves us in peace. (2) The enemy within ourselves is more dangerous. That enemy is our perverse and obstinate will. But in His mercy God endeavors to align our obstinate wills with His by a power firm and gentle. (3) Beneath all, however, is lurking the archenemy of the human race, the devil. His influence is not to be slighted; he is the adversary from the beginning. He swore enmity against Christ, and everyone who sides with Christ is his foe. It is the devil who is constantly inciting the world and the flesh to trouble us. The liturgy depicts this state of affairs in two pictures today, that of a *siege* and that of a *lighthouse*.

It would, however, be of little benefit if the Church merely pointed out to us the enemy and the battle lines. Wisely she supplies us with effective means for successful combat. When the city of the soul is besieged, she brings to it a mighty shield, an invincible protector, a savior, Christ Jesus the Lord. He is not distant; in holy Mass He is with us. During today's holy Banquet the Church sings the beautiful verse: "The Lord is my Firmament, and my Refuge, and my Deliverer!" Furthermore, the

Lord is a lighthouse giving us our true bearings. He gives light to our eyes that we may not veer off into the sleep of death.

Third stage. And lastly the Church clarifies the third and final stage, the journey's end. We must bear much suffering in this life, the Epistle says, but a glance forward to the glory of heaven will lighten the load. As pilgrims on earth we should cherish a holy homesickness for our heavenly fatherland; such a spirit will enable us to overcome more easily the hardships of life, for as St. Paul says so consolingly: "I do not regard the sufferings of this time worthy to be compared with the glory to come, the glory that will be revealed in us."

The apostle of the Gentiles then continues with a meditation upon nature. When he beholds nature he believes he sees in it a great longing for the glorification of the children of God: "Every creature groans and travails in pain" in order to attain transfiguration. Nature, however, is no more than a type. Life on earth with all its pain and temptation is only the travail from which a child is born, the glorified, transfigured child of God. Again, it is principally the holy Eucharist that accomplishes this process of glorification and transfiguration.

Each Sunday Mass, then, gives meaning and direction to life's pilgrimage. The holy Eucharist links together past, present, and future by bringing to perfection the graces of divine adoption received in holy baptism and by bestowing the strength needed to meet the harsh realities of daily living. It is our Light, our Shield, our Citadel of strength. The holy Eucharist prepares us for a happy future, for a blessed meeting with our returning Lord.

FIFTH SUNDAY AFTER PENTECOST

First you must be reconciled with your neighbor.
Then, when you come, bring your offering.

1. **Text Analysis.** A striking difference may be noted between the spirit of the liturgy today and that of previous Sundays. Our gratitude to Mother Church for this variety in the celebration

of God's holy mysteries. On previous Sundays the liturgy presented Christ in a series of tableaus: first as the good Landlord who invites His guests to a supper; then as the Good Shepherd who carries His little sheep into the heavenly sheepfold; and lastly as the good Fisherman who with His net draws the chosen fish into the bark of the Church.

Instead of painting another such picture for us today, Mother Church seeks to teach us a lesson, an important lesson, one that must become impressed deeply upon our hearts: *the lesson of love toward neighbor*. Before her mind is a community united in Christ through love — let us say, a family of Christians intimately joined to Christ through grace, a family, moreover, united among themselves by true neighborly love. And this family is now assembled for the holy Sacrifice which is being co-offered with the priest.

According to an ancient *Ordo*, today's Mass formulary was assigned to the first Sunday after the feast of the apostles Peter and Paul. The Epistle is taken from the First Letter of St. Peter, thus breaking the regular sequence. By way of exception the principal parts of the formulary are thematically unified in that the Epistle, Gospel, and Collect all treat the virtue of love. This theme the Collect summarizes very beautifully: in His love God prepares for us *bona invisibilia* that will bear fruit only if we too show love.

2. Holy Mass (Inclina Domine). In orderly sequence the chants of the Proper express the sentiments of a soul from petition in deepest need to joyous praise in blessed union with Christ. At the *Introit* procession the oppressed soul nears the sanctuary; from the depths of the heart she is imploring that her prayer for aid be granted. In the words of Psalm 26, a psalm of trust and confidence, the lowest note is struck: "Forsake me not, do not despise me" — an excellent disposition with which to enter the house of God.

The *Collect*, an exceptionally fine prayer formula, reminds us of the wonderful things God has prepared for those who love Him. Nevertheless, love of God is no human creation; it can be infused only by God Himself. This divine love is the object of our petition, and we ask it in such measure as to love God "in all things and above all things." How well this truth is phrased: to love God *in* His creation, yet *transcending* all creation! Our Collect certainly brings the Mass text to a theological crest, one that may even be regarded as a climax to these first Masses of the Pentecost season that turn on love.

In the *Epistle*, Peter, the prince of the apostles, whose feast comes at the end of June, stands before us as the preacher. He too teaches us how universal the love of God must be: "You should all be of one mind. Show sympathy toward one another and brotherly love. Be merciful, modest, humble. Never return evil for evil or abuse for abuse; on the contrary, pay back with blessings. For such is your vocation; and in the end you will inherit blessing." Think over these simple words. What does the Church ask of us? Unity. To be one in prayer, one in love, one in grace. We have but one Father in heaven; Christ is our only Mediator; He is our Head and elder Brother, and all of us are brothers and sisters.

Now in the Mass, which surely is the Christian's principal service toward God, we are to pray in unison to our Father, not each one for himself but all with a single voice. That is praying with the Church. And if we wish to pray as one, then we must also live as one. As in a good family all suffer when one member is sick, so too it should be among us Christians. We ought act in a sisterly, brotherly manner toward one another. We are brothers and sisters because through baptism we have become brothers and sisters in Christ. In a very true sense we have become blood-relatives — divine blood, divine life surges within us. Therefore we must suffer, must easily forgive, willingly yield to others and be humble.

Recall the last verse of the Epistle: "In your hearts worship Christ the Lord." These words point to a second union. The first union is that between Christian and Christian; the second is between Christian and Christ. In baptism we have "put on Christ," the apostle says. As a garment when put on becomes, as it were, a part of the wearer, so we have become intimately bound up with Christ. This Epistle, if perfectly practiced, would change our whole community life.

The *Gradual* goes a step higher on the ladder of confidence. We feel ourselves already out of danger; God is our protector, we are His slaves. The *Alleluia* verse tells of Christ the King who once won the Easter victory and now in great glory rejoices at the right hand of God, while we, the redeemed, exultingly shout *Alleluia*! The *Gospel*, culled from the Sermon on the Mount, delves still more deeply into the lesson of love. Hard words come from the lips of Jesus: hating one's neighbor is equivalent to murder in His kingdom; the heavenly Father will accept no gifts or sacrifices from my hands if I am hostile toward my brother.

Christ's Gospel-teaching still rings in my heart as I chant the *Offertory*. I am thankful to Him for my knowledge of and insight into the law of love; nevertheless, without Him I am unable to transform this love into action. Therefore Christ with His grace stands as a warrior at my side in the holy Eucharist that I may not waver. The *Secret*, a well composed community prayer, requests that what we as individuals have brought to the altar during the Offertory procession should be of benefit to all. Unmistakably this prayer points to the ancient practice of having the faithful bring suitable gifts to a table near the altar. These offerings were made and brought by the individual members of the community, yet all were to benefit thereby.

At the *Communion* we again pray Psalm 26, but the verse selected is not so much a petition as a cry resembling Peter's "Lord, it is good for us to be here." The moments following holy Communion are precious: "One thing I have asked of the Lord, this will I seek after: that I may dwell in the house of the Lord all the days of my life!" In the Communion Banquet we have attained the end proper to the holy Sacrifice, viz., union with Christ and union with fellow-Christians. The *Postcommunion*, petitioning that we may be cleansed from secret failings and delivered from the snares of enemies, expresses another of the Mass's multiple effects.

3. Divine Office. We may center attention upon the two main readings, the tragic death of Saul and the Sunday Gospel. The three greater antiphons (Lauds and Vespers) stem from these pericopes. On Saturday evening: "Mountains of Gilboa, neither dew nor rain must come upon you! For upon your slopes the shield of heroes met disgrace, the shield of Saul as though it had not been anointed with oil. How the valiant have fallen in battle! And Jonathan slain on the heights! Saul and Jonathan, so lovable, so very charming in life, now even in death have not been parted!" This is part of David's touching funeral dirge over Saul and Jonathan as given in the opening chapter of Second Samuel.

At Matins St. Gregory the Great asks: "How is it that David, who to those that did him evil would not return it, when Saul and Jonathan fell in war, cursed the mountains of Gilboa, saying: 'Mountains of Gilboa, neither dew nor rain must come upon you nor upsurgings from the deep! For upon your slopes the shield of heroes met disgrace, the shield of Saul as though it had not been anointed with oil'? It is because the word *Gilboa* has the (etymological) meaning of 'running down.' Now by Saul, anointed and dead, the death of our Mediator was foreshadowed. And the mountains of Gilboa well represent the proud uplifted hearts of the Jews, for by *running down* after the cravings of this world they became enmeshed in the death of Christ, that is, of 'the Anointed.' Because among them an anointed King died physically, they too became deprived of all the dew of grace."

At the *Benedictus*: "You have heard that it was said to the ancients: *Thou shalt not kill.* And if anyone did, he would be liable to judgment." At the *Magnificat*: "Should you be carrying your gift to the altar and chance to remember that your neighbor is at odds with you, put your gift down even at the very altar and leave. First you must be reconciled with your neighbor. Then, when you come, bring your offering, alleluia."

Discussing the Gospel, St. Augustine says: "For the Pharisees justice consisted in not committing murder; but for those who seek to enter the kingdom of God justice consists in never yielding to anger without good reason. Not to kill, then, represents a minimum morality; and one who accomplishes that will be called the least in the kingdom of heaven. By fulfilling the law not to murder, one does not straightway obtain title to greatness, and thereby become fit for the kingdom of heaven. Still he definitely has taken a step in the right direction; he will, however, attain perfection only when he no longer becomes irate without good reason. And having arrived at that stage, his chances to commit murder will be remote indeed. Therefore He who teaches us not to become angry does not in any way abolish the law against murder; rather, He brings it to perfection, for now we maintain innocence both in external actions by refraining from killing another as well as internally by restraining ourselves from anger."

4. Meditation. A. Community Sunday. On these first Sundays after Pentecost Mother Church exhorts us to foster and cherish the most precious of Christian virtues: *love* — love of God and love of neighbor. The present Sunday may be called "The Sunday of the Love of Neighbor." In the Gospel Christ spoke very seriously on the love of neighbor. Hating one's brother is tantamount to murder in the Christian community; and the heavenly Father will accept no offerings from a child who cherishes ill will. In the Epistle St. Peter touchingly counselled love of neighbor, and in the Collect we sincerely petitioned for the love of God above all and in all, especially in our brethren.

Nevertheless, the title "Community Sunday" would perhaps be better suited to the liturgy today, the fifth Sunday of the Pentecost cycle. For today the Church endeavors to cast a dual bond about her children, the bond of the love of God and the bond of the love of neighbor. We ought constitute a community welded into unity through the divine life of grace in Christ and through the love of neighbor among the separate members.

It is the will of Christ that we work out our salvation not as isolated individuals but rather in communion with the great family of the Church. Virtue is perfected by contacts with others. We form one Body, and as members of this Body we mutually aid one another. But we form not only that one great community, the Catholic Church; we should also feel ourselves as part of the smaller unit, the parish. From such awareness the finest stimuli toward both personal and social virtue can arise. We Christians ought pray in common, sacrifice in common; we ought afford mutual edification, having regard for one another, care for one another. The first phrase of today's Epistle provides a whole program for Christ-like community life: "You should all be of one mind. Show sympathy toward one another and brotherly love. Be merciful, modest, humble."

The focal point of spiritual life in a community and at the same time the fountain of all graces is the holy Sacrifice of the Mass. Sunday Mass provides the most noble expression of true community endeavor. It would be interesting and very useful to consider the entire Mass, delving further into each word or action that tells of or suggests this ideal. We must, however, be selective.

a) What perfect communion and solid unity stems from the Sacrifice Banquet! For no other reason is it called *communion,* that is, "a union with . . ." In the first place there is the union with Christ who says: "He who eats My flesh and drinks My blood remains in Me and I in him." Nevertheless, it must not be forgotten that holy Communion is also the best basis for union between men. Through the Body and Blood of Jesus we become in the highest sense blood-related; we become real brothers and sisters in Christ.

This would be a fitting place to note three "community acts" that should be fostered and exploited spiritually with regard to the Mass. Results, however, do not depend as much upon external performance as upon the accompanying spirit. I refer to the Offertory procession, the kiss of peace, and the love-feast or agape.

b) The Offertory procession. It is well established that at every Mass the early Christians held an Offertory procession at which they brought bread and wine to the altar as well as other gifts. Perhaps today's Gospel helped to occasion this Offertory procession, for Jesus says: "Should you be carrying your gift to the altar. . . ." Now what is the spirit of the Offertory procession?

The Sacrifice of the Mass consists in this that through the hands of the priest we bring to the heavenly Father the Flesh and Blood of Jesus Christ. Strictly speaking, our contribution to the holy Sacrifice is nil, since we can do nothing touching its essence.

Nevertheless, that this Sacrifice may also be our Sacrifice, we should bring the needed materials, the bread and wine that will be changed into the Lord's Body and Blood. These gifts, however, must represent one's own self, one's whole person. In the gift we give self. Now consider the wondrous exchange that ensues. Every one brings of his own, even, as it were, his very soul. But he lays it upon the Offertory table as a common gift. Therefore the Secret very appropriately petitions "that what each of us has offered may profit all unto salvation." The poor bring little, the rich much, while all benefit from the common sacrifice. This, however, is not the exclusive privilege of Offertory gifts — all the prayers and merits of individual Christians should be oriented unto everyone's good through the holy Sacrifice.

c) The kiss of peace. The kiss of peace may also be said to have been occasioned by today's Gospel. Christ our Redeemer commanded: "Should you remember that your neighbor is at odds with you, put your gift down even at the very altar and leave. First you must be reconciled with your neighbor." In deference to this command the Christians of earlier centuries gave to each other the kiss of peace before the Offertory. But in the Roman Mass it was placed before holy Communion. Nowadays the kiss of peace is retained only at solemn high Masses. How beautifully it reminds us that before the Giver of peace can come to my heart I must live in peace with those around me. My neighbor to whom I give the kiss of peace is, as it were, the representative of all men, especially of those with whom I do not get along too well. Therefore I express visibly forgiveness and love toward them before receiving holy Communion.

Consider the deep significance of the kiss of peace. The priest first kisses the altar upon which the Body of the Lord is lying. The altar is the symbol of Christ, it is Christ. The kiss, then, comes from Christ and descends upon all present. A twofold unity is thereby shown: unity in Christ and unity of Christians among themselves. What a glorious manifestation of Christian community!

d) The agape. Some liturgical circles [1] have adopted a practice to which more attention could be given, the *agape* or love-feast. After Mass the members gather for a common breakfast. This, however, must not be considered a mere social or secular affair, for it too belongs to the Mass. Christians of apostolic times concluded every Mass with a love-feast; they enveloped the holy Eucharist in love. The Christians of modern times would profit by resuming the practice. The family meal on Sunday could serve well as an *agape*, or continuation of the Mass. It would afford a splendid opportunity of practicing those community virtues of which St. Peter reminds us today in the Epistle — sympathy, patience, modesty, humility. In short, the love-feast in a liturgical circle or at home as the family meal would be an ideal way in which to foster a holy, brotherly and neighborly charity, as also to practice social virtue. Christ would be in the midst of such company. Parishioners, become a community of which the Holy Spirit is the soul, a community which carries Christ in its heart, which images the Catholic Church!

B. "Whoever hates his brother is a murderer." Do you recall that sentence from the Epistle on the second Sunday after Pentecost? At the time St. John's words may have made no great impression. Today our Savior says the same thing in the Gospel. The passage is taken from the Sermon on the Mount, which, as you know, sets forth the program and spirit of Christianity. In that sermon Christ point after point showed how the New Law rises heaven high over the Old. One such point in a passage that is somewhat difficult to follow is contained in today's Gospel. Jesus says: In the Old Law the fifth commandment read: "Thou shalt not kill." A murderer was to be arraigned before the local court and sentenced. In the New Law the fifth commandment really presents little difficulty, because no follower of Christ will commit murder. Nevertheless, there is in the New Law a sin that

---

[1] For example, St. Gertrude's, Klosterneuburg, Austria.

is comparable to murder, namely, hatred, enmity. Therefore whoever hates his brother has fallen under the law as if he had committed murder.

Among the Jews there was, moreover, a higher court, the Great Sanhedrin, before which the more serious crimes were brought. The Messiah was condemned by the Sanhedrin because the Jews accused Him of blasphemy. Our Gospel account continues: If hate is fostered and breaks into open insults (*Raca* means "fool"), then an ordinary court can no longer try the case; such a sin must be brought before the higher court. Yes, there even are sins against the love of neighbor which must be punished by nothing less than the flames of hell.

Do we understand what our Savior is saying? True, He is making allusions, allusions readily intelligible to the people of the time. If we pare off the allusions, His teaching is simple and clear: hardheartedness, hatred, enmity belong to the greatest of sins; they are equivalent to murder. Is it clear now how the beloved disciple John could write those awesome words: "Whoever hates his brother is a murderer! And you know that no murderer has eternal life abiding in himself"?

Our Redeemer has not yet finished speaking. He continues no less strongly. The heavenly Father will accept no gift or offering from any of His children who lives in enmity with his brethren. He will have nothing to do with such an individual. Christ repeats the lesson employing another allusion. Among the Jews the offering of tithes was a strict commandment; they were obliged to bring to the temple the firstlings and the tenth of all fruits and cattle. Jesus therefore says: "Should you be carrying your gift to the table of burnt-offerings and chance to remember that your neighbor is at odds with you, put your gift down even at the very altar and leave. First you must be reconciled with your neighbor. Then, when you come, bring your offering."

Forcibly though lovingly our blessed Savior has endeavored to impress upon our minds and hearts the importance of the greatest of the commandments. Hatred spells murder. It forces God to abandon His child and it excludes from membership in the Christian community.

SIXTH SUNDAY AFTER PENTECOST

Baptism — Eucharist

In accordance with ecclesiastical law, holy water is blessed every Sunday before the principal service in parish churches. The celebrant then proceeds to the altar, and after he has intoned the antiphon *Asperges me,* he sprinkles the altar and the people while the choir continues the verse. Translated, this antiphon says: "Sprinkle Your saving water upon me, Lord, to cleanse me; for if You wash me, I will become more white than snow." Immediately Psalm 50 is begun: "Have mercy on me, O God, in accordance with the greatness of Your mercy."

Now just what does all this mean? The holy water serves as a reminder of the baptismal water that cleansed our souls from original sin; it should now purify us from the sins of the past week; it should now re-cleanse the baptismal garment that perhaps became somewhat spotted. Accordingly we pray a penitential psalm asking that our baptismal robe "be made more white than snow." Furthermore, since sprinkling with holy water denotes a renewal of baptism, this ceremony is performed only on Sunday because Sunday is the day *par excellence* for the administration of this sacrament.

Such the significance of the rite. But how is it possible to renew baptism? Through holy Mass, through the holy Eucharist. Baptism has conferred divine life with all its concomitant blessings, but the holy Eucharist preserves and perfects that life. On the portal to every Sunday, therefore, two words may be inscribed in huge letters: BAPTISM — HOLY EUCHARIST. It would be particularly apropos today.

1. **Text Analysis.** It seems that the key to the formulary is had in the Collect. Here God is addressed as the divine Gardener; it is He who plants the germ of religion in our souls and brings it to maturity. The Easter-Pentecost season is like a garden in which the divine Caretaker places seedlings. These should now be growing, well protected from bugs and blight. Today's Mass

text enumerates various means employed by the heavenly Gardener to make His work successful. The Epistle lists the first of these, baptism. Baptism is the fountain emitting a constant flow of eternally life-giving waters. Every Sunday means baptism, the day for refurbishing baptism's graces. The second means employed comes to the fore in the Gospel, the holy Eucharist. By It the plantings are continually nourished, preserved, protected, cleansed.

The various chants of the Mass are helpful in voicing our heart's response to God's gardening. In the five chanted texts we can discern a gradation from conflict to victorious peace and rest, from distraught petition to the serenity of a soul aglow with celestial light. The first step is made at the Introit, *Ad te, Domine, clamabo*. The Gradual goes a step further, confident of a goodly answer. Trust in God becomes stronger as we sing the Alleluia verse — the third stage. The fourth takes us into the "marvels of Your mercies," Easter's graces (Off.). At last, with the Communion antiphon, we reach the summit, transfigured in God. Our hearts sing jubilantly: "I will approach and bring an offering of joy to His tabernacle! I will sing, I will give thanks to the Lord." Thus do the chants touch the life of Easter grace, that life about which the divine Gardener is so concerned. An excellent Mass formulary for Sunday because its every text turns our attention to the growth of that divine life bestowed at Easter.

2. **Holy Mass (Dominus fortitudo).** Characterize today's formulary as a genuine "Easter Mass." We are shown the relation that the liturgy of the Word bears to the liturgy of the Eucharist, how the doctrinal content of a Mass formulary mirrors that which actually takes place in the sacrifice-*mysterium*, i.e., the actualization of the work of redemption at the present time and its application to us. The *Gospel* in particular provides a fine picture-symbol for the Mass action. Every Sunday a great (Christian) multitude is gathered with Jesus in the parish church. Now as then He first preaches. He speaks to us in the Epistle, in the Gospel, in the sermon. After that He again says: "I have compassion on the multitude. The week is long, and if I send them away fast-

ing to their homes, they will faint on the streets of daily life."
Jesus is thinking of souls. Straightway He nourishes them, not, of
course, by multiplying ordinary bread but by changing it into
His own Body.

The *Epistle* puts us into the context of Easter blessings.
Through baptism we were all plunged into the likeness of
Christ's death; we became new men, walking in newness of life;
we died to sin to live only for God! All these Paschal blessings
should be refreshed in us today by means of the holy Eucharist.

Give a few extra moments today to the chants of the Proper.
Note and try to assimilate the spirit of the *Introit*, its trust and
confidence. We are God's "anointed" (in baptism), God's
"people," God's "inheritance." The consciousness of being God's
own elect, of having Him as "Shepherd," places this soul-stirring

prayer on our lips. Yes, "the Lord is the strength of His people, the all-powerful protector of His anointed. Save Your people, Lord, and bless Your inheritance; govern them and exalt them day after day" (pray the entire Psalm 27).

A profitable meditation could easily be made on the *Collect*. God must be my all, my beginning, my progress, my end. He is the good Gardener over my soul. He "sows" divine love in my heart, He "gives increase" of spiritual life, He "cherishes and protects" the plantings of virtue, He weeds and waters and "wards off" enemies.

The *Gradual* has no direct connection with the Epistle; in fact, it is cast in a contrary spirit, for the Epistle speaks of the redeemed while Psalm 89 voices the curse of the unredeemed. In structure the Gradual is antiphonal, i.e., its second verse begins the psalm, while its first verse gives the antiphon. Nor does the *Alleluia* with its pleading call for deliverance ring true to type.

The *Offertory* chant serves as the processional while we carry our gifts to the altar. It is a march that symbolizes our upright way of life, our experience of the "marvels of divine mercy." According to Schuster, the *Secret* formerly was couched in stronger terms: May God place the proper words in the mouth of His people so that their prayer is certainly heard. Our offerings are escorted heavenward by the common prayer of the faithful; such prayer is always effective.

The *Communion* is directly Eucharistic in theme (which is not always the case). The sacred Species are spoken of as the *hostia iubilationis* in a very joyful mood: "I will sing, I will chant a psalm to the Lord." In conclusion we may say that the chants are more joyous than on the previous Sunday, and our hearts are happiest as we sing the Communion. Like last Sunday, the *Postcommunion* is concerned with the negative effects of holy Communion, cleansing and protection.

3. **Divine Office.** The two topics proper to today's Office are David's sin and the Gospel miracle. Words spoken by the penitent David are employed as the *Magnificat* antiphon at Vespers on Saturday: "I beseech You, Lord, take away the iniquity of Your

servant, for I have acted foolishly." At Matins St. Ambrose delivers an admirable apology on David's sin: "How often each of us blunders during the course of every hour! Yet no one, at least not the ordinary person, gives any thought to acknowledging his sin. But David, great and mighty as he was, would not hide the knowledge of his guilt within himself for a moment but immediately and with immeasurable sorrow confessed his evildoing to the Lord.

"Could you find anywhere today a man of means and status who would not become resentful if reminded of his evil deeds? But David, illustriously ruling as king and privileged by many divine oracles, did not become embittered when an individual with no special mandate from on high upbraided him for sinning gravely; rather, with genuine groans he admitted his error. His heartfelt sorrow so moved the Lord that He said to David through Nathan: 'Because you have repented, the Lord has taken away your sin.' Note how swiftly forgiveness came; this proves how thorough and genuine the king's contrition had been, sincere enough to undo so horrendous a crime.

"When corrected by priests, other men aggravate their guilt by trying to deny or to excuse their actions; and thereby the sin, for which a remedy was administered in hope, becomes graver still. It is quite the opposite with the Lord's saints who strive to win the holy struggle and to run the course of salvation. These, if by chance they fall into sin because they too are human and stumble from the weaknesses of nature rather than from a lusting for sin, lift themselves up again to run with greater determination. Shamed by their sin, they now fight more strenuously; it would seem that their fall proved to be no hindrance at all, but rather an incentive to accelerate their pace.

"David sinned — as kings will. But he repented, he wept, he lamented — as kings will not. He acknowledged his guilt, begged forgiveness; prostrate on the earth he grieved over his deplorable state. He fasted, he prayed, and left to all later ages the proof of his repentance and heartfelt grief. A deed that ordinary persons would be ashamed to do, a king here publicly confesses! Those who are bound by laws will try to deny that they violated them; they will not humble themselves to ask forgiveness, as did this king who was bound by no man-made decrees. That he sinned shows he was human; that he begged forgiveness shows he wanted to do the right. To fall happens to everybody; only the few repent. To commit sin stems from our very nature, while to rid ourselves of sin is the surest sign of sanctity."

Both greater antiphons of the Sunday Office call to mind the miraculous multiplication of the loaves of bread. Noteworthy is the fact that these antiphons are almost identical: "I have compassion on the multitude. See, they have now been with Me three days and have nothing to eat. If I send them away fasting to their homes, they will faint on the way, alleluia" (*Magn. Ant.*). How well these beautiful words reveal the deep, human sympathy in the heart of Jesus.

For the Lessons of the third nocturn St. Ambrose appears again and explains the Gospel. "The food of heavenly favor was not distributed until after the cure of the woman suffering from hemorrhage (for she was to typify the Church), as well as after the apostles were called to preach the kingdom of God. But note to whom distribution was made. Not to the idle, not to those in the city, that is, to Jews or those attached to earthly affairs, but to such as sought Christ in the desert.

"Only those free from secular entanglements are received by Christ; and the Word of God does not speak to them about worldly things, but about the kingdom of God. It is to those who carry the open sores of physical suffering that He willingly applies His healing medicine. How fitting, too, that those whom He had healed of their wounds and suffering should likewise be freed from hunger through spiritual nourishment.

"No one, therefore, receives food from Christ unless he is previously healed. Those, then, who are invited to the banquet are cleansed by His very invitation. If one was lame, he is given the ability to walk so that he may come; if one was blind, he could not enter the Lord's house unless the light had been restored to his eyes. Thus, in mystery, the same sequence may be detected everywhere: first through forgiveness of sins wounds are healed; then food from the heavenly tables is givenly profusely.

"Nevertheless, this multitude was not yet nourished on the more solid Food, nor their hearts, weak in faith, nourished with the Body and Blood of Christ. Milk, Paul says, I have given you to drink, not meat; for till now you were not able, and even now you are not. The five loaves may well be compared to milk; but a more solid food is the Body of Christ and a more fiery drink is the Blood of the Lord."

St. Ambrose's words are an example of how the patristic writers commented mystically on holy Scripture.

4. **Meditation upon the Sunday Liturgy. A.** Baptism and the holy Eucharist. Today's liturgy features the two principal sacraments of our holy religion, baptism and Eucharist. In these two sacred acts we have the focal points of the liturgical life of the individual and of the community. Baptism and Eucharist lift the soul out of the darkness of the unredeemed into the light of divine life and constantly shape it unto greater participation in eternal glory. Let us see what Mother Church wishes to teach us about these two sacraments.

a) *Baptism.* Never does St. Paul speak more sublimely about the sacrament of baptism than today. It is not enough for him to say: Through baptism we have become children of God, we have received a new life. No, his words actually startle us. He says: Through baptism we become members of Christ, we become other Christs! He is speaking of the sublime mystery of the Mystical Body. Christ is continuing His mortal, earthly life in a mystical life, a life of which He is the Head, of which the Church is His Body, of which we are the members. Through baptism, St. Paul says, we become members of that Body, and thereafter we partake in all Christ's activities as well as in all the fruits of His works.

To put it more concretely: Through baptism I became a hand of Christ. The hand partakes in all that concerns the person of whom it is a member. If the person is rich, the hand will be soft and smooth; if the person is poor, the hand will be rough and calloused. Visualize the hand of Christ. It worked wonders. Upon the Cross it was pierced; it was placed in a grave; at the resurrection its scars shone brightly; at the ascension it entered heaven's glory. Now at baptism you became a hand of Christ; therefore you are reliving all that Christ did and suffered. You also partake in the fruits of His every act. With Him you are crucified; with Him you die to the old man; with Him you arise to a new life. And as Christ dies now no more, so also you are dead to sin, alive always to God.

What a tremendous wealth of genuine Easter theology may be drawn from Paul's few words! Each Sunday let us be "baptism conscious." With such sublime thoughts in mind we may cheerfully face any week's rough weather.

b) *Holy Eucharist*. What St. Paul says of the redeemed man is, to our sorrow, the ideal; for, in reality, even after baptism we remain subject to weaknesses and passions; even after baptism we stand in continual need of aid from above. For this reason Christ, who knew human nature, instituted a further sacrament, one meant to perfect that which baptism began — the holy Eucharist.

Today's Gospel-miracle is easily pictured. We see Christ surrounded by throngs of people who press close to hear His words, who will not be separated from Him. Towards evening He says compassionately: I pity these people. For three days they have persevered with Me, and now they have nothing to eat. If I allow them to return home hungry, many will fall exhausted on the way. So He fed four thousand with seven loaves and a few little fishes. All ate and were filled. Now what is the moral of the story?

To retell one of Christ's miracles is certainly not the Church's only object, for the Gospel at Mass is concerned not merely with the past but principally with the present. What Jesus did on that occasion He still does today. At that time He acted visibly, today He acts invisibly. At that time He nourished the body, today He nourishes the soul. At that time He gave men perishable bread, today He gives us all the true, living Bread that is Life and bestows life. Viewed in this light, it is easier to appreciate the import of the Gospel. We, the baptized, are journeying through

May the grace of our Lord Jesus Christ,

the love of God the Father,

and fellowship with the Holy Spirit

gladden your hearts ✚

the wilderness of life toward a heavenly fatherland. We need the Bread of Life not to fall and perish while on this journey.

See too how subtly the Gospel supplements the Epistle. The Epistle says: We are baptized Christians and as such free from sin. The Gospel adds: To preserve yourself from sin you need the Bread of Life. It is the holy Eucharist that completes, protects, and perfects the sacrament of baptism, that develops the whole Christian personality, that leads to the eternal goal.

c) *The fruits* of these two sacraments are described in the Collect of today's formulary. God is portrayed as the Gardener, the soul as His plant. We ask Him to "implant in our hearts the love of His holy Name." This He did already at our baptism. Baptism's graces are like seed-wheat. But the wheat-sprout is not immediately seen, neither is its stalk. The little seed must first bud and grow. "And grant us *growth* in the fear of God." This is the work of the Eucharist. When the sprout appears above ground, the gardener's task of watering and weeding will begin (*nutrias . . . ac custodias*). Here we have the work of the many Sundays of life. At Sunday Mass the divine Gardener goes through His garden aiding, guarding, and nourishing His plants. This He accomplishes by the Mass liturgy.

B. The "Redeemed Soul" and the "Unredeemed Soul." If we read today's profound Epistle meditatively, it almost seems that St. Paul wanted to say that sin was an impossibility for man endowed with the graces of baptism. He concludes very clearly: We are baptized into Christ's death, that is, we have died together with Him; the old man in us has been fastened to the Cross. As a result we ought consider ourselves "dead indeed to sin, but alive unto God in Christ Jesus our Lord."

It certainly would be paradise upon earth if after baptism no one would be subject to sin. In real life, however, it is quite different. Baptism doubtlessly bestows grace and effaces sin, but it does not transform us into angels. Before the fall Adam could easily overcome sin, since he had no inclination to evil; he was free from the flesh's inordinate desires. We, on the contrary, do not enjoy that blessed state. Sin, of course, is blotted out, but the tendency toward evil still remains. This tendency is constantly alluring us to sin, this tendency makes us groan under the yoke of personal weaknesses and passions. In everyday life the words of Goethe's Faust prove true: "Two spirits dwell within my breast." The one spirit is the *redeemed soul*, the other is the *unredeemed soul.*

It would be both interesting and spiritually advantageous to see how the liturgy during the course of an ecclesiastical year views not only the individual soul but also the whole Church as redeemed and as unredeemed. At no time, though, is either state present absolutely; and the liturgy sees both the Church and the soul now from one angle and now from the other. Often there are present elements from each. As long as we remain upon earth we will experience the impact of both. During Advent we will feel ourselves as unredeemed, if we properly understand and live the Advent liturgy. At Christmas-Epiphany we will feel redeemed. During Lent we place ourselves among the catechumens, the unredeemed. At Easter we constitute God's redeemed children.

In this way the liturgy seeks to unfold and develop all aspects of spiritual life. As unredeemed men we should become conscious of our helplessness, should practice humility; as redeemed men we should carry within ourselves an awareness of our Christian vocation. In the time after Pentecost both approaches receive attention, since both the redeemed and the unredeemed soul make their appearance. An example of this is found in today's Mass. Let us take the formulary and listen to the "two souls" expressing themselves.

In the *Confiteor* the unredeemed soul alone acknowledges her threefold *mea culpa*. Both souls chant the *Introit*; the unredeemed cries out: "Unto You do I cry, O Lord! O my God, do not be silent toward me, for if You are silent toward me I will become like them that go down to Sheol." But the redeemed soul comes to the fore, clinging to the Lord. Indeed she is weak, but God is her Strength, her Protector, her Shepherd, her Guide. Echoes from both can be heard in the *Kyrie* and *Gloria*. In the *Kyrie* the need of redemption is paramount; the *Gloria* witnesses to the joyous consciousness of redemption attained.

The redeemed soul prays the *Collect*, but she well knows that only God can make her fruitful through much toil and patience. In the *Epistle* only the redeemed soul speaks because the Apostle describes the ideal; we have died to sin, we live only for God. The *Gradual* is the response of the unredeemed soul to harsh reality. A gripping lamentation, Psalm 89, has as its theme God's eternity versus man's brief days. Here we meet deep tragedy. The psalmist asks: Why must we die? The answer: Because of sin. The redeemed soul receives instruction from the *Alleluia* verse; in distress, trust in the Lord from whom comes salvation. Even though you are redeemed, Christ says in the *Gospel*, you may fall by the way. I am aware of this and accordingly I am providing you manna upon your pilgrimage, the holy Eucharist.

Now the drama of the Mass of the catechumens is over and the Sacrifice proper begins. Both souls participate in the *Offertory* procession. The unredeemed soul pleads: "Perfect my going in Your paths, that my footsteps be not moved," while the redeemed soul confidently petitions: "Show forth Your wondrous mercies! For You save those who trust in You." Upon the altar lies immolated the divine Lamb of sacrifice. Standing about the altar, we call ourselves His holy nation, His redeemed people. But while preparing to receive the Bread of Life all our miseries and ills suddenly well up and the unredeemed soul cries out: "O Lord, I am not worthy . . . say only the word and my soul will be healed," the redeemed soul straightway adds, shouting for joy. And so is received the Bread which "cleanses" and "protects," which gives the strength needed to persevere.

Thus there is in the Mass a constant ebb and flow between the consciousness of redemption attained and the consciousness of dire need for redemption. We certainly are saved, redeemed, even though we carry the treasure in frail vessels. St. Paul himself affords us the finest example. When he thinks of his sins, he casts himself to earth; he does not regard himself worthy to be the least of the apostles. But this is only the *Kyrie*; his *Gloria* soon

follows. His redeemed soul lifts itself in joyful knowledge of its
high calling and exultingly sings: "I can do all things in Him
who strengthens me." My unredeemed soul keeps me meek and
humble, my redeemed soul gives me joy and strength and victory.

SEVENTH SUNDAY AFTER PENTECOST

Slaves of sin — Servants of God

It has been our practice on past Sundays to give special consideration to one dominant thought or scene characteristic of
the day's liturgy. We saw Christ as the Good Host (2nd Sunday),
as the Good Shepherd (3rd Sunday), as the Good Fisherman
(4th Sunday). The fifth Sunday concentrated on the love of
neighbor, while the sixth was entitled "Baptism — Eucharist."
Now, however, a sequence of Sundays is beginning that features
a series of contrasts; the kingdom of God is shown in opposition
to the kingdom of the world, the good Christian versus the bad
Christian. Various parables and pictures are employed in developing these antitheses. Mother Church is trying to draw a sharp
line of demarcation between the divine and the worldly. Surely
this is our greatest fault — to vacillate so easily between the things
of God and the things not of God. Not that we never have made
a clean, sharp break. We did that when asked at baptism: "Do
you renounce Satan and all his allurements?" These Sundays
after Pentecost challenge us to renew and observe inviolately that
decision.

1. **Text Analysis.** Notwithstanding the fact that the two
following Sundays are still oriented to the feast of the apostles
Peter and Paul, various signs indicate the beginning of another
series. One such sign is the Introit-psalm (46), which breaks the
sequence by nearly a score (Ps. 27 to Ps. 46; see table, p. 6).
More important, though, is the content change. Today's liturgy

introduces a theme that continues until the tenth, perhaps even until the fourteenth Sunday after Pentecost; it is a theme beloved by the early Christians, that of the "two ways" or the "two kingdoms" (7th Sunday: military review of the two kingdoms; 8th Sunday: discourse upon the kingdom of the devil; 9th Sunday: judgment upon the kingdom of the devil; 10th Sunday: the foundations of the two kingdoms, pride and humility; 14th Sunday: the two Masters).

The Readings today are evidently related to one another, for both treat of the two ways: servants of God — slaves of sin; good tree — evil tree; words (Lord, Lord) — action (the will of God). And in both, attention is directed primarily toward results, fruits. Also the two Orations (Coll. and Postc.) show an antithetical structure, negative (imploring deliverance from evil) and positive (beseeching the bestowal of blessings). A secondary theme is added in the Offertory and in the Secret, viz., the sacrifices of the Old Covenant typify the sacrifice of Christ.

The glory and exuberance of summertime find reflections in the Mass formulary with its allusions to light, joy, and the fruits of earth — realities from the world of nature that are employed to illustrate supernatural realities. The Church is our teacher, gathering us, her children, close and saying: "Come, children, listen to me. I am going to teach you the fear of the Lord." It would be easy to imagine her taking an apple from the table at which she is sitting and speaking to us of the good tree and the bad tree, the good fruit of virtue and the evil consequences of vice.

There is an inversion of tone and spirit if today's Mass is placed alongside those of previous weeks; for the formulary today begins with a joyous ring and ends with a cry for help.

2. Holy Mass (Omnes gentes). The spirit of a particular day's liturgy is very often crystallized in the *Introit*. Today it is joy, the joy of Easter with Christ our glorified King enthroned above us. The basis of this Easter joy is divine life, a blessing to which the whole of Psalm 46 is dedicated. God has crushed the enemy in us, He has chosen us as heirs; our only prayer and care must be to preserve the precious legacy of divine life, divine adoption. In the *Collect* God's children beseech their Father, who wisely and providentially watches over them, to bestow all that is needed to live rightly.

Standing before us in the *Epistle*, the great teacher of the Gentiles points to our past lives, reminds us of our good fortune as also of our grave duties (Rom. 6:19-23). The apostle flashes before us two pictures that are worlds apart; one is entitled "Slaves of Sin," the other, "Servants of God." Formerly, before conversion, we served the tyranny of sin and put all our strength in its service. Now we are serving God and therefore should place soul, body, and life itself at His disposal. This is true liberty, the fruit of which is sanctity, and the end eternal beatitude. "But now having been freed from sin and having entered God's employ, you receive holiness as your pay, and at the end, life unending." This is a sentence that we should mull over during the entire coming week!

In the *Gradual* it is Mother Church herself who wishes to teach us this slave-like service of God, this "fear of the Lord" that transforms us into "children of light." The *Alleluia* verse, too, is a lightsome Easter song. Culled from the Introit psalm and charged with holy joy, it is a genuine Alleluia chant.

The Apostle referred to the fruits of the twofold way of life. Now we hear the very same from the lips of the Master. In the *Gospel*, an excerpt from the Sermon on the Mount, Jesus warns against seducers or false prophets and bares the signs by which they may be recognized. Mother Church is enlightening her children on how to distinguish the true way of Christian life from the false. Just as the tree is known by its fruit, so the true Christian is known, not by his fervent words, but by his performance of God's holy will. The Gospel, moreover, could serve for a serious self-examination: Am I perhaps a victim of self-delusion? Am I really a good tree loaded with good fruit?

As prayers accompanying our oblation, the *Offertory* and *Secret* are excellent; reference is made to the Old Testament and we are reminded again of the superiority of the Mass-sacrifice.

The chant for the Offertory, a genuine oblation-hymn, asks God to accept Christ's present sacrifice as formerly He accepted the many Old Covenant holocausts "that it may be pleasing unto Thee." The thought-content of the Secret is in perfect harmony with the concomitant Mass-action (which is rather exceptional). Christ's Sacrifice is the fulfillment of the ancient animal sacrifices; may God sanctify this perfect oblation "with the same blessing as the offering of Abel."

The brief and simple *Communion* antiphon voices a petition without designating its nature. So we should formulate our own request based upon the Readings and prayers, e.g., strength and grace to fulfill the will of God, to be servants of God, to produce fruit. The final prayer follows a similar mold (*Postc.*).

3. Divine Office. Proper to today's Office are the accounts concerning the aged king David and his successor Solomon, taken from the Old Testament, and the Gospel story taken from the New. St. Jerome comments mystagogically upon the Sunamitess Abisag: "Upon reaching the age of seventy, David, the warrior for many years, began to suffer from senility and from the lack of body heat. Out of Israel's tribes the maiden Abisag from Shunem was therefore chosen to sleep with the king and keep warm his aged body. Now what are we to understand by the reference to that Sunamite, that virgin woman aglow with the vitality of youth, who was needed to warm a cold, old man and who at the same time was of such holy reserve as not to arouse his lusts when comfortable?

"Let the most wise Solomon explain his father's pleasure; let the prince of peace describe the embraces of the man of war: 'Get wisdom, get understanding. Never forget and never stray from the words of my mouth. Do not forsake wisdom and wisdom will protect you. Love her and she will save you. The first thing about wisdom is: Get wisdom; and whatever be your belongings, let understanding be among them. Embrace her, and she will embrace you and place upon your head a crown of blessings; with a garland of delights will she protect you.'

"Practically all one's physical strength vanishes as old age sets in; wisdom alone increases while everything else is on the decline — fasting, vigils, almsgiving, sleeping on the hard earth, multiple engagements, reception of pilgrims, aiding the poor, fervor and perseverance in prayer, visiting the sick, and manual labor, the source for alms. We will not prolong the list; you know how all physical activity wanes as the body loses its vigor.

"I do not mean to imply hereby that wisdom remains inert in young people or in adults enjoying full health — especially those who by labor, concentrated studies, holiness of life and frequent prayer to the Lord Jesus have attained true knowledge for themselves; nor that wisdom too does not actually fade away for many as the years overtake them. I mean, rather, that because of the continual struggle youth is subject to in their bodies and because of the incentives to vice and the lusts of the flesh, wisdom, like fire in green wood, smolders and cannot show forth its gleaming splendors. But for those who devoted their youths to honorable disciplines, who meditated night and day on the law of the Lord, old age brings mature knowledge and experience; as time passes they become wiser and wiser and reap the sweet ripe fruit of their earlier efforts."

The greater antiphons, culled from the Gospel, recount the similitude of the good and bad fruits: "Be on guard against fake preachers; they come to you clothed as sheep, but actually are rapacious wolves. By their fruits you can recognize them, alleluia" (*Ben. Ant.*). "A good tree cannot produce poor fruit; every tree that does not produce good fruit will be cut down and cast into the fire, alleluia" (*Magn. Ant.*). The homily upon the Gospel is presented by St. Hilary (*d.* 367), a Doctor of the Church.

4. Meditation upon the Sunday Liturgy. A. The Two Ways. What is the principal lesson the liturgy wishes to teach today? Briefly, it seeks to show us how to distinguish genuine Christianity from counterfeit Christianity. It labels for us the true and the false way of Christian life. This one lesson is the burden both of the Epistle and of the Gospel. The Epistle contrasts the slaves of vice with the servants of virtue, while the Gospel counters the Christian-in-words with the Christian-of-deeds.

1. (a) *Slaves to sin.* In the Epistle St. Paul reminds the Roman converts of their pagan past. They had been the subjects of a mistress who enslaved them, who made them serve false gods, as if they had no will of their own. That mistress was sin. Like a tyrant she compelled them to place their members, the powers of their bodies and souls in her service. In the Apocalypse St. John depicts her as the great courtesan Babylon: "I saw a woman sitting upon a scarlet-colored beast, full of blasphemous names and having seven heads and ten horns. The woman was clothed round about with purple and scarlet; she was gilt with gold, precious stones and pearls, and had a golden cup in her hand that was full of the abomination and filthiness of her fornication" (Apoc. 17:3–4). It is to this monstrous mistress that all sinners are subject, as the Savior Himself testified: "Whoever commits sin is the slave of sin." St. Paul therefore asked the converted pagans: What fruit did the tree of your life formerly bear? He gives the answer himself: Sin, vice, acts of which you must be ashamed. And the final outcome? Death, eternal death.

b) *Servants of God.* Changing the approach, St. Paul considers the new life of the Roman converts. He writes: You have broken the chains of slavery to sin, you have abandoned the service of your former mistress and have become the servants of another Lord, Christ, who is God. You must now place your whole strength, your soul, your spirit, your body in the service of God, even as formerly you placed all these in the service of sin. You are now slaves of God, you are God's property. A slave has no will of his own, he belongs wholly to his lord. So also the true Christian. In his letters St. Paul frequently calls himself the slave of Christ. And Mary, the Mother of God, in the holiest hour of her life, knew herself as the servant, the handmaid of the Lord. The prophets, too, spoke of the Messiah as the "Servant of Yahweh." This is the essence of Christianity, to be God's servants, which means to fulfill perfectly His holy will.

Then, continuing his discourse, St. Paul inquires: What is the fruit of this new tree, that is, your life as Christians? Here he can answer proudly: Its fruits are the virtues of holy living.

And the finale is not death, but life everlasting. Thus the great Apostle has not only taught us how to distinguish counterfeit Christianity from true Christianity, but he has at the same time filled us with enthusiasm and has spurred us on toward its realization.

2. It is comparatively easy to distinguish the slaves of sin from the servants of God, for whoever panders to sin must say, if he wants to be fair to himself: I am not true to Christ. A much more difficult problem is to distinguish the Christian who is clever at talking religion from one who really practices it. Satan is exceedingly diplomatic, and it is not his method to make advances in the frightful appearance of a devil. He much prefers to appear as an angel of light. Usually he does not rush out as a rapacious wolf but ambles along as a wolf in sheep's dress. Of those tactics precisely Mother Church wishes to enlighten and warn her children.

a) Most everyone has had personal experience of Satan's stealthy maneuverings. He seldom endeavors to tempt one to sin directly but prefers to allure his victims under the pretext of good. Alongside every true virtue, therefore, he places a sham virtue which in reality is an evil. He knows how to whisper to the miser: That is not avarice but prudent foresight, frugality. He knows how to urge those thirsting for revenge: That is not vengeance but justice, justice which you must further. And how ingeniously the devil capitalizes on the passion of lust, the lust of the eyes and the lust of the flesh, to deceive men is too well known to need examples. Yes, the devil is a hypocrite and a liar from the beginning, for under the appearance of good he deceived our first parents. We must be on our guard against his wiles. If he would only come with open vizard, one could recognize and oppose him. Therefore the Church warns us today against the wolf in sheep's clothing.

b) Our Redeemer, furthermore, gives the norms by which the true Christian may be distinguished from the false. First He speaks concretely, then abstractly. Concretely: the Christian resembles a tree. A tree's fruit proves its worth. Many a tree stands loaded with leaves; in the springtime it proudly displays a gay dress of blossoms. And still it is worthless because it bears no fruit. So our Savior observes: *By their fruits you judge them.*

A man does not prove himself a Christian by the foliage of fine speech, or by the blossoms of devout emotions, but by his fruits, his virtues. One does not become a real Christian by saying: Lord, Lord. No, in daily life one must give evidence by loving his neighbor, by patience, by accomplishing his duties, by resignation in suffering and sorrow. These are the fruits by which the true Christian may be recognized. These same norms of judgment are then reiterated in an abstract though brief and conclusive statement: "Not every one who says to Me: Lord, Lord, shall enter into the kingdom of heaven, but he who does the will of My Father." Yes, the infallible sign of a genuine Christian is obedient performance of God's commandments.

B. The contrasts found in today's liturgy may also be pictured in two scenes, a scene of war and a scene of peace.

1. The first, a war scene, is vividly described in St. Ignatius' book of "Spiritual Exercises." In your imagination picture the plains of Babylon. Upon a throne of fire and smoke the king of this world is sitting, Lucifer. He has convoked his soldiery and is giving them orders to go forth into every land, into every city, to lead astray and corrupt mankind. He commands them to lay snares and to plant nets to bring mankind under his dominion; moreover, he supplies them with methods of action. They are to arouse inordinate desire for earthly goods and for worldly honor; thereupon pride and insubordination will follow spontaneously. Note with what zeal these soldiers of Satan depart to fulfill their commission! And their wages? Death, everlasting death is the salary of Satan's soldiery.

Another and very different mobilization is in progress on the plains of Jerusalem. There too a throne is erected, but upon it is sitting the King Christ Jesus. "All nations clap their hands, for awesome is the great King over all the earth" (Intr.). He too is enlisting soldiers into His service and is sending them forth to win and to enlarge His kingdom. Their mission extends to every house in every nation; they too are given the methods by which men are to be brought to this new allegiance: contempt of the world, acceptance of suffering and of the Cross, humility. And the wages? Life, a lasting life in God.

Does Mother Church permit us to choose between these two encampments? No, the choice has already been made. Long ago at baptism we freed ourselves from the service of Satan when the priest asked: "Do you renounce Satan?" "I do renounce," we wholeheartedly declared, and today we renew our allegiance to the true King, Christ. The Church brings this scene before us to remind us to be grateful for redemption from the yoke of slavery. Sunday is Easter, the day of baptism! Renew your baptismal vows. Do not become traitors or deserters, standing with one foot on this side and with one foot on the other. Place yourself unreservedly under the flag of your heavenly Commander-in-chief.

2. The second scene. Before us now is a beautiful, well tended orchard having row after row of fruit trees. The caretaker or gardener and his assistants are there, working steadily. A little brook, flowing through the garden, supplies the needed moisture. The sun, soft and warm, is ripening countless rosy-cheeked apples. Now the owner of the garden approaches the caretaker; presently they stand before a little tree heavy with foliage but lacking fruit. Thoughtfully shaking his head, the owner says: "Look, for three years I wanted to see fruit on this tree and find none. Cut it down! Why does it occupy the ground?" But the caretaker answers: "Master, let it stay another year. I will dig around it and dung it. Perhaps it will bear fruit; if not, then after that you can cut it down" (Luke 13:7–9). So the owner allows himself to be persuaded. They go along farther, noting how heavily other trees are laden with excellent fruit, and their hearts are happy.

The meaning of this second scene? In the first there was an option between Christ and Satan; in the second we are in God's own garden, the Church. Every Christian is a tree, the caretaker is Christ, who does the planting and nourishing, the

pruning and the propping. From the wound in His breast upon the Cross a brook has sprung and flows via the sacraments through the orchard. The sun is the Holy Spirit, who ripens the fruit, the owner is God almighty. Today the Owner has come to inspect the work of His Caretaker. Now at Mass they are strolling through the orchard of the Church, reviewing the rows of trees. They do not want to see foliage (stylish clothes) but fruit (good works). Presently they stand before my own little tree. Leaves? Yes. Fruit? Well. . . . The Owner's face darkens, but Christ pleads for me. He pleads for me during this morning's Sacrifice, He points to His holy Cross. . . .

EIGHTH SUNDAY AFTER PENTECOST

Children of Light

The theme of today's liturgy and its development follow much the same mold as that of last Sunday. Again we stand as children of light opposed to the children of the world. The chants are more joyous, charged with more confidence than ordinarily.

1. **Text Analysis.** The first indication of a relationship between today's formulary and last Sunday's may be found in the psalms used for the Entrance Chant (Pss. 46–47). In the Lessons the antithesis between the two kingdoms is again made obvious, men of the flesh versus men of the spirit, children of the world versus children of the light. A typical example of the disgraceful conduct of carnal man is contained in the Gospel (the unfaithful steward). This contrast between the virtuous and the wicked also forms the basis of the Offertory chant: humble people — the eyes of the proud.

The prayers are positive in character, the chants redolent with trust and joy. Because of the Gospel, the formulary, at first glance, may indeed appear weighted and moralistic in tone, but deeper study will show it to be as buoyant and lightsome as an Easter Mass. The substratum upon which the entire thought-content rests is baptism grace (note how St. Paul assumes its importance in the Epistle). Effortlessly we sense that we are standing on sacred ground while praying the Introit, the sacred ground of Easter; for in baptism at Easter and now at holy Mass "we received God's mercy" in fullest measure. And this gives us solid reason to praise Christ "unto the ends of the earth."

The Collect affords occasion to ask for the ability always "to think and to act rightly"; this means genuine Christ-like conduct, a mode of living pleasing to our heavenly Father. The few words Paul has to say on living according to the spirit cut deep into the sphere of morality. The Gradual, the Mass's only text voicing suffering and need, is nevertheless surcharged with positive trust and confidence in God. With the Alleluia verse we resume our praise of Christ. With such precedent we are hardly in the mood to read the Gospel in anything but a brightsome light and to observe how the Church uses the story of the clever swindler as an example to spur on the children of light to make better use of their endowments. Humility, however, must not fall by the way because these endowments are not from men but from God (Off.). The remaining three prayers are Eucharistic in nature and show the transforming effects of the Bread from heaven.

Three areas of thought, therefore, may be isolated in this Mass formulary, viz., (1) the high dignity of a Christian, a man led by the spirit; (2) that dignity must be reflected in his activity; (3) the Eucharist confers effective aid. Could more be expected from one Sunday's liturgy?

2. Holy Mass (Suscepimus). Sunday is Easter, the Lord's day. This is the spirit with which we enter God's "temple" (*Intr.*). Before us we see the *majestas Domini*, the radiant Lord, and are grateful for the graces of Easter, the "mercy we have received." With Psalm 47 our voices break into praising the "great Lord" in the "city of our God" upon the mystical "mountain" of the altar. Thus the Introit again is a typical "entrance" into the Mass-drama. The feast of the Purification of the Blessed Virgin uses the same Entrance Chant.

Entirely consonant with the liturgy's primary message is the petition for correct thinking and upright living contained in the *Collect*; acknowledgment of human insufficiency together with the desire to live according to the will of God is the burden of this striking and meaty prayer. In the *Epistle* St. Paul again addresses us. The eighth chapter, the climax of the letter to the Romans, describes the Christian equipped with "the spirit." A comparison is made between the man of the flesh and the man with *pneuma*, spirit; the former centers his thoughts and ambitions upon the earthly and temporal like the clever steward, while the latter is a man of God, a man blessed with all the graces and privileges of revealed religion. He has the gifts of supernatural faith, of grace, of the divine indwelling; he is a child with a heavenly Father and has Christ as his Brother. Heaven and happiness are his inheritance! All this the Apostle includes in the word "spirit."

In the *Gradual* we place our trust in Christ, employing the same psalm (30) as last Sunday at the Communion. A genuine paschal note is again struck by the *Alleluia* verse, *Magnus Dominus et laudabilis valde*. It may be noted that the Entrance chant and the Alleluia verse of the present and preceding Sundays are taken from the same psalms (46; 47).

Unless the moral of the story be kept in mind constantly, the *Gospel* (the parable of the unfaithful steward) will occasion difficulties. Christ praises the unjust steward not for fraud but because of the cleverness and zeal with which he provided for his future, earthly career. The zeal of the children of this world in earthly affairs should serve as a model in our strivings after an eternal goal. Powerful forces are slumbering within us which must be utilized for eternity. Well may we learn from the wisdom of the worldly-minded.

Again in the *Offertory* we meet a prayer constructed antithetically, perhaps an echo to the Liturgy of the Word; God humiliates "the eyes of the proud" but exalts and saves "a humble people." With an act of humility upon our lips, we join our hearts to the Mass action. A lengthy *Secret* tells what our Sacrifice effects: it should sanctify ordinary daily life and lead men to eternal joy. Psalm 33 was the favorite song of Christians for centuries as they proceeded to the Communion table, because of the verse, "Oh taste and see that the Lord is sweet." The Greek word for "sweet" is *chrestos;* the similarity in sound with the word "Christ" gave rise to a play on the phrasing: "Oh taste and see that (it is) Christ *(chrestos)* the Lord!" The sacred liturgy concludes with a final plea for the "renewal of body and soul" *(Postc.)* in order that the man according to the flesh may truly be transformed into a man according to the spirit.

3. **Divine Office.** Because the Sundays at this juncture may occur in August, reference must be made to the section on Scripture readings (pp. 152–176) for comment on the Lessons from

the Old Testament. The Gospel affords the subject matter for
St. Jerome's homily as well as for the greater antiphons. "The
master said to his steward: What is this that I hear about you?
Give a report of your work, alleluia" (*Ben. Ant.*). "What am
I going to do now that my master is depriving me of the stewardship? To dig I am not able, and begging is beneath me. I know
what I will do in order that when I lose the stewardship, people
will invite me in" (*Magn. Ant.*). The dramatical in the liturgy is
here easily seen. During the day we are to relive the parable;
the liturgy assigns us the role of the steward, though, of course, as
children of God.

4. **Meditation upon the Sunday.** A. The Chants. Let us
remember that the chants of the Proper have life and meaning
only to the extent that they are used in union with their respective Mass actions. During the chanting of the Introit, for example,
the priest clothed in festal vestments and accompanied by minis-

ters or servers approaches the altar: he represents the "great Lord" who "in the city of our God" (the Church) is proceeding to "His holy mountain" (the altar) to make us the "receivers of His mercy" (the graces of the holy Sacrifice). What tremendous significance there is to the Introit thus understood!

The Gradual and Alleluia may be considered separately. The Gradual today is a prayer of petition, earnest and confident (Psalm 30 was prayed by Christ during His last agony). By nature the Gradual is not a joyous acclamation but a reflective prayer, an echo to the Epistle. The Alleluia verse again heralds the "great Lord" while the deacon readies himself for reading the Gospel; both he and the book of the Gospels are symbols of Christ appearing among us. And finally during the sacrificial Banquet the faithful in lengthy queues approach the Lord's table while the choir sings Psalm 33, the Communion hymn of the ancient Church. After each verse the whole congregation could well repeat the antiphon: "Oh taste and see that the Lord is sweet." Surely this lovely antiphon would make a deep impression if sung by all the assembled faithful. Happily it is becoming more and more evident that we will understand the missal better when the people also take an active part in the celebration of sacred mysteries.

B. The Golden Bridge from Earth to Heaven. The liturgy on the Sundays during the Pentecostal cycle develops three great themes. The first is that of baptism and its graces. We are baptized and in the graces of baptism we are to anchor; every Sunday means baptism repeated, a small Easter feast. The second theme, preparation for the Second Advent of the Lord, is treated in detail on the final Sundays of the season. The remaining theme, the burden of the Sundays midway after Pentecost, may be summarized in the phrase: *the conflict between the two camps.* Though placed in the kingdom of God, we remain surrounded by the kingdom of the world; and our souls, laboring under Adam's wretched legacy, waver continually to and fro between two allegiances.

By these three great themes the liturgy covers rather adequately the whole range of Christian life. In baptism the precious treasure of the spirit was conferred; today's Epistle describes some aspects of this treasure. Through it we are God's children; we may call God Father. Through it we have become temples of the Holy Spirit, heirs and brothers of Jesus Christ. Nevertheless, baptism has not translated us to a paradise without toil or trouble. No, the Church sends us out into a troubled world and commissions us to work and struggle. We must guard the holy land of our souls against hostile attack, must learn to know and conquer the enemy, and such is the task that will continue till we have taken our final breath.

Mother Church is, we may say, both the heroine who teaches us the art of warfare and our strong fortress and shield in the conflict. Through the holy Sacrifice she bestows aid which repeatedly frees the soul from the enmeshments of temptation. We may ask, how does the Mass effect this? Courage and strength and perseverance flow abundantly from the word of God in the Mass of the Catechumens, but in a still fuller measure from the Sacrifice proper. Of ourselves we are helpless creatures wholly unable to withstand the attack, but in the Mass Another battles for us, the Mightier (Christ) vanquishes the mighty. By means of the Mass we league ourselves with our Captain, Christ; His battle becomes our battle, His triumph our triumph. His is the wondrous strength that renders us invincible.

Having matured spiritually during the many weeks of the Pentecost season, the soul becomes ready to join the retinue of its heavenly Hero and King, Jesus Christ. Therefore on the final Sundays of the cycle the Church asks her children to direct their gaze to the Second Advent longingly and lovingly. In these three great themes we have the golden bridge that spans the years of life and reaches from earth to heaven.

To overcome the tension between man's higher and lower natures, two forces must unite and espouse each other in bridal union, God's grace and the human will. If either is lacking, nothing good will happen. The most sublime example of cooperation between grace and free will occurred at the Annunciation; the angel of the Lord saluted Mary with an *Ave* (grace) while Mary gave consent with her *Fiat* (will).

We have purposely placed grace prior to will because grace enjoys the primacy; it is the stronger and the nobler. This is an important point in liturgical piety. The human will is not to be placed in the foreground. Grant to grace primacy and precedence, and it will act; then, escorted and confirmed by grace, the will can accomplish great things. Pass in review what the human will can accomplish in the natural order of fallen nature. What will men not attempt when spurred on by passion, by politics, by the love of pleasure! The universe becomes too small for their journeys and the heavens too low for their banners! Now it is exactly because the children of the world put their wills to better use than the children of light that our Savior complains in the Gospel. The second point in liturgical piety, therefore, is that we show a determined will, for grace of itself can perform no human acts.

Every Mass is an espousal between will and grace in a twofold way. In the Liturgy of the Word we offer the words of our prayers and receive in return the Word of God. At the Offertory we lay our will upon the altar, which in the Sacrifice is bedewed with grace; while at the Communion grace and will unite as the consummation of the Sacrifice. The union of God's grace and man's will always spells triumph in the affairs of life!

C. For many persons the parable of the unfaithful steward occasions difficulties. The story concerns a rich landowner who had several farms or estates but entrusted them to the care of an overseer or steward, while he himself lived in the city. This general manager enjoyed almost complete control, and since justice was not his chief virtue, he began defrauding his employer in goods and money. Others, however, observed and reported his conduct, and after some time he was told to make a report pending dismissal.

Without work, without means of sustenance, what would he do? But he was shrewd, and unscrupulous too. So while still in office, having summoned the various tenants, he asked the first:

How much rent must you pay? He answers: A hundred barrels of oil (at that time rent was paid not in money but in kind). The steward quickly replies: Take your contract and change it to fifty. We may assume that the debtor did not hesitate doing it; for the year in question and perhaps for the year following he would then be legally obliged to pay only half the normal amount. The steward acted in this manner in order to gain the good will of the debtors. He was thinking that these people would later favor and support him when he would be jobless and low in funds.

At this point the parable ends and Jesus states the moral or lesson. He praises the steward because he acted shrewdly. But can the Savior really praise a swindler and a cheat? Would not censures have been more appropriate? Read closely. Jesus does not praise the steward for defrauding another; neither does He hold up his conduct as such as a model. That would have been impossible for the holy and sinless Son of God. What Christ praises is the shrewdness and ingenuity with which that man provided for his future earthly welfare. And this shrewdness Jesus places before us, His children, for imitation on the supernatural plane. Accordingly He concludes: "The children of this world (of whom the steward was an example) are wiser in dealing with their fellowmen than the children of light (i.e., we Christians)."

These words of our Lord may be illustrated by a further example. A man begins business. To make it successful he will work day and night; he will take risks, endure hardships, virtually enslave himself. And all for the sake of financial success. Or another example — sportsmen. What severe discipline they subject themselves to in order to win the pennant in a race, in football, tennis or basketball, etc. And the prices people will pay for amusement! That is the wisdom of the children of the world. What human energy is squandered and wasted upon trivia!

Now let us look at the wisdom of the children of God. We know that the value of holy Mass is infinite; we know that the sufferings of this world are not worthy to be compared to the joys of heaven; we know that for following our divine Savior and denying ourselves we will "receive a hundredfold reward and eternal life." All this we know, but with what zeal do we strive after these goods? Oh, how sluggish we are in regard to eternal salvation! Truly we may not fall so low as to befriend the vices of the world. Nevertheless, we would like to enjoy the goods and pleasures of earth without losing those of heaven. So we swerve from side to side, now toward the kingdom of God, now toward the kingdom of Satan. The Redeemer had a perfect right to say: "The children of this world are wiser in dealing with their fellowmen than the children of light."

Imagine what would happen if the following announcement were made: "All who attend Mass next Thursday will receive a quarter; and if one receives holy Communion too, he will receive a half dollar." Why, the Church would be crowded, perhaps even the aisles. And the distribution of holy Communion would take much longer than usual! But what are those few pennies in comparison to the spiritual benefits that Mass and holy Communion confer? And men bother so little about them. By the parable, therefore, Christ wished to teach us that as children of God we should pursue our eternal welfare with the same zeal and with the same shrewdness and with the same perseverance as the children of the world strive after social status and higher standards of living.

There are slumbering within us mighty forces which should be unleashed in the service of the faith. The human will can accomplish marvels if it only decides to do so. Let us place this precious gift in the service of Christ — not a fickle, vacillating will but one which, as the poet says, "can tear the stars from the heavens." Worldlings put us to shame. They have constructed architectural wonders, pyramids, skyscrapers; tremendous feats of engineering are the fruit of human determination. It is for us to accomplish far more amazing feats in the spiritual order. For this the one and only prerequisite is to place at God's disposal a strong human will.

NINTH SUNDAY AFTER PENTECOST

Christ weeps over Jerusalem

Today's liturgical scene is stark and threatening; it serves a needed warning on the real dangers in the dark sea ahead. There *is* a hell, and the chosen soul will be damned if it fails to practice its faith. That, in brief, is the liturgy's main message today. The faithlessness and rejection of the Chosen People are the theme common to both the Epistle and Gospel. Try to keep in mind throughout the week that impressive picture of Jesus weeping before the gates of God's chosen city. Gravity, seriousness, earnestness are not alien to the Christian spirit; allow them a position in the spectrum of virtues and awaken your spirit of penance; pray daily these words from the Canon of the Mass: "preserve us from eternal damnation."

1. **Holy Mass (Ecce Deus).** The texts of Sunday Masses aim to instruct; in addition, today's formulary gives grave admonition. The *Entrance Chant*, Psalm 53, mirrors the vicissitudes of Christian life. Even after Easter's conversion life continues as a battle which, it is hoped, will end in victory (as in the psalm). The initial verse, the antiphon, glories over the paschal victory repeated each Sunday, while the middle verse, with which the psalm begins, is easily oriented to the approaching week of conflict. Like thoughtless children we often ask for hurtful things; therefore the Church places on our lips a prayer in which we ask for those things only that are pleasing to the will of God (*Coll.*).

Lifting an admonishing finger, Mother Church continues. Baptism, membership in the Church, the sacraments do not in themselves guarantee salvation. Jewish history stands as a dreadful warning because it is the story of how a chosen people became a disinherited, rejected people. Pertinent passages from the sojourn in the wilderness are cited by St. Paul. He speaks severely, though kindly: "If anyone thinks he stands, he should be careful for he is on the point of falling. No temptation comes your way

except such as you can withstand. God can be trusted; He will
not permit you to be tempted more than you are able to bear;
but with the temptation He will open some avenue of escape
that you may be able to meet it."

Gradual and *Alleluia* chants have exchanged their proper roles
so that the former heralds the enthroned Lord while the latter
depicts hell's fierce battle against the souls of men; aid is requested in a petition surrounded by joyous *Alleluias*. The *Gospel*
narrates the touching story of Christ's entrance into Jerusalem
on Palm Sunday. Jerusalem symbolizes the baptized soul which
casts God's grace away from itself. What a warning! Jesus weeps,
Jesus the Creator and Judge weeps over the sins and infidelities
of His creatures. (Do not delay in cleansing the temple of your
heart.)

For the *Offertory* the soul, reflecting upon the Lessons, sings
the second strophe of Psalm 18. Yes, I have known the time of
"Your visitation," for "Your servant keeps Your justices." This
is my Offertory gift today. The *Secret*, a dogmatic prayer, helps
me to understand what the holy Sacrifice is and to esteem it
more highly, for "as often as the memorial of this Victim is celebrated, the work of our redemption is accomplished" (a wonderful statement, one that greatly clarifies the *mysterium* character
of the Mass). It would be difficult to sing a more appropriate and
beautiful hymn while at the *Communion* Banquet: "He who
eats My Flesh . . . abides in Me . . ." (note the contrast to the
Gospel!). And may the fruits of the Sacrifice be purity and unity
(*Postc.*).

2. **Text Analysis.** From the above observations let us make
a summary with stress upon practical spirituality. The Introit
will not permit us to adjudge the whole formulary in the somber
light of the two Readings. Psalm 53 tells of battle, of cries for
help, of fear; nevertheless, the antiphon senses a happy ending:
"See, God is my helper; the Lord is a shield for my soul." Approach the Mass with this briefing.

There is solemn gravity in her voice as the Church warns us in
the Liturgy of the Word: "If anyone thinks he stands, he should

be careful for he is on the point of falling. No temptation comes your way except such as you can withstand. God will not permit you to be tempted more than you are able to bear." This is the Mass's cardinal lesson. Everyone knows that there are occasions in life when the strongest motives are needed to overcome temptation. Such motives, not without the element of fear, come to the fore in the two Readings. Israel's forefathers never entered the Promised Land but died in the desert. Christ weeps over Jerusalem, the holy City, because she would not accept that which would really bring her peace. Now what do these Readings tell me? My soul is in danger. In fear and trembling I am to work out my salvation. As a responsory to the Lessons, the Alleluia verse follows quite naturally — the whole of Psalm 58, of course. (The Gradual would not be too appropriate.)

Mother Church, however, does not send us away with nothing more than sobering verbal admonitions. The second and more important part of the Mass, the Liturgy of the Eucharist, brings grace and joyous confidence. The Foremass met our needs as catechumens, the Sacrifice proper as members of God's family. The Church does not wish to threaten obedient children with hell fire, rather to show them the ways and means of salvation. Note this *contrast-connection* already in the Offertory. The Israelites in the desert and Jerusalem as a city did not accept God's peace proposals. Jerusalem turned the house of God into a hang-out for thieves. Temptation is not foreign to God's people, but His chosen ones about the altar meet temptation humbly and with determination to obey God's commandments. In fact, this spirit constitutes the oblation we bring to the altar at the Offertory today: "Your judgments are righteous, rejoicing the heart; Your commands are sweeter than honey and the honeycomb. That is why Your servant observes them."

This is the first response to the admonitions of the Foremass. We, God's children, know the things that spell peace for us. We obey God's will. By our own strength, however, it would be impossible to withstand the dangers threatening our peace of soul. We need the graces of Calvary, the Eucharist. How well it is worded for us in the Secret: "As often as the memorial of this Victim is celebrated, the work of our redemption is accomplished." As often as we offer Mass, we obtain the strength and grace that secure redemption.

Then as we approach the table of the Lord, when Christ indeed "visits" us, we chant His consoling words: "He who eats My Flesh and drinks My Blood abides in Me and I in him." What a wholly different tone and message than that in the Gospel! A new understanding of the Mass has come to us. The Church surely is anxious over our salvation and we must realize the spiritual dangers surrounding us; nevertheless, the Mass of the Faithful points out still more clearly the blessedness of our state and its inherent strength, the upright human will and the spiritual vitality derived from the Cross and the Mass Sacrifice.

3. Divine Office. Excerpts from the Gospel account are used as antiphons at Lauds and Vespers. "When Jesus drew near to

Jerusalem and saw the city, He wept over it, saying: If you only know . . . days will come for you when your enemies will throw a trench around you and encircle you and harass you on every side and beat you flat to the ground because you would not learn from the occasions when God visited you, alleluia" (*Ben. Ant.*). "It is written: My house is a house of prayer. You, however, have made it a hangout for thieves. And He was teaching daily in the temple" (*Magn. Ant.*). Regard these antiphons as divine admonitions. The homily on the Gospel is taken from St. Jerome.

4. **Meditation upon the Sunday.** A. Hell and the Liturgy. The question may be asked: What attention does the liturgy give to the topic of hell? To answer this, two periods in the history of the liturgy must be distinguished. (a) In ancient times the liturgy rarely mentioned hell. The Church of the martyrs, still in the glow of first fervor, longed for the Second Advent of the Lord; virginity and martyrdom were her ideals, while on all sides she was threatened with persecution. Under such conditions there was no need to use motives of fear as an incentive for religion, and therefore references to hell or damnation seldom occur in ancient liturgies.

(b) Later centuries, however, witnessed a great change. The Church became free and was protected by secular princes. Lukewarm and unworthy elements entered her fold; holy Mass and the sacraments no longer were esteemed so highly and the high morality of the age of martyrs began to wane. The Church, therefore, was obliged to strike harsher notes; she was forced to instill into her members the fear of punishment. During this period originated the liturgical texts treating more explicitly of judgment, damnation, and hell. From this period, too, dates today's Mass formulary.

This change in liturgical mood is most evident in the Mass for the Dead. The oldest parts of the *Requiem* are permeated with joyous thoughts and sentiments on the resurrection, with petitions asking for "eternal light" and "peace" for the deceased. But the *Libera* after the Mass, which presents the judgment scene so dramatically, is the product of medieval spirituality. This latter epoch is also responsible for the prayers in the Ordinary of the Mass that are based on motives of fear, such as the *Confiteor*, pleas for deliverance from eternal damnation in the Canon and before the Communion, and the *Domine, non sum dignus*.

Now what attitude should our piety take regarding the subject of hell? It would seem best to emulate the spirituality of the ancient Church. Most persons would rather act positively and consider Christianity from the brighter side. Sin and hell should hardly be our *principal* motivation. We want to be a holy people, a people who love their Father and are striving toward their Father's house. Yet it is necessary, too, to blend joyful love of God with a due measure of fear, respect, and awe. From time to time the doctrine of hell must be adverted to and used as an incentive toward assuring our salvation. "If anyone thinks he stands, he should be careful for he is on the point of falling."

B. Jesus Weeps over the City of Jerusalem. Let us first consider the setting of the Gospel account. It was the beginning of the last week of Jesus' earthly ministry. The first Palm Sunday had come. Accompanied by an interested retinue, Jesus proceeded from Jericho to Jerusalem for the celebration of the Pasch. He did not, however, enter the Holy City at once but remained in a little village, Bethany, about an hour's walk from Jerusalem. Here with the friendly family of Lazarus, Martha and Mary He stayed whenever He came to the City. Only a few weeks previously He had raised Lazarus from the dead, a miracle for which they naturally were very grateful. At the supper now prepared in honor of their divine Guest (a meal at which Lazarus too was present), Martha diligently did the serving while Mary anointed her Master's head and feet.

The same day crowds came from Jerusalem over Mount Olivet to Bethany in order to greet Jesus and also to see Lazarus, who had lain three days in a grave. When these people returned, Jesus accompanied them, receiving their homage as King of the Jews. In the neighborhood of Bethany the foal of an ass was procured and upon it the disciples put their garments. Then Jesus seated Himself upon the animal and the triumphal journey into the royal City began. Upon the way the crowd spread out their garments, broke off palm branches and sang jubilantly: "Hosanna to the Son of David, blessed is He who comes in the Name of the Lord, the King of Israel!" Previously, as at the multiplication of the loaves of bread, Jesus always withdrew from such popular demonstrations; why did He now permit royal homage to be given Him? Because He was now going to His passion, and He willed to embrace death as a King, freely.

During that solemn entrance a noteworthy incident occurred; it is narrated by St. Luke in today's Gospel. The royal procession was wending its way from Bethany over Mount Olivet, and as yet the Holy City could not be seen. Only when Jesus reached the summit of the Mount would Jerusalem with its temple lay suddenly before Him. Now the Jews loved their City with an intense love, and as often as pilgrims beheld it from a distance, they gave way to shouts of joy. Such, too, was the case in the present instance. The Jews were entering with the King of the Jews, with the true Messiah into the royal City, a new reason for unrestrained rejoicing. When Jesus had come to the top of the Mount and had glanced upon the City, He stopped indeed but did not cry out jubilantly. On the contrary, tears came to His eyes while He addressed the City sorrowfully: "If you only knew, particularly now, what really would bring you peace; but it is hidden from your sight."

Mysterious words! For a thousand years the prophets had been foretelling the advent of a Messiah, of a Redeemer for the royal City. Here in this City the heavenly King would reign. And it is this very City that now meets Him in a hostile spirit, this very City that long since had resolved upon His death, that already had erected a bloody scaffold for His crucifixion. Such base ingratitude brings tears to Jesus' eyes, although it is something else that makes Him weep so bitterly — His divine foreknowledge of the City's destruction. He continues: "The days will come for you when your enemies will throw a trench around you . . . and beat you flat to the ground, and the children within your walls; they shall not leave for you a stone upon a stone, because you would not learn from the occasions when God visited you."

These words of prophecy were fulfilled to the letter only forty years later when in the year 70 A.D. the Romans under the Emperor Titus besieged Jerusalem. The Jews resisted obstinately; the Romans became infuriated and retaliated with a frightful massacre when the City was taken. Temple and all were utterly destroyed, not a stone remaining upon a stone.

Thereupon Jesus descended the Mount into the City and entered the temple area. Here to His sorrow He must see how buyers and sellers were desecrating the holy place with goats and sheep, with screaming and bargaining. In righteous indignation He took a scourge and drove out those merchants, exclaiming: "It is written: My house is a house of prayer. You have made it a hangout for thieves."

The question may be asked: What moral does the Church wish to inculcate by retelling this incident? It would not be truths or mysteries related to the passion, since it is not the Lenten season. No, the Church, looking deeply into the heart of Christ, knows that her Founder wept because of another reason. Jerusalem, the chosen City, the City that because of its temple became the dwelling-place of God Himself, was a type and image of the soul. Through baptism and holy Communion the soul has become the temple of God, the city of the divine King Christ, a city richly blessed but which through sin "does not know what really would bring it peace."

The sanctified Christian soul that divorces itself from God through mortal sin resembles Jerusalem, the City that proceeded to crucify its Savior and King. St. Paul expressly says: "Those who fall away crucify again to themselves the Son of God, making Him a mockery" (Hebr. 6:6). With this in mind we can understand the Church's warning, an admonition given in all seriousness: *Even the baptized soul, the soul blessed with sanctifying grace may perish eternally.* Even the elect may go to hell! If the temple of your soul has become a "hangout for thieves" through sin, permit your Lord to drive out those intruders with the lash of His scourge!

TENTH SUNDAY AFTER PENTECOST

A taxgatherer in the Temple of God!

The spirit of the liturgy last Sunday was grave, serious, sobering; the gateway to hell was opened a trifle and we were permitted to glance in through the slit. We saw the tears in the eyes of our Savior as He beheld Jerusalem and the sinful souls of men. Today, however, Mother Church shows us consolingly how God floods man's sinful soul with divine grace if he but returns, humble and penitent. Humility is the liturgy's principal lesson; humility, the signpost infallibly pointing the way to the kingdom of God. It may help to bring this fundamental virtue of Christian life more strikingly home to your heart if you turn the parable into a paradox: "A proud saint is a devil, a humble sinner is a saint."

1.   **Text Analysis.** The present Sunday and the previous are

in some ways related (as also the 7th and 8th). Numerical order is followed in regard to the Introit psalms (53 and 54); and the tenor is penitential. Does today's Mass liturgy show unity in theme? Well, if the Gospel is taken as the mean of comparison, then the Collect and the Communion may be related to it. God is showing His mighty power through mercy and forgiveness (Coll.); He forgives and justifies the humble; accordingly we approach the Communion table in the spirit of penance (Ps. 50). However, it is only between these three texts that this relationship exists. The Alleluia takes us to the scene of the parable, Sion — Jerusalem. The remaining texts are quite general in thought content. It is rather difficult to fit the Epistle into the ensemble because its theme is foreign to all the other texts.

2. **Holy Mass (Cum clamarem).** Our participation in the Mass will become easier and more fruitful if we put the Gospel parable in the center of things and clothe ourselves with the spirit of the taxgatherer before we set out for church. Three times we will "go up to the temple to pray," taking the role of the publican. The first time is at the beginning of the day's liturgy. Conscious of our poverty and our sinfulness, we make our way to church. We bring nothing worthwhile, nothing except the conviction that of ourselves we are nothing. As expressions of our condition the texts of the Foremass serve well, with some exceptions; for they are the prayers of a humble soul. At the very entrance we "cast all our cares upon the Lord" and from Him await help and nourishment. At the *Kyrie* we humbly call: Lord, have mercy on me, a sinner. The same spirit continues in the *Collect*; God manifests His omnipotence best by forgiving and showing pity — it is the publican's prayer in classic Latin phraseology.

Perhaps even the *Epistle*, which seems so alien both to our way of thinking and to today's Mass formulary, may offer some points, e.g., the Holy Spirit will enter only the humble soul, for He seeks vessels empty of all selfish leanings. It may well be that present-day Christians experience so rarely the special charisms of the Spirit simply because they rely too much upon their own

abilities and love humility too little. Humbly, then, join your
voice to that of the Church as she pleads: "Protect me as the
apple of Your eye, O Lord. Hide me under the shadow of Your
wings." It is the still, small voice of the taxgatherer praying
within me.

Now it is time for the wonderful *Gospel* parable and its ringing climax: "He who exalts himself will be humbled, and he
who humbles himself will be exalted." It is a parable unique not
merely for its fine artistry but primarily for a theology inex-
haustibly profound. The parable is a resumé of the whole story
of God's dealing with men, and it also unveils the story of my
soul. On the great stage of history it reveals why Gentiles and
sinners were called to grace and salvation, while the Jews, self-
righteous and proud, fell from divine favor. As generations pass,
the parable repeats itself in the life of each individual. To us it
should bring home the lesson that the key to any supernatural
progress is humility. What is humility but the revelation of God
in Jesus Christ? This sublime virtue came to earth in the person
of the God-Man; in it everything that is good and great and holy
has its origin — all that pertains to the work of redemption.

With the *Offertory* there takes place the publican's second
"going up to the temple." Self-surrender, the soul of any offering
made to God, presupposes the virtues of humility and holy trust.
Today's Offertory antiphon (from Ps. 24 — familiar to us from
the first Sunday of Advent) is the prayer of a soul heroically
humble and fully reliant upon God. It would be helpful to have
read and studied the entire psalm beforehand. The gifts we
bring, the *Secret* reminds us, were first given to us — a further
reason for being humble. They were ordained for God's honor
and for our salvation. This, in fact, is the liturgy's whole *raison
d'être*, i.e., God's honor and man's salvation.

A third time we publicans approach the altar, to eat at the
table of the Lord. As we draw close there rises from humble
hearts the touching penitential psalm (50). It is the final act to
the drama of the parable. The publican within me prays: "O
Lord, I am not worthy that You should come into my presence."

And while the *Miserere* rises from trusting hearts, the humble publican receives the pledge of his justification. It remains only for the priest to announce the *Ite, missa est* before he may leave the temple and "go down to his house justified." The more humble and destitute and meek of heart I came to church, the greater will be the gifts of grace with which I depart.

3. Divine Office. The two greater antiphons bring to mind the Christian ideal exemplified in the humble publican. "The publican, however, stood afar off and would not so much as lift up his eyes toward heaven; he kept striking his breast, saying: O God, be merciful to me the sinner" (*Ben. Ant.*). "This man returned to his house justified rather than the other, because everyone who exalts himself will be humbled, and he who humbles himself will be exalted" (*Magn. Ant.*). In imitation of the publican we will pass this day, this whole week, deepening our spirit of humility.

The parable is commented upon by St. Augustine: "The Pharisee could at least have said: I am not as many men. What does *as the rest of men* mean, other than everyone except himself? I, he says, am just, all the rest are sinners. *I am not as the rest of men, unjust, extortioners, adulterers.* And at that very moment you take occasion for greater pride from your neighbor, the publican. *As that publican,* he says. I am unique, he thinks in his heart; he belongs to the crowd. I am not such as he is, for through my righteous acts I have proven that I am not unrighteous.

"*I fast twice a week, I pay tithes on all that I possess.* Try to find in his talk something he requests from God; you will discover nothing. *He went up to pray?* Certainly not to ask God for help but to praise himself. Not to petition God would not have been so bad, but to praise himself and moreover to mock another who did! *But the publican stood afar off.* It was he, nevertheless, who was really coming close to God. The voice of conscience kept him at a distance, while his piety urged him on. *The publican stood afar off,* but the Lord considered him very near. For the Lord is enthroned on high but looks kindly upon the lowly. The highbrows such as that Pharisee, *He recognizes from afar*. Yes, God knows such from afar, but He does not pardon them.

"Note now the publican's humility. Is it a negligible point that he stood afar off? Or that he did not lift up his eyes to heaven? He did not look so that he could be looked upon. He did not dare to gaze upwards; although his conscience pressed him down, hope buoyed him up. Read further. *He kept striking his breast*. He would punish himself, and therefore the Lord took pity on him. *He kept striking his breast, saying: Lord, have mercy on me the sinner*. Now you see who it is that prays. Why are you surprised when God forgives after he confesses?"

4. **Meditation upon the Sunday Liturgy.** A. The Humble Soul. On past Sundays the Church etched life in the kingdom of God in contrast-pictures. We easily recall how slaves of sin were contrasted with the servants of God, how the man of the spirit stood counter to the men of the flesh, how the good tree differed from the bad tree, how the children of light contradicted the children of the world. A similar contrast occurs today in the true-to-life parable of the humble taxgatherer and the proud Pharisee. Certain it is that Mother Church does not propose that we choose between them. No, we have already decided for Christ in baptism.

But if we look deeper into our hearts, we find enthroned there two principles, a lower one seeking to debase us and a higher one aspiring toward God, a pagan soul and a Christian soul, and each contends for mastery. Life's task is to triumph more and more over the pagan soul and to aid the Christian soul in realizing full and sole command. Focusing her light upon the inmost depths of our being, the Church reveals the little, humble, publican-soul within us, as also the proud, arrogant Pharisee-soul. And she unites herself with the former and leads it to the house of God. Let us study these two souls more minutely.

The lower soul is by nature autocratic, arrogant, rebellious, ever striving to be her own god. She has inherited pride as a sad legacy from Adam and Eve; they received it from Lucifer, who cried to God: "I will not serve. I will elevate my throne over the throne of the Most High." To our first parents Satan whispered: "You will be like God, knowing good and evil!" Pride is the mask of Satan's kingdom. In due time Christ, the second Adam, came to earth in the garb of humility. His work of redemption was one great act of humility. How beautifully St. Paul put it: "He emptied Himself, taking the form of a servant . . . becoming obedient unto death, even to death on a Cross" (Phil. 2:7–8). In words first uttered by Mary, the Mother of God, holy Church daily at Vespers voices her gratitude for this basic virtue in her repertoire: "He has put down the mighty from their thrones, and has exalted the lowly" (*Magn.*).

See, Mother Church is now taking the unassuming, humble soul by the hand and leads her toward the altar, for she wishes to bless her with the pledge of salvation. What is the proper spirit when going to church? The humble soul approaches the temple (i.e., the parish church) fully aware of her weaknesses and failings, realizing that she has nothing good of herself. She stammers out a single phrase: "Lord, be merciful to me!" This today is the Introit, the Confiteor, the Kyrie. Nevertheless, she is not crushed by the knowledge of her helplessness, because the liturgy points out to her the altar upon which Christ is enthroned and says: "Cast your cares upon the Lord, and He will sustain you!" Because she feels herself as an empty vessel, the Lord God willingly floods her first with the water of sacred doctrine in the Epistle and Gospel, and later, still more abundantly, with the wine of grace in the Eucharistic Sacrifice.

At the Offertory the modern-day publican takes a further step; till then he stood at the entrance; now he marches to the altar. But what shall I bring, he says blushingly, what shall I offer? I have nothing but faults and failings. Again Mother Church comes to the rescue. She points toward the altar, toward Christ in glory: "To Him lift up your eyes, have confidence in Him; for no one who trusts in Him is ever forsaken!" (hymn during the Offertory procession). Humility and deep confidence are our Offertory gifts today. Soon, at the consecration, Christ becomes present just as truly as when He appeared to the unbelieving apostle Thomas after the resurrection. Finally, at the sacrificial Banquet, Jesus approaches each publican-soul, each one of us, and says: "Go in peace, justified." Like Thomas I fall on my knees praying the *Miserere* meekly, confidently (Communion). I had come to the house of the Lord distressed and in sin, in greatest need of redemption; I return home rejoicing, knowing that I have been saved.

B. Pride and Humility. The parable of the pharisee and the publican, a parable so appealing, beautiful and true in every age, casts its consoling message over the entire day's worship (cf. antiphons at Lauds and Vespers). Originally our Lord employed it to show why the Jews, especially the Jewish leaders, the pharisees, could not find the way to the kingdom of God. Pride and arrogance obstructed their view, while publicans, pagans, and sinners found the heavenly kingdom simply because they had the needed predisposition, humility. At the present time Christ is shedding His light into our souls, pointing out the virtue fundamental to spiritual life and its opposing vice. Further, He shines this same light upon the two kingdoms and shows how the kingdom of God is grounded in humility, while the kingdom of hell rests upon pride. Let us consider these truths in greater detail.

a) When was the kingdom of hell established? It dates from the moment when Lucifer arrogantly retorted: *Non serviam*, "I will not serve. I will place my throne over the throne of the Most High." That cry opened the infernal pit. His diabolical kingdom was transplanted to earth as the serpent whispered into the ear of Eve: "You will be like God, knowing good and evil." Ever since those days pride is the prime statute of Satan's kingdom. Every sin is rooted in pride and every one who is proud and conceited, every one who wishes to be his own god becomes a citizen of this kingdom; he is incapable of being saved.

b) Now some points on God's kingdom. In what manner was it founded? Christ, the Son of God, became man and humility characterized His work. His advent to earth was encompassed by acts of humility. When the angel of the Lord brought the joyous message to Mary, she humbly answered: *Ecce, ancilla Domini*, "Behold, I am the Lord's servant." Her words stand as the eternal challenge to Satan's *Non serviam*. And as the holy bride of God, bearing God, came to Elizabeth, she sang humility's hymn, the *Magnificat*: "He has regarded the humility of His handmaid." Then she uttered for all ages the basic statute in God's kingdom: "He has put down the mighty from their thrones and has exalted the lowly. He has filled the hungry with good things, and the rich He has sent away empty." Today's parable of the publican and pharisee is a commentary upon Mary's words.

The humble King chose a stable as the house of His birth, and the crib as a cradle; beasts, the night, and the wind were His first attendants. Unassuming, unnoticed He goes through life, for He is come to bring the glad tidings to the poor and neglected. He would not, the prophet had said of Him, break the bruised reed or quench the dimly burning wick. His last act was to seal His life with humility's greatest triumph, death upon a Cross. "He humbled Himself, taking the form of a servant . . . becoming obedient unto death, even to death upon a Cross." Therefore the Church takes this virtue as absolutely fundamental, and traveling through the ages clad in the garment of humility, sings daily at sunset: "He has exalted the humble."

c) The thoughts and sentiments of the Church have been embedded in the liturgy. Humility, therefore, must be one of its principal features. And so it is. For through the whole liturgy runs a double motif, that of exaltation and that of humiliation. Or we may say that it is a single movement — through humiliation to exaltation. The moral Christ draws from His parable, "He who humbles himself will be exalted," may well be called the liturgy's informing principle. We will cite but two examples. During the Church's year of grace we abase ourselves twice and are twice exalted. Advent is a season of abasement, Christmas and Epiphany of exaltation. During Lent we humble ourselves only to be exalted again at Easter. The same structure is to be found in the Mass. In the prayer-service of the Liturgy of the Word (i.e., from the beginning to the Collect inclusively) we humble ourselves, while through the sacred Readings God raises us up. Our humble participation in the Offertory oblation is rewarded with the glory emanating from the Sacrifice Banquet.

Exaltation, glorification is the purpose of religion. But that end can be attained only through humility. Every act of humility merits exaltation, glorification. Life, then, can be one great exaltation secured through humiliation. But only at the finale will the promise of Christ be perfectly fulfilled: You humbled yourself in life. Now you will be exalted, transfigured by a crown of eternal glory.

ELEVENTH SUNDAY AFTER PENTECOST

Ephpheta — Be opened

In reviewing the Sundays of the Pentecost season, we should not try to seek for or to impose any systematic or artistic arrangement; for *a priori* schematic methods are alien to worship and liturgy. Nevertheless, no good reasons can be brought forward against an analysis of content; and analysis is often aided by a certain measure of classification, whether such classification was historically intended or not. At the beginning of the Pentecost sequence there occur three Sundays that can be called "Recruiting Sundays" (2nd, 3rd, 4th after Pentecost) because the Gospel each Sunday points out God's efforts toward having souls enlisted in the kingdom of heaven (viz., the parables of the Great Supper, the Lost Sheep, the Lost Coin, the Miraculous Catch of Fish). The three most recent Sundays (8th, 9th, 10th) formed a trilogy with emphasis on sin (viz., the story of the unjust steward, faithless Jerusalem, the penitent taxgatherer). The present three Sundays likewise have a common theme; they form a triad treating the sacramental grace-life of the Church as related to (a) baptism; (b) the healing power of the sacred mysteries; (c) gratitude for spiritual purification.

1. Text Analysis. As already noted, today's liturgy begins a series of three Sundays with stress on the primary sacraments in liturgical life. These three formularies break the "two ways" theme sequence proper to past Sundays (7th — 10th). Setting forth *mysterium* pictures of the Church's inner life, the Mass texts treat of baptism and the Eucharist; they are, therefore, more closely associated to the Easter mystery than other recent formularies. In the various prayers we may observe two threads of thought that lend a certain unity to the Mass, viz., Easter and summertime.

Easter. The formulary under consideration is another excellent example of an Easter or baptism Mass. The Readings bring Easter theology to mind, while the chants give voice to Easter sentiments. The Entrance Chant makes us realize the holy environment we are in; it is a sanctuary consecrated to God where the faithful stand in most intimate communion with one another; the "strength and power" that God gives to His people refer, of course, to the blessings of this morning's liturgy. After the Collect we hear Paul describing the great Easter mystery of the death and resurrection of Christ. At the end of his discourse he becomes very personal: "By the grace of God I am what I am. . . ."

During the Gospel I am standing at the baptismal font. Through its graces I received a new sense of hearing, a new tongue, a new ability to understand. The Mass is a classical example of how the ancient Church could achieve transcendent unity where text unity, strictly speaking, was absent, by keeping her heart close to the Easter theme of baptism and spiritual resurrection.

Summertime forms the setting for today's Mass liturgy. Because of this circumstance we have the joyous, festal spirit emanating from the chants. The Offertory hymn voices gratitude to the Giver of all gifts; the Communion antiphon teaches us how

The grace of God is life
everlasting in Christ Jesus

to honor God through the proper use of the goodly fruits of summertime, the crops that are being gathered into the barns and the ripening vineyards; for "now the heavy clusters are taking on luscious color upon the smiling hills of the Roman Campagna" (cf. Schuster). An inspiring Mass indeed for a beautiful summer morning!

2. Holy Mass (Deus in loco). The words of the *Introit* remind us what our parish church actually is. It is here that our God lives and reigns as King. It is our Father's house, the lovely home of God's children, where all are of one mind and heart, bound together by the bond of love. Here on the "Lord's Day" all gather round their Father and King. And He bestows strength and courage to continue the battle against the world, the flesh and the devil. So our setting of home and peace changes into a battleground (Ps. 67). Like a well-trained army Christians march through the world, the enemy fleeing at their approach.

These two settings, symbolizing Christian life, come before us again in the Kyrie and Gloria. For the joy of redemption attained (*Gloria*) is the reward for our longing cries for mercy (*Kyrie*). With a *Collect* the service of prayer closes. Cast in an unusual affectionate style, this prayer first acknowledges God's infinite goodness in granting blessings so superabundantly, then pleads forgiveness for known sins, and concludes by imploring those favors for which we hesitate to ask. It is a Collect in which the two principal petitions of the Our Father may be sensed; onward toward the kingdom of God — away from every semblance of sin.

Now listen to God's words. St. Paul rises to speak and from his lips come Easter tidings. We picture him as once he stood before the Church at Corinth heralding the greatest truth of the faith, viz., Christ died for our sins and He has risen again! The Apostle lists proofs for Christ's resurrection, adding his own experience last. For to him also did Christ appear. Once he was sick, deaf and dumb, a child born out of due time. Now he recounts how he received the grace of baptism and adds a personal reflection: "By the grace of God I am what I am; but His grace did not remain fruitless within me." Throughout his life St. Paul remembered how sorely he needed redemption.

Now imagine yourself standing before the baptismal font on the vigil of Easter. Deaf and dumb you come to Christ, your soul's Physician. He places His finger in your ear and on your tongue to heal you. And instantly you are able to hear and to speak, and your soul is illuminated for heaven. Joy is the dominant mood of the *Gradual* and *Alleluia.* The former is constructed antiphonally, i.e., the first verse constituting the antiphon for Psalm 27, which begins with the second verse. The newly baptized could well regard this antiphon as an Easter hymn.

Sincerest gratitude for redemption is the gift I bring to the altar as my *Offertory* oblation. Psalm 29, a noble thanksgiving hymn, is at the same time a song of self-surrender. The *Secret* beseeches divine mercy in order that the gifts offered may be pleasing to God and beneficial to us. And now in the Sacrifice proper the work of redemption becomes actuality and touches us here and now. We heard that Christ died for us sinners and rose again; now He is here upon this altar, the Lamb immolated and glorified. During the Mass the Lord of Easter comes to us as He once came to the five-hundred brethren upon the hillside, as He appeared to Paul on the way to Damascus.

In the Eucharistic Banquet my Savior approaches and says to me: There is still much blindness, much deafness, much dumbness in your soul. Always, however, as at baptism, He continues: *"Ephpheta,* "Be opened." New light pours into my soul! And He adds: What you received at baptism I wish to preserve in you, to confirm it and to enrich it unto the day of My Second Coming. The *Communion* antiphon unfurls a beautiful panorama of God's blessings in the fields and vineyards. But since mention is made specifically of wheat and wine, the liturgy wishes us to think of the spiritual fruits derived from the holy Eucharist. The Eucharist should make both soul and body (yes, even the *body*) strong and vigorous because it is a truly effective medicine (*Postc.*).

   3. Divine Office. The two greater antiphons, recalling Christ's cure of the man deaf and dumb, points to the cure from spiritual deafness and dumbness effected by the sacraments of baptism and holy Eucharist. Pope St. Gregory proffers the homily in explanation of the Gospel: "Why was it that God, the Creator of all things, when He sought to cure the deaf and dumb man, put His fingers into the man's ears and, spitting, touched his tongue with spittle? Simply because the Redeemer's fingers represent the gifts of the Holy Spirit. On another occasion He said, after casting out a devil: If I cast out devils by the finger of God, evidently the kingdom of God has come to you. This same passage is given by another evangelist in these words: If I cast out devils by the Spirit of God, the kingdom of God must therefore have come to you. By comparing these two texts we see that *finger* and *Spirit* are equivalent terms.

"Therefore, to put His fingers in the man's ears means to open the mind of the deaf person to obedience by means of the gifts of the Holy Spirit. But what is the implication of spitting and then touching the tongue with the spittle? That spittle from the mouth of the Redeemer symbolizes the wisdom that comes to us through divine teaching. For it is from the head that saliva flows into the mouth. Now when His wisdom, and He is Wisdom Itself, touches our tongue, then our tongues immediately become fashioned to preach His word.

"He looked toward heaven and groaned. No, it was not necessary that He should do this; for He Himself could give what He was asking for. But He was teaching us to petition Him who is enthroned in heaven to open our ears likewise through the gift of the Holy Spirit and to loose our tongues for preaching His words through spittle from His mouth, that is, through knowledge of the divine message.

"And He said to him: *Ephpheta*, that is, Be opened. His ears immediately were opened and whatever had held his tongue came loose. Note that it was to closed ears that the Lord said: Be opened. But when the ears of one's heart have been opened unto obedience, then the tongue too is straightway loosed from any constraint so that he might urge others to the performance of the good works he himself is doing. For this reason the evangelist rightly adds: He spoke plainly. Surely such a one speaks plainly who first obediently does that which he admonishes others to do."

4. **Meditation upon the Sunday. A.** *Ephpheta.* Since ancient times the Church has used our Gospel story as a symbol of baptism, because through baptism man first receives the power to hear (i.e., to understand) and to speak supernatural truths. Before baptism he resembles one who is deaf and dumb. He cannot speak to God in prayer because he has no faith; neither can he hear the voice of God. In regard to the kingdom of God he is deaf and dumb. But through baptism he becomes a child of God, he receives the life of sanctifying grace. The Holy Spirit, the Mediator between his soul and God, comes to dwell within him and supplies, one may say, the tongue that speaks to God and the ear that is sensitive to the divine voice.

Therefore, according to ancient practice, the priest at baptism performs an action similar to our Lord's in today's Gospel-cure. With saliva he moistens the ears of the neophyte and says:

"Ephpheta, which means, be opened." Then touching the nose he adds: "so that you may perceive the fragrance of God's sweetness." By these actions he wishes to indicate that through baptism one's ears are spiritually "opened," and that the sweet odor of a virtuous life will rise from the newly baptized.

What baptism initiated the holy Eucharist continues and perfects. The Church brings this Gospel miracle to our attention today and softly adds: You came to Mass poor, deaf, dumb. In the midst of the world's noise you could hear nothing of what God is saying to you; even now you stand here, a stuttering child unable to speak. But by the grace of today's holy Mass your ability to hear heavenly things is perfected anew, your tongue is loosed. Now you may grow mature spiritually in order that one day you may chant the praises of God along with the great choirs of angels. What baptism began, today's holy Mass should perfect!

The Epistle affords St. Paul an occasion to bring us his Easter message. Christ died for our sins; He was buried, and He arose. The Apostle then lists witnesses to the resurrection, e.g., Peter, the eleven apostles, the appearance of the risen Lord to five hundred brethren, many of whom were still living when Paul wrote. Very probably he was referring here to Christ's appearance upon the mount in Galilee, where for the last time He gathered together all His disciples. The risen Lord also appeared privately to the apostle James the Younger: of this the evangelists make no mention.

The final proof of Christ's resurrection noted by the Apostle of the Gentiles is the vision granted to him near Damascus: "And last of all He was seen also by me, as by one born out of due time; for I am the least of the Apostles, who am not worthy to be called an Apostle, because I persecuted the Church of God." Although the Savior appeared to Paul before the gates of Damascus and made him an Apostle, he remained meek and humble; he would not consider himself worthy to bear the honorable name of Apostle, but rather spoke of himself as one "born out of due time." Neither did he glory in personal accomplishments: "Only by the grace of God am I what I now am," a work of grace!

So also ought we to speak. Of myself I am nothing, yet through divine grace I am indeed great. If I could only say with Paul: "His grace in me has not been fruitless!" The words mean that Paul cooperated perfectly with God. How appropriate this Epistle is today! With the Gospel *mysterium* in mind, it is easy to see how the Church by the Epistle wishes to stress the message of Easter, while at the same time using the story of St. Paul's conversion as a type of our own conversion at baptism.

B. The Deaf and Dumb. It is always rewarding to study the literal sense of a Scriptural passage. Today's Gospel miracle occurred toward the end of Jesus' ministry in Galilee. In that district, too, Jesus was suffering keen disappointment, for He had done so much good, had preached, had worked miracles. And yet the Jews would not accept Him. When He had given the people bread, they wanted to make Him King; and they willingly brought to Him their sick. But when He tried to heal their souls, they hardened their hearts. From Judea evil-minded pharisees soon came and smothered any budding faith in Jesus. Consequently He withdrew more and more from the people and gave Himself to training and educating a few chosen apostles and disciples. For after His death these were to carry into all the world faith in Him and in His teachings.

On this particular occasion we meet the Messiah beyond the land of Israel in Phoenician territory, where the mighty cedars on high Lebanon tower to the heavens. Once the Phoenicians were the world's great merchants; they trafficked on the Mediterranean, even to distant Spain, where they traded their wares for amber and other rare products. In that same district occurred the unforgettable incident of the pagan Canaanite who implored Jesus to heal her sick daughter. At first He showed Himself unfavorably disposed, yet her humility and her perseverance forced Him, may we say, to grant her petition. Now as Jesus continued His journey southward and had come into the vicinity of the Sea of Galilee, the people were awaiting Him with their sick. Also at this time occurred the second multiplication of bread about which we heard some Sundays ago (Gospel on the 6th Sunday after Pentecost).

The particular incident with which we are at present concerned, however, is the miraculous cure of the deaf and dumb as recounted in today's holy Gospel. One doesn't realize immediately that the person involved in this miracle was mentally retarded, perhaps feeble-minded. Such persons often are the objects of common ridicule, and no one cares for them. But the Savior came for all men, and since these too have immortal souls, He resolved to heal both his body and soul. Of course, Jesus could have healed him with only a word, but He always endeavored to prepare those who were about to receive divine favors. For to Him the health of the body was only a sign of the health of the soul; and He wanted to be the Healer of souls.

But how could spiritual realities be made intelligible to someone who could neither hear nor speak, and moreover lacked intelligence? Jesus would use sign language. Observe closely how He proceeded. First of all He took him apart from the crowd because it would have confused the poor man to have so many people standing about. Then He touched his ears and tongue to show him that He wanted to heal those organs; next He looked heavenward and groaned to indicate that help could be obtained only from God on high and that he should ask with all his heart for a cure. The evangelist has even noted the exact Semitic word that Jesus used: *Ephpheta,* which in English means "Be opened." The cure was immediate. The man heard and spoke correctly, reasonably.

We are told that the people were astounded by the miracle. Because the man had been known to all, their joyous amazement was so much the greater. Loudly they shouted: "He has done all things well! He has made both the deaf to hear and the dumb to speak." How good our Savior is! All men may come to Him, no one is too unimportant for Him. Indeed, it is just the little ones, those despised by the world, who are His cherished ones. In this way He puts to shame the proud and haughty.

TWELFTH SUNDAY AFTER PENTECOST

Christ, the merciful Samaritan

During the coming week the picture of Christ as merciful Samaritan who nurses and heals the wounds of holy Church will be uppermost in our thoughts; and the commandment to which we will give zealous attention will be the first and greatest — that of love toward God and neighbor. So may it be a week framed by love and mercy.

1. **Content Structure.** A similarity that is quickly evident exists between the present Mass text and last Sunday's, even though today's formulary lacks a festive and joyous spirit. Thought unity too is hardly present, for neither the Readings nor the chants chime well together. The only perceivable sequence arises from the reference to Moses as a type in the Epistle and Offertory verse, and from the contrast between the old and the new Covenants (*Epist. and Gosp.*). Still the whole glistens like a colorful mosaic.

2. **Holy Mass** (Deus, in adjutorium). Today's Mass is far from being charged with that triumphant Easter joy proper to last

Sunday's text; rather we see mankind hastening to God's sanctuary sorrily in need of redemption. For centuries the *Introit* has been man's cry in distress; its first verses are used at the beginning of each hour of Divine Office, and the whole psalm is prayed in connection with the Litany of the Saints. (We will pray the entire psalm both for ourselves and in the name of unredeemed humanity.) In the *Collect* Mother Church teaches us to extend our hands in prayer "that we may run without stumbling towards the divine promises."

The Readings and the Offertory have this in common that they compare the new Covenant with the old and place the former high above the latter. Taken historically the *Epistle* is somewhat difficult to apply, but understood liturgically it describes not only the glory of the new Moses, Jesus Christ, who now in the holy Sacrifice steps before us in all the brightness of His splendor, but also the excellence of God's kingdom which the Holy Spirit is giving us through the instrumentality of Mother Church. Of ourselves we are helpless creatures because "our sufficiency comes from God," from Christ, from the *pneuma*, from the Holy Spirit "who bestows life." After our Sunday Mass we should be able to face daily life fearlessly, fortified, as we are, by the grace and glory granted to God's children.

The *Gradual* expresses heartfelt thanks for the glory that has been given to us. A rare combination is that had in the *Alleluia* verse: sorrow and distress in an Alleluia setting (pray the entire psalm, it is the saddest in the psalter). We may think of the Church in her present sufferings awaiting future resurrection; perhaps your own soul must sing in a similar key. Gradual and Alleluia have again exchanged their proper places today.

A *Gospel* extraordinarily rich in thought nuances compensates for the somewhat abstruse Epistle; more fortunate than the prophets and kings of old are we, for today in the Sacrifice we may again behold redemption's work accomplished; we are "they who see and hear" (recall last Sunday's *Ephpheta*). The parable became clothed with reality through Christ's work on Calvary, a reality that takes place again today at the altar, for while we are gathered together in this true πανδοχεῖον or "inn," Jesus pours oil and wine (i.e., the sacraments, holy Eucharist) into our wounds. In today's holy Mass we see our Redeemer, Jesus the good Samaritan, paying our ransom, paying the price of our health upon the Cross.

The *Offertory* singles out a figure from the Old Testament, Moses, the mediator and reconciler between Yahweh and the Israelites, a telling figure of our cross-laden Savior. The *Secret* and *Postcommunion* touch upon the expiatory character of the Mass and implore forgiveness. Again the *Communion* is a beautiful Eucharistic hymn, with a timely allusion to the harvest now in progress in field and countryside. The three principal parts of this Mass, Epistle, Gospel, Offertory, underscore its three major functions; like Moses, the great mediator, Christ, the merciful Samaritan, pleads for sinful men; He heals us from the wounds of sin, and He fills us with the brightness of His glory.

3. Divine Office. Since the thoughts of man's heart form the theme of his songs, Mother Church prompts her children to sing portions from the Gospel as the day's greater antiphons. In the morning eternal Truth answers our question with: "You must love the Lord your God with your whole heart, alleluia." In the evening the beginning of the parable is sung: "A certain man went down from Jerusalem to Jericho and fell among robbers; having stripped and wounded him, they went away, leaving him half dead." The homily on the Gospel is from the quill of St. Bede the Venerable (d. 735).

4. The Offertory. The text of today's Offertory, consisting of a single verse, forms but a tiny relic of the chant which the Roman Church once sang during the Offertory procession. Since the movement of an entire congregation would take considerable time, the greater part of an entire psalm was frequently employed. Gradually, however, the Offertory procession lost favor, with the result that less text was needed; some of these intermediate Offertories are preserved for us in ancient antiphonaries. Finally a single verse remained, that in our present missals.

Nevertheless, for a full understanding of the Mass the more complete text is often necessary. Of special importance is the so-called *repetenda*, the refrain or verse repeated after each strophe, which often betrays the theme. Both from a literary and a musical viewpoint today's Offertory belongs to the more significant chants in the missal. In its original form it reads:

Moses prayed in the sight of the Lord his God, and said:
    Why, Lord, is your wrath blazing up against your people?
    Do turn from the fierce anger within you.
Remember Abraham, Isaac, and Jacob;
    to them you swore to give a land flowing with milk and honey.

And the Lord was appeased from doing the evil
    he had threatened to inflict upon his people.

Then the Lord said to Moses:
    You have found favor before my eyes
    and for no one have I greater esteem.
In haste Moses flung himself upon the earth and prayed, saying:
    I know that you are merciful
    and that you blot out sins and injustices a thousand times.

And the Lord was appeased from doing the evil
    he had threatened to inflict upon his people.

Moses and Aaron spoke to the whole gathering of the sons of
        Israel:
    Draw near to God. The majesty of the Lord has appeared in
        the clouds;
    he has heard your murmurings in due time.

And the Lord was appeased from doing the evil
    he had threatened to inflict upon his people.

It is easily seen how dramatic the chant becomes when arranged in this manner, and how its message of Moses as type of Christ in His sacrifice of propitiation is brought into sharp relief.

5. Sunday Meditation. A. What the holy Sacrifice means

and what it effects can best be learned from the Mass text itself, for in it Mother Church has placed her most profound reflections. And certainly you know that it is her most earnest wish that you understand the Mass well and co-offer it with her to the best of your ability. In the Mass the river of redemption's graces flows unobstructed into your soul, perfecting the sanctification begun by baptism. Therefore, do not think that you have already plumbed the depths, that through baptism you have become a perfect Christian. At baptism the sprout was ingrafted; but its growth, its foliage, its flowers and its fruit are due to the holy Eucharist. Baptism and Eucharist are the two great fountains of divine life which assure your salvation. What today's holy Mass brings you specially is given in three pictures.

First picture. The Gospel recounts the immortal parable of the merciful Samaritan. By this parable Jesus wished to teach a lesson concerning the love of neighbor, but the Church uses it to illustrate His own activity at holy Mass. The man who fell among robbers is poor human nature robbed of its supernatural endowments, weakened in its natural powers, lying prostrate in utter misery. The Jewish Law passes by, for it can effect no healing. The humble God-Man, Jesus, the good and merciful Samaritan, comes and picks up the poor, wounded man. He pours oil and wine into his wounds, takes him to an inn, and cares for him. This is the work of salvation. It is also the work of the Mass.

Now let us see lying there not mankind but our own selves, myself, yourself. In baptism, at every Mass the Good Samaritan comes to you, picks you up. Your nature is still inclined to evil, you still bleed from many wounds, you are still weak and helpless and of yourself cannot "hasten to the divine promises" (*Coll.*). In the holy Eucharist, however, Jesus pours oil and wine into your wounds — oil, the sweet, and wine, the bitter tenets of Christian teaching. He dresses your wounds and cares for you as a father. Be convinced that at Mass your soul's wounds are healed. Doesn't this beautiful parable of the good Samaritan excellently sketch the fruit of today's sacred liturgy?

Second picture. The Gospel depicts the effects of the holy Sacrifice somewhat negatively; the Epistle presents its fruits more positively. The Epistle compares the old and the new Covenant. In the old Law the letter was paramount; in the new, spirit or πνεῦμα. St. Paul says: The countenance of Moses became so radiant from his interview with God that the children of Israel could not behold his face. But if the new Law is more perfect than the old, how indescribably more radiant must the face of a Christian be, since at each Mass he beholds the God-Man's face; incomparably more resplendent must the faces of God's children be after their meeting with Jesus at the holy Banquet. Yes, this is the fruit of holy Communion, that it transfigures us. Of course, as long as we are upon earth that glory is hidden, veiled; nevertheless it is present, and no one could face the sight of a soul in the brightness of that glory. Feel convinced that you depart from Mass into the workaday world with a face radiant, beaming, and a soul transfigured.

Third picture. The Offertory, heralding Moses as the mediator for the sons of Israel, forms the third tableau. While Moses was upon Mount Sinai speaking with God, the Israelites fashioned for themselves a gold-plated bull and worshipped before it. It was sufficient reason for Yahweh to break His covenant with them, but Moses pleaded in behalf of his unfaithful fellow men and the divine wrath abated. The message for us? Moses was the forerunner of Christ, the true and eternal Mediator and Peacemaker. Through every Mass (which is Christ's atoning sacrifice on Calvary made present here and now) "the Lord is appeased from doing the evil He had threatened to inflict upon His people."

Thus with startling clarity the effects and fruits of holy Mass are shown in three memorable scenes: the good Samaritan heals the wounds of our souls; we gaze upon Christ's glorified face and retain the radiance of that glory with us for daily life; and lastly, God wills to be appeased through the mediation of Christ, the divine Moses.

B. Christ and Christians. To the question, "About what does

the liturgy speak most?," the reply could quickly be given: The liturgy loves most to speak of the Bridegroom Christ and of His bride, the faithful; for the lips must tell that of which the heart is full. In the first half of the Church year the liturgical texts are constantly treating of and glorifying Christ. During Advent it is "He is coming"; at Christmas, "He is here, He has appeared"; at Easter, "He has died for us and has risen again; He has ascended into heaven and is sending the Holy Spirit." During the time after Pentecost, however, greater attention is accorded to His bride, to His Church. It should be profitable to consider briefly what today's liturgy has to say about us Christians and about Christ.

1) Christians. Again today the soul is pictured as she really is: on the one hand poor, pursued, sin-stained; on the other, a fortunate, transfigured child of God. With many petitions and with manifold needs we approach the house of God; the wicked enemy is following in hot pursuit. "O God, hasten to my aid. . . . I am needy and poor, Lord, stand by me." Too well do we know this aspect of human life. Of himself and by himself man is nothing, always afflicted and destitute; but the Collect already points to a brighter side: "with Thy grace are we able to serve Thee worthily." If we use God's gifts, a sublime destiny awaits us, an end called *promises* by the liturgy. We know what these promises are: grace here and glory hereafter.

In substance the very same point is made in the Epistle. True, of ourselves we are nothing, incapable to think or do anything; but with the grace of God we are strong. "Our sufficiency is from God." Then follows a comparison: as the face of Moses beamed radiantly after communicating with Yahweh on the mount, so the spiritual appearance of God's children is changed by communion with Christ Jesus their Lord. How the countenances of the just will shine in heaven when that glory becomes fully manifest! These are the promises after which we ought hasten! Every Sunday, every Mass leads us closer to that glory.

The twofold nature in the child of God is well shown in the Alleluia chant, for it is a song of sorrow in a joyous Alleluia setting: "Alleluia, alleluia. In Your presence, O Lord, my God and Savior, I cry day and night. Alleluia." Such is Christian life upon earth — pain and suffering transfigured by Easter Alleluias!

In the Gospel too the Church tells her children many things. She praises them as blessed because they partake of the Eucharistic mystery, because they are permitted to see and to hear their Lord. She places in their hearts the twofold commandment of love. She teaches them who their neighbor is, be he friend or enemy in need of assistance. Note too that the man who fell wounded among robbers represents mankind, mankind without Christ; yet he is given a Physician and Savior who is deeply concerned, who takes him to the inn of the Church and cares for him.

Let us summarize what today's Mass says of the individual Christian. Of himself poor, he goes through life subject to many needs and much suffering; yet in his soul he bears the beginnings of beatitude and hastens onward toward its perfect attainment. Of this the Alleluia is a fine expression: deep earthly suffering suffused and transfigured by Easter joy.

2) Christ. Now let us consider what the liturgy says about Christ. It places Him before us in two scenes, as Moses and as the Good Samaritan.

It is in the Epistle that Christ is first compared to Moses. The comparison is an ancient one, for Yahweh Himself used it when speaking to Moses: "I will raise up for them a prophet resembling you." And Christ spoke in similar terms: "Moses did not give you bread from heaven, but My Father gives us the true bread from heaven."

Between these two prophets there are many points of similarity. Moses fed the Chosen People with manna, he struck the rock with a rod, he led Israel through the Red Sea and through the wilderness into the Promised Land; he gave them the Law, he ordered the immolation of the paschal lamb. All these acts are readily applicable to Christ. But the Epistle employs a different approach. The radiant face of Moses prefigured our glorified Savior who in majesty is enthroned at God's right hand, who appears during Mass in all the splendor of His glory.

Another picture of Moses is given in the Offertory verse. It tells a whole story. When the Chosen People became unfaithful and worshipped before the golden calf, God determined to reject them; but Moses besought forgiveness and appeased the divine wrath. Here Moses prefigured Christ, who through His death upon the Cross became the great Mediator and Intercessor, and who at every Mass utters the perfect prayer of expiation.

Today's Mass presents Christ to us in still another picture, an exceptionally beautiful one, the parable of the good Samaritan. Who was the unfortunate victim of robbers? Mankind. And the priests of Levi and all the precepts of the old Law could provide no effective aid. Then Jesus, the divine Samaritan, appeared in the form of a humble servant, poured oil and wine in his wounds and carried him to an inn. Christ could not have portrayed His work more poignantly.

Whatever the liturgy wishes to tell us about Christ and about ourselves is excellently summed up in this parable. The souls of men, despoiled by robbers, are the objects of His special solicitude. Like the good and merciful Samaritan, He takes them to shelter and cares for them. Jesus is actually doing this now at holy Mass. The inn is the Church, the medicine is the holy Eucharist. Only permit Him to heal you!

THIRTEENTH SUNDAY AFTER PENTECOST

From Easter Eve to Sunday Mass

Two contrary moods dominate today's liturgy, the one grave, earnest, pleading, sad; the other joyous, thankful. Of special importance in understanding the Mass in its present form are the three chants taken from Psalm 73 (*Intr., Grad., Comm.*), which give the day its sombre, sober spirit; while the Gospel's drama-miracle is best understood as a vivid visualization of the sacrifice-mystery being enacted at the altar.

1. **Content Structure.** This Mass is the third in that trilogy which has the Church's life as its object, viz., baptism, sacramental living, holy Eucharist (see eleventh Sunday after Pentecost). Perhaps it is the antithesis between the old Law and the new, between Jew and Gentile found in the two Readings which gives today's formulary a certain inner unity and a semblance to last Sunday's. Again today the Gospel gives the Samaritans precedence over the Jews. The formulary's leit-motif is Psalm 73, a psalm lamenting a national disaster; some joyous strains, however, may be detected.

2. **Holy Mass (Respice, Domine).** Let us begin with the *Gospel.* We see ten lepers healed by Christ, nine of whom simply vanish after their cure, while the tenth, a Samaritan, returns singing his gratitude to the Lord. What does the Church wish to convey by the narrative? Here again we have a good example of "mystery" in liturgy, for it is not the Church's primary intention to inculcate a lesson on gratitude; she wishes rather to unravel the meaning of Sunday Mass and its sanctifying efficacy. Sunday is Easter, the day of baptism; and its Mass effects the renewal of baptismal graces. In the ten healed lepers we must see a figure of the baptized. Recall that in the ancient Church adults were baptized on Easter eve, and that ever since, the baptized in the eyes of the Church are considered men cleansed in the baptismal font from the leprosy of original sin. Moreover, every Sunday witnesses the renewal of the graces of baptism, for the Eucharistic banquet reinforces the substructure of baptism, completing and perfecting it.

The Eucharist too is subtly portrayed in today's Gospel. Of the ten who were healed one returned "with a loud voice glorifying God, and he fell on his face before His feet, *thanking* Him (εὐχαριστῶν αὐτῷ); "Eucharist" means giving thanks. Sunday Mass is a thanksgiving liturgy celebrated by the fortunate few who have been healed from the leprosy of sin. Let us sum

up the significance of Sunday. It is the day on which we should praise God with loud voices, a day of thanksgiving for the grace of baptism, a harvest day for the soul, a day on which it receives an "increase of faith, of hope, and of charity" (*Coll.*), an "increase of eternal redemption" (*Postc.*). So much for a better understanding of the Gospel.

In the person of the grateful leper have we been prefigured who now come to the holy Sacrifice. For this morning "the Lord enters a certain town," His Church. We "go to meet Him" and He heals us from the leprosy of sin, He seeks to give us freshening graces during the Sacrifice and its Banquet. This is the joyous and lightsome feature of the Gospel. There also is a sad, dark side — Jesus complaining over the ingratitude of "the other nine." These represent lukewarm Christians who, though baptized, no longer practice their faith, no longer offer Sunday Mass (in some countries nine out of ten might not be too high an estimate). This, our Savior's complaint, links the Gospel to the melancholy chant of Psalm 73.

A well-phrased *Collect* pleads for basic Christian virtues; "growth in faith, hope, and love" constitutes that renewal and deepening in the graces of baptism of which mention has been made. We plead not merely to be enabled to fulfill God's will but to *love* His commands. The *Epistle* (perhaps the most vexing passage in the whole missal) teaches that we have become God's children through grace alone without any merit on our part. At the *Offertory* procession we place in God's hands, together with the usual Offertory gift, our whole life's fortune: "My times are in Your hands."

At the consecration Jesus appears and heals us sinners from leprosy, while in the sacrificial Banquet He gives "increase in eternal redemption — *redemptionis aeternae augmentum*." And at the *Ite missa est* He sends us away as other Samaritans to act out a true Christian life: "Arise and go. . . ." But do take time to notice the excellent *Communion* verse which extols the holy Eucharist as the Manna full of sweetness. — This Mass could well be entitled "From Easter Eve to Sunday Mass," for its texts point up the intimate relation of Sunday Mass to holy baptism. Sundays are links in the chain binding the two great days of life, the day of baptism and the day of death — our two birthdays, that unto grace and that unto glory.

Certainly it is not the mind of the Church that we should touch upon the Gospel merely during the Mass; rather we ought use it as inspiration for the entire day. Therefore, as the sun rises at Lauds Jesus enters a certain town, i.e., the Church, and we, the lepers, go to meet Him: "As Jesus entered a certain town, there met Him ten men who were lepers. They stood afar off and lifted up their voice, saying: Jesus, Master, have mercy on us!" (*Ben. Ant.*). Our evening song voices our gratitude for being healed: "And one of them, when he saw that he was made clean, went back with a loud voice glorifying God, alleluia." There follows a thanksgiving canticle, the *Magnificat*.

3. Sunday Meditation. A. Psalm 73. To appreciate fully today's holy Mass it is necessary to know Psalm 73. It reads:

I. *Stricken by misfortunes*

Why, O God, have you rejected us so completely?
Why does your wrath flare up against the lambs
   in your own pasture?
Give some thought at least to your people,
   your own possession from the beginning,
   one which you redeemed as a personal inheritance.
Think of Mount Sion,
   which you made your dwelling-place.
Raise up your hand against their insolence,
   see how the enemy has desecrated the sanctuary.
How they who hate you swagger about,
   on the very sites of your sacred feasts!
Their standards they have erected as trophies;
   with axes they hacked down the gates as in a woods,
   with hatchet and ax they smashed their way in.
Your sanctuary they set on fire,
   desecrating to the dust the dwelling-place of your name.
Together they agreed, that hellish brood:
   "We will abolish God's feasts throughout this land."
No longer do we witness wonders as once we did;
   no prophet arises, and no one knows what still will come.

II. *Confident of divine assistance*

How long will the enemy continue to scoff?
   how long will he continue to blaspheme your name?
Why do you hold back your hand?
   and hide your right hand in your bosom?
Surely you, O God, have been our king for ages;
   marvels you have wrought in this land.
The sea, you have cloven it by your power,
   dragon heads, you crushed them on the waters.
You smote Leviathan,
   made him food for beasts in the wilderness.

You caused streams to flow,
  and dried up the ever-flowing rivers.
To you belongs the day, and to you the night,
  you fashioned the dawn and the sun.
You fixed the boundaries of the earth,
  summer and spring are your creation.

III. *The sufferer pleads*

Should, then, the enemy scoff at you,
  a godless people revile your name?
Do not abandon to wild beasts the souls of your
    faithful ones,
  or be utterly unmindful of your poor.
Your covenant, honor it;
  and do not permit the oppressed to be put to shame.
  Make the poor and the needy praise your Name.
Bestir yourself, O God, and safeguard your interests,
  note the insults sinners are constantly heaping
    upon you.
Do not disregard the haughty yelling of your foes,
  insolence that grows continually bolder.

This psalm, one of the gloomiest in the psalter, describes a sad
phase in Israelitic history. Enemies had penetrated into the
temple precincts, demolishing, destroying, desecrating. The
psalmist sought to console himself by recalling past marvels. God
had once freed His people from Egypt and had annihilated their
enemies. A meditation upon nature follows; the beauty of the
dawn, the sun, spring and its splendor are the works of God.
Strengthened by these considerations, he pours forth to heaven
a heartfelt plea for help.

We may ask, what are the Church's intentions in employing
this psalm? The desecrated temple represents God's holy kingdom, Christ's mystical Body, pursued by enemies, defiled
through sin. Mother Church is thinking of those children who

no longer fulfill their duty of thanksgiving on Sunday; and for these, our lukewarm fellow Christians, we will pray this psalm. Three times during the Mass we will link our hearts to its public recitation: upon entering the Lord's house, at the Gospel, and at the Communion. Our spirit of gratitude will help smoothen the lines of grief on the brow of Mother Church.

B. The Gospel story. Our Savior completed His mission in Galilee about four months before His death, not long after the transfiguration. Then He left that country, not to appear there again till after His resurrection. On His way to Jerusalem Jesus entered a town in whose neighborhood was a leper colony. The victims of that dreadful disease, still common in the Orient, literally rot away as member after member falls off. Because of its contagious character, Mosaic Law had decreed that lepers live apart and avoid all contact with the clean. When they wished to speak with someone, they were obliged to remain at a distance and give notice of their miserable lot. Ten such outcasts, all of whom belonged to the same colony, met Jesus as He journeyed along. "Standing afar off" they called upon Him to help: "Jesus, Master, have mercy on us" (the Greek original, *eleison*, is the same as in our *Kyrie, eleison*— Lord, have mercy). Without further ado Jesus sent them to the priests, whose office it was to declare lepers clean. For it was prescribed in the Law of Moses that anyone seemingly cured of leprosy must appear before the priests; it was their duty to make a thorough examination and to decide whether such was actually the case. After the examination the one-time leper was shorn and subjected to a thorough washing; then he presented an offering of two sparrows, three lambs and a food-offering according to the Law, and the priest declared him clean; only upon the completion of such ritual was he again allowed to associate freely with others.

But Jesus sent the ten to the priests unhealed. It was to try their faith, for He demanded some evidence of faith in connection with most any favor. All ten withstood the test and were healed upon the way. Of these, nine were Jews, and one a Samaritan. Upon realizing the miracle, the Samaritan returned to Jesus even before reporting to the priests; he thanked his Benefactor sincerely, falling down on his face before Him and praising God with a loud voice. This Samaritan, this stranger, this half-Jew put the other nine Jews to shame; for they did not consider it worth the trouble to return and show thanks. In sorrow Jesus noted their conduct and saw in it a type of the ingratitude and fickleness of the Jewish people, who cast away from themselves His mercy and grace, while strangers, pagans joyfully accepted the good news of the kingdom.

The miracle occurred soon after their departure from Jesus; they could easily have returned if they had wanted to pay their debt of gratitude. Reflect at some length upon Jesus' sorrowful complaint over the ingratitude of "the other nine." For this certainly is the key verse in the whole account. Jesus is seeking the gratitude of men, not for Himself, but for God. And He asks it especially from His own.

C. On gratitude. Gratitude is one of the more important virtues that should adorn a child of God. It is a sign of a noble soul, for only a good man will be grateful. There is a proverb about ingratitude being the world's reward. An egotistic, selfish society ignores this virtue. Thankfulness is related to faithfulness. Therefore let us be grateful to everyone who has benefited us, especially our parents. The evil others have inflicted upon us we will write in sand, but the good with which they have blessed us we will carve in marble!

In the first place we will be thankful to God not by way of some few isolated acts but with a constant spirit of gratitude. How beautifully it is put in the preface of the Mass: "It is truly fitting and right . . . that we at all times and in all places give thanks. . . ."

Think of the many blessings which have been accorded you. First, your natural faculties; your life is a chain of gifts, for without God you could not continue existing a split second. Every member of your body, eyes, ears, hands, are His gift to you. And visible nature in all its loveliness. Every flower, every blade of grass is calling: "I am God's gift to you." The splendor

of nature God created for your enjoyment. In fact, nature is
a picture book given you by your heavenly Father that in it you
may see a wholly different world. And still greater blessings are
yours, for you are God's own child, called by Him to heavenly
joys, to a divine kingdom. Church, sacraments, ecclesiastical
year, sacred liturgy, the Redeemer are all for you, given to you
that through them you may be eternally blessed. And so soon
you do cease your song of thanks?

So far you have been grateful from motives of self-interest;
proceed a step further now. You have reason and faith, and
through reason and faith God permits you to gaze upon His
glory, His love, His greatness, or at least to surmise His infinite
attributes. Therefore you ought pray in the spirit of the *Gloria*
at Mass: "We thank Thee for Thy own great glory," that is,
"for Thy own great glory" as you now know it and as you
shall learn to know it when once you shall see Him face to face.

A song of gratitude should be on our lips even in sufferings,
even when we do not understand the ways of God, for we know
that all that God wills is to our good. To be grateful when one's
heart is bleeding is truly heroic!

Now we can more easily see why the sacred liturgy, the prayer
of the Church, radiates gratitude. Each succeeding day of salvation is replete with prayers of thanksgiving. The Church's morning prayer (Lauds) and her evening prayer (Vespers) are *the*
prayers of praise and thanks. Especially in the evening is she
grateful when in that grand hymn of God's own Mother she
sings her gratitude for all the blessings of salvation: "My soul
magnifies the Lord!" Before the Son of God makes His appearance upon the altar at the consecration, the Church chants a
hymn of thanks, the preface: "It is truly fitting and right, rea-
sonable and salutary that *we give thanks* at all times and in all
places. . . ." Every Mass is concluded with the response: *Deo
gratias*, Thanks be to God! And the etymology of the word
Eucharist is "good thanks." Never forget that the nobility proper
to a Christian demands a spirit of gratitude toward God and
men.

FOURTEENTH SUNDAY AFTER PENTECOST

Seek first the kingdom of God

Because of its Gospel this Sunday is sometimes called "Divine Providence Sunday." Its Readings for the last time highlight the differences between the two kingdoms, an antithesis today between the kingdom of the flesh and of mammon and the kingdom of the spirit, of God (*Epist.* and *Gosp.*). From the contrast the moral lesson is evident: cling to God with your whole soul! The Communion verse would serve well as the spiritual motto for the week: "Seek first the kingdom of God, and all other things shall be given you besides." This text is also used as the Magnificat antiphon at the close of the day's Office. At sunrise we hear Christ's consoling words: "Do not be anxious, wondering: What are we to eat? or, What are we to drink? Your Father knows that you need all these things, alleluia" (*Ben. Ant.*).

1. **Content Structure.** It seems that a new group of three Sundays is beginning (indicated by the Introit psalms, 83, 85, 85), even though continuity in content is lacking. There is an obvious parallelism between the two Scripture Readings, viz., works of the flesh — fruits of the spirit; God — Mammon. The Collect's content betrays a similar structure: preservation from that which is harmful and assistance toward that which is good. The same pattern is noticeable in the Gradual: Lord — man, God — princes.

2. **Holy Mass (Protector noster).** Another inspirational, joyous Mass! This morning the soul is filled with bridal happiness after longing ardently to pass the "Lord's day" in the "courts of the Lord," in His "dwelling-place." Now she enters her "home," calling down God's blessing upon His "anointed" (individual souls; the members of the parish; the mystical Christ) in Psalm 83, one of the more glowing and fervent of entrance chants. Yes, today's *Introit* would be a most appropriate prayer for any visit to church: "How lovely is Your dwelling-place. . . . for Your courts my spirit burns within me. . . ."

In full accord with the thought content of the Readings and the child-like trust characteristic of the entire Mass we pray the *Collect*: Preserve Thy Church by Thy constant mercy, for without Thee we are weak, ever prone toward the spirit of the world. Man's soul is like a child learning to walk; without aid at every step, it tumbles to the ground. Your assisting grace, Lord, must effect two things: it must deter us from evil, as the angel deterred Lot from Sodom; and it must direct us to good, as a shepherd guides his sheep. In a word, grace upon grace is required to make us lead a saintly life (another thought-packed Oration).

Now the apostle Paul rises to instruct us, and today he tells us bluntly what is good and what is evil. He speaks of two kingdoms, the kingdom of the spirit and that of the flesh, the kingdom of grace founded and grounded in the soul by the Holy Spirit, and Satan's realm of sin. Within man's soul these two forces are battling, their trenches scarring the very core of every human heart. The apostle lists "the works of the flesh" as also the "fruits of the spirit," for every Christian is a tree planted by the Holy Spirit and destined to bear His priceless fruit. Life in Christ, it must be remembered, is no gay fling, rather a continuing struggle: "They who belong to Christ have crucified their flesh with its vices and its lusts!" Trust and confidence in God provide the "ultimate weapon."

Likewise in the *Gradual* may be seen two opposing principles, trust in God aligned against trust in princes. With the *Alleluia*, however, Easter jubilation floods in upon us, for in Easter's great Warrior our battle against the flesh is won. The Christian can make no compromises with the world, serving God to a degree while pilfering from Satan's dainties; for Christ demands utter reliance upon his Father's gracious providence in today's *Gospel*, certainly one of the loveliest passages in Holy Writ. What endless consolation this Gospel narrative of the birds God feeds and the lilies He clothes so gloriously has brought to needy men! Oh how the virtue of trust rings through the entire Mass!

If only we were conscious of being a holy people faithfully

guarded by God's angels against whom the world and all its
cohorts cannot prevail! Of this the *Offertory* verse seeks to remind us. Christian hosts are encamped about their King (viz.,
the altar), God's angels are constructing defences against the
enemy, the faithful receive strength and nourishment for the conflict from the altar. As the birds of the air and the lilies of the
field we are clothed and fed by the Lord in the Communion
Banquet; our response is a carefree: "Seek first the kingdom
of God, and all these other things shall be given you besides"
(*Comm.*). We rely on the Eucharist's power to cleanse and
strengthen as the means to reach our goal (*Postc.*). Yes, today's
is one of the most beautiful Masses in the Pentecostal cycle.

3. **Divine Office.** In the morning we hear from the lips of
our Savior the consoling words: "Do not be anxious, wondering: What are we to eat? or, What are we to drink? Your
Father knows you need all these things, alleluia" (*Ben. Ant.*).
The day's leit-motif has been selected as the Magnificat antiphon
(and also as the Communion): "Seek first the kingdom of God
and the holiness it implies; then all other things will be given you
besides, alleluia." The Gospel is explained by St. Augustine:

"No man can serve two masters. To clarify this statement our blessed Lord continued: For he will detest the first and love the second, or bear with the first and resent the second. The words must be applied correctly. Who the two masters are Jesus immediately indicated: You cannot serve God and mammon. The Jews called money mammon. The Phoenicians used practically the same idiom, since in their language mammon is equivalent to net profit. Now if one serves mammon, he actually worships as his god the one placed over earthly things because of his perversity, the one whom our Lord called the Prince of this world. Now man has no alternative but to hate that one and love the other, namely, God; or he will bear with the one and resent the Other's wishes. He who works for mammon must suffer under a cruel and killing master; enchanted by his own lusts, he subjects himself to the devil, whom he cannot love. For how could anyone love the devil? Still there are those who serve him."

4. Sunday Meditation. A. Psalm 83, the Introit psalm of this Sunday's Mass, must be numbered among the finest in the psalter. Without changing any of its phrases it is well suited for use as a daily prayer:

Yearning for God, vv. 2–5

How lovely is your dwelling-place,
    Yahweh Sabaoth!
With longing for the courts of Yahweh,
    my spirit burns within me.
My heart and flesh
    shout for joy to the living God.
The sparrow finds a house,
    the swallow a nest where she may put her
        young —
Your altars, Yahweh Sabaoth,
    my King and my God!
How fortunate are they who dwell in your house —
    ceaselessly they praise you.

The pilgrimage, vv. 6–8

How fortunate the man who looks to you for
    assistance,
    whose mind is set
    to cross the arid valley
    and reach the sought-for goal.
God gave the command,
    he will also give his blessing.
Step by step they go, their strength increasing,
    until they see in Sion
        the God of gods.

Consoled by God's presence, vv. 9–13

Yahweh Sabaoth, hear my prayer,
    give heed, O God of Jacob.
Look kindly upon our Shield, O God;
    with mercy upon your Anointed.
Truly, one day in your courts
    is better than a thousand elsewhere.
Much rather would I stand at the portals
    of the house of my God,
    than live in the tents of sinners.
For Yahweh, God, is a sun and a shield,
    a Lord who confers grace and glory;
No favor does Yahweh withhold
    from those who live virtuously.
O Yahweh Sabaoth,
    how fortunate is he who relies on you.

Originally this psalm was one of the songs pilgrims sang on
their journey to Jerusalem. For us "Jerusalem" is our parish
church with its altar as the site of sacrifice. Jerusalem, too, for us
is heaven. The psalm needs no further explanatory comment;
some of its verses are so soul-satisfying that we ought learn them
by heart. Pray it daily until you have become thoroughly familiar
with it. It will be a new jewel in your prayer treasury.

B. The Christian army about its King. If some artist wished

to express the principal thoughts of today's liturgy in a single scene, the Offertory hymn could serve admirably well for inspiration. It reads: "The angel of the Lord encamps round about those who fear Him and rescues them. Oh, taste and see that the Lord is sweet!"

Let us first note the highlights in the picture. It is the Offertory. The assembled faithful are offering the holy Sacrifice; they want to unite themselves with the offering of Christ, and for that purpose they march to the altar and place their oblation gifts there. Linked to these externals there is another area of truths. The altar is Christ, the King of God's kingdom; here He is enthroned, and about His throne are encamped His soldiery, the Christian hosts; and encircling the whole ensemble there maneuvers an army of angels who ward off the attacks of Satan's hordes; wholesome nourishment is furnished by the King Himself. Or we may arrange the lesson in this way: Christ upon the altar is the head of God's family; about Him His children are gathered; guardian angels watch over the group, protecting them from evil; the children receive the Bread of Life from their Father.

Now various details in the picture deserve consideration.

The Place. The rallying place for God's children is about the altar. God is their Father, Christ their King and good Shepherd. Holy Church is their Mother, the church building is their Father's house, their home upon earth. Oh, if only this would become abundantly clear that the church is our home! It is so beautifully worded in Psalm 83: "How lovely is Your dwelling-place, Yahweh Sabaoth! With longing for the courts of Yahweh, my spirit burns within me. . . . The sparrow finds a house, and the swallow a nest where she may put her young — Your altars, Yahweh Sabaoth. . . ." How we should want to hasten to church each Sunday to behold the face of our God after the week's turmoil and labors! There our aching hearts should find the peace and solace so desperately sought after. For what St. Augustine observed after years of sad experience still holds true: "Our hearts are restless until they find rest in Thee."

The Father. A second point for consideration is the trust and confidence stressed in the Mass formulary. Our relationship to God is likened to that of a child to its father. Especially is this true of the Gospel, in which Jesus encourages us to trust lovingly in divine Providence. He speaks of the birds, of the lilies which, though they neither sow nor spin, are nourished and dressed by His heavenly Father. Clothed in the resplendent beauty of divine childhood, are we not fairer than the lilies of the field or nobler than the birds of the air? Should we not then feel ourselves secure in God's hand, carefree and happy, knowing well that we have a Father who loves us, who cares for us? As an immediate proof of His love we have the Mass; in it at this very hour He is giving His Son for us.

Protection. God's family, God's army is surrounded, besieged by enemies, the battalions of hell. Here again the Church employs the familiar contrast of the two kingdoms. As long as we are upon earth, the conflict will rage within us. Which, however, will dominate, flesh or spirit? Gazing into the human heart St. Paul speaks of the works of the flesh and of the fruits of the spirit; and in the Gospel too mention is made of two masters, both of whom cannot be served. The Collect acknowledges that man is frail, weak, and consequently God must keep away all harmful things, must guide him toward that which is good. In this conflict, however, we need never rely upon our own strength for guardian angels are ever present to protect us.

The Bread. Angels are not the only ones aiding us in this spiritual battle; a mightier One than any angel enters the field, Christ Jesus our King. Long ago He vanquished mankind's primeval foe, "I have overcome the world," and His victory is our victory. He gives Himself as Bread for our nourishment: "Oh, taste and see for yourselves that the Lord is sweet." Here lies the key to the heart of each Mass. The Church brings to our mind the two rival kingdoms, not that we may choose between them, but to show that in this conflict our side possesses the only weapon which is invincible, the sacrifice of Mass, the Bread from heaven. With It we can be victorious over any enemy. How well St. Paul phrases it in today's Epistle: "They who belong to Christ have crucified their flesh with its vices and lusts." This happens at holy Mass, for in that sacred act, not only is Christ's death upon the Cross made present, but we too are affixed to the Cross to the degree of our union with Him.

The message of the Mass is also summarized in the day's spiritual motto: "Seek first the kingdom of God, and all other things will be given you besides" (*Comm.*). Stay close to Christ; let your primary concern be His kingdom. Then you will be strong, courageous, victorious; neither will your heavenly Father forsake you in your needs, be they of the body or of the soul.

C. The Epistle. It is St. Paul who addresses us. With the light of truth focused upon our hearts, he points out the two forces aligned against each other for battle. We may recall descriptions of the War with its foxholes, tanks, embankments, machine-gun nests. We may imagine our souls having a somewhat like appearance, a great battlefield, two hostile armies, runways and launching platforms. The Apostle calls one side *the flesh,* the other *the spirit.* What does he mean by "flesh"? Human nature inclined to evil, the sad legacy of our original parents, a marred personality that is ours to contend with throughout life, even after baptism. It is this nature bent toward vice and sin that is constantly misleading us. By "spirit" the Apostle means the whole ensemble of gifts and privileges given us in baptism, e.g., habitual grace; indwelling of the Holy Trinity; divine sonship; gifts of the Holy Spirit; faith, hope, charity; membership in the Mystical Body; forgiveness of sin, etc.

Doubtlessly these two must ever be in mortal conflict, with ourselves in the midst. It is a condition that never ceases from early morning to evening, although usually it resembles a cold war with only an occasional sally. Now and then, however, there occurs a general offensive, a day on which both sides fight to the finish. All reserves must then be called out, every muscle and nerve strained. It should be easy to see why God's kingdom on earth is called the Church Militant.

Two examples of a general offensive. First we will discuss an attack made by the forces of evil, then an offensive under God's initiative.

The holy hermit Antony had often been tempted and tortured by the devil. Once however when the attack was exceptionally violent, Antony called out loudly: "Here am I, Antony, and I will not flee your assaults, for no matter how long you continue your onslaughts, nothing will separate me from the love of Christ." Then he began singing: "If armies in camp should stand together against me, my heart will not fear." Satan redoubled his attacks. Antony remained firm. The Lord, however, would not forget His servant in the hour of crisis. The saint glanced upwards and saw the roof open and a beam of light descending upon him. Instantly the demons departed, his bodily afflictions ceased, and his cell took on its customary appearance.

Realizing that aid had come from heaven, Antony breathed more freely, regained composure, and then addressed the beam of light: "Where were you all the while? Why did you not appear to me sooner to quiet my pains?" A voice replied: "I was always with you, Antony, yet I waited to observe you fighting. Since you remained firm and did not waver, I will always be your helper and I will spread your glory far and wide." As the saint heard this he arose to pray; and a greater strength of body came to him than he had known previously.

Sometime during this season is celebrated the feast of St. Augustine. Till his thirtieth year he remained an unbeliever leading a scandalous life. His good and pious mother Monica was indeed praying constantly for him but with little more consolation than the words of a bishop: "A son of so many tears cannot go lost." And Augustine continued enmeshed in the world's sinful pleasures to her intensest sorrow. During a stay at Milan, however, the grace of God began its offensive, employing the sermons of St. Ambrose to soften the hard terrain. The life of the above mentioned Antony also had an influence. It made him soliloquize: "If this man was able to live so virtuously, why cannot I, I Augustine!" And holy Scripture, too, especially the letters of St. Paul, was prompting him back to

God. In the other camp strutted the prince of this world furiously defending his position. The lustful joys of the world beckoned to him in the persons of lewd women: "How can you live without us? If you serve God, you must forego us." So the battle raged, and Augustine knew not which side to favor.

One day while sitting in a garden he suddenly heard a boy's frail voice saying repeatedly: "Take, read." He regarded it as a sign from God. In his hands were the letters of St. Paul; the passage upon which his eyes first would alight would decide the future. He opened the book and read: "Know that it is now the hour for us to rise from sleep . . . the night is passed, and the day is at hand. Let us therefore cast off the works of darkness and put on the armor of light. . . ." The struggle was won. Augustine asked for baptism and became a fervent, saintly Christian.

It is true that Augustine's story is not ours in every detail; yet on a smaller scale a similar conflict rages day by day in every heart.

The battlefield. St. Paul enumerates the "works of the flesh," the sins into which our lower nature tends to lead us. They need not be repeated here, those vices which are the tools of Satan. It is obvious that we must be alert against even their subtlest intrusions.

Then the Apostle begins considering the brighter side and lists the works of the spirit. But note he uses a different word, *fruits* of the spirit. He has in mind a tree planted by our good God, a tree watered and nourished by our Savior, a tree whose foliage and fruit have been kissed and ripened by the blazing rays of the Holy Spirit. He sees this tree as present before him laden with fruit, the good fruits of "charity, joy, peace, patience, kindness, goodness, faith, modesty, continency." Doesn't your heart thrill as you read this inspiring passage? Note especially the first triad: charity, joy, peace! These are the sweetest and the finest fruits on the tree of Christian life.

Tell me, beloved Paul, how can I overcome my lower self and make my own such priceless fruit? "They who belong to Christ have crucified their flesh with its vices and lusts." But how can I nail my flesh to the Cross of my Savior, O Paul? "It has already been done. In baptism you were crucified with Christ unto death; moreover, you do it again every time you co-offer holy Mass, for this sacred act is nothing else than Jesus' death on the Cross repeated in your presence. Only permit yourself to be affixed."

Scripture Readings during the Pentecost Season

The following pages are devoted to comment upon the Scripture Lessons proper to each day during the season after Pentecost. These comments are given apart from the Sunday liturgy because during most of the period the Readings are related to the month and not to the respective Sunday. With regard to procedure, the same method will be followed as in the previous volumes; our efforts will be directed toward obtaining the greatest possible benefit from the various books of Sacred Scripture rather than adhering meticulously to the excerpts as contained in the breviary. This is in full accord with the spirit of the liturgy. Since access to a Bible and to Bible commentaries is presumed, the explanatory notes are usually very brief.

SCRIPTURE READINGS DURING THE FIRST WEEK AFTER PENTECOST

THE PROPHET SAMUEL

Monday (1 Kings 1:1–11). The Church now begins reading the four Books of Kings. Of these the first two are also called the Books of Samuel, because the prophet Samuel appears in them as the principal character. They present the memorable history of the Israelitic people from the birth of the last judge, Samuel, through the reigns of Kings Saul, David, Solomon; then the division of the kingdom into that of Judah and of Israel, down to the Babylonian Captivity. The devout reader will find much edification in these books.

The introductory chapters afford interesting meditation material. Opened are new windows on life, lives sown with sorrow.

We meet instances of God's intervention, and human acts ranging from noblest love of God and neighbor to the contrary extreme of priestly depravity. Accordingly, these accounts ring true to life; it almost seems that we knew those individuals personally. Genuine, solid theology, however, is not lacking; we are given an insight into the ways of God, who pursues and attains His purposes in union with or in spite of man. We see how God can turn all things into good, how He is long-suffering, and also just. *Noverim me, noverim te!* Knowledge of God and knowledge of self — such is the burden of the current Lessons from holy Scripture.

Tuesday (1 Kings 1:12–28). After years of prayer and suffering, Anna is blessed with a child, the great prophet and judge Samuel.

Wednesday (1 Kings 2:12–21). When Heli, the high priest, was old and weak, his two sons grieved him greatly by their scandalous conduct at the sanctuary.

Thursday. The feast of Corpus Christi, see p. 17.

Friday (1 Kings 2:22–36). The curse upon the unworthy sons of the priest Heli.

Saturday (1 Kings 3:1–19). In all things Samuel was the very opposite of the wicked sons of Heli. He served the Lord faithfully, conscientiously, and was "pleasing before God and men." Today's account describes God's first revelation to him. It is a moving story, one that tells us much about God and about His bearing toward the good and the wicked.

SCRIPTURE READINGS DURING THE SECOND WEEK AFTER PENTECOST

ISRAEL FIGHTS THE PHILISTINES

Sunday (1 Kings 4:1–18). A war had broken out against the Philistines. "So the people sent to Shiloh, from where they brought the ark of the covenant of Yahweh of hosts who sits upon the cherubim. The two sons of Heli, Ophni and Phinees, accompanied the ark of the covenant of God. Now as the ark of the covenant of Yahweh entered the camp, every Israelite cheered loudly, and the shouting echoed far and wide. The Philistines heard the noise of the shouting and became afraid. They said: The gods have come into their camp. Woe to us, for there was no such great joy yesterday and the day before. Woe to us. Who will deliver us from the hand of those high gods? . . . So the Philistines fought, and Israel was overthrown; every man fled, seeking his own safety. There was an exceeding great slaughter, and there fell of Israel thirty thousand footmen. The ark of God was captured and the two sons of Heli, Ophni and Phinees, were slain." A messenger brought the sad news to the aged Heli. The death of his sons shook him violently, but as he heard of the loss of the ark of the covenant, intense sorrow of soul overcame him. He fell from his chair, broke his neck, and died. He was ninety-eight years old, had judged Israel for forty years.

The ark of the covenant, upon which Yahweh was visibly present (*Shekinah*), was a type of the Eucharist; and as the former accompanied Israel, the latter accompanies the Church militant today.

Monday (1 Kings 5:1–12). The Philistines took the ark of the covenant, carried it to Ashdod, and placed it in the temple of Dagon (their national god, represented by the torso of a fish) aside the idol. Twice they found the idol cast down before the ark. In God's presence evil cannot endure.

Tuesday (1 Kings 6). The ark of the covenant is returned to the Israelites.

Wednesday (1 Kings 7). Samuel assembles the people and performs public penance.

Thursday (1 Kings 8:1–22). The people demand a king; Samuel is highly grieved and points out the folly of their way of thinking.

Friday. The feast of the Most Sacred Heart, see p. 33.

Saturday (1 Kings 9:1–17). With the establishment of the kingdom, Israel developed rapidly from a religious and political point of view. At the very beginning, however, a tragic figure held the sceptre, Saul, a man called by God, then rejected — Israel's first king! The story of his life is presented in a very vivid and realistic manner, with all its lights and shadows; in it we Christians may find much that is spiritually helpful. Today we read about his call to the throne. He went out to seek his father's she-asses and found a kingdom.

SCRIPTURE READINGS DURING THE THIRD WEEK AFTER PENTECOST

SAUL AS KING

Sunday (1 Kings 9:18–27; 10:1–9). Saul visits Samuel and is anointed king. The scene is so vividly portrayed that we easily feel ourselves present as witnesses.

Monday (1 Kings 10:17–27). Samuel allows the people to choose their king, knowing full well the outcome.

Tuesday (1 Kings 12:1–20). Samuel resigns his office of judge; his last words to the people reveal his spirit of impeccable justice and unselfishness.

Wednesday (1 Kings 13:1–14). After a brief period of success and glory, Saul's star begins to sink. He did not stand the test of obedience. Before engaging the Philistines, he failed to await Samuel's appearance. Thereby he showed greater trust in his own strength than in Yahweh. It was the beginning of his fall.

Thursday (1 Kings 14:6–46). At opposite poles to Saul's self-confidence stands his son Jonathan's feat of arms, accomplished wholly through trust in God. Saul's unadvised oath almost results in Jonathan's death.

Friday (1 Kings 15:1–11). A tragic chapter, Saul's rejection. Saul was not an obedient tool in the hands of God, he did not stand the test. By the prophet Samuel he was directed to inflict *herem* upon Israel's foe, the Amalekites. But out of covetousness he spared their king and much of their property.

Saturday (1 Kings 16:1–11). Saul turns more and more away from God. God ordains the selection of the boy David as king. Another spiritually instructive chapter.

SCRIPTURE READINGS DURING THE FOURTH WEEK AFTER PENTECOST

DAVID'S RISE TO GREATNESS

This week we meet the shepherd boy David, who through a memorable encounter with the giant Goliath suddenly became the hero of his people. Nevertheless, he was obliged to endure long years of persecution at the hands of Saul before he actually became Israel's undisputed king.

Sunday (1 Kings 17:1–16). David resolves to fight Goliath in single combat. At Matins St. Augustine comments on this encounter between David and Goliath: "For forty days the sons of Israel had been arrayed against the foe. Because of the four seasons of the year and the four corners of the earth, these forty days signify our present life during which we Christians never cease fighting against Goliath and his army, i.e., against the devil and his colleagues. But there could be no victory if the true David, Christ, had not appeared with His staff, that is, the Cross. Before the advent of the Lord, dear brethren, the devil was loose; but Christ upon His arrival did what is written in the Gospel: *No one can enter the strong man's house and*

My son, give me your heart,
and let your eyes keep My ways ✚

plunder his goods unless he first binds the strong man. Christ came and bound the devil. Now someone might say: If the devil is bound, how is it that he still is so powerful? Beloved brethren, it is true that Satan still is powerful; but only against the lax and the lukewarm, and against those who do not fear the Lord in truth does he have power. Nevertheless, he is bound, chained like a dog, and cannot bite anyone except those who with reckless self-reliance walk into his jaws. Now, brethren, anyone who is bit by a bound dog must certainly be a fool. Therefore, do not wander into his reach through sinful lusts and desires, and he will never be able to harm you. Oh, he can howl, he can foam at the mouth. But he can bite only those who wilfully place themselves in danger. The devil does not harm one by force, you must give your consent. Your consent he cannot demand, he can only entice."

Monday (1 Kings 17:25–37). Preparation for the encounter. Saul gives his assent.

Tuesday (1 Kings 17:38–51). Trusting in God, David meets and slays Goliath. Recall the typical explanation the Fathers of the Church attach to this incident.

Wednesday (1 Kings 18). Results of the victory. David is honored as Israel's hero. Saul is roused to jealousy and hatred against him.

Thursday (1 Kings 19). Jonathan endeavors to reconcile Saul to David.

Friday (1 Kings 20). A last fruitless attempt on the part of Jonathan to dispose Saul favorably toward David.

Saturday (1 Kings 21—31). These chapters may be read in a more cursory manner. David was forced to flee from Saul's presence. At Nob, the site of the tabernacle, he received from the high priest, Achimelech, bread and Goliath's sword. Then he went into the land of the Philistines. For several years Saul pursued him like an infuriated wild beast. David, however, enjoyed God's protection. Frequently Saul was close upon him, but David always succeeded in escaping. During those bitter days David perfected his virtue of trust in God; the psalms that date to this period in his life are expressions of his reliance and unbounded confidence in divine Providence.

At last Saul's end came. God had abandoned him. The occasion was a new war against Philistia. During the night before the decisive engagement, Saul betook himself to the witch at Endor and demanded that she conjure the spirit of Samuel. The prophet appeared and foretold the king's defeat and death. On the following day the two armies met on the hills of Gilboa, and the Israelites were routed. The Philistines pursued Saul and his sons; Jonathan and two of his brothers fell. Himself severely wounded, Saul took his sword and fell upon it.

Saturday Vespers. While the sun sinks in the west, we repeat David's lament over the two heroes, Saul and Jonathan: "Mountains of Gilboa, neither dew nor rain must come upon you! For upon your slopes the shield of heroes met disgrace, the shield of Saul as though it had not been anointed with oil. How the valiant have fallen in battle! And Jonathan slain on the heights! Saul and Jonathan, so lovable, so very charming in life, now even in death have not been parted!"

SCRIPTURE READINGS DURING THE FIFTH WEEK AFTER PENTECOST

DAVID, ISRAEL'S KING

Sunday (2 Kings 1). David is informed of Israel's defeat; griefstricken, he composes a magnificent dirge.

Monday (2 Kings 2—4). David is chosen king by the two southern tribes at Hebron; the other ten tribes remain loyal to the house of Saul, now under the leadership of Abner.

Tuesday (2 Kings 5). Abner is assassinated and David becomes king over all Israel.

Wednesday (2 Kings 6). David's first act was the solemn transfer of the ark of the covenant to Sion.

Thursday (2 Kings 7). David plans to build a temple to God, but upon the direction of the prophet Nathan enjoins the work upon his son and successor, Solomon.

Friday (2 Kings 8—10). David issues instructions governing divine worship and strives to have the sacred functions performed as solemnly as possible. Four thousand singers are chosen from among the Levites and divided into twenty-four groups. Various types of music become part of official liturgy. David himself composed a goodly number of psalms for public and private prayer; these psalms remain as a lasting monument to his piety and zeal for God's honor. According to the accompanying superscriptions, seventy-three of the one-hundred-fifty psalms were composed by David; furthermore, he may have written some of those for which no author is given.

Saturday (2 Kings 11). Who would have thought that David, the "man after God's own heart," after showing unprecedented zeal for the worship of the Lord, would have weakened and violated God's Law! Nevertheless, he did transgress grievously in two ways, adultery and murder. He sinned with Bethsabee and then arranged that Urias, her husband, be slain by the Ammonites.

But David repented of his sins. At *Vespers* we try to emulate his spirit of repentance: "I beseech You, Lord, take away the iniquity of Your servant, for I have acted like a fool."

SCRIPTURE READINGS DURING THE SIXTH WEEK AFTER PENTECOST

DAVID'S SIN AND ITS CONSEQUENCES

David, the beloved of God, sinned grievously; and the punishment that came upon him and his house cast its shadow over his declining years.

Sunday (2 Kings 12:1–10). In a very dramatic way Holy Writ depicts David's repentance.

Monday (2 Kings 12:11–25). Punishment: death of his child and misfortune upon his house.

Tuesday (2 Kings 13—14). David's punishment begins — Absalom murders his half-brother Amnon.

Wednesday (2 Kings 15:1–12). Absalom aspires to be king.

Thursday (2 Kings 15:13–37). Absalom revolts against his father. David is forced to flee.

Friday (2 Kings 16). David in flight; he shows himself great and noble in misfortune.

Saturday (2 Kings 18). David wins; Absalom's miserable end.

Saturday Vespers introduce us to Solomon, David's son and successor. Solomon was a type of Christ, the King of peace. "Sadoc the priest and Nathan the prophet anointed Solomon king in Gihon. And rejoicing they went up from there, saying: May the king live forever" (*Magn. Ant.*).

SCRIPTURE READINGS DURING THE SEVENTH WEEK AFTER PENTECOST

THE REIGN OF SOLOMON

During the coming week the Church presents Israel's third ruler, Solomon, the king of peace.

Sunday (3 Kings 1:1–15). After a strenuous life and forty years as king, David had become old and weak and felt the end approaching. The Bible preserves this anecdote of his last days: "Now king David was old and advanced in years, and when he was covered with clothes he was not warm. His servants therefore said to him: Let us seek for our lord and king a young virgin, and let her stand before the king and cherish him, and sleep in his bosom, and warm our lord the king. So they sought a beautiful young woman in all the coasts of Israel, and they found Abisag, a Sunamitess, and brought her to the king. The damsel was exceedingly beautiful, and she slept with the king and served him, but the king did not know her." At Matins St. Jerome endeavors to interpret and apply the passage (see p. 83).

Monday (3 Kings 1:28–40). Solomon is anointed king.

Tuesday (3 Kings 2). David's last instructions.

Wednesday (3 Kings 3). God appears to Solomon, who pleads for wisdom.

Thursday (3 Kings 4). The glory of Solomon's peaceful reign.

Friday (3 Kings 5). The construction of the temple.

Saturday (3 Kings 7—8). The dedication of the temple.

Saturday Vespers. "O Lord, You have granted the prayer of Your servant that I might build a temple to Your Name" (*Magn. Ant.*). The liturgy places Solomon's prayer upon Christ's lips (and upon ours); for in the Church (and in each soul) Christ has built unto His Father a glorious temple. This is what we are grateful for now in the Magnificat.

SCRIPTURE READINGS DURING THE EIGHTH WEEK AFTER PENTECOST

THE DIVISION OF THE KINGDOM

Solomon did not remain loyal to God. Yielding to his pagan wives, he consented to worship false gods and thereby brought his rule to an inglorious end. God punished his sins by dividing the kingdom at his death.

Sunday (3 Kings 9). God appears to Solomon a second time.

Monday (3 Kings 10). The queen of Saba visits the royal court at Jerusalem.

Tuesday (3 Kings 11:1–14). Solomon's infidelity is punished by the division of the kingdom.

Wednesday (3 Kings 11:26–43). Solomon dies and is succeeded by Roboam, his son.

Thursday (3 Kings 12). Roboam's harsh answer precipitates the division of the realm.

Friday (3 Kings 14). The northern tribes make Jeroboam king. A prophet announces his rejection by Yahweh.

Saturday (3 Kings 18). Elias. The contest between Baal and Yahweh on Mount Carmel.

Saturday Vespers. The coming week will be devoted to the prophet Elias and his disciple Eliseus. Both are mentioned in tonight's Magnificat antiphon: "When the Lord took Elias into heaven by a whirlwind, Eliseus cried: My father, the chariot of Israel, and its driver."

SCRIPTURE READINGS DURING THE NINTH WEEK AFTER PENTECOST

ELIAS AND ELISEUS

During the reign of Achab and Jezabel (875—853), Baal worship became the state religion of Israel. It was then that God sent among His people two illustrious prophets. Endowed with the gift of miracles and animated with a burning zeal for Mosaic religion, they resolutely opposed the king's evil innovations. Due to their efforts, true religion was not entirely uprooted; there remained a considerable group of faithful souls who would not bow to pagan idols. The two prophets were Elias and Eliseus.

From his birthplace, Tishbe in Gilead, Elias was called "the

Tishbite." About his family we know little; according to legend he was of the priestly tribe, remained single, and prepared himself by prayer and penance for his high calling. To him is due the preservation of monotheism in the ninth century, while his work as a herald of the one true God remained so vivid in the minds of the people that he spontaneously became the type of the Messiah's precursor. Even in external appearance there was a marked similarity between Elias and John the Baptist. Both wore rough garments, with a leather belt about the loins. Both dwelt in the wilderness. Both preached penance to the people, both opposed wicked rulers frankly and fearlessly; both were "burning lights" in the midst of a perverse generation.

Notable similarities also existed between Elias and Christ. Elias brought to an end a three-year drought and thereby restored the fruits of the earth. Dew and rain are often employed in the Old Testament as symbols of Messianic blessings. The food miraculously provided for Elias on the way through the wilderness to Mount Horeb symbolized the nourishment and strength redeemed mankind receives in the holy Eucharist. Jesus' fast of forty days in the desert had been prefigured by Elias' fast of forty days. Of particular importance is the prophet's wondrous assumption into heaven and the legend of his return to convert the Jews, types of Christ's ascension and Second Coming. For these many reasons the prophet Elias has always enjoyed high honor among both Jews and Christians.

Sunday (3 Kings 19). Elias was forced to flee from the wrath of the wicked queen Jezabel. Wearied by long hours of walking through the desert, he lay down under a juniper tree and fell asleep. Upon awaking, he saw near his head some bread and a vessel of water. He ate and drank, and strengthened by the meal, walked forty days and forty nights until he came to Mount Horeb.

Monday (4 Kings 2). The assumption of Elias, today's Bible story, is a figure of Christ's ascension into heaven. As Elias and Eliseus were walking east of the Jordan, a fiery chariot and fiery horses suddenly appeared and separated them; and "Elias went up by a whirlwind into heaven."

Tuesday (4 Kings 3). A great miracle-worker now comes to the fore, the prophet Eliseus. He labored in the kingdom of Israel, continuing the work of Elias. While the miracles of Elias manifested Yahweh's retributive justice, those of Eliseus showed His goodness toward the needy and afflicted.

Wednesday (4 Kings 4). Holy Scripture recounts a number of the miracles performed by the prophet Eliseus for the benefit and consolation of private persons; thereby faith in the one true God was preserved in Israel.

Thursday (4 Kings 5:1–16). We heard the story of Naaman's cure during Lent. Naaman is a figure of the newly baptized.

Friday (4 Kings 5:20–27). Giezi, Eliseus' servant, is punished for his sinful conduct.

Saturday (4 Kings 8:16–29). A sad passage upon the decadent state of Judah's kings. Judgment must come, for one king after the other acted in a manner displeasing to Yahweh. Nevertheless, Yahweh would not yet destroy the Southern Kingdom "because of David His servant to whom He had promised to keep a lamp before him forever."

Saturday Vespers. The Magnificat antiphon: "Joas did that which was right before the Lord all the days that Joiada the priest taught him." Joas was one of the few virtuous kings upon the throne of David.

SCRIPTURE READINGS DURING THE TENTH WEEK AFTER PENTECOST

THE DOWNFALL OF THE NORTHERN KINGDOM

It is not a pleasant story that the liturgy tells this week. Israel had proven obstinate, her leaders had become corrupt; the measure of God's wrath was full, and judgment could no longer be delayed.

Sunday (4 Kings 9:14–36). The murder of the wicked queen Jezabel.

Monday (4 Kings 11). Athalia reigns in Jerusalem.

Tuesday (4 Kings 12). Joas occupied the throne for forty years and "did what was right in the eyes of Yahweh." Nevertheless, the high places where the people sacrificed and burned incense were not abolished.

Wednesday (4 Kings 13). Sickness and death of the prophet Eliseus.

Thursday (4 Kings 17:1–18). The kingdom of Israel is destroyed by Assyria and the people led into captivity (722 B.C.).

Friday (4 Kings 17:19–41). Northern Palestine is colonized by foreigners later known as Samaritans.

Saturday (4 Kings 18). At Jerusalem, the "good king" Ezechias.

Saturday Vespers. The Magnificat is introduced with a petition from the prayer uttered by Ezechias when gravely ill, "I beseech You, Lord, remember how I have walked before You in truth, and with a perfect heart, and have done that which pleases You."

SCRIPTURE READINGS DURING THE ELEVENTH WEEK AFTER PENTECOST

DESTRUCTION OF THE SOUTHERN KINGDOM

At times there were exemplary kings upon the throne of David, as, for instance, Ezechias (721–693) and Josias (638–609). But these exceptions could not avert the impending catastrophe.

Sunday (4 Kings 20). The illness and miraculous cure of king Ezechias.

Monday (4 Kings 21). As a boy of twelve, Manasses succeeded his father Ezechias; he ruled from 693 to 639, and completely undid the work of his pious father.

Tuesday (4 Kings 22). Josias was chosen king of Judah after the violent death of his father Amon. He ruled for thirty years (638–609), and "did what was right in the eyes of Yahweh."

Wednesday (4 Kings 23). In the eighteenth year of his reign, Josias ordered that the temple liturgy be again solemnly observed and entrusted the care of the sanctuary to the high priest Helcias. Helcias found the Book of the Law that God-fearing priests had hidden in a building near the temple in days when false gods were honored.

Thursday (4 Kings 23—24). The idolatry and wickedness against which the good king Josias contended with great zeal and some success flourished again under his sons Joachaz and Joakim.

Friday (4 Kings 24). In 605 Nabuchodonosor, king of Babylon, appeared before Jerusalem and took Joakim and certain members of noble families (including the boy Daniel, who later became prophet) as hostages to Babylon. Some time later Joakim was permitted to return to Jerusalem, but when he entered into another unfriendly alliance, Nabuchodonosor besieged the city a second time. Joakim died before Jerusalem capitulated.

Saturday (4 Kings 25). Sedecias was Judah's last king (597–587). In 587 Nabuchodonosor destroyed the Southern Kingdom.

SCRIPTURE READINGS DURING THE MONTH OF AUGUST

The month of August in the liturgy. Ordinarily the liturgy pays no attention to months as specific units of time. Mother

Church is content with sanctifying the day, the week, and certain longer periods or seasons. Nevertheless, the months of August, September, October and November are treated as units in the distribution of Scripture Lessons in the breviary. To August the Church has assigned the Books of Wisdom; and they give the month a definite character. August is the month of summer's greatest heat, the month of bright days when light dominates over darkness — symbols of the clear vision and inner peace that reign when the spirit triumphs over the flesh. Now for such considerations the Wisdom Books of the Old Testament are very appropriate. For wisdom, according to Holy Writ, is not primarily knowledge but virtuous living. The Magnificat antiphons for Saturday during August seem to have been chosen with special care. Consider today's, for instance: "Wisdom has built herself a house which rests on seven pillars. The nations she has subjected to herself, and by her own strength she has trodden upon the necks of the proud and haughty!" In this antiphon, Wisdom, of course, signifies the Church; for the Church rests upon the seven pillars of the sacraments. It will aid us to understand the sapiential books if we keep this in mind. The Responsories throughout the month are based on Wisdom themes. August, therefore, has, as a unit of time, a recognizable liturgical character.

SCRIPTURE READINGS DURING THE FIRST WEEK OF AUGUST

THE BOOK OF PROVERBS

On the first Sunday of the month of August we begin a new series of books in the Divine Office, the Books of Wisdom. The Books of Kings symbolized the external growth and extension of Christ's kingdom. Another phase now receives stress, its interior development. To portray this the liturgy employs the

Books of Wisdom, a different volume each week. The first to be read is Solomon's Book of Proverbs, which consists of a collection of wise maxims that point the way to virtuous living. It is the piety or wisdom of the Old Law expressed epigrammatically. One cannot but benefit spiritually by reading the entire work.

Sunday (Prov. 1—2). The opening verses give the purpose of proverb literature:

> That men may appreciate wisdom and discipline,
>   may understand words of intelligence;
> May receive training in wise conduct,
>   in what is right, just and honest;
> That resourcefulness may be imparted to the simple,
>   to the young man knowledge and discretion.
> A wise man by hearing them will advance in learning,
>   an intelligent man will gain sound guidance.

Monday (Prov. 3). Fear God and love your neighbor.

> My son, do not forget my teaching,
>   and let your heart keep my commandments!
> For they will bring you length of days,
>   years of life and peace.
> Do not let mercy and truth leave you,
>   bind them about your neck,
>   and write them upon the tablets of your heart.
> Then you will find grace and rich rewards
>   from both God and men.
> Trust in the Lord with all your heart,
>   and never lean upon your own prudence.

Tuesday (Prov. 6). Condemnation of sloth.

> Go to the ant, O sluggard,
>   consider her ways, and learn wisdom!
> Although she has neither guide, nor master, nor captain,
>   she provides meat for herself in the summer
>   and gathers food for her needs in harvest time.

How long will you sleep, O sluggard?
  when will you rise from your bed?
"A little sleep, a little slumber,
  a little rest with folded hands!"
And want will confront you as a highwayman,
  poverty as a thug.

Wednesday (Prov. 8). Agelessness of Wisdom.
  The Lord created me at the beginning of His work,
    before He made anything from of old.
  I was fashioned ages ago,
    at the beginning, before the earth was made.
  The oceans did not yet exist,
    or springs bubbling over with water
    when I was born.
  The mountains had not yet been stationed,
    or the hills when I came into being.

Thursday (Prov. 10ff.). Between chapters 10:1 and 22:16 we find a collection of 375 proverbs called the "Parables of Solomon." Without exception they follow one rhythmic pattern, viz., two lines expressing one idea, usually by way of antithetical parallelism. Often several parables that suggest each other are grouped together. Among them are many spiritual gems.
  A wise son makes his father glad,
    but a foolish son is the sorrow of his mother.
  The slothful hand begets poverty,
    the industrious hand produces wealth.
  He who gathers in the harvest is a wise son;
    it is the good-for-nothing who sleeps in summertime.
  Hatred stirs up strifes,
    charity covers all offenses.
  Grief in man's heart discomfits him,
    a good word builds morale.
  A golden ring in a swine's snout:
    a woman fair and foolish (*physical beauty means nothing when one is spiritually corrupt*).

Friday (Prov. 25ff.). Space forbids more than few excerpts here (we recommend reading the complete text in the Bible).

Take away wickedness from the king's court
    and his throne will be established with justice.
He who speaks a word at the proper time
    resembles apples of gold on plates of silver.
As clouds and wind when no rain follows,
    so is the man who boasts and does not fulfill
        his promises.
When you find honey, eat moderately,
    lest being glutted you vomit it up.
A just man who falls down before the wicked
    is as a fountain troubled with the foot,
        or a polluted spring.
As a dog that returns to his vomit,
    so is the fool that repeats his folly.
As the door turns upon its hinges,
    so the slothful upon his bed.

Saturday (Prov. 31). The Book of Wisdom ends with the famous acrostic in praise of the virtuous woman. The Church applies the passage to holy women as the Lesson in the Mass *Cognovi* (Common of Holy Women).

SCRIPTURE READINGS DURING THE SECOND WEEK OF AUGUST

THE BOOK OF ECCLESIASTES OR QOHELETH

Saturday Vespers. "I dwell in the highest places, and my throne is in the pillar of a cloud" (*Magn. Ant.*). By this text the liturgy would teach us that in Wisdom we should see Christ, enthroned as King of the universe.

Sunday (Eccles. 1). This week we read the Book of Ecclesias-

tes or Qoheleth. The author's sober theme is that earthly pleasures
are vain and cannot bring peace to the heart of man. True happiness can be found only in God. According to Jewish legend,
King Solomon composed the book after his conversion at the end
of his life; scholars date its origin to the first century of the Hel-
lenistic era in Palestine.

> Vanity of vanities,
>   said Qoheleth.
> Vanity of vanities,
>   and all is vanity.
> What does a man retain of all the labor
>   by which he tires himself under the sun?
> One generation passes away,
>   and another generation comes:
>   only the earth stands firm forever.
> The sun rises, the sun sets,
>   it returns to the east only to rise again!

At Matins St. John Chrysostom offers a meditation on the
opening chapter of Qoheleth. "When Solomon was still en-
chained by the lusts of worldly things and enraptured by them, he
expended much time and money in constructing magnificent
palaces, in gathering vast sums of money, engaging singers, and
hiring all types of servants for table and kitchen. He spared no
effort to obtain happiness by planting splendid gardens, by having about himself only the most handsome and beautiful bodies,
and by pursuing, one might say, every possible avenue of pleasure
and self-gratification.

"But when he came to his senses again and was able to lift his
gaze from this deep, black abyss to the light of true wisdom, he
uttered those sublime words, words worthy of heaven itself, *Vanity of vanities, and all is vanity*. But we who have been called to a
nobler life are climbing to higher summits and are fighting on a
worthier battlefield. Therefore we are commanded to lead lives
similar to those incorporeal and spiritual beings whose home is
heaven."

Monday (Eccles. 2). Dissatisfied with spiritual values, Solomon describes how he sought peace and happiness in riches and earthly pleasures, but was foiled in his every attempt.

Tuesday (Eccles. 3). The tyranny of time.

Wednesday (Eccles. 4). Qoheleth reviews social conditions among men and finds nothing but want and suffering.

Thursday (Eccles. 5). Proverbs concerning one's relation to God.

> Speak not anything rashly,
>   and let not your heart be hasty
>   to utter words before God.
> For God is enthroned in heaven
>   while you are upon earth —
>   therefore let your words be few.

Friday (Eccles. 6).

> There is also another evil
> which I have seen under the sun
> and that is frequent among men:
> a man to whom God has given
> riches, and substance, and honor,
> and his soul lacks nothing of all that he desires.
> Yet God does not give him the health to eat thereof;
> but a stranger devours it!
> This, indeed, is vanity,
> and a great evil.

Saturday (Eccles. 7ff.). Do not postpone reading the entire book; it contains many excellent observations on human nature and conduct. "Remember your Creator in the days of your youth, before the time of affliction comes, and the years draw nigh of which you will say: They please me not! Before the sun, and the light, and the moon, and the stars turn dark . . . and the keepers of the house tremble . . . before the silver cord is snapped . . . and the pitcher breaks at the fountain . . . and the dust returns to the earth from whence it was taken, and the spirit returns to God who gave it. Vanity of vanities, says Qoheleth; all is vanity." Before concluding, the author summarized his teaching in one phrase: "Fear God and keep His commandments, for this is (the duty of) every man. All things that are done God will judge, whether good or evil."

SCRIPTURE READINGS DURING THE THIRD WEEK OF AUGUST

THE BOOK OF WISDOM

Saturday Vespers. "All wisdom is from the Lord God. Wisdom has always been with Him, it is eternal" (*Magn. Ant.*).

Sunday (Wis. 1). The Book of Wisdom was one of the last books to be added to the Old Testament canon; it treats in part of human wisdom (i.e., virtue, piety), in part of divine wisdom (which at times is described directly and at times personified). The first part of the book exhorts us to strive after moral wisdom.

Monday (Wis. 3—4). The tremendous difference between the death of a virtuous man and the death of a wicked man. Death for the upright man is merely a transition to endless life. Passages from these chapters are often applied to the death of martyrs.

Tuesday (Wis. 6).
Hear, therefore, O kings, and understand;
   learn, you who rule the ends of the earth.
Give ear, you who govern the people
   and pride yourselves over the multitudes
    of your subjects:
Sovereignty is given you by the Lord,
   and power by the Most High.
He will examine your works,
   and scrutinize your plans.

Wednesday (Wis. 7). And Solomon said:
> I myself also am a mortal man, like all others,
> and of the race of him that was first made of the earth;
> and in the womb of my mother I was fashioned to be
>   flesh.
> In the time of ten months I was compacted in blood,
> and when born, I drew in common air,
> and fell upon the earth.
> The first sound I uttered was a cry,
> like all others.

Thursday (Wis. 9—10). Give me that wisdom that sits on Your throne.

Friday (Wis. 13). The folly of worshipping idols! The passage contains the classic proof for God's existence.

Saturday (Wis. 15ff.). The final chapters of the Book of Wisdom (15–19) describe the role of wisdom in the history of God's Chosen People. Beginning with Adam, when divine wisdom manifested itself through creation and the promise of redemption, the author outlines the part wisdom played in the lives of Noe, Abraham, Lot, Jacob, Joseph and Moses. Considerable space is devoted to contrasting the Jews and the Egyptians, the wise and the foolish. The author brings his work to a conclusion with a hymn of praise to God, the Lord of creation and the Protector of Israel.

SCRIPTURE READINGS DURING THE FOURTH WEEK OF AUGUST

THE BOOK OF ECCLESIASTICUS OR SIRACH

Saturday Vespers. "In the street Wisdom is crying: If anyone loves wisdom, let him come to me and he will find her. And when he has found her, he shall be blessed if he retains her" (*Magn. Ant.*).

Sunday (Eccl. 1:1–10). Mother Church now puts into our hands the Book of the preacher Jesus Sirach, commonly known as Ecclesiasticus (i.e., Church-book, because in ancient times it was given to catechumens for instructions). Because its content is exceptionally practical, excerpts appear as Lessons in Mass formularies. The author of the book was Jesus, the son of Sirach (c. 180 B.C.). A companion to the Book of Proverbs, it consists of a collection of epigrams that synthesize the wisdom of the Old Law before its dissolution. Of its two major parts, the first (1:1—42:14) contains counsels for right and religious living; the second (42:15—51:38) praises God's greatness as manifested in nature, lists and praises the accomplishments of the Old Testament's most illustrious men, and closes with a canticle of thanksgiving to God.

Monday (Eccl. 1:11–35).
> The fear of the Lord is honor,
>> and glory, and gladness, and a crown of joy.
> The fear of the Lord delights the heart,
>> and gives joy, and gladness, and length of days.
> With him who fears the Lord
>> it will go well in the latter end,
>> and in the day of his death he will be blessed.
> The fear of the Lord is the beginning of wisdom,
>> it is created with the faithful and accompanies them
>> from the womb.

Tuesday (Eccl. 2). Fidelity to God is the topic in Eccl. 2:1—4:10. Wisdom, i.e., fear of the Lord, must prove itself by remaining faithful when put on trial by temptation.

Wednesday (Eccl. 3). Duties toward one's parents.
> The father's blessing establishes the house of the
>> children,
>> but the mother's curse roots up the foundation.

Thursday (Eccl. 4:1–10). Duties toward the poor.

Friday (Eccl. 4:20–31). True and false shame.

Saturday (Eccl. 5).
> Do not rely upon your possessions,
>> or say: I have enough to live on!
> Do not yield to the desires of your heart
>> so as to gratify its passions and lusts.
> And never say: Who has power over me?
> For God will surely punish you.

SCRIPTURE READINGS DURING THE FIFTH WEEK OF AUGUST

THE BOOK OF ECCLESIASTICUS OR SIRACH

In case the month of August has five weeks, the Book of Ecclesiasticus continues for another week.

Saturday Vespers. "My son, keep the commandments of your father, and forsake not the law of your mother; but always bind them to your heart" (*Magn. Ant.*).

Sunday (Eccl. 6). Principles for acting wisely.

Monday (Eccl. 7). In all your works remember your last end, and you will never sin.

Tuesday (Eccl. 8—10) On human relationships.

Wednesday (Eccl. 12). Beware of false friends.

Thursday (Eccl. 13). Insincerity and hypocrisy among the wealthy.

Friday (Eccl. 21). My son, if you have sinned, do so no more; but pray that your former sins may be forgiven. Flee from sin as from the face of a serpent; for if you come near, it will bite you. Its teeth are the teeth of a lion, robbing men of life. All iniquity is like a two-edged sword, there is no remedy for its wounds.

Saturday (Eccl. 36). There certainly are many more splendid passages in the Book of Ecclesiasticus than those indicated above. Chapter 36 begins with the canticle used at Saturday Lauds.

The Proper of the Saints

OUR CALENDAR OF FEASTS

Almost daily during the Pentecost season the Church observes a feast in honor of a saint. The saints, accordingly, accompany us quite closely throughout this period that is devoted to the practical aspects of Christian living. They serve as models for the practice of virtue and for the formation of sound moral norms. In the following pages our efforts will, therefore, be directed toward evaluating and applying the various feasts in relation to their bearing on everyday Christian life. Nevertheless, it would seem opportune at this point to add the following reflections.

Anyone who has been using the missal and breviary for many years in an effort to live in close harmony with the Church cannot avoid the thought that at the present time too many feasts of saints crowd the calendar. Feasts day after day tend to make spirituality restive, and piety less than completely Christ-centered. Many of the saints we meet are of too alien a stamp to hold our attention throughout the day — in Mass and the Hours of Office. And the Masses themselves, taken repeatedly from the Common, do not present sufficient variety, particularly in the Readings. In fact, the very nature of the Liturgy of the Word is jeopardized by such repetition, for its purpose is to further spiritual growth. The present situation can hardly be called ideal. With humble deference, then, do we look forward to a very thorough reform of the Proper of Saints in the missal and breviary.

The Sunday Masses, with changing Scripture pericopes, need to be read again during the ensuing week. The divine message would thereby become better understood and more effective. Holy Mass must be the "worship of God" rather than the cult of saints. Then, when a saint's feast would occur, especially that of a patron or a national figure, it would be truly impressive and purposeful. Pope St. Pius X took steps in this direction already a half century ago by initiating work on a calendar reform; and some religious Orders, the Benedictines, for instance, have succeeded in maintaining a more satisfactory arrangement down through the centuries. The rubric reform of 1955 did, in some measure, touch this problem by eliminating the octaves attached to certain saints' feasts. As part of our liturgical apostolate we will add our voices to the appeals being made for further reform.

June 1

ST. ANGELA MERICI, Virgin

Lead angelic lives

1. **St. Angela.** *Day of death*: January 27, 1540. *Canonized*: 1807; her feast was added to the calendar of the universal Church in 1861. *Grave*: in the Church of St. Afra, Brescia. *Life*. The saint was born in 1474 in the diocese of Verona. Early in life she dedicated herself to Christ as His bride. After the death of her parents, she desired to live solely for God in quiet and solitude, but her uncle insisted that she manage his household. She renounced her patrimony in order to observe most perfectly the rule for Franciscan Tertiaries.

During a pilgrimage to the Holy Land in 1524, she lost her eyesight temporarily. Pope Clement VII, whom she visited in Rome, desired her to remain in the Holy City. Later she founded a society for girls, under the protection of St. Ursula; this was the beginning of the Ursuline Order. St. Angela was almost seventy when she died; her body remained incorrupt for thirty days. Remarkable phenomena occurred at her burial in the Church of St. Afra.

Application. Angela means angel; and our patron saint transformed her name into a life program. This is why the Church prays that we may be inspired by her intercession and example to "lead angelic lives" (*Coll.*). The particular means to this end is detachment, renunciation of the things of the world, in accord with our state of life. Make some specific resolutions on this

matter today. Say a prayer too for the good of the Ursuline Order.
— The Mass is from the Common of Virgins (*Dilexisti*). See p.
406.

June 2

ST. MARCELLINUS, Priest; ST. PETER, Exorcist; ST. ERASMUS, Bishop; Martyrs

Present suffering — future glory

1. **The Saints.** *Graves*: the first two were originally buried
in the crypt of Tiburtius in Rome. The grave of St. Marcellinus
is now in Seligenstadt; that of Erasmus, in Gaeta, Italy. *Lives*.
The exorcist Peter was imprisoned under Diocletian; after he
had freed the jailor's daughter from the power of Satan, she and
the entire family became interested in the faith. Peter directed
them to the priest Marcellinus, who baptized them. For this deed
Marcellinus too was thrown into prison and treated atrociously.
Both were beheaded about the year 303. On an inscription Pope
Damasus relates how as a child he had listened to details of the
martyrdom as told by the jailor himself.

Erasmus was a bishop in Campania. Hot lead was poured over
him, but he remained unharmed; he was then clothed in a
glowing metal tunic, but again escaped all harm. He died a
natural death at the beginning of the fourth century. Erasmus
is one of the "Fourteen Holy Helpers."

Application. An exorcist, a priest, and a bishop, representing
three gradations in the sacrament of Holy Orders, bear witness
to Christ in blood. These men were put to death because they
zealously fulfilled their pastoral duties. A practical lesson we
could learn from them would be to foster a greater spirit of
cooperation between clergy and laity. Means to this end are
abundantly provided by the present liturgical revival.

2. **Holy Mass (Clamaverunt).** We hear the martyrs crying in the midst of their torments, but at the same time see them in glory; and our praise ascends to God in the words of the beautiful Psalm 33 (*Intr.*). The merits of the saints are a joy to us; their example, an inspiration (*Oration*). The *Epistle* restates the truth that the tears and harsh hardships of this life cannot be compared with the glory to follow. Paul would have us regard present suffering as the labor pains necessary to a birth into eternal life. Here the martyrs take the lead. In terms of the signs that will precede the final judgment the *Gospel* depicts the passion of Christ's followers. The Lord exhorts His faithful to act courageously, for He Himself will be their inspiration and support. The remaining Mass texts reflect the spirit common to Masses for martyrs.

June 4

ST. FRANCIS CARACCIOLO, Confessor

You are the God of my heart, the God who is my portion forever

1. **St. Francis.** *Day of death*: June 4, 1608. *Grave*: in the Church of St. Mary Major at Naples. *Canonized*: 1807. *Life.* Francis founded the Order of Minor Clerks Regular. In the course of time he became known as the "Venerable Father, the Preacher of the Love of God," a title merited for promoting devotion to the Blessed Sacrament and introducing nocturnal adoration in his community. He had a childlike love for the Blessed Virgin; his greatest joy was to be of service to his neighbor. God endowed him with the gift of prophecy and the discernment of spirits.

At the age of forty-four, while praying one day in the church at Loretto, he recognized that his end was near. Immediately he went to the monastery of Agnona in the Abruzzi, and exclaimed as he entered, "This is my final resting place." Shortly after, he was stricken with fever, received the last sacraments with deepest fervor, and quietly fell asleep in the Lord.

Application. The Church selects our saint's zeal for prayer and his spirit of penance for emphasis in today's Collect, and proposes these two virtues for imitation. "In imitating him grant that we may make such progress that we may pray without ceasing and constantly have our bodies under subjection." This is not an easy task; the liturgy, therefore, provides the needed assistance, the example of St. Francis, and the holy Eucharist.

2. **Holy Mass (Factum est).** The Mass texts, many of which are proper, point out the saint's heroic virtues, e.g., zeal for prayer: "My heart has become like wax melting within me, for the zeal of Your house has consumed me" (*Intr.*); "As the deer longs for the water brooks, so longs my soul for You, O God" (*Grad.*); "How great is the bounty of Your goodness, O Lord, which You have reserved for those who fear You" (*Comm.*). St. Francis' early death is alluded to in the *Epistle*: "Venerable age is not that of long time, nor counted by the number of years; but the understanding of a man is gray hairs, and a spotless life is old age. . . . Soon perfected, he fulfilled a long time for his soul pleased God. Therefore He hastened to remove him from the midst of iniquities." In the *Gospel* he is the watchful servant, with loins girt through penance and the lamp of God's love in his hand.

"You also must be ready, because the Son of Man will come at an hour that you do not expect."

June 5

ST. BONIFACE, Bishop and Martyr

For the restoration of religious unity in Germany

1. **St. Boniface.** *Day of death*: June 5, 754. *Grave*: at Fulda. *Picture*: as a bishop holding an ax, with a felled oak at his feet.

Life. A Benedictine monk was chosen by divine Providence to become Germany's great apostle and patron. Boniface's first missionary endeavor proved unsuccessful (716). Before attempting a second he went to Rome and received papal authorization (718). Under the holy bishop Willibrord he converted Frisia within a period of three years. On November 30, 722, Boniface was consecrated bishop by Pope Gregory II.

In 724 he turned his attention to the Hessian people, among whom he continued his missionary activity with renewed zeal. On an eminence near the village of Geismar on the Eder, he felled a giant oak that the people honored as the national sanctuary of the god Thor. Boniface used the wood to build a chapel in honor of St. Peter. This courageous act assured the eventual triumph of the Gospel in Germany.

The resident clergy and the priests dwelling at the court, whose unworthy lives needed censure, were constantly creating difficulties. Nevertheless Boniface continued to labor quietly, discreetly. He prayed unceasingly, put his trust in God alone, recommended his work to the prayers of his spiritual brothers and sisters in England. And God did not abandon him. Conversions were amazingly numerous. In 732 Gregory III sent him the pallium, the insignia of the archiepiscopal dignity. Boniface now devoted his time and talent to the ecclesiastical organization of the Church in Germany. He installed worthy bishops, set diocesan boundaries, promoted the spiritual life of the clergy and laity, held national synods (between 742 and 747), and in 744 founded the monastery of Fulda, which became a center of religious life in central Germany. In 745 he chose Mayence for his archiepiscopal see, and affiliated to it thirteen suffragan dioceses. This completed the ecclesiastical organization of Germany.

The final years of his busy life were spent, as were his earlier ones, in missionary activity. Word came to him in 754 that a part of Frisia had lapsed from the faith. He took leave of his priests and, sensing the approach of death, carried along a shroud. He was 74 years of age when with youthful enthusiasm he began the work of restoration, a mission he was not to complete. A band of semi-barbarous pagans overpowered and put him to death when he was about to administer confirmation to a group of neophytes at Dockum.

2. Holy Mass (Exsultabo). Inspiring proper texts bring to mind the life and virtues of Germany's venerable apostle. The Church hymns her joy over the conversion of the German people in the *Introit*. The psalm verse refers to and praises the saint's missionary work. The *Epistle* exhorts us to praise our forefathers in the faith, first among whom was Boniface. Their memory should continue on in the Church and we should walk in their footsteps. The holy martyr invites us in the *Gradual* to share, as he did, the sufferings of Christ while on earth in order that we may partake of Christ's joy and glory in heaven. In answer, as it were, to the Gradual we hear God's voice proclaiming Boniface's glory in the *Alleluia*.

Then Jesus Himself teaches us the eight beatitudes, eight royal roads to sanctity, and among them is that of martyrdom: "Blessed are you when men reproach you, and persecute you." Visualize the saint traveling through Germany under divine protection as you pray the *Offertory*. The *Communion* indicates his reward, a place on God's own throne — and we receive a pledge of this same reward in the Eucharist. The *Collect* recalls Boniface's missionary activity, and asks his protection. The Eucharistic Sacrifice effects our sanctification and increases our feast-day joy (*Secr.*). The *Postcommunion* implores the continual intercession of St. Boniface.

June 6

ST. NORBERT, Bishop and Confessor

We pray and offer sacrifice today for the Premonstratensian Order

St. Norbert. *Day of death*: June 6, 1134. *Grave*: at Magdeburg until 1627 when his remains were removed to the monastery of

Strahow in Prague during the Thirty Years' War. *Picture*: as a bishop with a monstrance in his hands. *Life*. Although a cleric, Norbert led a very worldly life for a number of years. The decisive change took place suddenly in 1115. While riding one day, he was overtaken by a thunderstorm. A flash of lightning struck the ground before him, the horse threw him, and he seemed to hear a voice upbraiding him for his conduct.

As in the case of St. Paul, the experience wrought a complete transformation. Norbert decided to give away his property and income rights, and to lead a life of abnegation, devoting himself particularly to preaching. In 1120 he founded the Order of Premonstratensians (the first monastery was at Prémontré) according to the rule of St. Augustine; approval came from Pope Honorius II in 1126.

In 1125, he was named archbishop of Magdeburg. On July 13, 1126, Norbert entered the city and came barefoot to the cathedral. About to enter the archiepiscopal palace, he was refused admission by the porter, who failed to recognize a bishop so poorly dressed. "You know me better and see me with clearer eyes than those who are forcing me to this palace. Poor and wretched man that I am, I should never have been assigned to this place," Norbert answered when the porter later sought his pardon.

The Bohemians honor St. Norbert as their national patron. The Mass, *Statuit,* is from the Common of a Confessor (see p. 397).

June 9

STS. PRIMUS AND FELICIAN, Martyrs

Fraternal love unto death

1. **Today's Saints.** *Day of death*: about 286. *Grave*: first at Nomentum (about twelve miles from Rome); Pope Theodore I (d. 649) transferred their relics to the Church of St. Stephen on

the Coelian Hill, where both saints are shown in mosaics. *Life*. At an advanced age the brothers Primus and Felician were beheaded at Nomentum (or Mentana). According to the legendary Acts of their martyrdom, they were thrown into prison by Diocletian. Felician was separated from his brother and subjected to cruel tortures. Then the magistrate called for Primus. "See," he said, "your brother has acted much more wisely than you; he listened to the emperor's wishes and now enjoys the greatest honor with him. If you follow his example, like consideration and favor will be shown you." Primus retorted: "What has happened to my brother, an angel has told me. Oh, that I, even as I am one in mind and heart with him, may not be separated from him in death!"

Both were then thrown to the lions, but the beasts crouched at their feet, fawning with head and tail. Of the twelve thousand persons who witnessed this marvel, five hundred together with their families embraced the faith. Finally the two brothers were beheaded. *Application*. Union with Christ through grace is the foundation of genuine love toward relatives and neighbors. This love will prove itself in time of trial.

2. **Holy Mass** (Sapientiam). The formulary is a mosaic from various Masses in the Common. The Church praises the wisdom of the saints, attested by their life and death (*Intr.*). The *Epistle* reminds us that now after their passion the holy martyrs are enjoying eternal life and are receiving due reward in heaven. In the *Gospel* Christ is grateful to His Father for concealing the good things of His kingdom from the mighty of this world while revealing them to the little ones. In a very real way this was fulfilled during the first centuries of the Christian era. The proud emperors have been forgotten, while Christ's poor, like our saints, are escorted through the streets of Rome in triumph and honor. The *Communion* attests that formerly the Mass had a different Gospel (John 15:12–16). The fruit of which Jesus is speaking in this liturgical context is martyrdom and its eternal crown.

June 10

ST. MARGARET, Queen and Widow

Pray for more good mothers

St. Margaret. *Day of death*: June 10, 1093. *Canonized*: 1251; feast since 1693. *Grave*: most of her remains are at the Escorial convent in Spain. *Picture*: a queen aiding the poor. *Life*. "She was born in Hungary (1046), where her father was living in exile, and likewise spent her childhood there as an unusually devout and pious girl. In the course of time she went to England, when her father was called to high office in his fatherland by his uncle, King St. Edward III. Fortune, however, soon reversed itself again (Margaret's father died suddenly in 1057), and upon leaving England a mighty storm — or better, divine Providence — brought her to the shores of Scotland. Upon instructions from her mother, Margaret married Malcolm III, king of Scotland, in 1069. The country was blessed by her holy life and by her deeds of charity for the next thirty years. Her eight children she zealously trained in the practice of Christian virtues.

"In the midst of royal splendor Margaret chastised her flesh by mortification and vigils and passed the greater part of the night in devout prayer. Her most remarkable virtue was love of neighbor, particularly love toward the poor. Her alms supported countless unfortunates; daily she provided food for three hundred and shared in the work of serving them personally, washing their feet and kissing their wounds" (*Roman Breviary*). St. Margaret is honored as a patron saint of Scotland.

Application. The *Collect* calls attention to "her love of the poor" and asks that "through her intercession and example God's love may grow from day to day in our hearts." Give special attention to this virtue on her feastday. "As long as you did it for one of these, the least of My brethren, you did it for Me," says the Lord. The Mass, *Cognovi*, is from the Common of Holy Women (see p. 408).

June 11

ST. BARNABAS, Apostle

Foster vocations

1. St. Barnabas. Strictly speaking, Barnabas was not an apostle, but the title has been bestowed upon him since very early times. His first name was Joseph; Barnabas (etymology: "son of consolation") was a surname. He belonged to the tribe of Levi. He was a Hellenist, that is, a Jew who lived outside of Palestine and spoke the Greek tongue. Born in Cyprus, he embraced the faith soon after the death of Christ, becoming a member of the original Jerusalem community. His first noteworthy deed was to sell his belongings and place the money at the feet of the apostles.

It is to his lasting credit that he befriended the neo-convert Paul and introduced him to the apostles when everyone was still distrusting the former persecutor. More noteworthy still was his service to the universal Church by being the first to recognize Paul's potential for the cause of Christ; it was Barnabas who brought him from Tarsus to teach at Antioch. The first missionary journey (about 45 — 48 A.D.) the two made together, and Barnabas seems to have been the leader, at least at the beginning (Acts 13 — 14). Barnabas' appearance must have been dignified and impressive, otherwise the inhabitants of Lystra would not have regarded him as Jupiter.

He was present with Paul at the Council of Jerusalem (*ca.* 50). While they were preparing for the second missionary journey, there arose a difference of opinion regarding Mark; as a result each continued his labors separately. Barnabas went to Cyprus with Mark and thereafter is not referred to again in the Acts of the Apostles or in any other authentic source. From a remark in one of Paul's letters we know that he lived from the work of his own hands (1 Cor. 9:5–6). The time and place of his death have not been recorded. It is claimed that his body was found at Salamina in 488 A.D. His name is mentioned in the Canon of the Mass since ancient times.

2. **Holy Mass** (*Mihi autem*). The missal treats our saint as
an apostle. In the *Introit* we express our respect for the "friends
of Christ, the princes" in His kingdom. The *Epistle* tells us of
Barnabas' first mission to Antioch; sent there by the apostles,
"He was a good man, full of the Holy Spirit and of faith." While
on this assignment he "went forth to Tarsus to look for Saul,"
and then spent a whole year with him at Antioch. Later on, Acts
tell us of their selection and consecration to the apostolate: "The
Holy Spirit said: Set apart for Me Saul and Barnabas unto the
work to which I have called them. Then, having fasted and
prayed and laid their hands upon them, they let them go." The
Gradual describes the two saints setting out on their journey.
The Lord Himself predicted the hardships of a missionary career: "I am sending you forth like sheep in the midst of wolves"
(*Gosp.*). They know that martyrdom is their portion. But for
this very reason the Church honors them as "princes," and
celebrates their coronation in heaven — an exaltation in which
we may share mystically by partaking in the Eucharistic Banquet.

June 12

ST. JOHN OF SAN FACUNDO, Confessor

Blessed are the peacemakers

1. **St. John.** *Day of death*: June 11, 1479. *Canonized*: 1690;
feast observed since 1723. *Grave*: at Salamanca, Spain. *Picture*:
as a hermit of St. Augustine, walking upon the sea. *Life*. John
came from a wealthy family. During a serious sickness he vowed
to embrace an ascetic way of life upon recovery. In fulfillment
of his resolve, he gave the better of his two garments to a beggar
who went about almost naked, and joined the hermits of St.
Augustine at Salamanca (1463); at the time that monastery was
universally respected because of its strict rule and discipline. He
was often granted the privilege of seeing Christ the Lord at

holy Mass and learning the deepest secrets directly from God
Himself, the secrets of men's hearts and the secret events of the
future. Through his prayers the seven-year-old daughter of his
brother was raised to life. His death was probably due to poi-
soning.

Application. John's special charism was to calm passions and
to restore peace. How quickly disputes and quarrels arise! Yet
we must practice the beatitude: "Blessed are the peacemakers."
Remember that the prayers for peace and the kiss of peace in
the Mass should not be empty ceremonies. The Mass, *Os justi*,
is from the Common of Confessors (see p. 402). The *Collect*
asks God, the Source of peace and love, for the gift of peace
through the intercession of St. John, our peace-loving saint.

2. Sts. Basilides, Cyrinus, Nabor, and Nazarius. Basilides
was a soldier in Rome, Nabor and Nazarius soldiers in Milan.
Their bodies were found on the present day by St. Ambrose. All
three died as martyrs under Diocletian. Cyrinus or Quirinus was
a famous bishop of Siscia. In the church of the Apostles in Milan,
St. Ambrose inscribed a number of edifying verses over the tomb
of St. Nazarius. The final lines are: "Whom the Cross leads to
victory, for him the Cross is the pledge of peace."

June 13

ST. ANTHONY OF PADUA, Doctor, Confessor

He always helps

1. St. Anthony's baptismal name was Fernando; to his name
in religion, "of Padua" is added because he died in that city and
was buried there. Few saints are more popular than Anthony,
and his power to grant practically every type of petition is widely
proclaimed. Born at Lisbon (1195), he first was associated with
the Augustinians; then he became a Franciscan at Coimbra

(1220). Desiring to die as a martyr, he sailed for Africa but was cast upon the shores of Sicily.

As a preacher in Italy he was highly successful. God confirmed his words with miracles, and often it became necessary to erect his pulpit in the open. Thousands flocked to hear him. Nature and grace had blessed him in a special way for the office of preacher, while his private life was a living Gospel. On June 13, 1231, he died at Padua, where his body is the object of great veneration. A year after his death he was canonized.

Down through the centuries St. Anthony has always been a very popular saint; in all wants the faithful confidently approach him. There is something extremely beautiful in this childlike devotion, proving that even in little things we should seek and find an answer from God. Still at times such devotion is not devoid of selfishness and superstition and needs to be refined and ennobled. The liturgical movement seeks to inspire a loftier, Christ-centered veneration of the saints. In the saints we honor God!

2. Holy Mass (In medio). The Mass is from the Common (p. 400), except for the *Collect*, *Secret*, and *Postcommunion*. These Orations give a touch of freshness to the formulary although no new approaches are presented.

June 14

ST. BASIL, Bishop and Doctor of the Church

"I saw the shepherd as he sent prayers to God for us on the wings of the Spirit" (St. Ephrem)

1. St. Basil. *Day of death*: January 1, 379 (today is the anniversary of his consecration as bishop). *Grave*: at Caesarea in Cappadocia. *Life*. St. Basil was born about 330, the oldest of four sons; three of his brothers became bishops, one of whom was St.

Gregory of Nyssa. His pious grandmother Macrina exercised a great influence upon his religious education: "Never shall I forget the deep impression that the words and example of this venerable woman made upon my soul." Between St. Basil and St. Gregory of Nazianzen (see May 9) an intimate friendship existed from youth to old age. Of Western monasticism St. Benedict was the father and founder, of Eastern monasticism, St. Basil.

As bishop, Basil was a courageous and heroic champion of the Catholic faith against the Arian heresy. Undauntedly he opposed the Emperor Valens, who was employing every possible means to make Arianism the state religion. Basil was a strong character, a burning lamp during his time. But as the fire from this lamp illumined and warmed the world, it consumed itself; as the saint's spiritual stature grew, his body wasted away, and at the early age of forty-nine his appearance was that of an old man. In every phase of ecclesiastical activity he showed superior talent and zeal. He was a great theologian, a powerful preacher, a gifted writer, the author of two rules for monastic life, a reformer of the Oriental liturgy. He died in 379, hardly forty-nine years old, yet so emaciated that only skin and bone remained, as though he had stayed alive in soul alone.

2. Holy Mass (In medio). The Mass is from the Common of Doctors (p. 400), with a proper *Gospel.* Today we come face to face with a teacher whose "mouth God opens in the midst of the Church" (*Intr.*). In the *Epistle* Paul speaks of his disciple Basil on the office of preaching and teaching; these admonitions of his master, Basil had faithfully followed. In the *Gospel* our Savior repeats His teaching on bearing one's cross. St. Basil did not shirk carrying his; he hated his own life and loved the Cross of Jesus.

3. Life. In 372 Emperor Valens sent Modestus, the prefect, to Cappadocia to introduce Arianism as the state religion. Modestus approached the holy bishop, upbraided him for his teaching, and threatened despoliation, exile, martyrdom, and death. To these words of the Byzantine despot, Basil replied with the peace of divine faith: "Is that all? Nothing of what you mentioned touches me. We possess nothing, we can be robbed of nothing. Exile will be impossible, since everywhere on God's earth I am at home. Torments cannot afflict me, for I have no body. And death is welcome, for it will bring me more quickly to God. To a great extent I am already dead; for a long time I have been hastening to the grave." Astonished, the prefect remarked: "Till today no one has ever spoken to me so courageously." "Perhaps," rejoined Basil, "you have never before met a bishop." Modestus hastened back to Valens. "Emperor," he said, "we are bested by this leader of the Church. He is too strong for threats, too firm for words, too clever for persuasion."

June 15

STS. VITUS, MODESTUS, AND CRESCENTIA, Martyrs

Humility is fundamental

1. **Today's Saints.** *Day of death*: June 15, 303 or 304. *Grave*: originally at Rome. The relics of St. Vitus were transferred to various places; an arm is in St. Vitus Cathedral, Prague. *Picture*: Vitus, alongside a cauldron of boiling pitch. *Life.* According to legendary Acts, the boy Vitus was baptized without the knowledge of his father. Having found out about it, his father had him beaten with rods by the magistrate. While his parent was considering more cruel punishments, Vitus, his teacher Modestus, and his nurse Crescentia fled to Sicily upon the command of an angel. But there, too, they were persecuted because of the faith. When thrown into a cauldron of burning oil, they, like the three youths, sang hymns of praise. Neither would wild beasts harm them. It is related that they were then quartered. Vitus is one of the "Fourteen Holy Helpers" (he is invoked against epilepsy and St. Vitus' dance).

Application. Today's *Collect* urges us to imitate our martyrs by practicing the virtue of humility: "By the intercession of Thy holy martyrs Vitus, Modestus, and Crescentia, we beseech Thee, O Lord, to prevent Thy Church from becoming proud-minded; rather, may she grow in humility in Thy sight, and by despising what is evil, perform with the freedom of love the things that are right."

2. **Holy Mass (Multae tribulationes)**. Almost all the texts in this formulary are proper. Like most ancient Masses, martyrdom is the object of praise. In the initial prayer the Church assures us that the martyrs are in the hand of God in spite of all their sufferings. And God will keep them for all eternity. Then follows a favorite psalm of the ancient Church, Psalm 33. Similar truths are contained in the *Epistle*. The lot of the just here on earth is to suffer; in the fire of suffering they must be purified like gold before God will receive them as an acceptable holocaust. In heaven, though, they will shine brightly, like torches, as they take part in the kingdom of Christ.

The *Gradual* echoes the Reading; the *Alleluia* is a true "praise the Lord" on the harps of the saints. The *Gospel* occurs nowhere else in the missal. The seventy-two disciples who had been sent out to missionize rejoice over the astounding miracles they could perform. And Christ acknowledges that He had given them power "to tread upon serpents and scorpions and upon all the might of the enemy." Much greater, however, should be their joy over the fact that they are children of God, that their "names are written in heaven." No doubt the Gospel was chosen with reference to the wondrous cures effected through the intercession of St. Vitus (he is implored, for instance, by persons who have been bitten by mad dogs or poisonous snakes). At the same time the Church teaches us the proper way of venerating the saints. The saints are not at our disposal primarily for our earthly needs; their principal task is to insure our eternal salvation. The glorified members of the Mystical Body are to aid the others in attaining glory.

For the *Offertory* we chant a favorite ejaculation of ancient

Christians: "Wonderful is God in His saints!" A verse from the Lesson serves as the *Communion*: "The saints are in peace!" The word "peace" is a synonym for "beatitude." Some of this beatitude or peace comes to our souls now in holy Communion. The final prayer reminds us that the Bread from heaven is a means of health for body and soul.

June 17

ST. GREGORY BARBARIGO, Bishop and Confessor

Preach the word — in season and out of season!

1. St. Gregory. St. Gregory's feast was inserted into the Church's calendar in 1960. The following account of his life is taken from the Breviary.

"Gregory Barbarigo, born at Venice of a very old family, obtained his degree in canon and civil law *magna cum laude* at the College of Padua. While attending the peace congress of Münster at the age of nineteen, he met the papal legate Fabio Chigi, and with his encouragement decided to become an ecclesiastic, and was admitted to holy orders. When Fabio Chigi became Pope under the name Alexander VII, he appointed Gregory bishop of Bergamo, and soon raised him to the college of cardinals, transferring him to the see of Padua. In entering upon his episcopal duties, he strove to model himself on St. Charles Borromeo. It was his lifelong endeavor to extirpate vices and cultivate virtues in obedience to the warnings and decrees of the sacred synod of Trent. In both dioceses he enlarged the seminaries. At Padua especially he improved the library and the press, from which books were published for distribution among the peoples of the Near East. He strenuously fostered catechetical instruction, and zealously traveled to every village of the diocese to teach and preach. He was distinguished for his works of charity and the holiness of his life. So generous was he to the needy and poor that he even gave away his household goods, his clothes and his bed to help them. Finally, after a brief fatal illness, he fell asleep peacefully in the Lord on June 18, 1697. As he was renowned for his merits and his virtues, Clement XIII added his name to the list of the Blessed, and John XXIII inscribed him among the Saints."

The Mass is from the Common of a Confessor Bishop (*Stat uit*).

June 18

ST. EPHREM THE SYRIAN, Doctor of the Church
STS. MARK AND MARCELLIAN, Martyrs
Be a harp of the Holy Spirit

1. St. Ephrem. *Day of death*: June 9, 373. *Grave*: at Edessa in Syria. *Life*. Ephrem, the deacon Doctor of the Church, easily ranks first among the Church fathers of his country. He was an untiring apologist for the Catholic faith against countless sects, especially the Arians; and in these struggles he knew how to combine fiery zeal with sympathetic love toward the heretics. He was a very prolific writer, the "golden mouth" of the Syrian Church, and an accomplished poet; the Eastern Churches have incorporated his sacred hymns into the liturgy. By the Syrians he is called the "harp of the Holy Spirit." He was a deacon in Edessa, where he settled after that city had become Persian in 363. The Mass, *In medio*, is from the Common of Doctors (p. 400).

2. "Harp of the Holy Spirit." A wonderful name! Ephrem comments beautifully upon the phrase in one of his hymns: "The call of the trumpets rouses the silent harps (departed souls): Awake, chant hymns, and praise the Bridegroom! What pandemonium when the graves will open! When one after another will seize his harp and intone hymns of jubilation: Praise be to Him who brings down to the dust — praise be to Him who raises

LORD, scatter
the forces of evil
and protect those
redeemed by Your Son,
CHRIST JESUS ✝

up again! May the harp of my soul be with those who praise the Lord at the resurrection!"

Every soul is a harp unto God, but this is particularly true of the saints; for their word and example keep resounding in the Church. Especially on their feasts do their harps become alive again. The Spirit of God surcharges them, the finger of God plucks the strings to the texts and truths of the holy liturgy. "It is good to praise the Lord, to sing to Him on ten-stringed harps."

3. Sts. Mark and Marcellian. *Grave*: in the catacomb of St. Callistus until the ninth century when their remains were transferred to the Church of Sts. Cosmas and Damian. *Life*. According to legendary *Acts*, these two saints were brothers, born at Rome, and deacons. On account of professing the Christian faith they were seized and their feet nailed to a post. When the judge addressed them: "Change your minds, you poor wretches, and free yourselves from such tortures," they retorted: "Never were we so full of joy at a banquet as now while we are suffering for Christ, in whose love we are just beginning to be nailed fast. May He allow us to endure such things as long as we are clothed with these corruptible wrappings." Day and night they passed in holy singing until they were finally put to death by arrows.

June 19

ST. JULIANA FALCONIERI, Virgin
STS. GERVASE AND PROTASE, Martyrs

May the holy Viaticum comfort and strengthen us
in our last struggle

1. St. Juliana. *Day of death*: June 12, 1341. *Canonized*: 1737; feast, 1738. *Grave*: at Florence, in the church of the Annunciation. *Picture*: as a Mantellate nun, a Host on the left side of her breast. *Life*. Juliana was born in 1270 of the illustrious Florentine family of the Falconieri when her parents were already well advanced in years. Her uncle, the saintly Alexius Falconieri, declared to her mother that she had given birth "not to a girl but to an angel." At the age of fifteen she renounced her inheritance and was the first to receive from the hand of St. Philip Benizi the habit of a Mantellate nun. Many women followed her example; even her mother placed herself under Juliana's spiritual direction.

St. Philip Benizi commended to her care and protection the Servite Order over which he had charge. So severe were her mortifications and fastings that a grave stomach ailment developed; she could take no food, not even the sacred Host. At the point of death she asked that a consecrated Host be placed against her heart. Then occurred the miracle to which the Collect and the hymn in the Breviary refer — the Host vanished, and Juliana died with a radiant face. After her death the picture of the Crucified, as it had been on the sacred Host, was found impressed upon her breast. The Mass, *Dilexisti,* is from the Common of Virgins (p. 406).

2. **Sts. Gervase and Protase.** These two brothers died as martyrs at Milan about the year 170. They belong to the illustrious saints of the ancient Church. Little is known about their lives. The finding of their remains by St. Ambrose is well attested (386). St. Augustine, himself a witness, describes the event very dramatically in his *Confessions* (9, 7). St. Ambrose requested to be buried alongside the bodies of Sts. Gervase and Protase. In the year 1864 their relics were found under the high altar of the old Milan basilica in a sarcophagus of porphyry, and together with the remains of St. Ambrose were honorably re-entombed.

3. **Holy Viaticum.** The pagans of ancient Rome were accustomed to place a piece of gold in the mouth of dead persons in order to enable them to pay Charon, the ferryman, for passage across the river of the dead. That was their viaticum. But Christians, already in earliest times, gave to those gravely ill the holy Eucharist to strengthen them on their last journey; they even placed the sacred Bread on the breasts of the dead. Though this

latter practice was never sanctioned by the Church, it proves early Christian faith in the resurrection of the body, of which the holy Eucharist is a pledge.

Communion given at a deathbed is called "Viaticum" — nourishment on the way. A different prayer is used when placing the sacred Host on the lips of a sick person than at the ordinary distribution of holy Communion: "Receive, brother (sister), the Body of our Lord Jesus Christ as nourishment on the way; may It preserve you against the wicked enemy and bring you to eternal life. Amen." Holy Viaticum may be received several times if the dying person lingers in his critical state. It may also be received on the same day that one has already received the blessed Eucharist. It stands to reason that for holy Viaticum the obligation of fasting does not hold. (It would be in place here to review the recent legislation of the Church on what is permitted to the ill before receiving holy Communion.)

Some solemnity should mark the occasion when holy Communion is brought to the sick. The priest bearing the Blessed Sacrament should be accompanied, and certain preparations should be made in the room where the sick person lies.

When possible, the Church wishes that the Blessed Sacrament be carried to the sick in a solemn manner. There will be a procession in which the faithful take part, informed by the ringing of a little bell. The pastor will be vested with surplice, stole and veil; servers will carry lighted lamps, the faithful, burning candles; even a small baldachin over the Blessed Sacrament will not be absent. A special indulgence has been granted for accompanying the Blessed Sacrament, one which remains in force even during a Jubilee.[1]

In the larger cities or in a non-Catholic environment, such a solemn carrying of the holy Eucharist to the sick cannot, of course, take place; but even in these circumstances it would be most appropriate if some special reverence were shown; others besides

[1] For accompanying holy Viaticum: with lights, 7 years; without lights, 5 years; for sending a substitute with a light, 3 years. For accompanying the priest bringing Communion to the sick, a plenary indulgence.

the priest should be devoutly present at the place where the Sacrament is administered.

In the sickroom certain preparations should be made for the great "visitation." There will be a table covered with a white linen cloth (this cloth will be readied while one is still in good health; it should be kept in a definite and known place along with other necessary articles, so that if illness comes suddenly, no lengthy search need be made). Upon the linen, candlesticks with lighted candles (blessed on Candlemas day) are placed, together with a crucifix, two small vessels of water, and a clean linen cloth, which may be placed on the breast of the sick person. Personal taste will dictate how to adorn the room. If the sacrament of Extreme Unction is to be administered, six small cotton balls should be placed on a plate, and on another some salt or bread crumbs for cleaning the priest's hands.

June 20

ST. SILVERIUS, Pope and Martyr

I have not been unfaithful to my duty, nor shall I

1. St. Silverius. *Day of death*: during December 537, on the island of Pontia. *Grave*: on the island of Pontia. *Life*. Silverius I, pope and martyr (536–537), refused to confirm the Monophysite Anthimus as patriarch of Constantinople after he was raised to that dignity by the Empress Theodora. Accordingly, the Empress ordered Belisar, the general of the imperial army stationed at Rome, to remove the Pope and clothe him as a monk. Silverius was exiled to Asia Minor, but on the counsel of the bishop of Patar was sent back to Rome by the Emperor Justinian. Through the intrigues of the anti-pope Vigilius, Belisar banished Silverius to the island of Pontia; while there he is said to have written Bishop Amator: "I am nourishing myself with the bread of trib-

ulation and with the water of affliction; but I have not been
unfaithful to my duty, nor shall I!" His death, according to one
tradition, was largely due to the privations of exile, but according
to another he was murdered at the instigation of Antonia, the
wife of Belisar. In any case, the Church has accorded him the
honors of a martyr.

2. **Holy Mass (Si diligis Me)** is from the Common of Sovereign Pontiffs (see p. 378).

June 21

ST. ALOYSIUS OF GONZAGA, Confessor

May we who have not imitated him in innocence follow his example of penance

1. **St. Aloysius.** *Day of death*: June 21, 1591. *Canonized*:
1726; feast 1842. *Grave*: at Rome in a chapel dedicated to his
honor in the church of St. Ignatius. *Picture*: as a Jesuit with a
cross, lily, and skull. *Life*. An angelic youth! Innocence intent
upon penance! "In a short time he accomplished the work of
many years!" St. Robert Bellarmine, who assisted him at his
deathbed, along with many others who knew him intimately,
have vouched that Aloysius never committed a mortal sin during
his whole life. His most outstanding virtue was angelic purity of
soul; through a special grace, it was never soiled by so much as
an impure thought. Two Popes, Benedict XIII and Pius XI,
have designated St. Aloysius as the patron of youth.

Aloysius was born in 1568 of an illustrious family; at the age
of nine he made a vow of virginity before the altar of the Blessed
Virgin at Florence. From the hands of St. Charles Borromeo he
received first holy Communion. His life was one of severest mortification. He could spend as long as five hours in prayer without
suffering the least distraction. After countering opposition from

his father for three years, he finally gained permission to enter the Society of Jesus (1585). In the service of the sick he contracted a grave illness and died in his twenty-fourth year, after being scourged on his death-bed according to his wish and put on the ground. *Application.* The Martyrology singles out his two greatest virtues: "Through contempt of a princely throne and innocence of life he won incomparable glory."

2. **Holy Mass (Minuisti).** The formulary, mirroring the life of St. Aloysius, is a good example of the style found in newer compositions. In the *Introit* we praise his angelic purity of soul: "You have made him a little less than the angels. . . . Praise the Lord, all His angels!" Cast in classic phraseology, the *Collect* orients our petition: in Aloysius God "united wonderful innocence with a like spirit of mortification," and then states the request proper: "may we who have not imitated him in innocence follow his example of penance" (the Latin style is most concise: *innocentem non secuti, paenitentem imitemur*). The *Lesson* from the Common is particularly apt today: "He could have sinned, but did not" — he, the son of a prince and at the royal court! The *Gradual* and *Alleluia* tell the story of his vocation: from the womb of his mother he was predestined; in his childhood he dedicated himself to God; in early youth he entered a religious Order despite severe and prolonged opposition.

The *Gospel* likewise was especially chosen; the angelic lives of the saints foreshadow their future life with the angels in heaven. Its closing sentences describe Aloysius' great love of God and neighbor. In the *Offertory* we behold our saint ascending the mount of heaven. A beautiful *Secret!* We see ourselves seated with Aloysius at the wedding feast, wearing wedding garments; the garment of our saint, however, is studded with glistening pearls (his tears of penance). In the Sacrifice Banquet we eat the "Bread of angels" and then petition that we too may "live like the angels," continually giving thanks to God (*Postc.*). Each text that is proper to this Mass could well serve as the subject for a profitable meditation.

ST. PAULINUS, Bishop and Confessor

I will prepare a lamp for My anointed

1. **St. Paulinus.** *Day of death*: June 22, 431. Though today's feast has always been observed, only in 1908 was it raised to its present high rank. *Grave*: first at Nola, later at Benevento, then in the church of St. Bartholomew at Rome. Pius X ordered the relics to be taken back to Nola. *Life*. In 353 Pontius Meropius Anicius Paulinus was born of a prominent Bordeaux family. He received his education in the school of the rhetorician Ausonius. At an early age he attained the dignity of senator and then of consul. As governor of Campania, he chose Nola as his seat. Here he was converted to the faith by St. Felix of Nola. He resigned his position and returned to Gaul, where St. Martin of Tours restored his eyesight.

Despite personal remonstrances, Paulinus was ordained a priest in Spain, and from there he returned to do honor at the grave of his sainted spiritual father. In 409 he became bishop of Tours. Paulinus was an author and poet; he corresponded with the great saints and scholars of his time, Ambrose and Augustine. During the Vandal invasion he used every possible means to feed the poor. When a poor widow asked for money to ransom her son, he gave himself into slavery. With God's aid he returned to his flock and died at the age of seventy-eight in 431. His last words were: "I will prepare a lamp for My anointed" (Ps. 131). His particular virtue was love toward the poor.

2. **Holy Mass (Sacerdotes).** The Mass, a mosaic from various Masses in the Common, to some extent mirrors the life of the saint. In the *Introit* and *Gradual* we come face to face with the venerable bishop. In the *Epistle* he preaches to us on the poverty of Christ: "Being rich, He became poor for your sakes, that by His poverty you might become rich." And in the *Gospel* we hear the same message from the lips of our divine Master: "Sell what

you have and give alms." Our saint practiced this counsel literally; his words, therefore, are more convincing.

He was "the faithful and wise servant whom the Lord places
over His household" (*Comm.*). For he distributed not only the
measure of Eucharistic wheat, but also the measure of ordinary
wheat in the "due season" of famine; and when he no longer had
anything to give, he gave himself into slavery. The *Secret* (unite
the sacrifice of perfect love with the perfect Sacrifice of the altar),
which is proper to the formulary, and the *Postcommunion* (Paulinus drew his piety and humility from the divine Fountainhead)
deserve time for lengthier meditation.

3. Divine Office. The Lessons of the second nocturn describe
the life of St. Paulinus. They are taken from the 1908 Brief of
Pope Pius X (an excellent example of critical and objective hagiography). The Readings of the third nocturn are culled from
a homily by St. Paulinus on his favorite virtue, poverty. "God
almighty could have made all men equally rich in worldly goods
from the very first day of birth, so rich that no one would be de-
pendent upon another. But He did not do it in order to test the
hearts of men. He created the poor to make men merciful, He
created the helpless to put the powerful on trial."

June 23

VIGIL OF ST. JOHN THE BAPTIST

Many will rejoice at his birth

1. The Vigil. Today we prepare for a feast that is part of the
basic structure of the Church year, the commemoration of the
birth of Christ's precursor. It is a kind of Advent, a second annunciation of the Savior's nativity, the first having been on March
25. The feast belongs to the redemptive cycle rather than to the
sanctoral cycle; it is a joyous anticipation of approaching salva-

tion. Its special mystery is to herald the birth of the Baptist, to proclaim the message brought by the angel Gabriel to Zachary in the temple.

More specifically the liturgy commemorates John's conception in the womb of Elizabeth his mother. Of this we hear as soon as we enter the church. The Gospel gives further details, and in the Office the matter is discussed by St. Ambrose. He observes that sacred Scripture praises not only certain holy persons but also their parents and cites as examples the stories of Samuel and Isaac; in the present instance the priestly family from which Zachary sprang is indicated, likewise his wife's family.

Actually the Lesson describes the call of the prophet Jeremias, but the liturgy accommodates the passage to John the Baptist; and it fits admirably, for the Baptist was sanctified in his mother's womb and sent to preach repentance: "Before I formed you in the womb of your mother, I knew you; and before you saw the light of day, I sanctified you and made you a prophet unto the nations. Lo, I have set you this day over nations and over kingdoms to root up and to pull down, to waste and to destroy, to build and to plant."

2. **Significance of the Feast.** The purpose of a vigil is, in part, to isolate the spirit of the coming feast and to underscore its significance. Let us, therefore, study the life of this great man whom Christ praised so highly. Rarely does holy Scripture treat in equal detail the life of a saint, recording his conception, birth, circumcision (Luke 1); his first public utterances, preaching and witnessing to Christ (Luke 3; Matt. 3; John 3:22–36); his imprisonment and martyrdom (Mark 6:14–29). Become better acquainted with these splendid New Testament passages.

Why is St. John the Baptist accorded such prominence in the liturgy? Even though he was a unique personality, his real greatness is due to his office as forerunner of the Messiah, to his work of preparing the way for the Redeemer. Christ is the Sun, John the dawn. The liturgy aims at presenting Christ's advent most dramatically, and therefore insists on having the precursor

precede. A few examples will clarify this statement. (a) Christ's
birth is celebrated in winter when the sun begins a higher course
through the heavens; but the birth of the Baptist is celebrated in
summer after the sun's course starts its decline. In symbol the
liturgy is actualizing the Baptist's words: "He must increase; I
must decrease." (b) During Advent, before the rising of the
divine Sun at Christmas, John's presence symbolizes the dawn.
(c) Each day at Lauds, before the sun, the symbol of the Eucharistic Sun, rises, the Church sings the praises of the precursor
in the *Benedictus*. (d) And finally, when the eternal Sun is rising
over the grave of a departed Christian, the Church again chants
the *Benedictus*. To this very day John is still the forerunner of
Christ in Christian worship.

3. The Martyrology. "At Philadelphia in Arabia the holy
martyrs Zeno and his slave Zena. As Zena was being bound with
chains, Zena kissed the fetters of his master and pleaded for a
share in his afflictions; accordingly, he too was seized by the
soldiers, and like his master, obtained the crown of martyrdom."

June 24

NATIVITY OF ST. JOHN THE BAPTIST

John was a lamp that burned and shone

Today's feast, a segment of Advent in the season of Pentecost,
makes us aware of the wonderful inner relationship between
the sacred mysteries; for we are still in the midst of one Church
year and already a bridge is being erected to the coming year of
grace.

1. The Feast. Ordinarily the Church observes the day of a
saint's death as his feast, because that day marks his entrance
into heaven. To this rule there are two notable exceptions, the
birthdays of Blessed Mary and of St. John the Baptist. All other

persons were stained with original sin at birth, hence, were displeasing to God. But Mary, already in the first moment of her existence, was free from original sin (for which reason even her very conception is commemorated by a special feast), and John was cleansed of original sin in the womb of his mother. This is the dogmatic justification for today's feast.

In the breviary St. Augustine explains the reason for today's observance in the following words: "Apart from the most holy solemnity commemorating our Savior's birth, the Church keeps the birthday of no other person except that of John the Baptist. (The feasts of the Immaculate Conception and of the Nativity of the Blessed Virgin had not yet been introduced.) In the case of other saints or of God's chosen ones, the Church, as you know, solemnizes the day on which they were reborn to everlasting beatitude after ending the trials of this life and gloriously triumphing over the world.

"For all these the final day of their lives, the day on which they completed their earthly service is honored. But for John the day of his birth, the day on which he began this mortal life is likewise sacred. The reason for this is, of course, that the Lord willed to announce to men His own coming through the Baptist, lest if He appeared suddenly, they would fail to recognize Him. John represented the Old Covenant and the Law. Therefore he preceded the Redeemer, even as the Law preceded and heralded the new dispensation of grace."

In other words, today's feast anticipates the feast of Christmas. Taking an overall view, we keep during the course of the year only two mysteries, that of Christ's incarnation and that of His redemption. The redemption mystery is the greater of the two; the incarnation touches the human heart more directly. To the redemption mystery the entire Easter season is devoted, from Septuagesima until Pentecost; and likewise every Sunday of the year, because Sunday is Easter in miniature.

The Christmas season has for its object the mystery of God-become-Man, to which there is reference only now and then during the remaining part of the year, e.g., on Marian feasts, especially that of the Annunciation (March 25) and today's feast in honor of the Baptist. In a sense, then, we are celebrating Christ's incarnation today. The birth of Jesus is observed on December 25 at the time of the winter solstice, while the birth of His forerunner is observed six months earlier at the time of the summer solstice. Christmas is a "light" feast; the same is true today. The popular custom centering about "St. John's Fire" stems from soundest Christian dogma and could well be given renewed attention. St. John's Fire symbolizes Christ the Light; John was a lamp that burned and shone. We Christians should be the light of the world.

2. **Holy Mass (De ventre).** The theme dominating the Mass is that of the precursor's call. Already in the *Introit* the Baptist steps before us and tells of his sanctification in his mother's womb. The liturgy accommodates to the Baptist passages from the Old Testament that recount the call of the prophets Isaias and Jeremias. The Readings of the first nocturn refer to the call of Jeremias, the *Lesson* of the Mass (and Introit) to that of Isaias. The message in both cases is the same: already before his birth John was commissioned by God to be a preacher of penance and the forerunner of the Messiah.

The *Gradual*, another borrowing from the Old Testament, is an echo to the Lesson; the *Alleluia*, a prelude to the Gospel, is taken from the New Testament. The birth and circumcision of the Baptist are announced by the *Gospel*. It is a memorable family feast as Zachary, miraculously cured of his inability to speak, circumcises the infant and sings the prophetic hymn of praise, the *Benedictus*, in which he beholds the "Dayspring from on high" about to visit man. Without the least shadow of doubt, Mary, God's blessed Bride, was present on this occasion. She was a type of God's other Bride, Mother Church, who now in the holy mysteries repeats this same drama in the order of grace. For in the holy Sacrifice the *Oriens ex alto* appears together with His precursor; and at the sacred Banquet I too become a *propheta Altissimi*, a prophet of the Most High, called to spend the entire day before "the face of the Lord," preparing His ways.

3. Thoughts on the Mass. The Mass is cast in a very personal "You — I" dialog or monolog form. Who is meant by these pronouns? In the first place, John. The liturgy is highly dramatic. John is present and speaks. He speaks in the Introit, he speaks in the Lesson (it is a favorite procedure of the liturgy to have the saint of the day or the stational saint address us in the Readings). We share his sanctification in his mother's womb (the point and purpose of the feast) through our Catholic vocation and through grace. Read the Gradual carefully. The second verse ends with: "And He said to me," a most unusual ending. It is evident that in ancient times the Gradual had a somewhat different cast; it was sung in antiphonal fashion.

Schola (God):

Before I formed you in the womb of your mother, I knew you.

The faithful: (repeating it meditatively)

Before I formed you in the womb of your mother, I knew you.

Schola (John):

The Lord put forth His hand, touched my mouth, and said to me:

The faithful (God):

Before I formed you in the womb of your mother, I knew you.

4. The Martyrology. "At Rome the commemoration of a countless number of holy martyrs who, wholly unjustly, were accused by Nero of having set fire to the city of Rome. This cruel tyrant condemned them to be put to death in various ways. Some were covered with the skins of wild animals and thrown to wild dogs to be torn into pieces; some were nailed to crosses; others were prepared as living torches and used as lights by night. All were disciples of the apostles, the firstfruits of those martyrs whom the Church at Rome, that rich field of witnesses to the faith, sent to heaven even before the martyrdom of the apostles themselves."

On the 27th of June a special feast is celebrated at Rome for these protomartyrs of the Roman Church. Out of reverence for the blood of the martyrs, Pope Pius V forbade holding shows in the Vatican. When an ambassador asked this Pope for a relic, he was given a little ground from St. Peter's Square. The ambassador complained, but the Pope pointed out to him that it was ground reddened by the blood of martyrs.[1]

June 25

ST. WILLIAM, Abbot

Mortification and solitude

St. William. *Day of death*: June 25, 1142. *Grave*: in a church the saint built and dedicated to Mary on Monte Vergine. *Picture*: after a statue of the saint placed among the founders of religious Orders in St. Peter's, Rome. *Life*. Abbot William hailed from Vercelli in Piedmont. At the age of fourteen he undertook a pilgrimage in shabby penitential clothes to the tomb of the holy Apostle James at Compostella, Spain. After his return he lived upon a deserted hill, where he practiced severe penances. On this "Hill of Vergil," called Monte Vergine after it was dedicated to the Blessed Virgin, William built a monastery and founded an order of Benedictine hermits. He performed many miracles. When tempted by a shameless woman, he threw himself into a bed of burning coals, but remained unharmed. Thereupon King Roger of Naples became one of the saint's admirers.

Application. William's pilgrimage to the tomb of an apostle was the turning point of his life. Is it not easily possible for you to make a pilgrimage to some holy place in your neighborhood now during the summertime? First of all, however, are you familiar with the relics in your own parish church? Remember that any visit to a church is a pilgrimage to the grave of a saint! The Mass, *Os justi*, is taken from the Common of Abbots (see: p. 401).

[1] Schuster, *Liber Sacr.*, 7, p. 267.

June 26

STS. JOHN AND PAUL, Martyrs

Two olive trees, two candlesticks aglow before the Lord

1. **Sts. John and Paul.** *Day of death*: June 26, year unknown. *Grave*: at Rome, in their own house, which later became a basilica in their honor. *Life*. The *Acts* of these two martyrs, which historians regard as spurious, contain the following: "The two brothers, John and Paul, were valets to Constantia, the daughter of Emperor Constantine. For their excellent work she bequeathed to them a considerable sum. This they used to aid poor Christians. When Julian the Apostate (361-363) invited them to become members of the inner circle of the imperial household, they refused and boldly explained that they did not relish close association with one who had fallen away from Jesus Christ. The Emperor gave them ten days to reconsider their position, threatening them with death if at the end of this time they refused to do his bidding and sacrifice to Jupiter. The brothers used the interval to distribute what remained of their possessions to the poor so that they could begin their journey home to God with less hindrance, while at the same time benefiting many who would 'receive them into the everlasting dwellings' (Luke 16:9). Their choice was death, and they were beheaded in their own house."

Both John and Paul were highly venerated by the Roman Church. They are mentioned in the Canon of the Mass and in the Litany of the Saints. Their particular virtue was love toward the poor. The following, at least, is historically certain: these two court officials were martyred and buried in their own house. Byzas and Pammachius transformed this house into a church dedicated to the two martyrs. Excavations have proven these points. Beneath the church were found their home, the tombs, and the place of execution. (Cf. the stational observance on Friday after Ash Wednesday where the saints appear very realistically in our midst.)

2. Holy Mass (Multae tribulationes). The Mass is old and has many proper texts. Psalm 33, the "trust-in-God" psalm, is sung as we enter. The just (by which term the old liturgies understood the martyrs) suffer many tribulations, but God delivers them. The *Collect* invites us to share in the joy of the feast; common faith and common martyrdom are more effective in making brothers than the bonds of blood. The *Lesson* calls our saints *viri misericordiae*, men of mercy, a reference to their love of the poor. The *Alleluia* dwells upon their spirit of brotherliness: "This is the true brotherliness which conquers the sins of the world! They followed Christ and now possess a glorious heavenly kingdom." In the *Gospel* Christ challenges us to a fearless confession of His Name, and pledges to reward us before the angels of God. Both saints accepted the challenge — and received the reward.

3. The Divine Office contains some texts proper to the feast (antiphons and responsories); these usually allude to brotherliness and love toward the poor, characteristics of John and Paul.

Responsory:

℣. Two olive trees, two candlesticks aglow before the Lord.

℟. The Ruler of all the world.

June 28

VIGIL OF STS. PETER AND PAUL

A night vigil at St. Peter's grave

1. The Vigil. Again today let us imagine ourselves present at an ancient Roman vigil. Christians are gathering at the grave of Peter the Rock. It is evening, and they intend to remain throughout the night. They have brought along their sick; at the tomb of the apostle these will find relief. The divine services

With celestial gifts You have
lavishly enriched Your children,
almighty God — preserve them
in Your grace ✚

begin. The saint is vividly present in their minds; he, the bearer
of the keys of the Church, arises from the grave; they behold
him as a disciple of Christ, as an apostle. They see him walking
on the waves of the sea, hand in hand with his Lord; they see
him during the night of the passion, weeping bitterly; they see
him kneeling before the risen Lord: Do you love Me more than
these? They see him as the leader of the infant Church and in
his imprisonment by Herod; they listen to his encyclicals, his
words on "the royal priesthood" of the faithful; they watch the
trial before his martyrdom. And in the midst of these scenes the
congregation breaks in, chanting psalms and hymns. Now it is
toward morning and the "Word becomes flesh" in the sacred
mysteries; the holy Sacrifice is offered and the graces of redemption flow through the hand of Peter into the hearts of all
assembled. Thus in spirit should we keep the feast, like the
ancient Church.

2. Holy Mass (Dicit Dominus). It seems that this vigil Mass is
older than that on the feast itself. The principal theme, the Lord's
prophecy concerning Peter's death on a cross, is announced already in the *Introit*. Psalm 18, the accompanying psalm, has been
called *Apostolus* since ancient times because it is so easily applied
to the work of the apostles. The *Lesson* recounts Peter's cure of
the man born lame. Peter, the head of the Church, says to us
today, every day: "In the Name of Jesus Christ, arise and walk."
The *Gospel* setting is the Sea of Genesareth. There the risen and
glorified Savior had prepared a richly symbolic meal for His
disciples; there Peter was elevated to the office of chief shepherd
of the Church; and there his martyrdom is now foretold. "This
He said to signify by what manner of death he should glorify
God." You too should be another Peter. At the *Communion*
banquet the Master will ask you: "Do you love Me more than
these?" "Lord, You know that I love You!"

June 29

STS. PETER AND PAUL, Apostles

Today Simon Peter ascended the wood of the cross,
*   alleluia!*
Today the key-bearer of the kingdom of heaven
*   went joyously to Christ!*
Today the apostle Paul, the light of the world,
*   bent his head for the Name of Christ*
*   and received the crown of martyrdom, alleluia!*

The Roman Martyrology announces the feast in the following words: "At Rome, the birthday of the blessed apostles Peter and Paul, who suffered under the Emperor Nero. In this city the former was fastened to a cross, head downwards, buried in the Vatican, and honored by all the world; the latter was be-headed and buried on the road leading to Ostia and receives the same honor." Since in ancient times the feast of a saint was always celebrated near his tomb, two liturgical services took place on the present day — at the tomb of Peter in the Vatican and at that of Paul. At the present time, however, the two liturgies are united. Nevertheless, since the Mass and Office give greater prominence to St. Peter, tomorrow, June 30, is dedicated specially to St. Paul.

It is difficult for us to realize the festivity with which this feast was celebrated in Rome. It was like a second Easter;[1] it was the birthday of Christian Rome and marked the triumph of Christ's victory over paganism. Rome's provincial bishops came to the Eternal City to celebrate the feast together with the Pope. As at Christmas, three services were held, at the graves of the two apostles and at their temporary depository in times of persecution. The two apostles were never separated; they were the two eyes in the Church's virgin-face.

1. **Peter's name** at first was Simon. Christ Himself gave him

[1] Schuster, *Liber Sacr.* 7, p. 279.

the name Cephas or Peter when they first met and later confirmed it. The name was meant to show both his rank as leader
of the apostles and the outstanding trait of his character — Peter
(in Hebrew *Kephas*) the Rock. Peter was born in Bethsaida on
the Sea of Galilee. Like his younger brother Andrew, he was a
fisherman and dwelt at Capharnaum. Peter's house often became
the scene of miracles, since the Master would stay there whenever He was teaching in that locality. Together with his brothers
John and Andrew, Peter belonged to the first of Jesus' disciples
(John 1:40–50).

After the miraculous draught of fish on the Sea of Galilee,
Peter received his definitive call and left wife, family, and occupation to take his place as leader of the Twelve. Thereafter we
find him continually at Jesus' side, whether it be as spokesman of
the apostolic college (John 6:68; Matt. 16:16), or as one specially
favored (e.g., at the restoration to life of Jairus' daughter, at the
transfiguration, during the agony in the garden). His sanguine
temperament often led him into hasty, unpremeditated words
and actions; his denial of Jesus during the passion was a salutary
lesson. It accentuated a weakness in his character and made him
humble.

After the ascension, Peter always took the leading role, exercising the office of chief shepherd that Christ had entrusted to
him. He delivered the first sermon on Pentecost and received the
first Gentiles into the Church (Cornelius; Acts 10:1). Paul went
to Jerusalem "to see Peter." After his miraculous deliverance
from prison (Easter, 42), Peter "went to a different place," most
probably to Rome. Details now become scanty; we hear of his
presence at the Council of Jerusalem (Acts 15:1), and of his
journey to Antioch (Gal. 2:11).

It is certain that Peter labored in Rome as an apostle, that he
was the city's first bishop, and that he died there as a martyr,
bound to a cross (67 A.D.). According to tradition he also was the
first bishop of Antioch (see February 22, Chair of St. Peter). He
is the author of two letters, the first Christian encyclicals. His
burial place is Christendom's most famous shrine, an edifice

around whose dome are inscribed the words: *Tu es Petrus, et super hanc petram aedificabo ecclesiam meam* (Matt. 16:18).

2. **Holy Mass (Nunc scio).** The vigil emphasized Peter's martyrdom, the feast stresses his role in the Church. Christ's words, "You are Peter and upon this rock I will build My Church," give the theme. The Mass begins with Peter's reflection, "Now I know for certain that the Lord has sent His angel and rescued me from the power of Herod. . . ." This deliverance occurred during the night. Recall that in ancient times the Mass took place at dawn, *in aurora*.

The *Lesson* describes Peter's miraculous deliverance; this incident typifies God's protection of the papacy and the Church. In the *Gospel* we witness the scene at Caesarea Philippi, when Christ laid the foundation of His Church.

The Church's bridal song serves as the *Offertory* hymn (Psalm 44). Christ is the Bridegroom, the Church is bride and mother; the apostles are the sons placed as princes over all the earth. The *Secret* describes the saints' part in the holy Sacrifice: we bring the oblation to the altar while they, especially on their feastday, adorn these gifts with intercessory prayer for our protection and purification. At the *Communion* the Rock upon whom Christ built His Church is again with us. But the Savior also speaks to me; I too should be a rock upon which He may build, and it is the holy Eucharist that will make me firm and solid. The *Postcommunion* also clarifies the part the saints take at the sacrificial drama; the Eucharist and the intercession of the saints are two complementary forces at our service in attaining salvation.

3. **Divine Office.** The psalms of Matins together with their antiphons are taken from the Common of Apostles, a Common that very probably had its origin in today's feast. Exceptionally dramatic and beautiful responsories place before our eyes various scenes from Peter's life. The Breviary Lessons tell how Peter healed the man born lame (Acts 3:1–16). The feast's three Readings, therefore, form a triptych; at either side a scene showing how Peter enjoyed miraculous power and protection; in the center the promise of promotion to the primacy: "You are Peter."

During the second nocturn we listen to a sermon delivered by Pope St. Leo on today's feast. "It is indeed true that the whole world shares in every holy solemnity, for the one true faith demands that whatever happens for the spiritual benefit of all should be commemorated by all in common joy. But today's feast, apart from the liturgical observance accorded it throughout the world, must be kept in our city (Rome) with extraordinary jubilation; for here, where the apostles ended their lives so gloriously, the greatest happiness must prevail on the day commemorating their martyrdom.

"These are the men through whom the Gospel of Christ first came to you, O Rome. And whereas you had been a teacher of error, now you have become a disciple of truth. These two men are your true fathers, your true shepherds; by transplanting you into the kingdom of heaven, they have given you a better and happier foundation than those two who first laid your walls. The one whose name you bear (Romulus) defiled you by murdering his brother. But our founders raised you to such a pinnacle of glory that you have become a holy nation, a chosen race, a city of priests and kings, and the capital of all the world by being the See of Peter.

"Indeed, through the Christian religion you are exercising your authority over lands and peoples more remote than during the time of your greatest imperial might. For even though you extended your sovereignty over land and sea by many triumphs, nevertheless that which became subject to you through fighting and war is relatively insignificant in comparison to that which the peace of Christ has brought under your sway."

> O happy Rome! who in thy martyr princes' blood,
> A twofold stream, art washed and doubly
>   sanctified.
> All earthly beauty thou alone outshinest far,
> Empurpled by their outpoured life-blood's
>   glorious tide.
>
> —*Vesper Hymn*

June 30

COMMEMORATION OF ST. PAUL, Apostle

*By the grace of God I am what I am, and His grace in me
has not been fruitless*

These words sum up the whole life of today's saint. For in St. Paul we see exemplified the primacy of grace, as well as man's cooperation. God called the future apostle without any merit on his part. He accepted the call, and that with all his powers. To-day's feast is a canticle on the efficacy of grace. In ancient times a second Mass was celebrated on June 29 in the church where St. Paul lies buried; it was deemed improper to separate after death two who had been joined in death. Only since the eighth century has a special observance commemorating St. Paul been kept on the present day.

1. **St. Paul.** Friends of the liturgy should know and study the life and writings of this great apostle, for no other inspired writer speaks to us more frequently during the year. Paul, known as Saul (his Roman name) before his conversion, was born at Tarsus in the Roman province of Silicia about two or three years after the advent of the Redeemer. He was the son of Jewish parents who belonged to the tribe of Benjamin, was reared according to the strict religious-nationalistic party of the Pharisees, and enjoyed the high distinction of Roman citizenship.

As a youth he went to Jerusalem to become immersed in the Law and had as teacher the celebrated Gamaliel. He acquired skill as a tent-maker, a work he continued even as an apostle. At the time of Jesus' ministry he no longer was at Jerusalem; neither did he see the Lord during His earthly life. Upon returning to the Holy City, Paul found a flourishing Christian community and at once became its bitter opponent. When Stephen impugned Law and temple, Paul was one of the first at his stoning; thereafter his fiery personality would lead the persecution. Breathing threats of slaughter against the disciples of Jesus, he was hurrying to

Damascus when the grace of God effected his conversion (about the year 34 A.D.; see January 25, Conversion of St. Paul).

After receiving baptism and making some initial attempts at preaching, Paul withdrew into the Arabian desert (c. 34–37 A.D.), where he prepared himself for his future mission. During this retreat he was favored with special revelations, Christ appearing to him personally. Upon his return to Damascus he began to preach but was forced to leave when the Jews sought to kill him. Then he went to Jerusalem "to see Peter." Barnabas introduced him to the Christian community, but the hatred of the Jews again obliged him to take secret flight. The following years (38–42) he spent at Tarsus until Barnabas brought him to the newly-founded Christian community at Antioch, where both worked a year for the cause of Christ; in the year 44 he made another journey to Jerusalem with the money collected for that famine-stricken community.

The first major missionary journey (45–48) began upon his return as he and Barnabas brought the Gospel to Cyprus and Asia Minor (Acts 13—14). The Council of Jerusalem occasioned Paul's reappearance in Jerusalem (50). Spurred on by the decisions of the Council, he began the second missionary journey (51–53), traveling through Asia Minor and then crossing over to Europe and founding churches at Philippi, Thessalonia (his favorite), Berea, Athens, Corinth. He remained almost two years at Corinth, establishing a very flourishing and important community. In 54 he returned to Jerusalem for the fourth time.

Paul's third missionary journey (54–58) took him to Ephesus, where he labored three years with good success; after visiting his European communities, he returned to Jerusalem for a fifth time (Pentecost, 58). There he was seized by the Jews and accused of contemning the Law. After being held as a prisoner for two years at Caesarea, he appealed to Caesar, was sent by sea to Rome (60 A.D.). Shipwrecked and delayed on the island of Malta, he arrived at Rome in the spring of 61 and passed the next two years in easy confinement before being released. The last years of the saint's life were devoted to missionary excursions, probably in-

cluding Spain, and to revisiting his first foundations. In 66 he
returned to Rome, was taken prisoner, and beheaded a year later.
His fourteen letters are a precious legacy; they afford a deep insight into a great soul.

2. Holy Mass (Scio cui). In spirit we approach the basilica in
which are preserved the relics of the great apostle of the Gentiles.
It is located just outside the gates of the Eternal City. Often during the year we gather here because St. Paul's Outside the Walls
is a favorite stational church. Many generations of Christians have
received grace and strength at this tomb.

We can understand and offer today's holy Mass best if we remain aware of Paul's presence and participation in the Sacrifice.
Mystically we unite ourselves to him; his words become our
prayer. Immediately in the *Introit* he speaks *and* I speak: "I have
put my trust in Him who will protect the grace reposing in me
unto that Day." Psalm 138 gives me the joyous assurance that I
have been predestined from eternity — with Paul. The *Collect*
reminds us of St. Paul's mission as teacher of the nations. In the
Epistle the apostle personally describes his call to that dignity.
While still a persecutor, he was chosen to be an apostle, the
illustrious preacher to the Gentiles.

In the *Gradual* Paul and I reflect on the operation of grace. The
Alleluia is an acclamation in honor of the great missioner. Then
the Lord foretells the persecution, scourgings, betrayals, even on
the part of one's own family, that will be the portion of the
apostles — all of which proved so true in Paul's life. And we are
standing at his tomb! At the *Offertory* we bring the sacrifice of
our lives to the altar, our saint at the lead; and with him we
receive a portion of the hundredfold reward during the *Communion* Banquet. Thus at the apostle's grave may we share our
common suffering and glory. In my opinion, this is the deepest
import of a martyr's feast, of any feast in the sanctoral cycle: to
share in the saint's labors and reward!

3. Divine Office. Matins is rich in passages from St. Paul's
Letters which show the harmony between grace and free will.
This too is the topic of the second nocturn Lessons taken from

St. Augustine's work on grace and free will: "While he was still stained by sin and had nothing to his credit before God, the apostle Paul received grace from God, who repays evil with good. Nevertheless, shortly before dying a martyr's death, he wrote to Timothy: I am already being poured out in sacrifice, and the time of my deliverance is at hand. I have fought the good fight, I have finished the course, I have kept the faith. He regards all these accomplishments as his own and awaits a crown as reward, even though grace had come to him in the midst of evil deeds.

"Note how he continues: For the rest, there is laid up for me a crown of justice which the Lord, the just Judge, will give to me on that Day. Could the just Judge bestow on him a crown if a merciful Father had not granted him grace? How could this crown be a crown of justice without the grace that blots out sin? And how could this crown be regarded as merited if grace that was not merited had not first been granted? Let us look more closely at the apostle's merits, the deeds for which he says the just Judge will give him a crown. Were these merits his own, obtained by his own efforts, or were they gifts from God? I have fought the good fight, he says, I have finished the course, I have kept the faith. The first of these accomplishments would not involve any good deed if good thoughts did not precede. Recall what he wrote to the Corinthians on this subject: We are not sufficient of ourselves to think anything as from ourselves, but our sufficiency is from God.

"In the light of this principle let us consider his various statements. He says: I have fought the good fight. But, may I ask, with whose strength did he fight? Was it by his own ability and power, or did it come from above? Impossible that this well-versed teacher of God's Law did not know the passage in the Book of Deuteronomy which says: Do not say in your heart: It is my own power and the strength of my own hand that has obtained for me this wealth (8:17). Remember then it is the Lord, your God, who gives you the power to acquire wealth. Now is there any value to a good fight if victory does not follow? But who gives victory if not He of whom Paul wrote: Thanks be to God who has given us the victory through our Lord Jesus Christ" (1 Cor. 15:57).

July 1

FEAST OF THE MOST PRECIOUS BLOOD

Divine Blood, the price of our redemption!

The feast of the Most Precious Blood continues the mystery of redemption proper to Good Friday and to feasts such as Holy Cross, Corpus Christi, and Sacred Heart. The observance was placed on the first Sunday in July by Pius IX in 1849, as the whole month was formerly dedicated to the Precious Blood. The Breviary reform of Pius X assigned the feast to the present date.

The liturgy of the feast, stressing history and dogma rather than mystery and drama, does not follow classic molds. The prayers, however, are noteworthy in that the dogma featured is a fundamental of our holy faith. The feast offers us another opportunity to reflect upon the sufferings of Jesus. Christians of ancient times commemorated today's mystery in the liturgy of Passion Sunday.

1. **Holy Mass (Redemisti nos).** The *Introit* transports us to heaven, where we hear the redeemed sing their glorious thanksgiving hymn: "You have redeemed us with Your Blood. . . ." Presently we join them, continuing with Psalm 88 in praise of God's mercy and fidelity. To those divine attributes the Blood of Christ has certainly borne witness.

In the *Collect* we pray that the power of our Savior's Blood may protect us from earthly misfortunes so that we may enjoy its fruits in heaven. The *Epistle* is the same as that on Passion Sunday; the blood of animals sacrificed in the temple lacked power, for that ritual was essentially prefigurative. Transcendently greater is the efficacy of Christ's bloody sacrifice! The text continues, unraveling before us the magnificent picture of the divine High Priest as He enters heaven's Holy of Holies in festive fashion to effect eternal redemption. It is His own Blood that He offers as the price.

The *Gradual* voices our reflections upon the Epistle. That High

Priest is Jesus Christ; He has come in water and blood, signs that
bear witness to His divinity. The *Gospel,* identical with that on
the feast of the Sacred Heart, describes the lancing of the departed Savior's sacred side. That our Redeemer shed all His Blood
during His sacred passion is attested by an open and pierced
heart! This act, so charged with mystery, likewise implies by
way of symbol the formation of the Church — through blood and
water. When we begin the Sacrifice proper, we are reminded by
St. Paul that not only ought we venerate the Blood of Christ at a
distance, but we should partake of it eucharistically, drinking
from the "chalice of blessing" (*Off.*). The *Secret,* too, helps to
clarify the import of Christ's Blood in the holy Sacrifice, Blood
that "speaks better than that of Abel."

Today is not the first time that the liturgy entertains thoughts
about the end of the world at the end of the Mass. The *Communion* antiphon compares Christ's two advents. In the first He
took away sins by becoming a victim for sacrifice; in the second
He will come in glory "unto the salvation of those who are awaiting Him." To link these lofty thoughts with the Eucharist is easy.
For here too Christ comes, and with something from each advent: from the first, Blood; from the second, wondrous salvation stemming from His sacred side. The *Postcommunion*
borrows phrases from two passages in sacred Scripture (Is. 12:4
and John 4:14), and the blend has not been an entirely happy
one. The Savior's Blood is the fountain of salvation; it should
gush over unto our eternal life.

2. Divine Office. Matins especially is rich in illustrations pertaining to the sacred Blood; the Hour traces the mystery's history
from type to fulfillment. St. John Chrysostom's homily is worthy
of special note. "Do you wish to know the power of Christ's
sacred Blood? Let us then review its Old Testament antecedents,
let us recall what prefigured it, listening to what sacred Scripture says. Take the story of the tenth plague. The scene is Egypt,
and God has foretold the death of all Egypt's firstborn at midnight because they retained His firstborn people. But that His
chosen nation would be spared — for they were living together in

the same land — God devised a visible sign that would save them. A wonderful symbol, one which vividly brings home to us the power of blood! Now the divine wrath is striking the land, now the Destroyer is hurrying to every home! What does Moses do? He says: Slay a yearling lamb and smear the doorposts with its blood. Such advice, O Moses? Is sheep blood capable of delivering a human being? Yes, he says; not, of course, because it is blood, but because it foreshadows the Blood of the Lord. For just as the statues of kings which lack life and speech in times past delivered men with spirit and mind who embraced them — not, of course, because they were cast of bronze, but because they represented the king himself — similarly brute blood saved the Israelites, not by its own merits but because it pointed to the advent of divine Blood.

"And the Destroyer passed by the homes whose entrances were smeared with blood and dared not enter. Likewise the devil must now flee from the soul sealed, not with the blood of an ancient type, but with the very Blood of Christ, the divine Lamb. If the Destroyer fled in terror from the mere figure, with what unimaginable fright will Satan shrink away when he beholds the true reality!"

3. Meditation. Let us classify the matter which the liturgy presents on the subject of the Precious Blood under the following headings: (a) types from the Old Testament; (b) scenes from the life of Jesus; (c) symbols.

a) *Three types from the Old Testament.* The Church takes us back to the beginning. Cain and Abel are making an offering. Abel's sacrifice is pleasing to God, Cain's is not. This gives rise to the sin of hatred, and fratricide is its resolution. The thirsting earth soaks up Abel's blood as it shouts to heaven for vengeance. This shouting prefigured the scene on Calvary, where Christ's Blood cried to heaven for the redemption of mankind.

Millenia pass, and now we see Israel oppressed by Egypt. God commands the people to kill a lamb and to sprinkle the doorposts with its blood; houses thus besprinkled are spared by the messenger of death. But where the doors are not reddened with the blood of the lamb, all male firstborn from king to slave die. This blood on the doorposts was a type of the Blood of Christ. Can the blood of a lamb save a man? No, but as a figure of the Redeemer's Blood it certainly does. For when the Destroyer sees the thresholds of a human heart marked with Christ's sacred Blood, he must pass by. And another soul is saved.

In a vision the prophet Isaias saw a man treading out grapes (in the Orient, trampling upon grapes in the wine-press was the usual means of extracting the juice). The prophet asked the man: "Why are your garments so red?" "The wine-press I have trodden alone," he answers, "because from the nations there is no one with me." The trodder of the wine-press is Christ, His garments crimsoned by the Blood of redemption.

b) *Scenes from history.* The Church reminds us of the first drops of blood that flowed for our redemption on the day when Jesus was circumcised.

It is night on Mount Olivet, and the moon is shining. We see the holy face crimsoned with blood during the agony in the garden.

Unhappy, despairing Judas casts the blood-money down in the temple. "I have betrayed innocent blood!"

Our meditation continues as the Church leads us into the scourging chamber and shows us the Lord in deepest humiliation; under raw strokes the divine Blood spurts out over the floor. Christ is led before Pilate. Pilate shows the blood-covered Body to the crowds: *Ecce homo!* We go through Jerusalem's streets following the bloody footsteps to Golgotha. Down the beams of the Cross blood trickles. A soldier opens the sacred side. Water and Blood.

c) *Two symbols.* Adam is sleeping an ecstatic sleep. God opens his side, removes a rib and forms Eve, the mother of all the living. But our view transcends this action and in spirit we behold the second, the divine Adam, Christ. He is sleeping the sleep of death. From His opened side blood and water flow, symbols of baptism and the Eucharist, symbols of the second Eve, the Church, the Mother of all the living. Through blood and water Christ willed to redeem God's many children and to lead them to an eternal home.

At Jerusalem a service in Yahweh's honor is taking place on the Day of Atonement. The high priest is making his annual entrance into the holy of holies to sprinkle the blood of bucks and bulls upon the covenant in expiation for the sins of the people. The Church shows us the higher meaning of this rite. Our divine High Priest Christ on the first Good Friday entered that Holy of Holies which is not made with hands nor sprinkled with the blood of bucks and bulls; there He effects, once and for all, with His own Blood man's eternal redemption. This message is the burden of today's Epistle.

A finale. Holy Church transports us to the end. The heavenly liturgy is in progress. Upon the altar is the Lamb, slain yet alive, crimsoned by His own Blood. Round about stand the countless army of the redeemed in garments washed white in the Blood of the Lamb. Hosts of the blessed are singing the new canticle of redemption: "You have redeemed us out of every tribe and tongue and nation by Your Blood."

Now from vision to present reality. How fortunate we are to have divine Blood so near to us, to offer it to the heavenly Father for the sins of the whole world! Why, we are even permitted to drink it!

July 2

THE VISITATION

My soul magnifies the Lord

1. **The feast of the Visitation** commemorates Mary's visit to Elizabeth. Of medieval origin, it was kept by the Franciscan Order before 1263, and soon its observance spread throughout the entire Church. The liturgical texts have undergone several redactions; the present date to the reform of Clement VIII (1592–

1605). In thanksgiving for his safe return to the Papal States,
Pius IX in 1850 elevated the feast to a double of the second class.
In the East a Marian feast had long been observed on July 2.
This precedent and the proximity of the Nativity of St. John the
Baptist determined the present date for the feast of the Visitation.
For the birth of the Baptist and the visit of God's Mother with
Elizabeth are not unrelated. Soon after the annunciation Mary

went to her cousin Elizabeth in the hill country of Judea, where
the memorable meeting of the two holy women occurred; the
occasion witnessed the composition of the *Magnificat*, so often
used and so highly esteemed in the liturgy. Mary stayed with
Elizabeth about three months; without doubt she was present at
the Baptist's circumcision and heard Zachary burst forth in his
sublime hymn of praise, the *Benedictus*. Then she returned to
Nazareth, where a great trial was awaiting her.

2. Holy Mass (Salve). Alongside texts common to Marian Masses, there are certain prayers that are proper. Praising Mary, we enter the house of the Lord. A fourth-century Christian poet, Sedulius, has supplied the words with which we praise her. The *Orations* are the same as on the feast of Mary's birth. Her divine motherhood marks the beginning of our salvation; may today's feast increase our inner peace. Under the guise of bridal love the *Reading* pictures the dignity of Mary's divine motherhood and her love toward Jesus; her journey through the hill country of Judea is described poetically in the verse, "Ah, here my beloved is coming — leaping over the hills, bounding over the ridges." The *Gospel* relates the same historical event in simple prose: "Mary arose and went with haste into the hill country, into a city of Judah." In the holy Sacrifice we share the good fortune of God's blessed Bride and become like to her; for the Lord visits us as He visited the Baptist and Elizabeth, granting grace and enlightenment.

At the *Offertory* we chant a beautiful hymn of praise to the Mother of God: "You bore the Creator of all things; you gave birth to Him who made you while remaining a virgin forever." Upon leaving His Mother's womb, Christ did not violate her virginal integrity; rather, He sanctified it. Now in the holy Sacrifice may His presence in us cleanse us from the stains of sin and make us holy (*Secr.*). At the *Communion* we become like the Mother of God; we praise her body because it carried the Son of the eternal Father and are not unaware of the identical thing that we are doing. May the Food of heaven be a means of salvation for the twofold life within us, the bodily and the spiritual.

3. Divine Office. The Lessons at Matins, a passage from the Canticle of Canticles, are easily accommodated to today's mystery (2:1–17). The Canticle of Canticles is one of the three books of holy Scripture referred to as the "Books of Solomon" in the liturgy. In highly poetical language Yahweh's relation to Israel is described in terms of Solomon's love toward a shepherd maid. The principal points are: the longing of both for most intimate union; hymns and dialogs in which they bespeak their mutual affection; the obstacles standing in the way of their union. This Old Testament relationship typified Christ's love for the Church and for the individual soul that is united to Him. We Occidentals must not be scandalized at the unrestrained, even sensual modes of expression. Today's Office gives one of the better known passages.

> Listen! My beloved!
>   Ah, here he comes —
> leaping over the hills,
>   bounding over the ridges.
> My beloved is like a gazelle,
>   or a young fawn.
> See, now he stands
>   behind our wall;
> he is looking in at the window,
>   he is gazing through the lattice.
>
> And now my beloved begins to speak —
>   he says to me:
> Arise, my love,
>   my fairest one, and come.
> For the winter is over, surely;
>   and the rains are past and gone.
> Flowers can be seen on the earth,
>   it is the season for singing;
> the call of the turtledove
>   may be heard throughout the land.
> The fig tree is putting forth its fruit,
>   fragrant perfumes rise from blossoming vines.
> Arise, my love,
>   my fairest one, and come.

4. Sts. Processus and Martinian. During the time when Sts. Peter and Paul were prisoners in the Mamertine, legend says that two jailors together with forty others were converted through the prayers and miracles of the holy apostles. They were baptized with water that suddenly sprang out from a rock. The jailors then wished to help the apostles make their escape. Both died as martyrs for the faith (about 67 A.D.). Their relics now lie in St. Peter's, Rome.

5. The Magnificat. Today's feast occasioned the composition of the *Magnificat*, one of the Church's finest and most highly esteemed thanksgiving hymns.

The *Magnificat* is the hymn chanted by the Blessed Virgin in thanksgiving for the privilege of becoming the Mother of God and for God's goodness in redeeming mankind. To understand this prayer more perfectly, it would help if we visualized ourselves present at the great hour in which it was first uttered. Mary had received the message from an angel that she was to be the Mother of the Son of God. She cannot fully understand that great grace and has no one to whom she can pour out her bursting heart. She goes into the hill country of Judea to visit her cousin Elizabeth, who was favored with a somewhat similar blessing. Divinely enlightened, Elizabeth greeted and received Mary as the Mother of her God. Now Mary can no longer restrain the lofty emotions within her soul; she gives vent to a heart overflowing with gratitude. She prays the *Magnificat*. She thanks God for the great dignity that has come to her and for the redemption that it brings to men. Her song falls into three strophes:

First strophe: (a) gratitude for the graces and honor bestowed upon her;
(b) praise of God's power, holiness, mercy;
Second strophe: praise of God's rule over mankind (how He acts toward the humble and the proud);
Third strophe: the fulfillment of the Messianic prophecies.

First strophe. (a) With a joyous heart I magnify the Lord. Why? Because He has conferred upon me, a lowly, unworthy servant, an unparalleled grace, the dignity of divine motherhood. The effects of this grace distinguish me from all mankind. (b) God, the almighty and merciful One, has elevated me to the heights. My selection, which inaugurated the work of redemption, is the greatest act of divine power; thereby is revealed His holiness, His horror for sin, and His unbounded mercy towards sinful men.

Second strophe. After enumerating God's attributes, Mary passes from the consideration of her own selection to the divine plan of salvation and in the second strophe develops the essential characteristics of predestination in the economy of salvation. God's power shows itself in reducing to nought the haughty pride of the mighty and in taking to Himself the world's weak and lowly ones.

Third strophe. After these reflections Mary joyfully assures us that God will redeem Israel because of His mercy and fidelity — because of His mercy, since Israel could not help herself if left alone; because of His fidelity, since God promised redemption to the prophets and patriarchs.

Like all Old Testament or early Christian poetry, our hymn is very simple in form. The rhythm of thought, expressed in classic Hebrew parallelism, is easily discernible. Perhaps Mary's "heart-song" received a more perfected poetic form during her three-month stay in the house of Zachary.

The *Magnificat* very early found its place in the liturgy; already in the fourth century it formed part of the Office, and one tradition credits St. Benedict for having introduced it into Vespers.

July 3

ST. IRENAEUS, Bishop and Martyr

Father of Catholic dogma

1. **St. Irenaeus.** St. Irenaeus, who contributed in no small measure to the acceptance of the authority of Rome, was the distinguished disciple of St. Polycarp; and the latter received his religious training directly from the apostles. His name, Irenaeus, i.e., "peacemaker," sums up his life's work.

Born in Smyrna about the year 140, he made great progress in virtue and knowledge under bishop Polycarp. Later he went to Gaul, became bishop of Lyons. In the Easter controversies between the Asiatic bishops and Pope Victor I, Irenaeus took the role of mediator and peacemaker. Of his prolific writings — he is called the "father of Catholic dogma" — there still remain *Five Books Against the Heretics*. In the third book (III, 3, 2) our saint, who was instructed by a disciple of the apostles, presents an important and glorious apology on the succession of Roman bishops and on the Roman Church as the faithful, constant, and surest guardian of divine revelation. One famous passage reads: "On account of the extraordinary dignity of the Roman Church, every church must conform itself according to her." According to a later tradition Irenaeus died as a martyr about the year 202.

2. Holy Mass. Practically all the texts of the Mass are proper and allude to the life of St. Irenaeus. There is point and purpose to the fact that numerous prayers and chants contain the word "peace," a word-play on the saint's name. "In peace and righteousness he dwelt with Me" (*Intr.*); "With those who hated peace I was peaceable" (Ps. 119:7). The word occurs twice in the *Collect*; it is found in the *Gradual*, in the *Secret*, and in the *Postcommunion* (the last two prayers are from the ancient *Missa pro pace*). The *Epistle*, words of Paul to his disciple Timothy, should here be regarded as admonitions from John's disciple Polycarp to Irenaeus, his faithful student. The *Gospel* (Matt. 10:28–33), taken from Christ's discourse to the disciples before He sent them on their first mission, was put into practice literally by our saint; he was not afraid in the presence of his enemies but heroically professed the Name of the Lord.

3. The Magnificat. Let us continue our meditation upon Mary's hymn, the *Magnificat*. There is much that can be noted regarding its use in the liturgy.

The *Magnificat* brings Vespers to a climax. At sung Vespers this is very easily seen. For then a greater solemnity is accorded to the *Magnificat* than to the other psalms, and the altar is incensed while it is chanted. The *Magnificat* is a prayer of thanksgiving; it is, in fact, the Church's most sublime expression of joyful gratitude. Who is it that speaks? The Church and the soul, borrowing the words and sentiments of the highest among God's creatures in heaven and on earth, Mary. Mary is, we may say, our "go-between," our representative and model in giving thanks to God. Why is the Church thankful? Primarily for the day's graces, because God attaches special graces to the feasts of the Church year. Each soul, too, has its own personal reasons for thanking God. In the *Magnificat* the Church and individual souls are grateful for all the graces and benefits received. Our reason for this spirit of gratitude is much the same as Mary's. Mary carried the Savior under her heart; the Church carries the mystical Savior in her heart together with all the graces of salvation. Each individual also carries his Savior in his heart, be it through grace or be it through the morning's holy Communion. Church and soul place all their spiritual dowry together and joyfully thank God, their Savior. All Mary's thoughts and sentiments expressed in this canticle may easily be accommodated to the Church and to the individual member.

My soul magnifies the Lord, and my spirit rejoices in God my Savior (Jesus). The reason? God was concerned about His little, poor servant. The soul, a beggar as the result of original sin, knows its sinfulness, the weakness of its will, its inclination to evil. Not by natural right but by divine favor can heaven come. And the Church, is she not outlawed, despised? Nevertheless, God has exalted her; all nations call her blessed! The Church has become the Mother of nations. The "poor" soul has become a temple of God, a child of God! What distinction, what high privilege is sanctifying grace!

Great things He has done to me, the almighty, the holy One, the merciful One. *The Church:* how many are her converts, how many are become her children, how many she has escorted to heaven! *The soul:* what manifold graces and blessings have already been received, together with the special inspirations proper to the feast! God has shown His MIGHT as the healer of hearts, His HOLINESS in victory over sin, His MERCY through forgiveness — but only, of course, to His faithful ones.

In the second strophe our canticle gives instruction and consolation. *Instruction*: stay little, remain a stranger to earth, be humble. Think on the great model, Mary. God has exalted the lowly maid, the hungry He has filled with good things. The instruction is short, yet its lapidary phrases reveal the foundation of God's kingdom. That foundation is *humility*. Mary's hymn also affords *consolation*. The Church's enemies are raging, dragging her into the dirt, disowning and disinheriting her; the rich, the sated, the proud pass by with sneers. Notwithstanding, in the fading light of daily Vespers we are assured midst the smoke of incense: "He scatters the proud, the mighty He tumbles from their throne, the rich He sends empty away." And the Church has always kept God's truth. The proud have fallen from their thrones, while she speaks with the experience of two millenia. What a consolation for us! Here likewise it is true: "Heaven and earth shall pass away but My words shall not pass away."

With the final stanza we voice our gratitude for the great work of redemption and predestination. We are "Israel His child." Gratefully we recall God's fidelity and mercy. Through sin we became debtors; still God has kept His promise. This very day He has acted to fulfill His word. And I am grateful from the depth of my heart!

July 5

ST. ANTHONY MARY ZACCARIA, Confessor

To Christ through the spirit of the apostle Paul

1. **St. Anthony.** *Day of death*: July 5, 1539. *Canonized*: 1897. *Grave*: at Milan, in the Church of St. Barnabas. *Life*. Anthony, born in upper Italy (1502), pursued the studies of the humanities and medicine before realizing that he was called to be a spiritual physician. Ordained to the priesthood in 1528, he dedicated himself with fatherly love to strangers, to the oppressed and poor. He was regarded as "father" and "angel" by contemporaries. He founded a community of Clerks Regular, which he named after

his favorite apostle, St. Paul. They are now known as Barnabites. He spread devotion to Christ suffering and dying upon the Cross, added exposition of the Blessed Sacrament to the Forty Hours' devotion in 1534, and furthered more frequent reception of holy Communion. He died at the early age of thirty-six in 1539.

Application. "To Christ through the spirit of the apostle Paul." Is not this the sincerest aim of every true liturgist? About a hundred times during the Church year the apostle of the Gentiles speaks to us in the Readings of the Mass, as today; and many times more in the Divine Office. "That in the spirit of the holy apostle Paul we may learn the all-excelling science of Jesus Christ" is the plea we make today in union with St. Anthony.

2. Holy Mass (Sermo). The Mass, which is proper, summarizes Anthony's various activities. The *Introit* tells of his simple yet powerful way of preaching according to the spirit of St. Paul. The *Epistle,* a pastoral admonition of Paul to his beloved disciple Timothy, the liturgy applies to Anthony Zaccaria and insinuates that Anthony lived and worked wholly in accordance with the apostle's spirit (*Coll.*) In the *Gospel* we hear the Lord's counsel to the rich young man: "Follow Me." This was our saint, and he accepted. Nor do the less important chants and prayers lack inferences to the life and work of Anthony Zaccaria.

3. The Martyrology. "At Rome, St. Zoa, martyr. She was the spouse of St. Nikostratus. While praying at the grave of the holy apostle, she was seized by bailiffs from Emperor Diocletian, chained and thrown into a dark hole. Then with a cord about her neck made from her own hair, she was suspended from a tree. Under her a slow, smoky fire was enkindled. Loudly praising her Savior, she died from suffocation.

"At Cyrene in North Africa, the holy martyr Cyrilla. During Diocletian's persecution glowing coals and incense were placed in her hands; but to avoid every appearance whereby she might seem to offer sacrifice to the gods, she preferred to continue holding the hot coals in her hands rather than to shake them off by some slight movement. She was then cruelly lacerated and died a bloody death for her heavenly Bridegroom."

July 7

STS. CYRIL AND METHOD, Bishops and Confessors

How lovely are the feet of those who herald
the tidings of peace

1. Today's Saints. *Day of death*: Cyril, February 14, 869;
Method, April 6, 885. *Grave*: Cyril, at Rome in San Clemente;
Method, at Velehrad in the Church of St. Mary. *Life*. Cyril and
Method, the apostles of the Slavs, were brothers who hailed from
Thessalonia. After receiving an excellent education, they were
sent by the Eastern Emperor Michael III (842–856) into the kingdom of Grand-Moravia; through great effort and in spite of tremendous difficulties they converted the Slavonic nations. They
translated the Bible into Slavonic and devised a kind of writing,
called *glagolitic,* which even to the present day is used in the
liturgical services of some Eastern rites.

In 867 the two brothers came to Rome, were met by Pope Hadrian II (867–872) and the whole papal court. They gave a report
of their labors but encountered opposition on the part of jealous
clergy who took offense, it was said, because of their liturgical innovations. Cyril and Method explained their methods and from
the Pope himself received episcopal consecration (868). Soon
after, Cyril died at Rome, only forty-two years old, and was buried
in St. Peter's; later his body was transferred to San Clemente,
where his remains still rest. His funeral resembled a triumphal
procession.

Method returned to Moravia and labored as a missionary
among the Hungarians, Bulgarians, Dalmatians, and the inhabitants of Carinthia. Falling again under suspicion, he returned to
Rome and defended the use of the Slavonic language in the liturgy. The Pope bestowed upon him the dignity of archbishop.
After his return to Moravia, he converted the duke of Bohemia
and his wife, spread the light of faith in Bohemia and Poland, is
said to have gone to Moscow (after the erection of the See of Lem-
berg), and to have established the diocese of Kiev. After his re-

turn he died in Bohemia and was buried in the Church of St. Mary at Velehrad, the services being conducted in Greek, Slavonic, and Latin.

2. Holy Mass (Sacerdotes). The Mass is in part taken from the Common of Bishops (p. 399), and in part composed of proper texts. All the prayers are in the plural because two saints are commemorated (the liturgy pays attention even to such details; cf. *Intr., Epist., Grad., Gosp., Off.*). The Liturgy of the Word brings to our attention the high office of bishop that our saints received from the High Priest (*Epist., All.*), points that lend depth to the Mass. Christ the High Priest offers His Sacrifice; united to it is the life sacrifice of two holy bishops. The priest at the altar takes the place of Christ and His saints, and the lay priests present likewise have their role to play.

The *Gospel* on the mission of the seventy-two disciples includes the missionary apostolate of Cyril and Method. The same thought underlies the chants at the *Offertory* and *Communion.* We are amazed at the fruit garnered by these two apostles to the Slavs and praise God for the miracles wrought through His saints (*Off.*). We also discover where exactly the saints receive their strength, namely, in the quiet hours of dawn when Christ speaks to them at Mass (*Comm.*).

The liturgy loves to celebrate feasts honoring the apostles and patrons of the various nations. Today on the tree of the Church it is the mighty limb of the Christian Slavonic peoples. The Mass is a sacrifice of thanksgiving and petition — thanksgiving because the Slavs by nature are religious and inclined to Christianity; petition because many Slavs — over a hundred million — have strayed from the unity of the Church. May these people with their deep faith, a people who now must suffer such heavy trials, find the way back to the one true sheepfold!

3. Meditation. Christ's missionary commands have been fulfilled during the course of time by many missioners and apostles. All have not been granted the same measure of success. Some have reaped little, others seemingly much. Today's saints made an unusually great catch of fish and deserve the name "Apostles to the

Slavs." Their extraordinary success resulted from two factors: first, the grace of God, without which all human work is worthless. For in His good Providence, God chose these two men to spread His Gospel among the Slavs and bestowed on them all needed graces. The second factor was human effort. With what marvelous zeal, with what pains and patience our saints gave themselves to their work! Hundreds of miles of trackless country they crossed on foot; and they met with continual opposition, not only from the pagans but from their own brethren.

Another observation. As part of their apostolate, Cyril and Method initiated a kind of liturgical movement. They realized how much more effectively they could approach the Slavs if they celebrated the divine services in the vernacular and if they gave them the Bible in their own language. This, however, occasioned opposition from ecclesiastical quarters and resulted in complaints to the Pope, even some clamor for their imprisonment! But they persevered; they vindicated their methods at Rome and continued their liturgical and Biblical work.

Application. We too are missioners. Every man must first attend to his own soul, but he must work for the souls of others also. To us is committed the liturgical apostolate as a pastoral work for the good of souls. That is our mission. We too must count on opposition. But we must likewise persevere because we know that it is God's holy will.

July 8

ST. ELIZABETH, Widow, Queen

Elizabeth, mother of peace and of your people, give us peace

1. **St. Elizabeth.** *Day of death*: July 4, 1336. *Grave*: in the convent of the Poor Clares at Coimbra, Portugal. *Life.* A saint on the nation's throne! Born in 1271, Elizabeth, Queen of Portugal,

was a model mother both for her own family and for her people. Her particular charism was that of peacemaker (*Oration*: "Thou didst favor St. Elizabeth . . . with the grace of appeasing the fury of war").

The Divine Office notes the following events from her life. Already at her birth it appeared how in the future she would be a successful peacemaker among kings and kingdoms; for at that happy event her father and grandmother were reconciled, although previously they had been at odds. She gave her hand in marriage to King Dionysius of Portugal (1279–1325). Her married life was marked by zeal for virtue. She constantly strove to educate her children in the fear of God, to please her husband, and most of all, to please God. During practically half of the year she fasted on bread and water. Certain monies she wished to distribute to the poor changed into blooming roses in the middle of winter, so that her act would remain unknown to the king. After the death of her husband she became for widows a model of every virtue, even as previously she had been a model maid for maidens, and a model wife for wives. In patience and resignation she attended the funeral wearing the garb of the Poor Clares.

2. Holy Mass (Cognovi), from the Common of Holy Women, p. 408. Elizabeth's special gift, that of restoring peace, is recalled at the *Collect*. The Office honors our saint by a number of proper antiphons: "You are the glory of Jerusalem, you are the joy of Israel, you are the honor of your people" (*Ben. Ant.*). "Elizabeth, the mother of peace and of her people, now triumphs in heaven. Give us peace!" (*Magn. Ant.*).

> She has opened her mouth to wisdom,
> and the law of clemency is on her tongue.
> She has looked well to the paths of her house,
> and has not eaten her bread idle.
> Many daughters have assembled great riches,
> you have surpassed them all.
> Favor is deceitful, beauty passes;
> but the woman who fears God deserves to be praised.
> — *Lesson*.

July 10

THE SEVEN BROTHERS, Martyrs
STS. RUFINA AND SECUNDA, Virgins, Martyrs

Martyrs' Day
(an ancient inscription, characterizing today's liturgy)

1. **Today's feast** commemorating seven brothers who were martyred together with their mother about the year 162 belongs to the oldest of the martyr-feasts of the Roman Church. In ancient times it was even preceded by a fast and a vigil and had four Mass formularies.

During the persecution decreed by Emperor Marcus Aurelius (161–168), seven brothers, sons of the saintly Felicitas, were tempted to renounce their Christian faith; the prefect Publius first used flattery, then resorted to atrocious torments. But they remained steadfast, and their mother encouraged them in confessing Christ. Different types of death were allotted them. Januarius died under the scourge, Felix and Philip were beaten with clubs, Silanus was cast from a rock, Alexander, Vitalis and Martial were beheaded. Four months later their mother, too, suffered martyrdom. Burial took place in different cemeteries. During the eighth century Silanus and his mother were taken to the Church of St. Susanna at Rome, where they still rest. Alexander came into the possession of the abbey church of Farfa.

The two sisters Rufina and Secunda, Roman maidens, refused to marry after they had consecrated themselves to God. Led before the judge, Rufina was first beaten with rods; during the ordeal her sister said to the judge: "Why do you honor my sister with such torments and leave me dishonorably untried? Let us both suffer the same torments that we may both bear witness to one faith." They were finally beheaded in the forest of Buxetum, called Silva Nigra; in their honor the name was changed to Silva Candida. A church, which finally became a cathedral (St. Rufina), was erected there. Since the twelfth century their bodies rest in the Lateran.

2. Holy Mass (Laudate pueri). The Mass is very old and has its own text honoring particularly the heroic mother who exhorted her sons to martyrdom. As the service begins, the *Introit* flashes before us the inspiring scene of that fortunate mother surrounded by seven sons in heaven. Here on earth she indeed was made childless, barren; but now she dwells in heaven, the joyful mother of sainted sons. The *Reading* is the well-known "praise of the valiant woman." "Her sons rise up and call her blessed . . . many daughters have assembled great riches, but you have surpassed them all. Favor is deceitful, beauty passes; but the woman who fears God deserves to be praised."

In the *Gradual* we hear the seven brothers praising God like birds that have escaped the snare; their martyrdom was a deliverance from the mesh of earthly life (we are reminded of the Holy Innocents). In metered verse the *Alleluia* tells of true fraternal love kept inviolate even unto a common death. Particularly fitting is the choice for the *Gospel*. It relates an episode from the life of Christ. Word had come to our Lord that His Mother and brethren were standing outside awaiting Him. But He uses the occasion to say: "See, these are My mother and My brothers! Whoever does the will of My Father, he is My brother, My sister, My mother." What would the liturgy have us understand? The holy martyr-mother, her seven sons, and the two sisters have become by dying for the faith (the will of the Father) mothers, brothers, and sisters of Christ; and we who bind ourselves together with these martyrs in the holy Sacrifice share their glory; we too become mothers, brothers, sisters of Christ! Again, when we approach the Banquet table we hear from the lips of Christ: "Yes, through the Eucharist you share in the dignity of being brothers, sisters, and mothers to Me." We are blood-relatives of Christ because we drink His Blood.

3. Divine Office. To make our joy on this feast perfect, the Office gives us a homily by Pope St. Gregory I which he himself delivered "to the people in the basilica of St. Felicitas on her feast-day." It is such a magnificent homily that I would like to reproduce the complete text, but space limits us to the following summary: "The Gospel that has just been read, beloved brethren, is quite short, but it is rich in spiritual allusions." Jesus acts as though He did not know His Mother or His relatives, and designates those as His mother and His relatives who bear a spiritual relationship to Him rather than a physical one. Continuing the theme, Gregory applies this relationship to the synagogue and the Jews on one hand, and to the Gentiles on the other. The synagogue and the Jews, who were related to Jesus by blood because He was of their nation, remained standing outside; and He did not recognize them because they would not believe in Him. But the Gentiles He embraced and regarded as members of His family because they responded to His invitation.

It should cause us no surprise that the Lord calls those who do the will of His Father His brothers and sisters, for we know that after the resurrection He referred to His followers in similar terms: "Go, and tell My brethren . . . " (Matt. 28:10). The problem is somewhat different, however, as to how He could call someone His mother. Gregory puts it this way: "We should not be ignorant that anyone who has become a brother or sister to Christ through faith becomes His mother through preaching. For he becomes like to the Lord if he makes the Lord come to life in the hearts of those listening. And he becomes Christ's mother if through his words the love of Christ is enkindled in their hearts. As an example take St. Felicitas, whose feast we keep today. As a Christian she was a handmaid of the Lord; and as herald of the faith she was a mother unto Christ."

Thus far goes Gregory's homily at Matins. He continues, in the original sermon, with a eulogy to that heroic mother who confirmed her sons in the love of their heavenly fatherland and thereby gave a second, a spiritual birth to children she once had borne according to the flesh. "Brethren, here within a woman's body behold a man's heart. . . . Should I call this woman a martyr? She is more than a martyr! Before her she has sent seven pledges to the kingdom of God; seven times did she die before her own death. With the first she embraced martyrdom, and consummated it with the eighth. Grief-rent but undaunted, that mother witnessed the death of her sons, for to the pain in her heart was joined the joy of hope. . . . Therefore has St. Felicitas triumphed over other martyrs; she died for Christ as often as her sons died before her. Her love for Christ required more than only her own death."

July 11

ST. PIUS I, Pope and Martyr

A good shepherd sheds his blood for his sheep

1. **St. Pius I.** *Day of death*: July 11, about 155. *Grave*: at Rome, in the Vatican. *Life*. Pope Pius I ruled from 140 to 155. The third Lesson at Matins contains the legend that he decreed Easter should always fall on a Sunday (contrary to those who wished it to be celebrated on the fourteenth of Nisan). He is also reputed to have transformed the house of Senator Pudens into a church and to have given it the name of "The Shepherd," making it his own titular church. There he often celebrated the holy Sacrifice and himself baptized many. During his pontificate Hermas, his brother, wrote "The Shepherd," one of the oldest extant patristic writings.

Application. A sovereign pontiff stands before us today who was likewise a "good shepherd" with all the Gospel implications of the name. He, the first of the popes to bear the name Pius, shed his blood for his sheep "by a glorious martyr's death." During the second century, thinking in "Good Shepherd" terms was common; his own brother reflects this mentality by a book entitled "The Shepherd," and Pius' titular church was given the name *Pastoris*, i.e., "of the Shepherd." How closely the liturgy and pastoral work were joined already at that early date.

2. **Holy Mass (Si diligis Me),** from the Common of Sovereign Pontiffs (see p. 378).

July 12

ST. JOHN WALBERT, Abbot

STS. NABOR AND FELIX, Martyrs

Love your enemies, do good to them who hate you

Today's worship and work are dominated by a single theme, *love your enemies*. The Church favors the practice of emphasizing a saint's primary virtue and presenting it for imitation. The life of St. John Walbert offers a vivid and unusual example of heroic love of enemy.

1. St. John Walbert. *Day of death*: July 12, 1073. *Canonized*: 1193; feast 1679. *Grave*: at Passignano, a monastery near Florence. *Life*. Our saint was born of a noble Florentine family about the year 995. His father was arranging for him to become a soldier when Hugo, the only other child, was murdered by a relative. It was Good Friday, and Walbert, accompanied by an armed escort, met the murderer in a narrow pass. There was no way to avoid one another. They met, and the murderer, with arms crossed on his breast, threw himself at Walbert's feet. Moved by his plea for mercy and the remembrance of Christ's dying act of forgiveness, he spared the murderer's life and lifted him up as a brother.

Walbert continued his journey. Arriving at the Church of St. Minias, he prayed before a picture of the Crucified which appeared to move its head toward him. Thereupon he determined to dedicate his life to God in spite of his father's opposition. He cut off his hair, took the habit of a monk, and in a short time attained such perfection that his life and work were a model for others. He became the founder of the Vallombrosian monks, a branch of the Benedictine family.

2. Holy Mass (Os justi). The Mass, from the Common of Abbots (p. 401), has a proper *Gospel* on the love of enemies. Christ says in the Sermon on the Mount: "You have heard it said: You must love your neighbor but hate your enemy. Now I say to you: Love your enemies, do good to them who hate and persecute you.

Then you will be children of your heavenly Father, who makes the sun rise upon the good and the bad, and the rain fall for the just and the unjust." Let us seriously examine our conscience on this point. Let us recall that the Church places the kiss of peace before holy Communion; it is her way of teaching us that the Prince of Peace cannot come to our heart unless we are at peace with our fellowmen. Love of enemy is our *Offertory* gift; it is also the divine Gift received in return.

3. Sts. Nabor and Felix. "At Milan the death of the holy martyrs Nabor and Felix, who suffered in the persecution of Maximian. They were Christian soldiers in the army of Emperor Maximian Hercules. Because of their Christian faith they were tried in Milan and beheaded in Lodi, Italy, (303 or 304). Their bodies were interred in Milan" (*Martyrology*). When Emperor Frederic Barbarossa captured Milan in the twelfth century, he gave the sacred relics to Reinald, archbishop of Cologne. Soon after, Reinald transferred the bodies of the holy martyrs to his episcopal see, where they are still venerated in one of the cathedral's magnificent chapels.

4. The Divine Office gives us St. Jerome's comment upon the Gospel: "Many persons interpret God's commandments according to their own weaknesses rather than in the light of the strength given to the saints, and come to the conclusion that the commandments cannot be kept. In order to be virtuous they think it is sufficient to refrain from hating enemies; but to love them sincerely — that is expecting too much from human nature. Now everyone should know that Christ would not impose the impossible; but He does require perfection. David already had met this requirement in his attitude toward Saul and Absalom; and the martyr Stephen prayed for enemies who were stoning him. Paul went so far as to wish to be anathema in the place of his persecutors. We have here a doctrine that Jesus not only preached but practiced: 'Father, forgive them for they know not what they do.' For other good works, apart from that of love, there are excuses; you may say that you cannot fast, or forego marriage, or distribute all your property and money among the poor. But no excuse holds when it concerns the love of enemy. You cannot say: I will not love my enemy."

The biography of the saint, the Gospel of the Mass, and the homily afford reading and meditation material on this one truly important lesson.

July 14

ST. BONAVENTURE, Bishop and Doctor

The Seraphic Doctor instructs us in Christian mysticism

1. **St. Bonaventure.** *Day of death*: July 15, 1274. *Canonized*: 1482. *Grave*: at Lyons. His remains were burned by fanatical Calvinists in 1562; only his head was saved. *Life.* "In Bonaventure we meet a unique personality. He was unsurpassed in sanctity, wisdom, eloquence, and gifted with a remarkable skill of accomplishing things, a heart full of love, a winning disposition, benevolent, affable, pious, charitable, rich in virtue, beloved by God and man. . . . The Lord endowed him with such a charming disposition that everyone who saw him was immediately attracted to him." In these words the historian of the Council of Lyons concludes his account on St. Bonaventure.

At an early age he was a celebrated teacher and a powerful preacher. At thirty-six he was called to the highest post among the Franciscans, the Order which honors him as a second founder. He was an important figure at the Council of Lyons. His virtue and wisdom, his versatility and mildness were major factors in attaining the happy result that the Greeks so easily returned to the unity of the Church.

Bonaventure was a subtle scholastic and a profound mystic. Because of the latter he is known as the "Seraphic Teacher." In philosophy he was the principal leader of the Platonic-Augustinian school of Franciscan thought; as such he stood opposed to the Aristotelianism that was making its way into the schools of the time (Thomas of Aquin). Bonaventure's *Life of St. Francis* was a favorite book of the Middle Ages. When St. Thomas was told about Bonaventure's work, he said: "Let us allow one saint to labor for another." His contemporaries are said to have believed that no one was "more handsome, more holy, or more learned" than he. — The Mass (*In medio*) from the Common of Doctors, p. 400.

2. Doctor of the Church. What is meant by the words "Doctor of the Church"? To certain saints who have been outstanding in learning and writing the Church has granted the title "Doctor." This honor is not entirely due to wisdom and knowledge; their manner of living, too, is highly important. Such a person must be a *doctor vitae*, a teacher of life (Coll.). Twenty-nine so far have received this distinction, the last being St. Lawrence of Brindisi. It would seem to be the teaching of the Church that her doctors, even as her virgins, are receiving a special degree of glory in heaven. The liturgy of the Mass honors them by granting them a *Credo*.

Now what in particular does a Doctor of the Church teach us? Two things: to teach and to listen. Just as there is a common priesthood of the laity, so it is also justifiable to speak of a common teaching office of all the faithful. Technically, the bishops alone form the teaching Church, *Ecclesia docens*; priests and laity are "the taught," *Ecclesia discens*. However, a layman often has the opportunity, yes, the duty of instructing others. The mother of a family is a natural catechist to her children; and frequently this important duty is most nobly discharged. It is a most excellent service to instruct others either through the spoken or the written word. Especially in our day has it become necessary for the laity to be leaders or teachers in catechetical, liturgical, and social programs.

Secondly, the "teaching Church," speaking through her doctors, needs a humble and receptive audience. Are you doing your part here? Do you *listen* to sermons? Do you *read* instructive, religious books? Are you interested in the Bible, the Old Testament too? As an educated Christian, how familiar are you with the writings of the fathers and doctors of the Church?

July 15

ST. HENRY, Emperor, Confessor

A German emperor among the saints

St. Henry. *Day of death*: July 13, 1024. *Canonized*: 1146. *Grave*: in the Cathedral of Sts. Peter and Paul at Bamberg. *Picture*: as emperor, with a lily and a church. *Life*. Henry and his wife Cunegunde — holiness on the throne of Germany! As sovereign ruler (1002–1024), Henry II tempered a powerful personality with kindly forbearance. The Breviary contributes these details. All his projects were accompanied by prayer. Before battle he saw on occasion how his guardian angel and other martyr-saints and patrons fought in his behalf and protected his life. Against barbarians he would war more with prayer than with arms. He effected the conversion of the pagan Hungarians to Christianity by giving his sister to King Stephan as wife, with the stipulation that he be baptized. He financed the construction of churches and the foundation of monasteries. On one occasion he sent the imperial crown-jewels to the Abbey at Cluny to be offered to the Lord. In marriage he preserved absolute purity of body and mind, and when at the point of death, he sent his wife Cunegunde back to her family still a virgin (this statement contradicts the conclusions of modern historical research). In the Roman liturgy St. Henry has a lasting memorial in that the Creed was introduced into the Mass at his request.

Application. "Just as You enabled him to overcome the enticements of the world by Your overflowing graces, so through his example enable us to shun the temptations of this world and come to You pure of heart" (*Coll.*). It is our duty to live chastely, soberly, uprightly, according to our state in life. Nothing is of greater benefit to the liturgical movement than a pure heart. — The Mass (*Os justi*) is from the Common of Confessors, p. 402.

COMMEMORATION OF THE BLESSED VIRGIN MARY OF MOUNT CARMEL

Thy head is as Carmel

1. Mary of Mount Carmel. Today is the principal feastday of the Carmelite Order. Through the efforts of the crusader Berthold, a group of hermits living on Mount Carmel were organized into an Order after the traditional Western type about the year 1150. Oppressed by the Saracens, the monks slowly emigrated to Europe. During the night preceding the sixteenth of July, 1225, the Blessed Virgin is said to have commanded Pope Honorius III to approve the foundation (cf. fifth Lesson at Matins). Since the Carmelites were still under constant harassment, the sixth General of the Order, St. Simon Stock, pleaded with the Blessed Virgin for some special sign of her protection. On July 16, 1251, she designated the scapular as the special mark of her maternal love. That is why the present feast is also known as the feast of the Scapular. The scapular, as part of the habit, is common to many religious Orders, but it is a special feature of the Carmelites. A smaller form of the scapular is given to lay persons in order that they may share in the great graces associated with it. Such a grace is the "Sabbatine privilege." In the so-called *Bulla Sabbatina* John XXII affirmed that wearers of the scapular are soon freed from the flames of purgatory, at least by the Saturday after death. The latest confirmation of the *Bulla Sabbatina* was promulgated by the Sacred Congregation of Indulgences, July 4, 1908.

Application. The Blessed Virgin scapular should remind us that Christians have an apostolate against current extremes and extravagances in modes of dress. Clothes are a symbol of the person. Like the Christian heart, dress must be chaste and simple, for one judges the interior from the exterior. It should not be necessary to add that special attention be given this matter when preparing for church attendance.

2. Holy Mass (Gaudeamus). In part the Mass is from the Common (Gospel; see p. 376), in part it is composed of proper texts. We begin with a joyful shout. We are celebrating a feast in Mary's honor; yes, even the angels in heaven are taking note (*Intr.*); and the Church adds her finest nuptial hymn, Psalm 44. The priest enters, clad in festal robes, a type of the heavenly bride going to her divine nuptials (this very common Introit originated in the Greek liturgy).

In the *Lesson* Mary stands before us as our instructor and describes her office of protectress: "I am the mother of fair love, of fear, of knowledge, and of holy hope. . . . Come to me, all of you, and be filled with my fruits." The *Gospel* is the well-known passage from the Marian Masses in which Christ praises His Mother as blessed and includes all those who mother God spiritually through hearing and keeping His word. By way of exception the *Offertory* and *Communion* are petition prayers composed by the Church. Let those who have a Little Office of the Blessed Virgin pray it as part of today's liturgy.

July 17

ST. ALEXIUS, Confessor

For love of Christ he left house and father and bride

1. St. Alexius. To what extent the life and *Acts* of this saint are historical, whether this "man of God," as he was and is called in the Orient, lived in the East or at Rome — these are questions we here must pass over. The story of St. Alexius, one of the most edifying in Christian hagiography, presents a glorious illustration of that Christian ideal of perfection which for Christ's sake embraces poverty and humiliations. Is it possible to be more heroic than to live for seventeen years under the steps in one's own house, to endure the wanton affronts of one's father's slaves, to remain as an unknown beggar to father, mother, and a bride

still longing for her spouse? And for Alexius all this was moti-
vated by an insurmountable love of Christ! Even supposing the
legend to lack an historical kernel, it still would be marvelous to
find a religion that could create such an ideal.

The Breviary gives these details. Alexius belonged to a noble
Roman family. Prompted by a special divine illumination and
moved by an ardent love for Jesus Christ, he left his maiden
bride upon their wedding day and began a pilgrimage to the
more illustrious churches of Christendom. He had devoted seventeen years to this pilgrimage and was at Edessa, a Syrian city,
when his holiness was revealed by a picture of the Blessed Virgin
that uttered his name. He left the place and by boat arrived at
the port of Rome. His father received him as a traveling stranger
and he remained there seventeen years, living under the stairs
of the house unrecognized by anyone. Only after his death were
documents found giving his name, family, and a kind of auto-
biography. He died July 17, 417, during the pontificate of Pope
Innocent I.

2. Holy Mass (Os justi). The Mass, in part from the Common
(cf. p. 402) in part proper (*Gosp., Epist.*), stresses poverty. We
have brought nothing into the world, neither can we take anything out. Having food and clothing, let us be content. Those
who wish to become rich will fall into temptation and into the
snares of the devil because the love of money is the root of all
evil (*Epist.*). How powerful these words sound coming from
the lips of St. Alexius, for he actually lived them in all their
bitter implications. His stay in his father's house was the great
temptation which he withstood (*All.*). He left all and followed
the Lord; therefore now, at the regeneration when the Son of
Man is sitting on the throne of His majesty, he rules with Him.
To the very letter Alexius lived those words about leaving one's
father, house, and wife for the Name of Christ (*Gosp.*); now he
receives the hundredfold and eternal life. In the Mass we may
share his glorification, especially at the Communion Banquet.

The Church of Sts. Boniface and Alexius on the Aventine in
Rome possesses a number of memorials of our saint; in the crypt

may be seen the place of his death, the well at his father's house, and the staircase under which he lived those many years.

July 18

ST. CAMILLUS DE LELLIS

I was sick and you visited Me

On the next three days the Church commemorates saints who were heroic in the practice of charity — Camillus, Vincent, and Jerome Aemiliani. It is not an accidental sequence, because these feasts do not correspond to the days on which the three saints died. The first practiced heroic love toward the sick, the second toward the poor, the third toward orphans.

1. **St. Camillus.** *Day of death*: July 14, 1614. *Canonized*: 1767. *Grave*: at Rome, in the Church of St. Mary Magdalen (under a side altar on the Epistle side). His mother was nearly sixty years old when Camillus was born (1550). As a youth he gave himself to the sinful pleasures of this world. His conversion dates from the feast of the Purification, 1575. Two attempts to enter the Capuchin Order were frustrated by an incurable sore on his leg. In Rome he was received in a hospital for incurables; before long he was put in charge because of his ability and zeal for virtue. He brought to the sick every imaginable kind of spiritual and bodily aid.

At the age of thirty-two he began studying for Holy Orders and was not ashamed of being numbered with children. After ordination to the holy priesthood he founded a congregation of Regular Clerics, the "Ministers to the Sick." As a fourth vow the community assumed the duty of caring for the plague-ridden at the risk of their lives. With invincible patience Camillus persevered day and night in the service of the sick, performing the meanest of duties. His love shone forth most brightly when the city of Rome was stricken by epidemic and famine, and when the plague raged at Nola. Having suffered five different maladies,

HE MUST INCREASE,
I MUST DECREASE!

which he called God's mercy, he died in Rome at the age of sixty-five. On his lips was the prayer for the dying: "May the face of Christ Jesus shine gloriously upon you." Leo XIII declared him the heavenly patron of hospitals and added his name in the litany for the dying.

2. Holy Mass (Majorem hac). The Mass is an example of the newer type of formularies that summarize the life and virtues of the saint. The *Introit* furnishes the title and theme of the Mass: "Greater love than this no one has, that he sacrifice his life for friends." Psalm 40, the psalm for the sick, follows. The theme of the Entrance Antiphon is developed in the *Epistle* and *Gospel*, both taken from writings by the Apostle of love. The first accents love of neighbor, the sign of the divine life within us: "We know that we have passed from death to life because we love the brethren. . . . In this we have known His love that He laid down His life for us; and we too ought to lay down our lives for the brethren. . . . Children, let us not love in word nor in tongue, but in deed and truth." In these few sentences St. John has plumbed the depths of the commandment of love.

In the *Gospel* the Master Himself speaks; it is His farewell address: "This is My commandment, that you love one another as I have loved you. Greater love than this no one has, that he sacrifice his life for friends." Christ's words cannot but impress us deeply. His words do not remain mere words — in the holy Sacrifice they become "deed and truth," for we "renew the work of Jesus Christ's immeasurable love" (*Secr.*). The *Communion* gives a preview of the parousia. The Lord is speaking: "I was sick and you visited Me — as long as you did it to one of these My least brethren, you did it to Me." In the final petition we ask for a happy death; may today's holy Communion nourish us on our final journey.

3. St. Symphorosa. "In Tivoli (middle Italy) St. Symphorosa, the wife of the holy martyr Getulius, together with her seven sons. Under Emperor Hadrian she was repeatedly struck in the face; then she was suspended by her hair, and lastly, tied to a rock, was thrown into a river. Her sons were bound to a pillar and their members disjointed with windlasses; thereupon, in various ways, they suffered martyrdom" (about the year 138). (*Martyrology*). Their bodies were placed in the Church of St. Michael near the fish market in Rome.

4. Prayers for the Dying in the Liturgy. "That we may conquer the enemy in the hour of our death and obtain the heavenly crown," is our principal petition today. At this point may I ask — how familiar are you with the prayers for the dying as given in the liturgy ? Do you possess a sick-call set, with a cross, candles, a white tablecloth, etc., in case the last sacraments must be administered ? Are you aware that the Church has special prayers which should be said during the final moments before the soul's departure? Unfortunately these prayers are hardly ever explained by those having the care of souls. Express your desire now to responsible persons that you want a priest to assist you at the hour of death with the full liturgical ritual.

And do become acquainted, while you are still healthy, with the ritual for the sick and dying. Most people find it very consoling. A litany first invokes the various patrons of a happy death. Thereupon follows that final, stirring imperative: "Go forth from this world, O Christian soul, in the Name of God the Father almighty, who created you; in the Name of Jesus Christ, the Son of the living God, who suffered for you; in the Name of the Holy Ghost, who has been poured forth upon you. . . ." Another prayer, in litany form, reminds God of Old and New Testament saints whom He saved from danger and distress; for example, "Deliver, O Lord, the soul of Thy servant, as Thou didst deliver Susanna from an unjust condemnation." And after the sick person has breathed forth his soul, those about petition for a blessed journey home: "Come to his (her) aid, O saints of God; come forth to meet him (her), angels of the Lord, receiving his (her) soul, presenting it to the Most High." Familiarity with these texts will aid us in being interiorly prepared when our own last moment arrives.[1]

---

[1] A ten-cent booklet entitled *The Last Rites for the Sick and Dying*, containing the full text for Communion to the Sick and the last sacraments, may be obtained from: The Liturgical Press, Collegeville, Minnesota.

ST. VINCENT DE PAUL, Confessor

The charity of Christ impels us

1. **St. Vincent.** *Day of death*: September 27, 1660. *Canonized*: 1737. *Grave*: at Paris, in the monastery of St. Lazarus. *Picture*: Vincent, holding a foundling in his arms. *Life*. St. Vincent de Paul, the founder of the Lazarists (Vincentians) and the Sisters of Charity, is the patron of all charitable organizations. His name, Vincent (*vincens*), means "conquering," and through love did he conquer every type of obstacle. Already as a boy he showed great concern in the poor. For some years he herded his father's sheep. Then he studied theology, fell into the hands of the Turks after his ordination, was made a slave, converted his master and fled with him to Rome and France. He was appointed pastor, then grand-almoner to the galley slaves. For some forty years he guided the Visitation nuns.

Innumerable were his works of charity, e.g., freeing Christian slaves, caring for orphans, neglected children, fallen women, galley slaves, sick pilgrims, tramps, and beggars. As counsellor to the French king he exercised considerable influence upon choices for high ecclesiastical offices. He remained mild, humble, and poor, even when fifty million francs passed through his hands. It has been said that he would have been the only one who could have prevented the French Revolution.

2. **Holy Mass (Justus ut palma).** Apart from the Collect and the Gospel (on the mission of the seventy-two disciples), the Mass is from the Common (p. 403). To his feastday Mass the founder of a religious Order does not come alone; his whole family is present, resembling a great limb which branches out from the tree, Christ, and ever produces new fruit. In today's liturgy the work of redemption is perfected in that we re-enkindle in ourselves the fire of our saint's heroic love and draw out a like strength from the holy Eucharist. It is also important to note how the text of the Common is colored by the life of a given

saint. This morning we see Vincent as the palm and cedar in God's great and wonderful forest (*Intr.*). In the *Epistle* Vincent speaks to us, puts us to shame; he was despised, persecuted, treated like an outcast — we seek honor, strive to be wise. In the *Gospel* we see him and his missionary priests (the Vincentians) going forth into all the world; we accompany them at least with our prayers ("Pray the Lord of the harvest that He send laborers") and our alms. The *Communion* Banquet again is the "pledge of the hundredfold reward and eternal life."

July 20

ST. JEROME AEMILIANI, Confessor
ST. MARGARET, Virgin and Martyr

The spirit of divine childhood

1. **St. Jerome Aemiliani.** Day of death: February 8, 1537. *Canonized*: 1767; feast, 1769. *Grave*: at Somasco (Lombardy) in the Church of St. Bartholomew. *Life*. The third model for the practice of charity, Jerome Aemiliani, the "father of waifs," hailed from Venice. First a military officer, he fell into the hands of the enemy during battle and was cast into a dreadful dungeon. Miraculously delivered through the intercession of the Blessed Virgin, he hung on her altar the chains with which he was bound; then he devoted himself to the practice of the works of mercy in Venice, caring especially for orphans and establishing special homes for them. His principal house was at Somasco, after which his newly founded Congregation of Clerks Regular (of Somasco) was named. While serving the plague-ridden, he died on the 8th of February, 1537, at the age of fifty-seven. *Application*. Orphans need our personal love. The interest of government or church agencies is not sufficient. Every child wants a human heart to cling to. Remember that the Father of all orphans

is God, who will reward your love for the homeless by divine adoption.

2. Holy Mass (Effusum est). The formulary exemplifies both the perfections and failings of the newer liturgical compositions. The composer sought to stress the importance Christian love has in the making of saints. With the help of a concordance it was not too difficult to find Scripture texts pertaining to charity and to the lot of widows and waifs. The *Introit* describes the miserable lot of orphans. The *Epistle* urges kindly consideration for the poor, promising a reward: "Break your bread to the hungry . . . for then your light will break forth like the dawn." At the *Gospel* it is our Savior Himself, children's greatest Friend, who repeats His kindly plea: "Suffer the little children to come to Me . . . for theirs is the kingdom of heaven." The saint commemorated is represented by the rich young man to whom Jesus said, "Come, follow Me." (Note how the liturgy uses sacred Scripture; actually the rich young man did not accept Christ's invitation, but that detail is glossed over by the liturgy).

From the Book of Tobit we have an exceptionally appropriate *Offertory* antiphon. The prayers and sacrificial gifts which we carry to the altar an angel offers to God on a golden vessel! At the *Communion* Banquet Mother Church instructs us on the nature of true religion: "Clean and immaculate service to God the Father consists in visiting the fatherless and widows in their tribulation and in keeping one's self unspotted from this world." Wouldn't observing this ideal make a perfect "thanksgiving"? From this Mass we learn that serving God in a Christian way does not consist in liturgy alone but includes love and the way one lives.

3. Divine Office. At Matins we read from one of St. John Chrysostom's homilies. Today he tells us why we must "become like little children." "A child's soul is subject to no base passions. A child does not harbor grudges, but will go to an enemy even as to a friend, as though it never suffered at his hands. No matter how often mother has punished her child, it will seek her and esteem her most highly. Show it a queen gaily clothed, the child will not choose her but its mother in broadcloth and will prefer her so dressed to any sovereign in glittering attire. For the child bases its choice not on poverty or wealth but on love. Nor does it ask more than is needed, for when it has enough it no longer clings to mother's breast. The child does not worry over things that worry us, money, for example, and such like; nor is it happy over such temporal pleasures as please us. To the child physical beauty goes unnoticed. Now our Redeemer said, *For of such is the kingdom of heaven*, so that we, by using our free wills, should acquire those good habits which infants have by nature."

4. **St. Margaret.** "At Antioch the death of the holy virgin and martyr Margaret (ca. 307)" (thus briefly the *Martyrology*). In the Greek Church St. Margaret has been highly venerated since ancient times. She is often pictured with a dragon. According to a legend, the devil appeared in the form of a dragon to tempt her. She is honored as one of the "Fourteen Sainted Helpers" (see Vol. 5, p. 162).

July 21

ST. LAWRENCE OF BRINDISI,
Confessor and Doctor

ST. PRAXEDES, Virgin

Practice the corporal works of mercy

1. **St. Lawrence.** "Lawrence was born at Brindisi in the kingdom of Naples. When a young man he entered the Capuchin Order, acquired a thorough knowledge of philosophy and theology and became proficient in several languages, ancient as well as modern. After his ordination to the priesthood he took up the office of preaching, in which he labored indefatigably throughout almost all of Italy and other European countries. Possessed of unusual prudence and the gift of counsel as well, he was given

authority over the whole Order, and he was often employed by the Supreme Pontiffs for very important diplomatic missions. Indeed, it has been attributed principally to St. Lawrence that the Christian princes joined their forces against the assault of the Turkish troops. The Christian army engaged the Turkish forces in Hungary and, with Lawrence himself riding before the army, armed with a crucifix and giving a rousing address to the soldiers and generals, won a most renowned victory. In spite of the pressure of so many great activities he practiced the virtues of a religious in a heroic degree. Whatever spare time he had he would devote to prayer, wonderfully combining the interior life with the external and active life. Finally he died as it were in the line of battle in 1619 at Lisbon, whither he had been sent by the people of Naples to put their case before the King of Spain, pleading forcefully for Christian freedom and justice. He left behind many writings which were devoted to the defense of the Catholic faith against heretics and to the explanation of the Sacred Scriptures. Pope Leo XIII enrolled him among the Saints, and Pope John XXIII declared him a doctor of the universal Church" (*Breviary lesson*).

The Mass is from the Common of a Doctor (*In medio*).

2. St. Praxedes. *Day of death*: July 21, about 160. Grave: at Rome, in the catacomb of Priscilla at the side of her sister. Pope Paschal I (817-824) transferred her body with those of many other martyrs (about 2300) to the ancient Church of St. Praxedes, which as a result became one of the more notable churches in the Eternal City. *Life*. A virgin saint from the earliest Christian times who placed her goods and her services at the disposal of the Church! The life of this saint, like that of most other early Christian saints, remains concealed in the obscurities of legend.

Praxedes, it is said, was the sister of St. Pudentiana (feast on May 19); she was devoted to the practice of works of mercy, particularly towards martyrs, during the reign of Emperor Antoninus (138-161). "Some she kept in hiding in her house, others she encouraged to profess the faith heroically, and the dead she buried. To those languishing in prison she brought needed assistance. When she no longer could endure the sight of the cruel oppression to which Christians were subjected, she implored the Lord to take her from this vale of tears if such were His holy will. It was. On July 21 the Lord called and gave her heaven as the reward for her piety and love of neighbor. Her body was placed in the catacomb of Priscilla in the tomb of her father Pudens and her sister Pudentiana" (*Roman Breviary*).

Application. No matter how high a standard of living may prevail, there always remain abundant opportunities for practicing the corporal works of mercy. It is not the Christian approach to leave the physical needs of others, whether in your own community or in a distant country, to state agencies. When did I last with my own hands "clothe the naked . . . feed the hungry . . . harbor the harborless"?

3. Holy Mass (Loquebar). The Mass is taken wholly from the Common of Virgins, but not wholly from one formulary. The reason for this is that our saint, though living in times of persecution, was not actually martyred. As the liturgy begins, Praxedes stands before us and recalls her "testimonies," the spirit of her interior life, her abandonment to the will of God. In the *Oration* we ask similar graces for ourselves.

Then Paul speaks, and through him the Church, concerning virginity. He offers us sublime thoughts upon which to meditate. First he declares that virginity is the more perfect state of life. Married life, too, is holy and desirable. That which is most necessary, however, is the spirit of virginity which manifests itself in detachment from earthly things. More at length he describes this spiritual virginity: "The time is short. Therefore the married should live as if they were not married; the sad as if not sad; those rejoicing as not rejoicing; the rich as poor . . . for this world as we see it is passing away." The message is simple — be detached from anything that hinders attachment to Christ. The *Gospel* on the buried treasure and the costly pearl is easily applied to the incomparable values inherent in virginity and sanctity. Praxedes found that treasure, that pearl, and gave all to obtain it. At the *Communion* this same Gospel passage has reference to the Eucharist, the one treasure and the one pearl beyond price. *Postcommunion*:

> You have nourished Your children, Lord,
>   with the holy Eucharist.
> Now through the intercession of the saint
>   whose feast we are keeping
> please make our souls more fervent.

July 22

ST. MARY MAGDALEN, Penitent

Apostle to the apostles

1. St. Mary Magdalen. Persons who lived in the company of Jesus are accorded special honor by the Church. In the missal and breviary Mary Magdalen bears the surname "Penitent," the only instance of this particular title in the books of the Church. Who was this woman? The Gospels tell of three women (whose lives have been integrated into one): (1) the "Sinner," who with her own tears washed the Savior's feet at the banquet given by Simon the Pharisee (Luke 7:36ff.; today's Gospel); (2) Mary of Bethany, the sister of Lazarus and Martha (Luke 10:38ff.; John 11:2, 12:3; the feast of St. Martha will be celebrated on July 29); (3) Mary Magdalen, a member of Jesus' entourage from whom seven devils were driven out (Mark 16:9; Luke 8:2); it was she who was very prominent at Christ's death and resurrection. Although certain writers do not distinguish the three individuals from one another but regard them as one and the same person, scholars seem to have established as historically certain that three different women appear in these Gospel passages. In the Eastern Church the three are honored with separate feastdays.

Mary Magdalen enters history in the eighth chapter of St. Luke's Gospel as one of a group of women ministering to the physical needs of Jesus and His disciples. The evangelist adds parenthetically that "seven devils had gone out" from her. During the passion she tarried with Mary and John beneath the Cross, took part in the burial. She was privileged to be the first to see the risen Savior and also the first to bring the message of His resurrection to the apostles (John 20:18). This is the reason why she is called *apostola apostolorum*, "apostle to the apostles," and, until 1955, received a Credo in the Mass. Apart from the Blessed Virgin, she was the only woman so honored. Later "tradition" embellished her life with the most amazing fictional details, (e.g., making her the fiancée of St. John the Apostle — *The Golden Legend*).

It may be interesting to add that the Greek Church observes today's feast as that of "The Little Apostle" but makes no reference to Mary Magdalen as a sinner or penitent.

2. Holy Mass (Me exspectaverunt). The Mass offers a fine "mystery-action" by which we may identify ourselves with the saint. At the *Introit* we free ourselves with Mary Magdalen from the poisonous embraces of the world (symbolized by going to church) and walk the way of innocence with Christ: "Blessed are the immaculate in the way." The *Lesson*, taken from the Canticle of Canticles, invites us to imitate the great love of our penitent: "I found Him whom my soul loves! I held Him and would not let Him go. . . . Put Me as a seal upon your heart, as a seal upon your arm; for love is strong as death."

The *Gospel* describes that immortal scene in which a repentant woman washed the feet of Jesus with her tears and dried them with her hair, and heard the consoling words: "Many sins have been forgiven her because she loved much." In the holy Sacrifice this scene becomes a mystical reality, for with our *Offertory* gifts we approach the banquet of the Lord, moisten His feet with tears of contrition, and anoint them with oil (the Lord receives this service in the form of charitable acts toward His poor). In the *Sacrifice-Banquet* we hear the words of pardon, for the Eucharist is the visible sign of divine forgiveness.

July 23

ST. APOLLINARIS, Bishop and Martyr
ST. LIBORIUS, Bishop

When the Prince of pastors appears
you will receive a never-fading crown of glory

1. **St. Apollinaris.** *Day of death*: July 23, about the year 75.
Grave: at Classe near Ravenna, where even to this day a basilica
rich in old mosaics stands to his honor. *Life.* A martyr-bishop of
the apostolic Church who is hardly known to us! According to
a seventh-century report, Apollinaris was a disciple of St. Peter
and became the first bishop of Ravenna; the Breviary describes
the many torments and sufferings which he suffered for the faith
at the hands of pagan priests and even fellow Christians.

At one period the Roman emperors of the West resided at
Ravenna, thereby conferring upon the city a passing importance
that was extended to matters ecclesiastical. Certain later arch-
bishops sought to capitalize upon that fact and began to withhold obedience to the See of Rome. Support for their pretensions
was gained by details on the foundation of the Church of Ravenna by Apollinaris, Peter's disciple. Humility and obedience
to the Roman Pontiff are prominent points in the Mass formulary; that Apollinaris was Peter's disciple is indicated clearly
enough, and Peter himself speaks in the Epistle. The message
Christ gives likewise concerns humility.

2. **Holy Mass (Sacerdotes Dei).** It is an old Mass with a number of proper texts; the two Readings in particular are not found
in the Common. From them one may sense that the liturgy is
honoring the high dignity of a bishop. It is for that reason that
the "priests of God" and the "holy and humble of heart" (laity)
are invited to praise God in the *Introit*.

In the *Epistle*, Peter (or better, Peter's disciple) speaks to us.
He refers to himself as "a fellow presbyter and a witness to the
sufferings of Christ" and also as "a partaker of that glory which
is to be revealed." He directs his words primarily to his succes-

sors in the episcopate but includes all pastors: "Feed the flock of God that has been entrusted to you, taking care of it not because you must, but with a sincere interest, as God wishes it. Nor for filthy lucre's sake, but eagerly; neither lording it over the faithful, but becoming a model for the flock. Then when the Prince of pastors appears, you will receive a never-fading crown of glory." (In the church at Ravenna where St. Apollinaris is buried a mosaic in the apse represents him as a bishop surrounded by his flock in a blooming paradise.) And now addressing the laity, the bishop seeks to instill obedience, humility, sobriety, watchfulness, and resistance to the devil. From the lips of a martyr these are gripping words.

The *Gradual* and *Alleluia* praise Apollinaris as the "anointed" representative of the High Priest according to the order of Melchisedech. The *Gospel* shows us our Lord with His disciples at the Last Supper. He is giving a homily on humility and on suffering and rejoicing in union with Him. Apollinaris took these words seriously. He is great because he was little before the world and continued with Christ in His temptations. Therefore he now "eats and drinks in the kingdom of the Father and sits upon the (heavenly) throne." Through the Mass we take part in both his sufferings and his glory.

3. **St. Liborius** was bishop of Le Mans (348–397), where he labored with signal success. He is said to have healed sufferers from "gravel and allied complaints," and for this reason his feast was introduced by Pope Clement XI, himself a victim who was cured through the saint's intercession. The earliest historical reference dates to the ninth century when his remains were transferred to Paderborn, Westphalia, to aid in the conversion of the Saxons; they are still there at present.

4. **Living Out the Mass.** Daily Mass is a powerhouse from which we are to draw instruction and strength. Take today's Epistle; regard it as a sermon from St. Apollinaris' lips and strive to live it. How many profound truths are touched upon! And not instruction merely, for the Eucharist affords the needed grace to fulfill, to put into practice the instruction given.

July 24

ST. CHRISTINA, Virgin and Martyr

I am a fruitful olive tree in the house of the Lord

St. Christina. *Day of death*: July 24, about the year 300.
Grave: at Palermo, Sicily. *Life*. We must distinguish two saints
by this name; the native city of one was Bolsena; the other lived
in Tyre and is venerated by the Orientals as a martyr who suffered most unusual torments. Both feasts occur today. Of the
Western saint the *Martyrology* says: "At Bolsena in Tuscany
the death of the holy virgin and martyr Christina. To show her
faith she broke the gold and silver idols in her father's house and
distributed the proceeds to the poor (as an eleven-year-old girl).
For that act she was torn with hooks at her father's order, was
gruesomely maltreated by a series of torments, and finally cast
into the sea, after being tied to a heavy stone. An angel, however,
delivered her. Later, under another judge who succeeded her
father in that office, she suffered still greater torments in proof
of her constancy. She was thrown into a heated oven where for
five days she remained unharmed; finally she consummated her
victorious passion by being pierced with arrows after her tongue
had been cut out."

Application. There still are children who have the courage to
tell their father and mother that certain things do not belong in
a Catholic home, who take the responsibility upon themselves
for removing neo-pagan pictures and books — whatever might
be the consequences. May God increase their number.

July 25

ST. JAMES, Apostle

My chalice you shall drink

1. St. James the Elder. *Day of death*: about Easter in the year
42 (today's feast commemorates the translation of his remains).

Grave: his grave was still being honored at Jerusalem during the sixth century; since the ninth century his relics have been venerated at Compostella, Spain, a place of pilgrimage that for centuries has ranked next to Jerusalem and Rome. *Life.* The apostle James the Elder belonged to the select group of three whom Jesus loved most. He was one of the first to be called, and with his brother John was known as one of the "sons of thunder." He was granted to see Christ transfigured on Tabor and to witness His deepest agony on Olivet. He was the first among the apostles to "drink the chalice of the Lord," that is, to suffer martyrdom, being beheaded in the year 42 A.D. under Herod. "And he killed James, the brother of John, with the sword" (Acts 12:2). Of his apostolic labors we know nothing. Legend says the following. As the executioner who was leading the apostle to the block saw how courageously he was accepting death, he too acknowledged the Christian faith. He bade James forgive him. The apostle kissed him and said, "Peace be with you!" Both were beheaded.

2. **St. Christopher,** one of the "Fourteen Sainted Helpers," has been highly venerated since ancient times in both the Eastern and Western Churches. The older martyrologies say that he suffered death for Christ; in more recent centuries piety has woven garlands of legend about his name. Christopher has become a giant who wished to enter the service of the most powerful of lords. He first thought that the emperor qualified; later he selected the devil, and finally he discovered Christ to be the most powerful Sovereign over all the world. From then on he served Him with greatest fidelity.

Because Christopher was of giant stature, he practiced charity by carrying pilgrims across a certain river. Once a child asked to be taken across. He complied as usual. While carrying the child on his shoulders through the river, it became heavier and heavier, and finally he could hardly support it. Then the revelation was made: "You are carrying the Lord of the world!" It was Christ (*Christopher* means "Christ-carrier").

The legend has the nature of a symbol. Bishop Vida gives the following exposition: "Because you, O Christopher, always carried Christ in your heart, the artists place Christ on your shoulders. Because you suffered much, they paint you standing deep in the waters. And because you could not accomplish this without being large of stature, they have made you a giant, bigger than great temples; therefore do you live under the open heavens during the greatest cold. And since you conquered all that is difficult, they have given you a blossoming palm as traveling staff."

3. Holy Mass (Mihi autem). We worship at Compostella today, since the spirit of the liturgy always celebrates Mass at the tomb of the day's saint. It is an excellent occasion to observe how the life and activity of a saint continues its influence down through Church history. Who could measure the faith and piety enkindled at this shrine!

Along with prayers from the Common Mass for Apostles (see p. 377), today's formulary contains several beautiful texts that are proper. In the *Introit* James and the other apostles come before me as Christ's FRIENDS and as PRINCES in God's kingdom; and I honor them. Divine selection is the object of praise in the psalm, both James' call and mine. God, You alone know my life, in Your Providence You have so ordained things that I am now Your child!

In structure the *Collect* does not follow type, but its thought-content is no less full. What do we ask for? That God sanctify and shepherd His people. As once the Jews, when building the temple, carried a trowel in one hand and a sword in the other to ward off enemies, so may God build His temple — Church and soul — by conferring sanctifying grace and by warding off temptations. Thus a twofold good is attained: (a) Christians will lead lives rich in virtue, and (b) worship God in peace. May this happy state of affairs be obtained through the intercession of St. James.

The *Epistle* affords Paul an opportunity to speak severely, almost harshly: We apostles are dedicated to death, are considered fools, go hungry, naked, without honor in the world; and you Christians hesitate to follow us. Is it not strange that the Church, on a day dedicated to honor an apostle, chooses a *Gospel* passage that seemingly does him no credit? Now the Church has chosen the passage because in it Jesus foretold James' martyrdom. Moreover, match the two Lessons. In the Gospel James asks for a seat in the Messiah's earthly kingdom; in the Epistle Paul tells how he drank the chalice of the Lord, how he suffered dishonor, poverty, how he became the outcast of men. A more striking contrast can hardly be imagined than that between what the two apostles asked for and what awaited them.

For the *Gradual* we chant the Church's wedding hymn. We say to the Church: Mother, these are your dearest children, for they are the princes in God's kingdom. Then in the *Alleluia,* Christ addresses the apostles: "I have chosen you out of the world that you should go and bring forth fruit and that your fruit should remain!" These same words Jesus addresses to me. The *Offertory* procession reflects the apostle's journey — we see James traveling to Spain, following the course of the sun. The *Secret* continues the theme: May the blessed passion, *beata passio,* of the apostle make the gifts offered acceptable to God. At *Communion* time we behold James encircled by heavenly glory, in which we too may share already now. "You who have followed Me shall sit upon thrones." What was denied to James on earth is given to him most perfectly in heaven. But not only is such his good fortune. To us also Christ made the same promise. For the Gospel applies to all Christians, both as to drinking the chalice (receiving the holy Eucharist and sharing in the sufferings of Christ) and to be enthroned at the right hand of the Lord.

4. **Reigning with Christ — Drinking the Chalice with Christ.** The petition put to Jesus by Salome, the mother of the sons of Zebedee, was characteristic of an ambitious person. Nevertheless, it did occasion a reply that we may well take to heart. James and John wanted to be high officials in Christ's kingdom. Jesus expressly says that such is not His to give; it is the Father alone who grants all privileges. He is teaching that the call to grace, the various states of life and vocations are determined by divine predestination. Whether you are rich or poor, whether you are an

employer or an employee, whether you are healthy, strong and
handsome or weak, sickly and handicapped — God has willed it
so. Nor can you change it. It is the type of life God planned for
you.

These vicissitudes divinely ordained for you constitute the
chalice of the Lord that you are to drink. There is no need to
identify Christ's words with martyrdom, and John himself was
not put to death. By the words, "drink the chalice of the Lord,"
understand simply the following of Christ. So be with Him at
table (Eucharist and worship); be with Him under all the crosses
of life. The one presupposes the other. Yes, it is in our power to
drink the chalice of Christ. His law must ever guide our wills, His
way must be the road we travel, the Cross must be our delight,
His ignominy and disgrace our ignominy and disgrace — or better, our glory. Union with Christ means drinking the chalice of
the Lord.

July 26

ST. ANNE, Mother of the Blessed Virgin Mary

"Anne," that is "grace"

1. **St. Anne.** "The mother of the Blessed Virgin Mary" is the
official title which the liturgy bestows on St. Anne; this too is her
greatest claim to greatness. Accordingly the feast is not primarily
one in honor of a saint but one commemorating the work of redemption, a feast in honor of our Lord Jesus Christ.

Anne, the grandmother of our Lord according to the flesh! Yet
sacred Scripture makes no mention of her, does not even give her
name. The apocryphal *Proto-evangel of James* is the earliest
source for the story of the pious and just couple, Joachim and
Anne. They were wealthy and generous, and they divided their
annual income into three portions, the first going to the poor, the
second to the temple, while the third was kept for their own needs.

One great sorrow weighed heavily — they were denied the blessing of children, although they had petitioned God incessantly for
years. Scorn and contempt were Anne's portion from acquaint-
ances, while Joachim, upon bringing his offering to the temple,
was cast out publicly as one barred from divine favor. With heavy
heart he betook himself to solitude and unburdened his plight to
God. An answer came in the message of an angel: "Thy prayer
is heard, Joachim. A daughter shall be born to thee and thou shalt
give her the name Mary; she shall be dedicated to the Lord from
childhood and be filled with the Holy Spirit." At the same hour
Anne was granted a similar vision. Both hurried to the temple to
thank God, and beaming with joy, entered the golden portals of
the sanctuary.

What kernel of truth lies at the bottom of this legend we do not
know; nevertheless, it teaches that great men must mature in the
school of suffering and that everyone who shares in the work of
redemption must be a bearer of the Cross. Even if we knew nothing about Anne, could we picture the mother of Mary, the grandmother of Christ other than as a noble, courageous, saintly
woman? The Lesson describes the "good wife" who provides for
her family, for her servants, who helps the poor, serves her husband. The Gospel reveals the source and the mystery of Anne's
greatness; she found the treasure, viz., the love of God. To insure possession of it she gives all, places all her strength in its service. A final thought. Let us think of our grandmother today
with gratitude. See this good and kind woman sitting in her humble room with the rosary in her hand, praying for her children
and grandchildren. Next to God we owe our faith principally to
our mothers and grandmothers. To them our gratitude.

2. **Holy Mass (Gaudeamus).** The Mass, to a great extent, is
from the Common of Holy Women (p. 408). When the Church
wishes to keep a feast more solemnly, she frequently introduces it
by some choice text with which we are familiar: "Let all of us rejoice in the Lord on this feastday in honor of St. Anne. In her
honor the angels are rejoicing and praising the Son of God." It is
in a joyous mood that we gather together in order to honor St.

Anne through the Sacrifice of her Grandson. And not only the earth, in heaven too, this feast is kept (*Intr.*).

The variable chants are taken almost entirely from the Church's wedding hymn, Psalm 44, Christ's nuptials with the Church. The entrance of the clergy is the wedding march. Anne is the bride; we follow. At the *Offertory* procession we bring bridal gifts. On the gift-table (the altar) lie the bride's adornments; now the royal bride is standing next to the bridegroom (altar) in her wedding apparel. The *Reading* is the well-known passage from the final chapter of the Book of Proverbs: "A good housewife, who will find her?" Today we have found her in the person of St. Anne. And what is the meaning of the *Gospel's* pearl and the treasure? Love of God in Anne's case; for us, love of Christ and His kingdom. "Anne" means "child of grace"; its signification may be played upon in the *Collect*. Again today the holy Sacrifice should transform our souls into other Annes, i.e., other children of grace.

3. The Model Christian. Because no historical data on St. Anne has come down to us, the Church approaches and presents her as the model housewife. The two Readings describe the model Christian. Where are the points of contact? While listening to the Epistle, we think of Anne as the perfect mother and wife. All the tasks and duties falling to the mother in a home she performed well and ably. From early morning till on into the night she is busy. Her hours of sleep are shortest. Everyone is the object of her solicitude — her husband, her children, domestics; nor does she neglect the poor who ask for her aid. Into her heart flow the troubles and needs of all about her. Truly she is a mother to all. Translated into its spiritual context, the first Reading teaches: the good Christian will be practical and prudent in his state of life; he will master his vocation and show it by virtuous acts.

But this challenge to be a model Christian is not quite enough. For outside the faith there are many who live properly according to their state of life. The Gospel proposes a second challenge: the kingdom of God must become your first and greatest objective, your greatest treasure, a priceless pearl in your estimation, for

which you would actually bargain off anything, everything — self
included. By these two parables Christ pointed out the absolute
and total claims the kingdom of God makes upon the soul. Here
precisely do we have the dilemma facing most Christians; for we
too often wish to play both sides, to enjoy what the world and the
flesh offer as also the peace of Christ. Such a spirit makes one
lukewarm, neither hot nor cold, and these Christ vomits from
His mouth. Christ demands unreserved service, one's heart whole
and entire. It is not a simple task to meet this double challenge
and perform perfectly all the duties of one's state in life, while at
the same time placing the kingdom of God before any other consideration. Its perfect accomplishment calls for the genius of a
saint.

July 27

ST. PANTALEON, Martyr

For Christian doctors

1. **St. Pantaleon.** *Day of death*: July 27, around 305. *Grave*:
first in Constantinople, now in St. Denis, Paris; his head at Lyons.
In Ravello at Amalfi there is a vessel containing his blood, which
at times liquefies. A picture in the Church of S. Maria Antiqua
dates to the year 708. *Life*. A celebrated "fee-less physician" from
Nicomedia who placed his skill in the service of God's kingdom!
According to legend he was the emperor's ordinary physician. He
is said to have strayed from the faith because of the voluptuous life
at the court, but the zealous priest Hermolaus, by pointing out the
example of his virtuous mother, effected such a change that Pantaleon distributed his goods among the poor and devoted his talents for healing to the most wretched and poor among the sick.

Because of his Christian faith he was seized by order of Emperor Maximian, tied to the rack and scorched with torches. But
in these tortures Christ appeared, granting him further strength.
Finally a stroke of the sword ended his sufferings (*Martyrology*).
He is the patron of physicians and belongs to the "Fourteen

Sainted Helpers." *Application*. The health and well-being of the body is a legitimate concern of the Christian, though, of course, secondary to that of the soul. Numerous indeed are the blessings and prayers in the liturgy directed to the well-being of the body. Liturgy is the service of God by the whole man — body too. The Mass, *Laetabitur*, comes fourth in the Common of Martyrs (see p. 387). Among the Greeks our martyr is called Panteleemon; this name is said to have been given him by Christ Himself, with the message that he should be a channel of divine mercy to all.

July 28

ST. NAZARIUS AND COMPANIONS, Martyrs

The martyrs cross the Red Sea

It is a rare occurrence that saints with different vocations and from various centuries are commemorated together.

1. **Sts. Nazarius, Celsus, Victor I, and Innocent I.** *Day of death*: July 28, though in different years. *Grave*: the first two at Milan, the last two at Rome (St. Peter's). *Life*. We celebrate today the feast of four saints from various states of life and from different centuries. Nazarius was baptized by Pope Linus; according to legend he instructed and baptized the boy Celsus, both of whom were beheaded for the faith, one at Trier and the other at Milan (about the year 68). St. Ambrose interred the remains of the former in a grand tomb about the year 395.

Pope St. Victor I, an African (189–198), labored for unity regarding the date of the Easter celebration. Perhaps he is the author of the Muratorian fragment, the oldest witness to the New Testament canon.

St. Innocent I, Pope from 402 to 417, ranks among the more illustrious pontiffs of the first centuries. His decrees have proven quite important to history. As a memorial of Christ's stay in the tomb, he ordered a Saturday fast. His letter to Bishop Decentius of Gubbio is significant in liturgical history because it treats of diptychs, the kiss of peace, and the sacred *fermentum*. At his time Rome was besieged by the Gothic king Alaric. Pope Innocent appealed to Emperor Honorius at Ravenna for help; during his absence Rome was taken and sacked. Innocent has been compared to Lot, whom God led from Sodom before the city was destroyed. (St. Nazarius' feast was observed on the 12th of June.)

2. The Mass, for the most part, is from the Common of Martyrs (*Intret*), explained on p. 388. Only the *Lesson* is proper. Aptly it compares martyrdom to Israel's passage through the Red Sea. For it is a sea of blood through which martyrs pass to the banks of eternity, guarded by a cloud of grace by day and by a pillar of faith at night. And the sea covers their enemies. Note, too, the theology contained in the *Secret*: "May we please God by the gifts brought hither; and by these gifts received back again may we receive new life." Here we have another of those inspiring concepts of ancient Christianity; in the Sacrifice Banquet our Offertory gifts come back to us, consecrated.

July 29

ST. MARTHA, Virgin
ST. FELIX AND COMPANIONS, Martyrs

Martha, Martha, thou art troubled about many things —
but one thing is necessary

1. St. Martha. Apart from a few remarks found in the Gospel, we know nothing about St. Martha that is historically certain. The story that she journeyed to Spain with Lazarus and Mary Magdalen and remained there is later fiction. The Gospel represents her as the motherly type of a woman; the words of Jesus ring in our ears today, and in the midst of earthly activities they recall life's highest purpose: "Martha, Martha, thou art troubled about many things. But one thing is necessary!" In Martha and Mary, two sisters, the two ideals of Christian piety are typified, the active and the contemplative. (The feast is of very late origin.)

2. Mass and Divine Office. The Mass is from the Common of Virgins (*Dilexisti*), p. 406. Only the *Gospel* is proper. An exposition of the Gospel, which tells of Jesus' visit at the house of Mary and Martha, is given by St. Augustine at Matins: "The words of our Lord Jesus Christ which are proclaimed in the Gospel bring home to us the message that there is ONE thing for which we ought strive in the midst of the many activities of earthly existence. For it we work at present not as citizens but as aliens, because we are still on the way and not at our destination; and with a yearning spirit because its full enjoyment is still distant.

"Nevertheless, we must be determined to strive after this ONE thing with all seriousness, making allowance for no respite or diversion, so that its attainment may be absolutely assured. Martha and Mary were sisters, not only by blood but sisters in spirit. Both were attached to the Lord, both served the Lord wholeheartedly when He was with them. Martha welcomed Him as special guests are welcomed; nevertheless, it was the servant that welcomed the Lord, the sick that welcomed the Physician, the creature that welcomed the Creator. She welcomed Him and provided nourishment for His body so that she would be nourished in spirit. . . . Thus was the Lord received as a guest who came to His own and His own would not receive Him; but to as many as did receive Him, He gave the power of becoming sons of God, for He took them as slaves and made them free, He redeemed them as captives and made them heirs. Now none of you should say: Oh, how fortunate were they who could welcome Christ into their own homes! Stop crying, stop complaining because you were born at a time when you no longer could see the Lord in the flesh. By no means does He deprive you of that privilege. What you do for one of these My least, He says, you do for Me."

3. The Call of Ringing Church Bells. Christ's words to Martha were in no way intended as a condemnation. But the Savior did want to slacken the speed with which that restless woman was hurrying about the house. "Please don't make such a big meal; a light lunch will be enough for Me. I didn't come in order to eat.

My interests touch the kingdom of God and the needs of the soul. In this am I really concerned. Therefore My words of praise for Mary, who does the better thing in sitting down by Me to listen and to speak of heavenly things."

Through the centuries the Church has used Christ's words to Martha as she warns and pleads: Children, do not lose yourselves in material, earthly concerns. What does it profit if you should master the whole world — to the detriment of your soul? It could be said that the Church has no other interest than to divert men from being engulfed in the meshes of the profane. On Sunday in particular she would whisper this message into the ears of every Christian. And I can prove this from the liturgy. For at the solemn consecration of the church bells this Gospel is read. Why? The bell is the voice of the Church, the liturgy is implying. And the message that is ever pealing out is none other than Christ's: O men, you are busy about many things. You are pursuing a mad rush for money and positions. The one important matter is the salvation of your soul. This message is rung out by the church bells at early morn, at noon, and at night, by their tolling at a funeral, by their joyous clanging on Sunday, inviting all to worship God. Yes, it is our resolution to become more like Mary, choosing the better part, sitting at the feet of Jesus and listening.

4. **Mary and Martha.** The two women of today's Gospel are often referred to as types of the active and contemplative life. In God's economy the house of Bethany symbolizes the Church; there are "Martha souls" and "Mary souls." The one class serves God mediately by their state of life, the other immediately by prayer and interior recollection. In the occupations of the active life, which certainly are to the service of God, the danger of external dissipation and of losing oneself in earthly concerns is dangerously great. Therefore down through the ages has rung Christ's warning call: "Martha, Martha, thou art troubled about many things. But one thing is necessary."

We must therefore regard Mary's work in the Church as essentially higher, and cherish and further it in order that we may not become too engrossed in secular affairs. This holds true for

(a) the individual Christian, (b) for the family, (c) for the parish, and (d) for the universal Church.

a) The individual Christian is ordinarily a "Martha-soul" because of his state in life. He must work and worry from early morning till late evening to earn bread for his family. Applicable to him are the words of Christ, "Martha, Martha . . . ," because for such a man the danger to be wholly absorbed in temporal affairs is very great. Now and then he must become a "Mary-soul." How important and beneficial would be the proper celebration of Sunday, the Mass, sermon, prayer. How easily the Sunday liturgy could be made into an hour at the feet of the Savior at Bethany. How fruitful a good morning prayer, an evening devotion with Scripture readings, meditation, prayer. Living with the Church will further this contemplative side and make it into a praiseworthy habit. Such hours of more intense interior recollection are necessary to all persons following an occupation.

b) In the family there seems to be a division that is more natural, that of *Ora et Labora.* The father of the family will be given more to the *Labora,* the mother to the *Ora* without, however, failing too much with regard to the other. Perhaps there is an old grandmother sitting in the rocker who can do nothing more than pray for the family. Her "Mary-work" is most important and only in eternity will it be known what she has done for the family, how many graces she has occasioned. How beneficial the practice of having one member of the family attend holy Mass daily in order to obtain the blessings of the holy Sacrifice upon the whole family! We ought emphasize the contemplative side of liturgical life in the family.

c) In each parish too there should be a group of interior, pious souls who form the heart of the parish's life. Those devout persons who come to Mass daily, who like the prophetess Anna "never leave the temple, but by fastings and prayers serve night and day" (Lk. 2:37), must not be contemned as of little importance. They are the "Mary-souls" of the parish who have "chosen the better part." Only let the pastor educate them properly and lead them to true participation in the holy Sacrifice and in common prayer. He should daily celebrate with them a community Mass; be it ever so simple, he should instruct them on how to pray portions of the Divine Office. Yes, this could be the ideal: the parish church, as the place for the recitation of the canonical Hours in common. These "Mary-souls" are a truly great driving power in the spiritual life of the parish.

d) In the Church universal the Religious Orders bear Mary's burden. May they always remember their highest and most important duty. Notwithstanding their pastoral and missionary interests, the interior life and the cultivation of the liturgical services constitute their greatest mission. It is for them the "better part" and thereby they accomplish most in the Church of God. It is their peculiar obligation as members of Christ's Body. They are to counteract the dangers of worldliness in the Church, to preserve clean and rich her interior life. When in past history the life of the Church seemed threatened by extinction, it was the Religious Orders who were the traitors. And usually it was the Religious Orders who again brought new life to the Church. Let us esteem the religious life very highly. See how the words of Christ, "Martha, Martha . . . ," like a warning and a plea sound down through the centuries, urging us to free ourselves from the profane and to search out and cling to the inmost soul of the Corpus Christi Mysticum.

July 30

STS. ABDON AND SENNEN, Martyrs

Blessed are they who suffer persecution for justice's sake

1. **Sts. Abdon and Sennen.** *Day of death*: July 30, about 250. *Grave*: at Rome, in the cemetery of Pontianus. In the seventh century their relics were translated to the church above ground. Gregory IV translated their bodies to St. Mark's in 826. *Life*. According to legend Abdon and Sennen were two Persians who, under Emperor Decius (249–251), were accused of burying on

their estates the bodies of martyrs; for this reason they were thrown into chains at the Emperor's command. As they persistently refused to offer incense to the gods and candidly confessed Jesus as their Lord and God, their imprisonment was made more and more unbearable, and when Decius returned to Rome they were led bound in his triumphal procession. They were dragged before the idols in the capital city, only to spit upon them. Cast to the bears and lions, they were not attacked. Finally they were put to death with the sword. Their bodies were secretly taken away by Christians, and the deacon Quirinus buried them in his house, the cemetery of S. Pontian, where an old mural of them may still be seen. They are depicted in Persian clothing, receiving from the Lord the crown of victory.

Application. The corporal work of mercy, "to bury the dead," today's saints fulfilled to the letter, and it brought them a glorious martyr's death for Christ. They gave burial to martyrs and themselves were lovingly buried as martyrs. In our day, efficiency and commercialism have to a great extent displaced personal and loving service to the bodies of the dead. Is this the Christian ideal?

2. Holy Mass (Intret). In part the Mass is from the Common of Martyrs (p. 388); the Lessons and Orations are proper. Today's Mass is an example of how dramatic the sacred liturgy can be. Four roles may be distinguished in this drama: the holy martyrs, Christ, we the faithful, and the Church. Let us imagine ourselves at the grave of our saints. During the night-vigil the acts of the martyrs were read and now we are about to re-enact the holy Sacrifice. The choir gives expression to our emotions — fundamentally human ones. We hear the lamentations of the martyrs, bound and groaning in prison; we see their blood flow. Human nature straightens itself and cries for justice.

Now the Church speaks, and she seeks good things for her children. The martyrs have acquired great merits for themselves; they are of benefit for expiating the sins of fellow Christians (*Coll.*). It is time for the *Epistle*, and the martyrs themselves step forward; they describe their Christ-life to comfort us: "Brethren, let us exhibit ourselves in all things as the ministers of God, in much patience, in tribulation, in necessities, in distresses, in strifes, in prisons. . . ." They had actual experience of what these words imply, and they exhort us to "martyrdom" according to our state of life: "in labors, in watchings, in fastings, in chastity, in longsuffering, in sweetness, in charity unfeigned." No matter what our lot, whether rich or poor, despised or honored, our aim should be to serve the Lord. Again they point to their own lives: "As deceivers and yet true, as dying and behold we live, as needy yet enriching many, as having nothing and possessing all things."

From the mouth of martyrs these words have an authentic ring. But we, the choir, have different ideas on martyrdom: "Glorious is God in His saints and wonderful in His majesty" (*Grad.*). "The souls of the just are in the hand of God" (*Allel.*). Then Christ, the King of martyrs, rises. From His lips we hear the beatitudes. He calls our saints blessed: "Blessed are they who suffer persecution for justice's sake. Blessed are you if men persecute you; rejoice and be glad for your reward is great in heaven" (*Gosp.*). But the choir re-echoes the theme: "Wonderful is God in His saints" (*Off.*). Now the Sacrifice proper may begin. Christ's Sacrifice on the tomb of the martyrs! A double sacrifice, and yet but one, for Head and members are joined. Mother Church is pleading that the chains of the martyrs loose the bonds of our sins.

July 31

ST. IGNATIUS, Confessor

All for the greater honor and glory of God

The Society of Jesus was the providential bulwark against the heresies of the sixteenth century. On all sides it accomplished great things — in furthering Christian life, in the education of the young, in the care of souls. The Society produced men who kept burning the fire of its founder (Ignatius means "fireman"). Through his *Exercises,* Ignatius converted countless souls and afforded a means of spiritual renewal for both religious and laity. The *Spiritual Exercises* is a book for the formation of saints, practical at all times, and has, as someone has said, produced more saints than it contains letters.

1. **St. Ignatius.** *Day of death*: July 31, 1556. *Grave*: his body rests at Rome in the Church del Gesu that adjoins the first profession house of the Jesuits. *Life.* Ignatius, born in 1491, was first a page at the Spanish court and followed a military career. His conversion took place during his recovery from a wound received at the siege of Pampelona (1521). He made a pilgrimage to Montserrat, did severe penances at Manresa, where he composed the *Exercises.* Then as an adult he began priesthood studies (1528–1535), gathered together companions of a like mind, laid the foundations of his Society in the chapel of Montmartre in Paris (1534), and began his work of reform, which included all angles of religious life. Once he said that if God left him the choice, he would prefer working for the service of God and neighbor, uncertain of being saved, rather than to die with the assurance of immediate glory. St. Philip Neri and many others often saw the face of the saint beaming with heavenly delight. Finally in his sixty-fifth year he returned to his Lord, whose GREATER HONOR AND GLORY he always had upon his lips and strove to further in all his works.

2. **Holy Mass (In Nomine Jesu).** The Mass, in its various texts, gives pointed expression to the life and maxims of our saint. Already the *Introit* proclaims the motto of the Society: *Omnia ad majorem Dei gloriam,* "All for the greater glory of God!" In the *Epistle* Ignatius himself recounts his solicitude for the Gospel and challenges his sons (and us also) to imitate him. The *Gospel,* describing the mission of the seventy-two disciples, places our saint in the company of the great missioners who carried the Name of Christ throughout the world. The *Communion* chant is quite striking: "I have come to cast fire upon the earth,

and what will I but that it be kindled?" *Ignem* — Ignatius! He was a true Prometheus who brought divine fire to earth. Where may we receive this fire again and again when the heart grows cold? In the Eucharist. The *Secret* says that "God has disposed that these most holy mysteries are the fount of all holiness."

3. Two Types of Piety. In the course of centuries two types of piety may be noted as permeating the religious life of the Church. We may call the one "objective" piety, the other "subjective." Religion and piety establish a relationship between God and man. Now according as emphasis is laid upon the human side or upon the divine side, piety becomes subjective or objective. In general, we may say that the Oriental prefers objective piety, piety of a more passive type, that is, he lets himself be led and carried by God, with the human element in the background.

Western or Occidental piety is more active and subjective. The Occidental wants to work with his own will, wants to let the human element have its share in the service of God. The individual with his entire emotional make-up seeks expression. It can also be said that the primitive Church preferred objective piety, while recent times are more inclined to subjective types. Ignatius of Loyola is one of the spokesmen for piety stressing the human aspect which is dominant in our day. To St. Ignatius we are indebted in that he has shown what mighty forces lie dormant in man, that he has shown us ways which cleanse and deepen our inner lives.

Liturgical piety takes another path, stresses the divine, the communal, the cultic, and thereby effects a salutary equilibrium. Objective and subjective, communal and individualistic, active and passive, grace and will in right proportions, emphasis and balance, give the ideal for which we should strive. Ignatius has voiced this very beautifully in the following words: "In all your works have so great a confidence in God as if He alone, without your cooperation, accomplished all things; nevertheless, employ your whole strength with such zeal as if results hinged upon you alone."

THE MACHABEAN MARTYRS

1. **The Machabean Martyrs.** The seven Machabean brothers, together with their mother, were martyred about the year 164 B.C. by King Antiochus Epiphanes. The mother in particular deserves to be admired for the heroic fortitude with which she encouraged her children to suffer and die. Their remains were venerated at Antioch. After the church which was built above their resting-place was destroyed, they were taken to Rome; during the renovation of the high altar of St. Peter in Chains (1876), a sarcophagus dating from the fourth or fifth century was found; lead tablets related the relics to those of the Machabean martyrs and their mother.

Seldom does it happen that the Roman Church venerates Old Testament saints in the Mass and Office; it is much more common in the Greek rite. Martyrdom before the advent of Christ was possible only through faith and hope in Christ. Today's feast is among the oldest in the sanctoral cycle. In the second Book of Machabees, sacred Scripture recounts the passion and death of the Machabees in a very edifying manner. St. Gregory Nazianz discusses why Christians honor these Old Testament saints:

"They deserve to be universally venerated because they showed themselves courageous and steadfastly loyal to the laws and traditions of their fathers. For if already before the passion of Christ they suffered death as martyrs, what heroism would they have shown if they had suffered after Christ and with the death of the Lord as a model? A further point. To me and to all who love God it is highly probable that according to a mystic and hidden logic no one who endured martyrdom before the advent of Christ was able to do so without faith in Christ."

August 2

ST. ALPHONSUS LIGUORI, Bishop and Doctor

With the Lord there is plentiful redemption (Ps. 129)

1. St. Alphonsus. "To bring the good news to the poor" was Christ's mission upon earth. While on His travels our Lord made the sad discovery that the ordinary people were indeed of good will but that they were straying about as a flock without a shepherd. "The harvest indeed is great, but the laborers are few." A similar experience has been the lot of saintly men throughout the history of the Church; and therefore they gathered workers and sent them as missioners among the people. During the Middle Ages, St. Francis of Assisi and St. Dominic; in more recent times, among others, St. Alphonsus Liguori, who founded the Congregation of the Most Holy Redeemer (Redemptorists). The members of this community, following Christ's example, were to "bring the good news to the poor" in cities and throughout rural areas.

Day of death: August 1, 1787; canonized, 1839; declared a Doctor of the Church, 1871. *Grave*: in the church of the Redemptorists at Pagani near Nocera in the Campania. *Picture*: as a bishop with bowed head, rosary in hand. *Life*. St. Alphonsus was born of noble parentage at Naples in 1696. He first gave himself to the practice of law. A misjudgment in the presentation of a case brought him to realize the emptiness of the world and the dangers inherent in his profession. He bade good-bye to the world, became a priest in 1726, and in 1732 founded a community to assist him in his work.

His zeal for souls was most extraordinary, as shown by his manner of preaching and through numerous edifying and scholarly writings. He bound himself by vow never to waste a moment of time. Great was his love and devotion to the Blessed Virgin, in whose praise he composed an excellent volume still praised in our day (*The Glories of Mary*). Among the people he zealously promoted devotion to the passion of Jesus and to the most holy Sacrament of the altar. To wonderful innocence of life, which he never stained by grievous sin, he added severe penances. Only out of obedience did he accept the bishopric of St. Agatha of the Goths (1762), but in 1775 he returned again to his community, as poor as he had left it. He died peacefully in the Lord at the venerable age of ninety years.

2. Holy Mass (Spiritus Domini). Again a Mass with proper texts that portray the life of the saint. In the *Introit* we hear the aims of the saint's Congregation: "To bring the good news to the poor." In the *Epistle* the venerable founder exhorts his sons to battle in the army of Christ, and to labor in the vineyard of the Lord. The *Gradual* and *Alleluia* tell of his zeal for the conversion of sinners. The *Gospel* on the sending of the seventy-two disciples is often applied to saintly missioners; Alphonsus and his sons are following faithfully in the footsteps of Christ's disciples. In the saint of the day Christ the High Priest appears before us at the *Communion*. The *Offertory* brings to mind ancient Offertory processions.

3. Pope St. Stephen. *Day of death*: August 2, 257. *Grave*: at Rome in the catacomb of St. Callistus; in the ninth century his body was taken to the Church of St. Praxedes. *Life*. Stephen I, a Roman, was Pope (254–257), during the reign of Emperor Valerian and Gallienus. We are told that he forbade clerics to wear the sacred vestments outside of church. Through his efforts many were converted to Christ, particularly a number of prominent Roman families. In sacred history Stephen is known through his stand on the question of heretical baptism: "Let there be no innovations regarding converts from heresy; follow tradition" (Cyprian, Ep. 74, 1).

A legendary account of his martyrdom is given in the Office (actually Pope Stephen may not have suffered martyrdom at all): "As the persecution became more severe, Stephen called together the clergy, exhorted them to steadfast perseverance in the faith, and, in the crypts of the martyrs, celebrated Mass regularly and held sacred meetings. When the pagans had seized the Pope and had dragged him to the temple of Mars in order to force him to offer sacrifice, he openly denied that he would give such honor to devils as belonged to the one true God. At his words an earthquake rocked the temple and the idol of Mars crashed to the floor in pieces. The guards who held Stephen fled panic-stricken, and the Pope returned to his brethren in the catacomb of Lucina. He instructed them further in the divine precepts and strengthened them with the sacrament of Christ's Body. There, while performing the sacred mystery, soldiers again arrived from the emperor and beheaded him as he was sitting in the bishop's chair. His body and the blood-drenched chair were buried by the clergy in the catacomb of St. Callistus."

August 4

ST. DOMINIC, Confessor

With his burning torch he will enkindle the earth

1. **St. Dominic.** *Day of death*: August 6, 1221. *Canonized*: 1234. *Grave*: at Bologna, first in the Church of St. Nicholas; since 1267 in a church dedicated to him as patron. *Picture*: a Dominican with the rosary, or with a dog carrying a torch in his mouth. *Life*. The *Martyrology* gives the following: "At Bologna (upper Italy) the holy confessor Dominic, the saintly and learned founder of the Order of Preachers. He preserved his virginity inviolate and gained for himself the grace of raising three dead persons to life. By his word he crushed heresy in the bud and led many souls to piety and to religious life."

Born about 1175 in Castile (Spain), Dominic hailed from the illustrious Guzman family. First he was a canon regular at Osma; then he founded the Dominican Order, which was approved in 1216. Alongside the Franciscans, it became the most powerful Order in medieval times, giving the Church illustrious preachers, e.g., St. Vincent Ferrer, and contemplatives, e.g., Sts. Thomas of Aquin and Pius V, and contributing immeasurably to maintaining the purity of the faith. Through the example of apostolic poverty and the preaching of the word of God the Friar Preachers were to lead men to Christ. To St. Dominic is attributed the origin and spread of the holy rosary.

The two contemporaries, Dominic and Francis, effected a tremendous spiritual rejuvenation through their own spiritual personalities and through their religious foundations. Of the two, Dominic was the realist who surpassed the other intellectually and in organizational talent. His spirit of moderation, clarity of thought, and burning zeal for souls have become the heritage of the Dominican Order. Legend has contributed the following rare anecdote as preserved in the Breviary: "During pregnancy, Dominic's mother dreamed she was carrying in her womb a little dog that held a burning torch between its teeth; and when she had given birth, it set the whole world on fire. By this dream it was made manifest beforehand how Dominic would inflame the nations to the practice of Christian virtue through the brightness of his holy example and the fiery ardor of his preaching." He died at Bologna upon hearing the liturgy's prayer for the dying: "Come, ye saints of God, hasten hither, ye angels!"

2. Holy Mass (Os justi). Parts of the Mass are taken from the Common of Confessors (explained on p. 402), parts from other Masses in the Common (Epistle and Communion). The *Epistle* (from the Common of Doctors) recalls the zeal of our saint for preaching: *Praedica verbum* — preach the word of God (Order of Preachers), and likewise reminds us of the "crown of justice" which the true soldier receives at death as the prize of triumph.

3. The Dominican Liturgy. In ancient times, and even during the Middle Ages, various churches, dioceses, religious Orders, and even monasteries had their own peculiar liturgical rites (e.g., the Spanish, African, Gallican liturgies). The sixteenth century, however, witnessed a powerful movement toward unity along liturgical and rubrical lines, a direction officially sanctioned and furthered by the Council of Trent. With the publication in 1570 of the *Missale Romanum* (which is still in use), Pope Pius V restricted these practices to such venerable rites as the Ambrosian, or that at Lyons and Braga. Some religious Orders were also allowed to retain unique, century-old observances. Of these a well-known example is that of the Dominicans.

Dominican liturgical practices stem from the French-Gallican Church, particularly that of Paris. Until the year 1228, every Dominican convent adapted itself to the rite of the diocese in which it was located. Naturally a variety of observances did not work out well at the time of a general chapter. Accordingly, under the fourth General of the Order, John of Wildhouse, there began a movement to introduce a single rite for all Dominican houses. At the first general chapter at Köln in 1245 it was decided that, working conjointly, representatives of the German, French, English and Lombard provinces should submit a single ceremonial. The following year their work was considered and two years later adopted (1248). Since that date we may speak of a Dominican rite, although there were later modifications. Accordingly they could retain their practices when Pope Pius V (1568–1570) abolished all variants not enjoying a tradition of at least two hundred years.

The most important differences between the Dominican and the Roman Mass ritual occur in the prayers at the foot of the altar, the Offertory, and Communion. According to the Dominican ritual, the Offertory oblation is prepared at the beginning of the Mass. After this preparation the priest says the prayer *Actiones nostras* and descends to the foot of the altar to say the preliminary prayers. In place of Psalm 42 the first verse of Psalm 135 is said. A short *Confiteor* follows with a lengthier *Misereatur* and the *Absolutionem*.

Ascending the altar-steps, the priest says only the *Aufer a nobis*. At the altar the priest signs the altar and himself with the Sign of the Cross, goes to the Epistle side and begins the Introit. Since the chalice was already prepared at the beginning of the Mass, the Offertory is shorter than in the Roman rite. The priest first says the prayer *Quid retribuam,* then taking the chalice with the paten continues with the *Calicem salutaris*; the *Suscipe, sancta Trinitas* is said at the offering of the bread. After a short *Lavabo* follows the *In spiritu humilitatis* and the *Orate, fratres,* without the *Suscipiat*; the *Domine, exaudi* brings the Offertory to a close.

The Communion too is different. After the *Pax Domini* follows the *Agnus Dei.* Then a short prayer which implores the fruit of holy Communion and concludes with the *Domine Jesu Christe, Fili Dei vivi.* The priest receives, then says the *Corpus et sanguis*; after the absolution the *Quod ore sumpsimus.* The blessing is given in the following form: "May the blessing of almighty God, the Father, the Son, and the Holy Spirit descend upon you and remain forever." Of note, too, is that the Dominicans pray with outstretched arms. Other differences could be cited. During Eastertide there is a double Alleluia versicle; the first part has reference to the feast, the second to the season. For Christmas, Epiphany, and the feasts of Sts. Dominic and Francis there are special Sequences. The feasts are classified as follows: III lessons simple; semi-double; double; wholly double II class; wholly double I class.

Other practices peculiar to the Dominican rite may be found, especially in the calendar of saints and in the Divine Office.

August 5

DEDICATION OF OUR LADY OF THE SNOW

Mary—Theotokos

"At Rome on the Esquiline Hill, the dedication of the Basilica of Mary of the Snow" (*Martyrology*). We celebrate today the dedication of one of the four most illustrious churches of Rome. While each diocese and parish keeps its own dedication anniversary, the Church universal commemorates the consecration of the four great Roman basilicas, the mother churches, we may call them, of Christendom, viz., St. John Lateran, St. Peter, St. Paul Outside the Walls, and St. Mary Major. By means of these feasts the Church seeks to link all Christians with the Holy See.

St. Mary Major is important to Christendom for three reasons: (a) it stands as a venerable monument to the Council of Ephesus

(431), at which the dogma of Mary's divine Motherhood was solemnly defined; the definition of the Council occasioned a most notable increase in the veneration paid to Mary. (b) The basilica is Rome's "church of the crib," a kind of Bethlehem within the Eternal City; it also is a celebrated station church, serving, for instance, as the center for Rome's liturgy for the first Mass on Christmas. To this basilica we make a spiritual pilgrimage annually on the first Sunday of Advent, Ember Wednesdays, the vigil of Christmas, and the feast of St. John the Evangelist. In some measure every picture of Mary with the divine Child is traceable to this church. (c) St. Mary Major is Christendom's first Marian shrine for pilgrims. It set the precedent for the countless shrines where pilgrims gather to honor our Blessed Mother throughout the world. Here was introduced an authentic expression of popular piety that has been the source of untold blessings and graces for Christianity in the past as in the present.

1. Dedication of St. Mary Major. The beginnings of St. Mary Major date to the Constantinian period. Originally it was called the Sicinini Basilica; it was the palace of a patrician family by that name before its transformation into a church by Pope Liberius. The story of its origin is legendary, dating from the Middle Ages. The Breviary gives this version: "Liberius was on the chair of Peter (352–366) when the Roman patrician John and his wife, who was of like nobility, vowed to bequeath their estate to the most holy Virgin and Mother of God, for they had no children to whom their property could go. The couple gave themselves to assiduous prayer, beseeching Mary to make known to them in some way what pious work they should subsidize in her honor.

"Mary answered their petition and confirmed her reply by means of the following miracle. On the fifth of August — a time when it is unbearably hot in the city of Rome — a portion of the Esquiline would be covered with snow during the night. During that same night the Mother of God directed John and his wife in separate dreams to build a church to be dedicated to the Virgin Mary on the site where they would see snow lying. For it was in this manner that she wanted her inheritance to be used.

"John immediately reported the whole matter to Pope Liberius, ind he declared that a similar dream had come to him. Accompanied by clergy and people, Liberius proceeded on the following morning in solemn procession to the snow-covered hill and there marked off the area on which the church in Mary's honor was to be constructed."

Under Pope Sixtus III (432–440) the basilica was rebuilt, and upon the occasion of the definition of Mary's divine Motherhood by the Council of Ephesus, consecrated to her honor (432). He decorated the apse and walls with mosaics from the lives of Christ and His blessed Mother, which even to this day beautify the church and belong to the oldest we possess (the unique work on Rome's ancient mosaics by J. Wilpert reproduces most of them in color). As early as the end of the fourth century a replica of the Bethlehem nativity grotto had been added; on this account the edifice became known as "St. Mary of the Crib." To the Christian at Rome this church is Bethlehem. Other names for the basilica are: Liberian Basilica, because it dates to the time of Pope Liberius; St. Mary Major (being the largest church in Mary's honor in Rome); Our Lady of the Snow, because of the miracle that supposedly occasioned its erection.

2. Holy Mass (Salve, sancta Parens). Dedication anniversaries ordinarily use the Mass for the Consecration of a Church from the Common. But today we have a Blessed Virgin Mass, the well-known *Salve, sancta Parens* (explained on p. 375). The reasons are evident.

3. Mary — Theotokos. As remarked above, today's station church was consecrated by Pope Sixtus III in memory of the happy conclusion to the Council of Ephesus, at which Mary was proclaimed Mother of God. Ever since 1931, when the Church observed the fifteenth centenary of Ephesus, we have become more conscious of the importance of this Council and of Mary's primary title. We could point out how the divine Motherhood mystery dominates all Marian liturgy; for the *Theotokos* doctrine has kept Mariology Christo-centric in the Church's worship. Although recent popular devotion to Mary has become to a certain extent soft and sentimental and has, one may say, erected its own sanctuary around Mary as the center, devotion to our Blessed

Mother in the liturgy has always remained oriented to Christ. In the liturgy the divine Motherhood has always been the bridge from Mary to Jesus. One need only examine Matins in honor of Mary or the Masses from her Common to be reassured. Everywhere Christ takes the central position, and Mary is the Christ-bearer.

Take, for example, the five chants proper to today's Mass; they all treat of *Dei Genitrix.* At the *Introit,* in the words of the ancient Greek poet Sedulius, who most certainly composed these lines in memory of the Ephesian decree, we greet the Mother of Him who rules the world: "Hail, O holy Mother! You gave birth to the King who rules heaven and earth forever." The *Gradual* glorifies Mary's virginal Motherhood: "O virgin Mother of God, He whom the whole world cannot contain enclosed Himself in your womb and became man." Likewise the *Alleluia*: "After child-birth you remained an inviolate virgin. Mother of God, pray for us." At the *Offertory* we greet Mary and Christ with the angel's *Ave.* At the *Communion* we hear chanted: "Blessed is the womb of the Virgin Mary that bore the Son of the eternal Father."

May our devotion to Mary with deep, true, and loving affection remain solidly constructed upon dogma that is Christo-centric. For such is the fruit of a living faith in Mary's divine Motherhood.

August 6

THE TRANSFIGURATION OF CHRIST

Tu Rex gloriae, Christe!

Today we have a votive feast that was introduced into the West by Pope Callistus III (1457) after the victory of St. John Capistran over the Turks at Belgrade. In the East, where it is a summer feast of highest rank in honor of Christ the King, it was celebrated on this date already in the fifth century. The original Office, of which only the antiphons and responses remain in present Breviaries, was composed by the Dominican James Gil.

1. **Gospel Background.** Today we celebrate the marvel of

In this we have the proof of God's love—

He has sacrificed His life for us

our Lord's transfiguration, a miracle that the Fathers of the Church numbered among the greatest God worked in attestation to Christ's divinity. It was during the second half of His public ministry. Already Calvary's Cross was casting its shadow when Jesus ascended Mount Tabor one evening with His three favored disciples. Night. Jesus prays. His companions drowse away. He continues in prayer, and through the cloak of human nature the brightness of His divinity beams forth. He becomes radiant, glorified. The apostles awake to the blinding light and are witnesses to the miracle. (Instead of the usual Scripture reading, it should be interesting and profitable to compare the four accounts of the transfiguration, viz., Matt. 17:1-9; Mark 9:29; Luke 9:28-36; these three narratives describe the transfiguration; the fourth is to be found in St. Peter's Second Epistle, 1:10-21).

2. Holy Mass (Illuxerunt). Already at the *Introit* the bright rays of Christ's transfiguration strike us, rays that traverse the entire earth and fall upon both the good and the wicked. Psalm 83, "How lovely are Thy tabernacles, O Lord of hosts," makes allusion to Peter's words: "Lord, it is good for us to be here. . . . Let us set up three tents." In the *Oration* we ask to be co-heirs of the "King of glory," i.e., to share His transfiguration. In the *Epistle* St. Peter speaks as an eyewitness of the event: "This is My beloved Son in whom I am well pleased. That voice we ourselves heard borne from heaven when we were with Him on the holy mount."

Let us cull out the dramatic element in the formulary. In the Epistle St. Peter reports to us the transfiguration as he saw it; during the reading of the *Gospel* we behold Christ transfigured, glorified. By means of the Sacrifice proper and especially the sacred Banquet, the transfiguration becomes an actuality through the sacrament; the glorified Christ appears and we are sharers of His glory. In the *Offertory* the Church tells us that today we shall see "glory and magnificence in the house" of the Lord. The *Secret* voices our plea that the "splendor of His transfiguration cleanse away the stains of our sins" (as the sun dissipates disease). Holy Mass is our hour on Tabor. Returning to our places of work in the world, we carry along the graces received in the inmost sanctuary of our hearts: "Tell the vision to no one" (*Comm.*).

3. Divine Office. The "prayerbook of the Church" features splendid texts today. The Invitatory announces that we are celebrating a feast in honor of Christ the King: "Christ, the King supreme in glory — Him let us adore." The psalms of Matins are well chosen, for kingship themes are never absent. "Made a little less than the angels, You have crowned Him with glory and honor; You have set Him King over the works of Your hands" (Ps. 8). Psalm 28 echoes God's voice in a thunderstorm; our thoughts turn to "the voice from the clouds" on Tabor: "This is My beloved Son." Psalm 44 shows us the glorified King (Christ) and the glorified Queen (the Church).

Notice, too, the precision and clarity with which St. Leo covers the mystery in his Matins homily: "The primary purpose of the transfiguration in the mind of Jesus was this: that His disciples should not take offense when He would die on the Cross nor that the humiliation of the passion He so freely embraced should shatter their faith; for the majesty of His hidden dignity had previously been manifested to them. Nevertheless, the Lord is no less mindful of His holy Church; for by that same act He sought to flood her with hope in the transfiguration of the whole Mystical Body; because the glorification of the Head must some day beam forth unto the glorification of every member." Yes, this is the one great concern of the Church and the aim of all liturgy — to make the members of the Mystical Body participate ever more fully in Christ's divine glory.

4. **Pope St. Sixtus II.** Today is also a feast of martyrs, Pope Sixtus II (257–258) and his deacons. During the Decian persecution Pope Sixtus continued to celebrate the sacred mysteries in a chapel above the catacomb of St. Callistus. A surprise arrest was made, and after finishing the holy Sacrifice the Pope was beheaded along with the four deacons who had assisted him. Two others were martyred on the same day, and the archdeacon Lawrence three day later.

5. **The Meaning of the Transfiguration** (a) for the apostles, (b) for us, and (c) for the liturgy.

a) For the apostles the transfiguration formed part of their training. It should have disposed them to believe in the divinity of Christ, even during His passion and death. In particular, the three favored apostles should have become sufficiently mature to remain faithful during their Master's deepest humiliation on Olivet and Calvary.

b) For us the transfiguration is, and will always remain, heaven's testimony to Christ's divinity. All the miracles of Christ served this end, to reveal the divinity of Christ. Jesus passed His life on earth as a poor, ordinary, simple Jew. But at the transfiguration, one may say, He threw off the dark mantle of humanity and revealed Himself in full divine splendor. In spirit we gaze upon Him glorified and say: "Lord, I believe. Thou art the Christ, the Son of the living God." Yet another truth is proclaimed in today's mystery, viz., some day we too will be glorified. Using words from St. Paul, the Breviary tells what today's feast anticipates: "We eagerly await a Savior, our Lord Jesus Christ. He will refashion the body of our lowliness and conform it to the body of His glory."

c) Lastly, what is the import of the transfiguration to the liturgy itself? Remember, the liturgical texts not only serve to give instruction; their principal function is to signify that which actually takes place. What once happened during the night on Mount Tabor happens again every time the holy Sacrifice is offered. We may see only the simple appearances upon the altar, but with the eyes of faith we behold the glorified Christ; we see, in fact, the King of glory with His court, the saints of the Old and New Covenant. Liturgy actualizes in our very presence the sanctifying act of Christ at His transfiguration.

It is, therefore, not only Christ who becomes transfigured — He allows me to share His glory. The holy Eucharist is the sacrament of transfiguration, for it is "the seed of glory." The purpose of the liturgy is the divine transfiguration of the participants. Understand the Gospel as a description of what the liturgy strives to effect and to perfect. Awareness of these truths seems presupposed by an ancient mosaic in the Church of St. Apollinaris at Ravenna. St. Apollinaris is pictured standing in paradise, surrounded by his congregation (twelve lambs); above him there is a veiled representation of Christ's transfiguration (*crux gemmata*), in front of which are three lambs (Peter, James, John), Moses and Elias. The whole design cries out: *Through the liturgy this congregation of St. Appollinaris is being transfigured into Christ.*

August 7

ST. CAJETAN, Confessor

Trust in divine Providence

1. St. Cajetan. *Day of death*: August 7, 1547. *Canonized*: 1671; feast 1682. *Grave*: at Naples, in the Church of St. Paul.

Life. Cajetan, a co-founder of the Theatines, received the office of protonotary at Rome from Pope Julius II when still quite young. After he was ordained priest in 1516, he left the papal court and dedicated himself entirely to the service of the Lord. With his own hands he cared for the sick. Such zeal did he show for the salvation of his fellowmen that he was surnamed the "huntsman for souls."

In order to raise the standards of ecclesiastical discipline among the clergy, Cajetan founded in 1524 a community of Clerks Regular who were to lead an apostolic life. They were to look with disdain upon all earthly belongings, to receive no income, to accept no salaries from the faithful; only from that which was freely offered were they allowed to retain the means of livelihood. Thus they were to rely unreservedly upon divine Providence.

St. Cajetan often prayed eight hours daily. He was particularly active during the Breviary reform under Pope Clement VII. He was kind, mild, but above all, humble. He asked God that no one should know the place of his burial. While attending the Christmas celebration at St. Mary of the Crib, he is said to have been given the grace of receiving from Mary the Child Jesus into his arms. During the sack of Rome by the soldiers of Charles V in 1527, he was tortured and cast into prison because he refused to surrender certain church monies which, in fact, he had distributed among the poor. An insurrection filled him with such grief and sorrow that he took sick and died.

2. Holy Mass (Os justi). Apart from the Collect and the Gospel, the Mass is from the Common of Confessors (explained on p. 402). In the *Collect* the Church isolates the principal virtue of our saint, utter trust in God and longing for heaven, and places it before us for imitation: "Because of his intercession and example may we always trust in You and desire only the things of heaven." In the *Gospel* Christ announces to us the "glad tidings" of God's Providence: "See the birds of the sky? Never do they sow or reap or fill up granaries. Still your heavenly Father feeds them. Surely you are much more dear to Him than they! And see the wild flowers — how they grow! Neither do they work nor weave; but I say to you that Solomon in all his glory never was arrayed like one of them."

In today's logbook the Church enters two imperatives. The first is found at sunrise: "Do not be anxious, saying: What shall we eat? or, What shall we drink? Your Father knows that you need all these things." The second comes at sunset: "Seek first the kingdom of God and His justice! Then all these things will be given you besides."

3. St. Donatus. "At Arezzo in Tuscany the death of the holy bishop Donatus. Besides other miracles, he restored, by means of his prayer, a chalice broken by pagans, according to the account of Pope St. Gregory I. He was slain under Julian the Apostate about the year 363" (*Martyrology*). A proper *Oration* points up the dignity of the priesthood. Christ is called the "glory of His priests," because the priestly character renders the soul like to Him. *Postcommunion*: God has made us "both sharers and stewards of His holy mysteries"; with the help of St. Donatus may we profit from our fellowship with him in the faith and in the practice of virtue.

4. Particular Examen — the Liturgical Way. The exercise known as the "particular examination of conscience" introduced by St. Ignatius has become part of present-day piety. It consists in that a particular virtue or vice is isolated and made the special object of scrutiny during the examination of one's conscience. This practice is a means unto perfection. The Church has been doing something similar for quite some time. When a saint is outstanding in a particular virtue, she focuses attention on that virtue and urges its imitation. We have a good example of this today. How does the Church proceed?

In a fourfold way: (1) First she sketches the life of the saint and calls attention to his most outstanding virtue; this at Matins. For words instruct but example moves. St. Cajetan gives us an example of absolute trust in God. (2) The Church wants us to pray. In the Collect we pray for that virtue; and we pray not merely once — during the course of the day we repeat the same prayer six times, at the end of each Hour. It is the day's principal prayer, the climax to each Hour. (3) The virtue in question is brought up for consideration in a special manner during holy Mass. The Church instructs us about it in the Foremass; from the lips of Christ we hear the beautiful passage on the providence of the heavenly Father toward His children. Then, in the Liturgy of the Eucharist, the Church bedews her teaching with grace from the sacrificial Banquet. The Oblation and Communion grace that is special today is trust in God's Providence. (4) Lastly, as a song in our hearts the Church would have us carry along the Gospel's primary message through the day. At sunrise, therefore, our voices chant the words, "Do not be anxious. . . ." And at sunset, "Seek first the kingdom of God. . . ." Thus does the Church show her genius in fostering growth in virtue.

August 8

ST. JOHN VIANNEY, Confessor
STS. CYRIAC, LARGUS, SMARAGDUS, Martyrs

They shall lay their hands upon the sick and they shall become well

1. St. John Vianney. *Day of death*: August 4, 1859. *Grave*: his well-preserved body remains enshrined at Ars. *Life*. The humble pastor of little Ars, who was canonized by Pope XI during the jubilee year of 1925, is now venerated throughout the universal Church. Born in 1786 of simple peasants, he was reared in a Christian way during the upheavals of the French Revolution. First a cowherd, later a schoolmaster, then a seminarian. He was ordained priest in 1815. Soon thereafter he was appointed pastor of Ars, at that time a tiny community of about five hundred persons who, for the most part, had fallen away from the practices of religion. Here until the end of his life he displayed an indefatigable activity that was exceptionally rich in blessings

He was untiring in the confessional. Whole trains of pilgrims came regularly to Ars; their number has been estimated as twenty thousand annually. His unusually severe life, his lovable and simple manner joined with supernatural strength and unction under a humble exterior, effected this influx from all grades of society. An ideal for all priests! He died on August 4, 1859. *Application*. The Collect praises his zeal for souls, his spirit of prayer and penance, and asks that by his example and intercession we too may win the souls of our brothers for Christ. The Mass is taken from the Common of Confessors (*Os justi*, p. 402).

2. St. Cyriac and Companions. *Day of death*: March 16, ca. 309. *Grave*: their remains were interred on the Salarian Way by the priest John. On the present day Pope St. Marcellus transferred them to the villa of Lucina on the Ostian Way. Later they were brought back to Rome and placed in the Church of St. Praxedes and in other churches. The transfer of St. Cyriac's relics to Neuhausen near Wurms has no basis in history. *Life*. The *Acts* concerning these martyrs give many fictional details. Together with Sisinius, Largus and Smaragdus, Cyriac languished a long time in prison. Among the miracles that Cyriac worked was that of freeing through his prayer Arthemia, the daughter of Emperor Diocletian, from an evil spirit. Thereupon he was sent to the Persian king Sapor and performed a similar miracle in favor of his daughter Jobias. But after baptizing the king and 430 of his entourage, he returned to Rome. Upon orders from Maximian the Emperor, he was arrested, chained, and dragged to prison. Four days later he was taken from confinement, drenched with seething pitch, and tortured on the rack; in company with Smaragdus and twenty other Christians he finally was beheaded on the Via Salaria near the gardens of Sallust."

Popular piety has numbered St. Cyriac among the "Fourteen Sainted Helpers." The existence of a martyr with this name seems well attested by the trustworthy *Depositio Martyrum* of 354. The remaining details in the above account are pure fiction. But the story may bring to mind that endless series of heroic souls who suffered for Christ even more dreadful tortures than those fiction describes.

3. Holy Mass (Timete). From some early century comes this beautiful Mass with proper texts related to the life of St. Cyriac. The formulary can be better understood if in spirit we place ourselves in the company of the ancient Church at the grave of our holy martyr. On the day preceding the anniversary of his martyrdom, Christians would come to the chapel at the grave, bringing along their sick and passing the night in vigil with them. Miracle-cures at a martyr's tomb were not infrequent. The *Gospel* and *Communion* were selected for that reason. Moreover, the accounts about St. Cyriac describe the wonderful cures he wrought.

Though miracles at martyrs' tombs no longer are as numerous as formerly, they still do occur. The *Communion* lists two miracles that are wrought daily by the holy Eucharist and the intercession of martyrs, viz., devils are cast out and spiritual diseases are healed. By its very nature the holy Eucharist can do this. Psalm 33, the favorite Communion chant of the ancient Church, runs through the Mass in motif fashion. It is sung three times, at the *Introit, Gradual*, and *Communion*. The *Epistle* we must regard as a sermon from the lips of the deacon Cyriac; he is thankful to God for two reasons: (a) because we welcome his message as God's word (one of the duties of deacons is that of preaching); (b) because in suffering and persecution we have remained steadfast. (Do his words actually apply to us?)

4. Attitudes toward Miracles. Very often the Breviary relates miracles wrought by the saints. How should we evaluate these accounts? Are we bound to believe them? May we regard them as fictitious? The first point in this regard is that miracles not contained in sacred Scripture do not belong to the deposit of Catholic faith. Accordingly we are under no obligation to believe them. Such miracles must stand the test of credibility. If founded upon sufficient evidence we accept them. If not, we withhold our consent. It is easy to see that in the Breviary narratives of the lives of the saints many unhistorical details are included; it may well be that these details were never intended to be taken as historical data but as imaginative embellishment to foster piety.

History has always been more an art than a science; only in recent centuries has the idea become prevalent that history excludes fiction. A scientific analysis of this modern approach would provide sufficient evidence for the fictitious nature of that position. We are still in the kindergarten stage in the matter of applying sound principles of hermeneutics to liturgical, patristic, and hagiographical texts.

The fact that miracles have happened in the Church and will continue to happen comes as the joyous conclusion to today's Gospel: "And these signs shall attend those who believe: in My name they shall cast out devils. . . ." Our Savior expressly says that the power to work miracles will always remain with the Church in witness to the truth she professes. Therefore we ought not be adamant in unbelief. But why are miracles seemingly so infrequent? In the early Church they occurred quite regularly. This question is answered in today's Office. Miracles were a necessity to the infant Church. To increase the number of the faithful, the new religion required divine confirmation repeatedly. Something similar is done in the natural order. When we plant young trees, we water them until they become firmly rooted. But then we stop. Miracles, therefore, take place more seldom now because the ordinary ways of grace prove sufficient.

However, let us not forget that miracles of grace still occur, miracles that are wrought in the depths of the soul. Of such miracles of grace every pastor is aware, also every Christian. Here on a loftier plane take place all the wonders of which Christ speaks; devils are driven out, i.e., sins and passions are overcome; men speak in a new tongue, i.e., the language of love and prayer; sicknesses are healed, i.e., spiritual ills of every type. Today's Communion teaches us that these spiritual miracles are wrought by the Eucharist. Believe firmly in the Church's power to perform miracles!

VIGIL OF ST. LAWRENCE

Lavishly he gives to the poor

1. The Vigil. The Roman Church is preparing to celebrate in a worthy manner the heavenly birthday of one of her greatest heroes. Familiarity with the Church year has made us familiar with the youthful deacon Lawrence; he is, for instance, the patron of catechumens and as such accompanies them yearly into the arena of the great Lenten fast (station on Septuagesima Sunday). His martyrdom upon the gridiron is often used as a symbol of the battle against our lower nature; to this end in the prayers after Mass we pray "that God may extinguish in us the flames of our vices even as Lawrence overcame the fiery flames."

It is hardly possible for us to realize fully what a vigil-service meant to the early Christians. On the evening before the feast the faithful came to the chapel where the saint was buried and brought with them their sick. The Roman vigil consisted mostly of readings, chants, and prayers by the bishop; of this we have an excellent example at the Easter Vigil service. The holy place of burial, the readings from the *Acts* of the martyrs, the sincere prayers of the faithful made the martyr-saint live again in their midst. At sunrise they celebrated the holy Sacrifice and partook of the Eucharistic "funeral meal" and thereby united themselves mystically with Christ and the holy martyr.

The death-knell to this venerable service was sounded when it became customary to relegate the vigil to the morning of the previous day. Nevertheless, with effort we may retain something of its spirit. A vigil is a day of penance. Those who are accustomed to receive the sacrament of penance frequently will likewise avail themselves of the opportunities offered on vigils and Ember days. A vigil is an occasion for cleaning house spiritually — a day of fasting in the broad sense, a day of prayer, a day of mortification, of ascetical acts. And almsgiving always accompanies fasting. (Today's vigil is mentioned as far back as the fourth century in the *Life of St. Melania*.)

2. Holy Mass (Dispersit). The formulary dates to an early century and seems to accent that which *preceded* Lawrence's martyrdom, viz., (a) the distribution of the goods of the Church among the poor (*Intr.* and *Grad.*); (b) the call to follow the Lord (*Gosp.* and *Comm.*); (c) earnest prayer (*Epist.* and *Off.*). The *Offertory* describes the spirit with which St. Lawrence came before the judgment seat of God: "My prayer is pure. Therefore I ask that my voice be heard in heaven; let my supplication ascend to the Lord." Today we are the "poor" upon whom the Lord bestows the treasures of the Church through the hand of our saint (*Grad.*); but to us also comes the call to follow the path of the Cross (*Comm.*); then too we beseech God to grant us the strength needed to follow this path (*Coll.*) and joyously thank Him for being "our helper and protector": "You preserved me from the oppressive flames that surrounded me, so that in the midst of the fire I was not consumed" (*Epist.*). This applied literally to St. Lawrence; it applies also to us in any affliction. For Mass formularies as old and venerable as today's we ought cherish a deep reverence; they are like the tools used by great masters.

August 10

ST. LAWRENCE, Martyr

The blows of the executioner, flames, torments, chains,
the faith of blessed Lawrence alone could conquer.
Weeping, Damasus has decked this altar with gifts,
in admiration of the merits of so illustrious a martyr!
— Inscription of Pope Damasus on our martyr's tomb

1. St. Lawrence. This young deacon and heroic martyr is numbered among those saints who were most highly venerated by the ancient Roman Church. Next to the feast of Sts. Peter and

Paul, that of St. Lawrence ranked highest in the Roman sanctoral cycle. "From the rising of the sun unto its setting," says St. Leo, "whenever the glory of Levites beams forth in splendor, Rome is deemed no less illustrious because of Lawrence than Jerusalem because of Stephen."

Even though we have no genuine account of St. Lawrence's martyrdom, we do possess considerable evidence from most ancient times regarding the particulars of his passion. Legendary *Acts* tell how Lawrence was a disciple of Pope Sixtus II (257–258), who dearly loved him because of his special talents, but principally because of his innocence; in spite of his youth, the Pope numbered him among the seven deacons of Rome and raised him to the position of archdeacon. As such, Lawrence had the immediate care of the altar and was at the side of the saintly Pope whenever he offered the holy Sacrifice; to him also was confided the administration of the goods of the Church and the responsibility of caring for the poor.

During the persecution of Emperor Valerian (253–260), Sixtus II and his four deacons were martyred. Very ardently Lawrence desired to die with his spiritual father and therefore said to him: "Father, where are you going without your son? Where are you hastening, O priest, without your deacon? Never before did you offer the holy Sacrifice without assistants. In what way have I displeased you? In what way have you found me unfaithful in my office? Oh, try me again and prove to yourself whether you have chosen an unworthy minister for the service of the Church. So far you have been trusting me with distributing the Blood of the Lord."

This loving complaint of joyous self-oblation Sixtus answered with words of prophecy: "I am not forsaking you, my son; a severer trial is awaiting you for your faith in Christ. The Lord is considerate toward me because I am a weak old man. But for you a most glorious triumph is in store. Cease to weep, for already after three days you will follow me" (see August 6). After these comforting words he admonished him to distribute all the remaining Church goods allocated to the poor. While Lawrence was dispersing these items in the house of a certain Narcissus, a blind man named Crescentius asked for healing help by the imposition of hands. The holy deacon made the Sign of the Cross over him and the man began to see.

From his relations with Pope Sixtus, it was known that he acted as the steward over the Church's property. He was arrested therefore and placed under the watch of a certain Hippolytus. There in prison Lawrence cured the blind Lucillus and several other blind persons; impressed thereby, Hippolytus embraced the faith and died a martyr (see August 13). Ordered by the authorities to surrender the treasures of the Church, Lawrence asked for two days time during which to gather them. The request was granted and he brought together in the house of Hippolytus the poor and the sick whom he had supported. These he led to the judge. "Here are the treasures of the Church!"

Lawrence was tortured, scourged, and scorched with glowing plates. In the midst of excruciating pain he prayed: "Lord Jesus Christ, God from God, have mercy on Your servant!" And he besought the grace of faith for the bystanders. At a certain point the soldier Romanus exclaimed: "I see before you an incomparably beautiful youth. Hasten and baptize me." He had observed how an angel dried the wounds of Lawrence with a linen cloth during his passion.

Again during the night he was dragged before the judge and threatened with immediate death. But he replied: "My God I honor and Him alone I serve. Therefore I do not fear your torments; this night shall become as brightest day and as light without any darkness." When placed upon the glowing gridiron, he jested with his executioners and the cruel tyrant. " Now you may turn me over, my body is roasted enough on this side." Shortly after this had been done, he cried again: "At last I am finished; you may now take from me and eat." Then turning to God in prayer: "I thank You, O Lord, that I am permitted to enter Your portals." To comfort him during his torments God said to him: "My servant, do not be afraid. I am with you." He was put to death upon the Viminal Hill and buried on the Tiburtinian Way.

Such the passion and death of this Christian hero, a story that in the Roman Breviary is told by the antiphons and responsories. Already in Constantine's time there was erected over his grave a church that belonged to the seven major basilicas of Rome, St. Lawrence Outside the Walls.

2. Today's Celebration. We will try to draw out from this feast its full liturgical richness. The Divine Office, notwithstanding an external simplicity, is highly dramatic and stimulating. First Vespers may be regarded as a festive reception for the saint. Matins, cast in classic lines, strikes home powerfully. "Crowned a martyr, blessed Lawrence is keeping triumph in heaven! Come, let us adore the Lord" (*Invitatory*). The psalms, though quite common and familiar, are framed with such vivid antiphons that we seem to be witnesses to the scene. The Readings of the first nocturn formulate the saint's thanksgiving prayer at his martyrdom; thereupon follow further antiphons describing his passion, and finally Pope St. Leo's homily.

With special devotion we pray the psalm Lawrence said while suffering upon the heated grid: "You are putting my heart to the test and searching it by night. You are testing me by fire, but no wickedness is found in me" (cf. *Gradual*). Rising with alacrity from bed to chant Lauds with our saint, we sense new meaning in the morning psalm (62): *Adhaesit anima mea post te,* "My soul becomes entwined about You, as with flames my flesh is consumed for You, my God."

Then holy Mass. What a glorious holocaust: Christ — Lawrence — the Christian community! These three constitute the oblation; the mystery is that of the buried kernel of corn (*Epist.* and *Gosp.*). The seed is Christ, "put to death through the malice of the Jews but multiplied through the faith of millions." The seed is Lawrence, hidden in the soil but multiplied through his example and intercession; countless Christians have become inflamed with love towards Christ because of him. And lastly, the seed is the holy Eucharist; it is sown in the field of human souls to spring up multiplied in all the activities of truly Christian lives. Here too it holds true: "He who sows sparingly will reap sparingly, while he who sows bountifully will also reap bountifully."

If we live a life that is rich and full liturgically and Eucharistically, we have sown the seed "bountifully," and there is solid hope for an abundant harvest. So throughout the day, at my side stands Lawrence, the youthful hero of holy love for Christ. And when a sorrow or a temptation comes, he says to me: "It's still a far way to the gridiron!" One of the official thanksgiving prayers after Mass asks that "God may extinguish the flames of lust within us even as He enabled Lawrence to conquer the flames of fire." In the Lateran palace there was a chapel in honor of St. Lawrence where the Pope divested and made his thanksgiving; that practice gives the background for the prayer.

3. Pope St. Leo's Homily at Matins. "When the fury of pagan might was being hurled against the elect members of Christ's Body, and in particular against those in holy Orders, that godless magistrate proceeded with full violence against the Levite Lawrence, who was illustrious not only for his ministry at the sacred rites but also for his administration of the Church's material goods. By arresting him he foresaw a twofold advantage for himself: he hoped to force him to surrender the treasures of the Church and to forsake the true religion. That avaricious magistrate, that enemy of the truth, equipped himself with a double weapon — with greed to rob and with godlessness to take Christ away. He ordered the upright guardian of the sacred treasures to hand over the monies of the Church upon which his heart was so greedily set. And the chaste Levite showed him where he stored them. Into his presence he brought a great number of good, poor people, those for whom he provided food and clothing from the Church's inalienable goods; thereby he had rendered it the more inviolate to the degree it was better expended.

"Angered by the frustration of his plans for easy prey and burning with hatred against a religion that advocated such dispersal of wealth, he proceeded to snatch away a still more precious good. From the holy deacon who possessed no earthly wealth he sought to take that supreme treasure which makes one rich for eternity. He commanded Lawrence to deny Christ and put his courage and constancy to severest test by the most gruesome tortures. When initial cruelties brought no results, more violent ones were applied. Finally he commanded that those limbs, torn and lacerated by countless strokes under the lash, be placed over fire and roasted. Upon an iron grate aglow from the flames beneath, his body was placed and slowly rolled about, extending the agony and making the pain more intense.

"O monstrous cruelty, you are gaining nothing, attaining nothing! A mortal body will be consumed by your tortures, and while Lawrence enters heaven you will stand there helpless alongside your fire. The fire of love for Christ cannot be burned away by your kind of flame, because the fire that burns under the grate is weaker than that which smolders in Lawrence's breast. O persecutor, you believe in venting your rage against the martyrs; but you are only making their crown the more glorious as you intensify your torments. Your very ingenuity has added to the honor of those who conquer, for even the tools of torture serve to enhance their triumph!

"Dearly beloved, we must therefore rejoice in holy joy and be happy in the Lord over the sublime passion of this singular individual whom He has placed before us as protector and model. For the Lord indeed is wonderful in His saints. Thereby He has spread His majesty throughout the world, so that everywhere, from the rising of the sun unto its setting, wherever the glory of Levites beams forth in splendor, Rome is deemed no less illustrious because of Lawrence than Jerusalem because of Stephen."

August 11

STS. TIBURTIUS AND SUSANNA, Martyrs

Witnesses to Christ

1. **Sts. Tiburtius and Susanna.** *Day of death*: August 11, about the year 303. *Grave*: Tiburtius was buried in the cemetery on the Lavicanian Way; Pope Gregory IV transferred the body to St. Peter's. Susanna rests in a church dedicated to her honor at Rome. *Life.* A sense of reverential awe and deep respect fills us whenever we meet the martyrs of the ancient Church. Yet it is often very difficult to give a strictly historical account of their lives. Nevertheless, even though we do not know all the biographical details, they are for us representatives of that "army of light," the martyrs, witnesses to Christ. And we want to be inspired by their example.

Today the *Martyrology* tells this: "At Rome, between the two laurel trees, the death of the holy martyr Tiburtius. During the persecution of Diocletian the magistrate Fabian forced him to tread barefoot upon burning coals. As it only served to make him profess the faith more boldly, he was ordered to be led outside the

city until the third milestone and there beheaded. . . . At Rome,
the holy virgin Susanna. She came from an illustrious family, and
was the niece of the saintly Pope Caius. At the time of Diocletian
she won the palm of martyrdom by being beheaded."

2. Holy Mass (Salus autem) for the feast is from the Common
of Martyrs (see p. 391). Only the *Epistle* is proper (Heb. 11:33–
39). This brief passage covers the whole gamut of suffering to
which the martyrs were subjected — all in order to give testimony
to Christ. Listening to it makes us feel small. What sacrifices do
we bring for the faith? Note, too, how this selection becomes so
much more incisive if in spirit we place ourselves at the martyr's
tomb, seeing his wounds bleeding afresh.

3. What Do Martyrs Tell Us? Even though centuries separate
us from the ancient martyrs and the extant accounts of their lives
and sufferings are not always worthy of credence, the liturgy
tenaciously, even enthusiastically, fosters their cult. The martyrs
are the Church's foremost heroes, they are the nobility in God's
kingdom, the most illustrious members of Christ's Mystical Body.
What is martyrdom? Martyr means "witness," i.e., to Christ.
Originally martyrs were called confessors, i.e., one who proclaimed himself a disciple of Christ (see today's Gospel: "Whosoever shall confess Me before men. . . . "). The Christian who
proclaims his faith in Christ by sharing with the poor his property, his position in life, and his time and efforts is in a very true
sense a martyr.

The martyr practices the three theological virtues in a perfect
manner: faith, by proclaiming and bearing witness to it with his
blood; love, for who would surrender his life for something he
does not cherish? "Greater love than this no one has, that one lay
down his life for his friends"; and hope, because no one would
renounce the joys and goods of life, even life itself, without expecting a higher good and a nobler existence.

One point more — the martyr stands closest to Christ. He fulfills literally Christ's imperative on taking up one's cross and following Him. He identifies himself with the Savior in suffering
and in death. He fills up in his body the sufferings which are

lacking in the Mystical Christ. The Mystical Christ, even as the historical Christ, has an appointed measure of suffering to contribute, and this the martyrs in particular bear for the whole Mystical Body. Therefore they are the principal benefactors of the Mystical Christ, the Church.

From what has been said, we easily see the great benefits which may be derived from cherishing the ideal of martyrdom and venerating those who attained it. To most Christians, God does not grant the grace of actual martyrdom; but its essential traits every Catholic should and must possess. All Catholics must profess their faith, even to the loss of earthly goods. Try using the Sunday *Credo* as your official profession of faith — to be actualized during the ensuing week. All Catholics must show their love for Christ, if not through sacrificing their lives, at least through acceptance of the sufferings sent by God. In hope all Catholics must raise their gaze above this earthly life to the future one. And lastly, they must venerate suffering as a holy gift, even love it. The sufferings of life are to be borne in the spirit of martyrdom. As there is a priesthood common to all and a special priesthood, so too there is a common and a special martyrdom. This latter, which forms the "shining host of martyrs clothed with white garments and palms in their hands," we wish to join at each martyr-feast by our presence at the altar with the King of martyrs.

August 12

ST. CLARE, Virgin

O Lord, do not deliver over to beasts souls that praise You

1. **St. Clare.** *Day of death*: August 11, 1253. *Canonized*: 1255; feast, 1670. *Grave*: for six hundred years her body remained buried in the Church of the Poor Clares at Assisi until Pius IX in 1850 ordered the grave to be opened and the relics to be raised. The remains, in particular the head with all the teeth,

were found perfectly intact. *Picture*: as a nun holding a vessel containing the holy Eucharist. *Life*. A delicate veil of holy, Christ-like love envelops the life of this co-worker of St. Francis of Assisi. She is the foundress of the Poor Clares, the cloistered, contemplative female branch of the Franciscan Order.

The Breviary says of her: "Following the example of St. Francis, she distributed all her possessions among the poor. She fled from the noise of the world and betook herself to a country chapel, where St. Francis himself sheared off her hair and clothed her with a penitential garb (on March 18, 1212, at the age of eighteen). Then she resided at the Church of St. Damian, where the Lord provided for her a goodly number of companions. So she established a community of nuns and acted as their superior at the wish of St Francis. For forty-two years she directed the nunnery with zeal and prudence, her own life serving as a constant sermon for her sisters to emulate. Of Pope Innocent IV she requested the privilege that she and her community live in absolute poverty. She was a most perfect follower of St. Francis of Assisi.

"When the Saracens were besieging Assisi and were preparing to attack the convent, St. Clare asked to be assisted as far as the entrance, for she was ill. In her hand she carried a vessel containing the blessed Eucharist as she prayed: O Lord, do not deliver over to beasts the souls that praise You! (Ps. 73). Protect Your servants, for You have redeemed them by Your precious Blood. And in the midst of that prayer a voice was heard, saying: Always will I protect you! The Saracens took to flight."

Heroic in suffering (she was sick for twenty-seven years), she was canonized only two years after her death. Thomas of Celano coined the saying: *Clara nomine, vita clarior, clarissima moribus.* In the Missal we follow the beautiful bridal Mass, *Dilexisti,* from the Common (explained on p. 406).

2. Holy Poverty. Clare was the first flower in the garden of the Poor Man of Assisi. Poor in earthly goods, but rich in her utter poverty, she was a replica of Jesus, poor in the crib and on the Cross. At her time the Church generally and many Church men were enmeshed in financial matters and political maneuvering. Through the renewal of the ideal of poverty, St. Francis effected a "reform of Christian life in head and members."

In our twentieth century there still remain large areas with millions suffering under extreme poverty. Poverty in itself is no virtue; but it should be made into a virtue. Let us recall a few of the examples and texts from holy Scripture which show how precious poverty is and what deep reverence we should have toward it. Christ was poor. His entrance into the world and His departure from it took place in circumstances of greatest need. He had no house wherein to be born, no crib; no house wherein to die, no deathbed. Poverty stood watch at birth and remained to see His death. "The foxes have dens and the birds of the air have nests; but the Son of Man has nowhere to lay His head" (Matt. 3:20).

He chose poor men as His disciples, men who were obliged to abandon even that little which they possessed. He came "to bring the good news to the poor" (Luke 4:18). In declaring the charter of His kingdom (Sermon on the Mount), His first article was: "Blessed are you poor, for yours is the kingdom of God. Blessed are you who hunger now, for you shall be satisfied" (Luke 6:20–21). Of His disciples He demanded poverty. He once said to them: "Amen, I say to you, with difficulty will a rich man enter the kingdom of heaven. And further I say to you, it is easier for a camel to pass through the eye of a needle than for a rich man to enter the kingdom of heaven. The disciples, hearing this, were exceedingly astonished and said: Who then can be saved? And looking upon them, Jesus said to them: With men this is impossible, but with God all things are possible" (Matt. 19:23ff.).

Now, the phrase "kingdom of heaven" or "kingdom of God" does not mean God's kingdom in heaven but God's kingdom upon earth, the Church. Christ was saying: "With difficulty will a rich man be a Christian!" Experience has proven the truth of His words. St. Paul was obliged to confirm this point to the Corinthians: "Consider your own call, brethren. There were among you not many wise according to the flesh, not many mighty, not many noble. But the foolish things (in the eyes) of the world has God chosen to put to shame the wise, and the weak things of the world has God chosen to put to shame the strong, and the things that are not, to bring to naught the things that are; lest any flesh should pride itself before Him" (1 Cor. 1:26ff.). In these words St. Paul laid down a fundamental tenet of Christianity which holds for all times: *Only the poor are true children of God* — it requires special blessing for the rich to be genuine Christians.

These considerations should make poverty more attractive and lovable to us again. Whoever has poverty as his companion should embrace her, live joyfully with her, and be grateful for her realm of spiritual riches. And those who have money must cherish the spirit of poverty. How we ought to love a certain responsory that keeps recurring throughout this month:

> Two things I have asked of Thee,
>   deny them not to me before I die:
> Give me neither beggary nor riches!
> Allow me only the necessities for life.

At least we can be moderate and frugal, and thereby find the way to the spirit of Christian poverty. St. Clare, help us.

August 13

STS. HIPPOLYTUS AND CASSIAN, Martyrs

The white-robed army of martyrs praises You

1. **St. Hippolytus.** The biography of this saint has been greatly obscured by legend, which has made him a soldier, the prison-warden of St. Lawrence, and a martyr. Actually he was a disciple of St. Ireneus, a priest and an illustrious teacher in the Roman Church. Later, sorry to say, the first anti-pope. Because of his rigorism he became involved in a controversy with Pope Callistus I (217–222), but atoned for this failing by martyrdom. He is the author of numerous works and attained popularity even in the Eastern Church.

Happily the schism did not last long. Together with Pontian, the rival Pope, he was exiled to the "death island" of Sardinia, where both died. The remains of Hippolytus were accorded a special burial place near that of St. Lawrence on the Tiburtinian Way. Later his body was transferred to the cloister of the Holy Redeemer upon the Leteninian Hill near Riezi. A marble statue of classic cast was found in the catacomb near St. Lawrence.

2. St. Cassian. At Imola, on this same day, the martyr Cassian underwent cruel torments. With hands bound behind his back, the judge delivered him over to his students to be pricked to pieces with iron styles. The small wounds from those little rascals lengthened his time of torment but also made his crown more glorious. He suffered during the persecution of Diocletian (*Breviary*). In the bishop's chapel at Ravenna there is a mosaic of St. Cassian that dates from the fifth century.

The Mass is from the Common of Martyrs, *Salus autem,* explained on p. 391.

3. The Liturgical Life of Christians at Rome in Post-Apostolic Times. It may scandalize us moderns to learn that St. Hippolytus fell into a quarrel with the lawful Pope. His contemporaries, however, did not judge him so harshly. Moreover, we may say with St. Augustine: "Branches too numerous or luxuriant upon the Christian tree, the heavenly Surgeon cut off with the knife of martyrdom."

Our interest in the liturgy makes St. Hippolytus' book, *The Apostolic Traditions,* particularly precious because it shows the liturgical life of the Christian at Rome in the first centuries. In it we find a description of the ancient Mass with the oldest texts, also the prayers at baptism, at the agape, etc. What interests us most, however, is the liturgical life of the early Christians. We shall center our attention upon three points: the Eucharist, the Divine Office, and the reading of Scripture. Daily Mass at that time was unknown, for only on Sundays was the holy Sacrifice offered. The faithful took the consecrated Bread home with them. And they were bidden to "watch carefully that no one not of the faith eat of the Eucharist. or that a mouse or something else come upon it, or that part of it spoil. It is the Body of Christ, the Food of all the faithful, and it should never cause disgust" (*ch.* 29). There was no difference between ordinary bread and that set apart for the Eucharist.

The Christians were admonished to come often to church in order to be instructed in the word of God: "They should remember that they are hearing God speak through the instructor. . . . The God-fearing Christian should feel that he is suffering a great loss if he does not go to the place where he will be taught the faith. And when an occasional speaker comes, let no one of you miss going to church . . . you will hear things of which you had never thought and benefit from that which the Holy Spirit gives you through the mouth of His preacher; thus your faith will be strengthened through what you hear. Therefore let everyone endeavor to go to church in that place where the Spirit is actually speaking. But if on some particular day there be no instructions, let everyone take up the holy Scriptures at home and read such a portion as to him seems beneficial" (*ch.* 32).

Of special value are the admonitions given to the faithful on prayer. From these we see that the Christians of the first centuries observed hours of prayer almost as found at present in the Divine Office. Concerning *Prime*: "All the faithful, men and women, upon rising in the morning before beginning work, should wash their hands and pray to God." *Terce*: "When you are at home, pray at the third hour and praise God. But if you are away when this hour comes, pray in your heart to God. For at this hour Christ was nailed to the Cross." *Sext*: "In a similar way you should pray again at the sixth hour. For at the time when Christ was nailed to the Cross, there came a great darkness. Prayer should therefore be said in imitation of Him who prayed at that hour, viz., Christ before His death." *None*: "The ninth hour too should be made perfect by prayer and praise . . . in that hour Christ was pierced by the spear." *Vespers*: "Once more ought you to pray before you go to bed."

Matins: "At midnight rise from your bed, wash yourself and pray. If you have a wife, pray together in antiphonal fashion. If she is not yet of the faith, withdraw and pray alone and return again to your place. If you are bound by the bond of marriage duties, do not cease your prayers, for you are not stained thereby. It is necessary that we pray at that hour (i.e., Matins), for at that hour all creation is resting and praising God. Stars, trees, water are as if they were standing still; all the hosts of angels are holding divine services together with the souls of the just. They are praising almighty God at that hour." What an inspiring passage!

Lauds: "In like manner rise and pray at the hour at which the cock crows . . . full of hope look forward to the day of eternal light that will shine upon us eternally after the resurrection from the dead." Motivation for these "hour prayers" of the early Christians was the conviction that daily they were reliving Christ's death and resurrection. Every new day was a day of resurrection, and daily they were raised with Christ on the Cross. It is an example that should spur us on to give the Mass, the Breviary, and the Bible the place of honor in our lives.

August 14

VIGIL OF THE ASSUMPTION
ST. EUSEBIUS, Confessor

We will prepare ourselves for a great feastday in Mary's honor

1. **The Vigil.** Today provides the opportunity to prepare for the summer's greatest feast, a kind of spiritual harvest festival!

Originally, vigils consisted in a celebration during the night preceding the feast; but when the service was relegated to the morning of the previous day, the vigil became a day of preparation, a day of spiritual acclimation and interior purification.

a) *Spiritual Acclimation.* What is the liturgy celebrating? First of all, Mary's *dormitio* or "falling asleep" to this life and world. The Church celebrates with great enthusiasm the "death-day" of her saints, for it is their birthday (*natale*) into heaven. Formerly today's feast was actually called *Dormitio Beatae Mariae Virginis.* Historically, of course, it is not the actual day of Mary's departure from this world. In the Greek Church the memory was celebrated originally on the eighteenth of January; it was transferred to the present date by Emperor Mauritius (582–602).

The Church, however, is not content with merely commemorating the death of Mary; rather, she is celebrating her entrance into heaven. That ascent of the Mother of God the liturgy pictures as a bridal march, a triumphal procession. We can even go a step further and include her coronation as Queen of all saints This would, however, be more in accordance with popular devotion and medieval mysticism; it is an aspect that the liturgy does not emphasize today because the accent is Christo-centric in the various prayer-forms.

Lastly, the Church celebrates the unique fact of Mary's bodily assumption into heaven. Concerning Mary's death we have no historically certain records; even the place where she died is not known (one tradition ascribes it to Ephesus, another to Jerusalem). Since the feast of All Saints, 1950, the century-long Catholic teaching that Mary was taken up bodily into heaven must be accepted as an infallibly defined dogma of faith.

b) *Interior Purification.* According to the present discipline of the Church, vigils are days of penance, days of interior purification. They provide for the penitential implications of the feast. If in spirit we are to ascend heavenwards with the Blessed Virgin tomorrow, we should today loosen ourselves from the earthly bonds that chain us to this world. If with Mary we are to make body and soul a worthy temple of the Son of God tomorrow (*virginalem aulam — Coll.*), we should today cleanse the citadel of our soul from the filth of sin. If with the most blessed among women we wish to "choose the better part, the one thing necessary" tomorrow, we should today scuttle all anxious care over the temporal, the earthly. Yes, let us prepare worthily for a great day in honor of our Lady!

2. **Holy Mass (Vultum tuum).** A touch of the lyrical enhances the beauty of our vigil Mass. The Queen-Bride is addressed in the *Introit;* we, the princes of the people, go forth to meet her, paying homage. The dogma-laden *Collect* reminds us how God Himself chose the "virginal palace" in which He deigned to live.

Mary's dignity as Mother of God constitutes the foremost reason for her exalted position on earth and in heaven; to this the *Gradual*, the *Offertory*, and the *Communion* bear witness. The *Lesson* surely ranks among the finest poetry from Scripture that the liturgy accommodates to Mary: "I am the mother of purest love, of fear, of faith, and of holy hope. Come to me, all you that desire me, and be filled with my fruits; to meditate upon me is sweeter than honey." From the lips of our blessed Mother comes this invitation to share her graces! Our response will be immediate and positive.

The *Gospel* contains the familiar passage telling of the "woman from the crowd" who invoked blessing upon the Mother of God. The Savior accords a similar blessing to all "who hear the word of God and keep it." Thus Christ Himself indicates the way by which we may become like His Mother. The *Offertory* echoes the Gospel and develops its message a step further.

3. St. Eusebius. *Day of death*: August 14, about the year 350. *Grave*: at Rome, in the cemetery of St. Callistus; later in the church dedicated to his honor. *Life*. According to the *Roman Martyrology*, the priest Eusebius was locked in a room of his house upon the command of the Arian emperor Constantius II. Here he passed seven months in constant prayer until he died. The liturgy venerates him as a confessor and priest. The church dedicated to his honor at Rome serves as station church on the Friday during the fourth week of Lent.

August 15

THE ASSUMPTION OF THE BLESSED VIRGIN MARY

Today the Virgin Mary is taken up to heaven!
Rejoice, for she reigns with Christ forever!

Now toward the end of the summer season, at a time when fruits are ripe in the gardens and fields, the Church celebrates the most glorious "harvest festival" in the Communion of Saints. Mary, the supremely blessed one among women, Mary, the most precious fruit which has ripened in the fields of God's kingdom, is today taken into the granary of heaven.

The ideal would be to keep the entire day liturgically in union with the Church, if possible by participating also in the Divine Office. New texts and new slants have been introduced into the various formularies since the formal definition of Mary's assumption, and these in particular merit our attention.

1. **Divine Office.** The feast extends from Vespers to Vespers, an Hour that through its antiphons proclaims the mystery commemorated, Mary's assumption and her sanctity as Mother of God. Matins, the Church's prayer through the night, gives dramatic expression to the dogmatic truths associated with the feast; from the Office formerly in use the psalms and responsories have been retained, but the Lessons for the most part are new selections. The hymn, *Surge!*, is a new composition. The antiphons and a series of fine responsories bespeak the glories of the heavenly Queen and Bride. Selections from both the Old Testament and the New are found as Lessons in the first nocturn, an entirely unprecedented procedure. The first Lesson is from the Book of Genesis, the Proto-evangel; the remaining two are from the fifteenth chapter of First Corinthians — St. Paul's vivid description of the resurrection of the body. As a result, the Canticle of Canticles has been, practically speaking, eliminated from the liturgy; formerly it was read each day during the octave of the Assumption.

During the second nocturn we listen to St. John Damascene, a Doctor of the Church, as he delivers a sermon on Mary's bodily assumption into heaven: "To the temple of the Lord not made by hands there today has come to rest Mary, a holy tabernacle, re-enlivened by the living God. David her father rejoices, and with him choirs of angels and archangels; choirs of Virtues and Principalities are glorifying her; choirs of Powers and of Dominations and of Thrones sing exultingly to her; the Cherubim and the Seraphim praising-chant her glory. For today the immaculate Virgin, undefiled by earthly affection, whose nourishment was heavenly thoughts, returns not again to the world with re-enlivened body but is assumed into the tabernacles of heaven.

"How could that one taste death from whom the true Life flowed out to all? Yet she did fall under the law inflicted by Him whom she bore, and as a daughter of the old Adam she suffered the old sentence of death, even as her Son who is Life itself. But now as Mother of the living God, she is fittingly taken up to heaven by Him. For how could death feed on this truly blessed one who had eagerly listened to the word of God; who at the Archangel's salutation, filled with the Holy Spirit, conceived the Son of God; who without pain gave birth to Him; whose whole being was ever consecrated to her Creator? Could hell receive such a one? Could corruption destroy a body in which Life had been brought forth?

"For her, beloved brethren, a way is prepared to heaven — a way that is straight and fair and easy. For if Christ, the Way and the Truth, has said: Where I am there also shall My servant be, does it not follow that His Mother is surely with Him?" (This homily of St. John Damascene has been somewhat abbreviated in the new Office for the Assumption.) Excerpts from the papal decree on today's mystery form the text for the sixth Lesson.

The Lessons of the third nocturn present a homily by St. Peter Canisius — or better, a sermon on truths related to the feast; for the Gospel on Martha and Mary no longer serves as part of the Mass formulary.

There are changes too throughout the Hour of Lauds. The hymn and the chapter from the Book of Judith are new, but the antiphons for the psalms and the *Benedictus* have not been altered. In the rising sun the liturgy today beholds Mary's ascent into heaven: "Who is this that comes forth as the rising dawn, fair as the moon, bright as the sun, awe-inspiring as an army set in array?"

2. The Blessing of Produce from Field and Garden. Since ancient times vegetables have been blessed on this day, yet its relation to the feast is not readily evident. In the Office, Mary is likened to fine-smelling fruits and flowers, and according to legend flowers were found in her grave in place of her body.

Most probably some pre-Christian Germanic harvest festival was Christianized and associated with her assumption.

3. Holy Mass (Signum magnum). When the dogma proper to today's mystery was solemnly defined in 1950, a new Mass formulary was promulgated that puts into even greater relief Mary's incomparable dignity and privileges. A cosmic picture from the Apocalypse is flashed before us at the *Introit*: "The woman, clothed with the sun, the moon at her feet, a crown of twelve stars about her head." Could there be a more sublime and inspiring representation of heaven's Queen than this, aglow with the radiance of the celestial orbs?

Mary was the first who shared her Son's glorification in fullest measure, body too; surely, then, do we have ample reason for breaking forth in "a new canticle." In the liturgy the word "new" has a most singular connotation in that it refers to the supernatural — the life of grace here on earth, and hereafter the "new heaven and the new earth." Our "new canticle" is sung in praise of the bodily exaltation of God's Mother, the *mirabilia* divinely wrought in her favor. If we took all of Psalm 97 into consideration, our thoughts would spontaneously regard Mary as the first glorified member of the human race that entered the courts of heaven. Thereby "the Lord made known His salvation and revealed His righteousness to all the world." By faith "all the ends of the earth see the salvation of (wrought by) our God." Thereupon paeans of praise ascend in Mary's honor from all creation. For all creation sees in her the firstfruits of its own final transfiguration into glory: "Sing praise to the Lord upon the zither . . . the sea must roar and all that it fills, the whole earth and its inhabitants. The rivers must clap their hands, the hills sing together for joy." Could there be a more magnificent overture to the Mass drama?

After formally declaring that the "immaculate Virgin and Mother of the Son of God" was "assumed body and soul into heaven's glory," the new *Collect* continues with a double application and petition; may we, while here on earth, "be ever mindful of heavenly things" and hereafter "come to share her glory." By these phrases the Collect pinpoints the feast's significance to practical-minded persons. It is the same objective that was put before us on the feast of Christ's ascension, viz., "to let our hearts dwell in heaven."

From the Book of Judith comes the selection for the first Scripture *Reading* (an excerpt from the Old Testament which, with minor modifications, already occurred in the Missal on September 15). The eulogy Israel accorded the heroine Judith is applied to the "serpent-crusher" of the New Dispensation: "With His own strength has the Lord endowed you, because through you He has vanquished our enemy" (through giving birth to Christ, the Conqueror over death and hell). Mary, therefore, is "blessed above all the women on earth . . . for God directed her to behead the prince of our enemies." It is not difficult to sense the allusion to the Vulgate text of Genesis: "She shall crush thy head." In this indirect but nonetheless definite manner the Epistle points to Mary's role in salvation-history; as the stainless Mother of the Redeemer, hers was a significant contribution to Satan's undoing. The final verse of the Reading is added from a later chapter in the Book of Judith: "You are Jerusalem's glory, Israel's joy, a halo over our people" (Jerusalem typifies the Church; Israel, Christendom). The selection for today's feast was indeed a happy choice.

The field of battle changes into a peaceful bridal scene as the Mass continues with the *Gradual*. The Mother of God, as the King's daughter and royal Bride, enters heaven's bridal chamber. We hear the divine wooing: "Listen, daughter, look, turn your ear. The King yearns for your beauty." We are witnesses as "the King's daughter, all glorious and clothed in robes of spun gold" marches into the heavenly nuptial halls. Our celebration comes to its dramatic climax with the *Alleluia* chant. Framed by heaven's own song, the *Alleluia*, our voices sing praise as "Mary is assumed into heaven; the armies of angels are exulting."

Fresh vistas are opened by the new *Gospel* chosen for today's formulary. The former Gospel described the conflicting activities of the two sisters, Martha and Mary, and was not apropos because no reference was made to the Blessed Virgin. The present pericope takes us to Elizabeth's house, the sequel to the annunciation and Gabriel's *Ave*. "Blessed art thou among women and blessed is the fruit of thy womb." The acclamation gives form and substance to the cry in Judith: "Blessed are you, O daughter, above all women." In response we hear from Mary's lips the opening strains of her wondrous *Magnificat*. Was this canticle Mary's first song upon entering in triumph heaven's glory?

For the *Offertory*, Genesis 3:15 serves instead of the usual psalm text: "I am putting enmity between you and the woman, between your descendants and hers." Again we may note a connection with the Reading. Judith "beheaded the prince of the enemy"; at the gates of paradise God spoke in terms of Mary as the "serpent-crusher."

The spirit of the feast colors the *Oratio super oblata*. The initial word *Ascendat* slants our thoughts to the Virgin Mother's assumption, but the following phrases relate it to the Offertory gifts that should ascend into the divine Presence. With the next sentence, however, we ask that Mary's assumption make our hearts "aflame with the fire of love." The glowing coals, the ascending incense as the *oblata* are censed, become present symbols of our *Secret* prayer.

Heaven opens before us at the Eucharistic Banquet, and we behold the Mother of God transfigured in glory, singing the *Magnificat*: "All generations call me blessed, because He who is mighty has done great things for me." There is no reason why we should not fill in the entire *Magnificat,* our best hymn in gratitude for mankind's redemption.

Postcommunion: "May we be brought to the glory of the resurrection through the intercession of the Blessed Virgin Mary." As the Mass liturgy comes to a close, Mother Church loves to turn our thoughts toward heaven and its beatitude (see, e.g., Postcommunion on Corpus Christi: "the eternal enjoyment of God's presence"). Now, in summary, let us count up the various scenes or events this new Mass formulary has flashed before us: at the beginning, the grand tableau of the woman clothed with the sun; at the walls of Bethulia, the heroine Judith; the celestial nuptial march of the royal Bride; the lovely young Virgin-Mother tripping over the hill country of Judea and rapping at the door of the priest Zachary's house; the prophetic vision of the "serpert-crusher" at the portals of a lost paradise; the revelation of the heaven of heavens with Mary, Queen of the Universe, singing her *Magnificat.*

4. The Martyrology lists several saints whose names we quickly recall. "At Rome on the Appian Way, the acolyte St. Tarcissus. While carrying the holy Eucharist, he was met by pagans. They began to question him as to what he carried. But, considering it an outrage to abandon pearls to dogs, he refused to tell. They knocked him down with clubs and stoned him to death. Though his murderers searched his hands and clothes thoroughly, they found no trace of the most holy Sacrament. His remains were gathered by Christians and honorably interred in the cemetery of St. Callistus."

"At Albarcale in Hungary, King St. Stephen of Hungary. Adorned with great virtues, he was the first to gain his realm for the faith. The Blessed Virgin herself accompanied him to heaven on the feast of her assumption. But a decree of Pope Innocent XI ordained that his feast be celebrated on September 2, because on that day the well-equipped fortress of Buda was finally recaptured by Christian armies, evidently through the aid of this saintly king" (1684).

"At Rome, the holy confessor Stanislaus Kostka. He was Polish by birth, became a member of the Society of Jesus. Having attained perfection at an early age, he possessed what could be regarded as the accomplishment of many years. Pope Benedict XIII canonized him."

August 16

ST. JOACHIM, Father of the Blessed Virgin

Lavishly he gives to the poor

1. St. Joachim. The father of the Blessed Virgin and the grandfather of our divine Savior! "By their fruit you will know them. Only the good tree produces good fruit!" Joachim stands before us as an upright, honest, "just" man; legend eulogizes his kindness toward the poor. It is said he divided his yearly income into three parts, assigning one part to his own living expenses, a second to the temple, and the third to the poor (the reason why the phrase, "Lavishly he gives to the poor," is repeated three times in the Mass).

Nevertheless, he was not exempted from suffering; for a long time no child was granted him. Even the priests tried to forestall him from sacrificing in the temple. Because of his childless condition, they believed that Yahweh's curse had fallen upon him. While sorrowing over his plight, grace came to console him: "The Lord is nigh unto them that are of a contrite heart" (Ps. 33), and an angel foretold the birth of Mary, the "child of grace." "For nature did not dare to precede grace; rather nature would continue waiting until grace had brought forth its fruit" (*Breviary*).

2. Holy Mass (Dispersit). St. Joachim's chief virtue, love of the poor, is the burden of the *Introit* and *Gradual*. In both, the "hymn of the just man" (Ps. 111) is appropriately accommodated. Joachim is the "man found without blemish, one who did not go after gold"; as a result, "all the church of the saints de-

clare his alms" (*Lesson*). The genealogy of the Messiah is traced
by the *Gospel*. Though Joachim is not actually mentioned (it is
conjectured that he is referred to as Heli in St. Luke's genealogy),
the liturgy wishes us to think of him as the grandfather of the
Lord, which is his unique title to veneration. By means of the
holy Sacrifice we share our saint's glory (*Off.*) and receive the
grace to imitate his virtues, especially his love of the poor and
patience in suffering; thereby we become more worthy of being
related to Christ. In conclusion we today are thankful to Joachim
for the divine wheat, Christ: "He gives them their measure of
wheat in due season" (*Comm.*).

3. Psalm 111 may be called the "hymn of the just man,"
because it outlines the just man's ideal according to the Old Law.
St. Joachim would be an example of what the psalmist had in
mind. Nevertheless, the Christian too can see his ideal in this
psalm. (In its original text Psalm 111 is alphabetical, i.e., each
of the twenty-two half-verses begins with a successive letter of the
Hebrew alphabet; this accounts for the somewhat disconnected
character of the contents.) Now let us study the composition
verse by verse.

> Good fortune to the man who reverences Yahweh,
>   who is delighted by His precepts.
> His children will be respected throughout the land,
>   because a pious generation is always blessed.
> His house is the abode for wealth and renown
>   and his virtue continues forever.
> A light unto the upright beams in the darkness:
>   the All-merciful, who is kind and gracious.
> Success to him who lends with sympathy,
>   who conducts his business justly —
>   never will he founder.
> The just man is remembered forever,
>   he need not be frightened by malicious rumors.
> Firmly his heart trusts in Yahweh;
>   he does not tremble, his heart remains strong,
>   till he gazes down upon his foes.

Lavishly he gives to the poor;
>   his upright acts will continue forever;
>   his horn is exalted in glory.
The sinner sees it and is vexed;
>   gnashing his teeth, he is consumed by jealousy.
>   For the plans of the wicked perish.

Now, how does the psalm describe the truly "just man"? First, note its two major divisions: love of God and love of neighbor. The just man "fears" God; not a slavish fear, but a reverential, loving fear, because he is delighted by God's commandments. The just man's conduct at home is detailed; and it is noted that in darkest suffering and misfortune God beams forth like a light. In simpler words, the just man has strong confidence in God in the midst of affliction.

Then, as the psalm describes his relationship to fellowmen, two points are stressed: sympathetic kindliness and justice. The just man acts kindly toward the needy and poor, he gives alms willingly, lavishly. (We know how highly almsgiving was praised in the Old Testament — the case, for instance, of Tobias 4:7ff.; 12:8ff.) Moreover, he bases all his transactions upon strict justice. Yes, he has enemies who plot to ruin him, who attempt to smother his cry, yet he does not fear; his pure conscience is like a smooth shield from which harmful arrows glide off. God is his protector and in Him he trusts. Although the tone of the psalm is that of the Old Testament, it is easily possible to read it in the light of the New.

August 17

ST. HYACINTH, Confessor

Into Your hands, Lord, I rest my spirit

1. **St. Hyacinth.** *Day of death*: August 15, 1257. *Canonized*: 1594; feast, 1625. *Grave*: in the Dominican church at Cracow.

Life. While a canon at the cathedral of Cracow, Hyacinth journeyed to Rome, was impressed by the preaching and miracles of
St. Dominic, and from the hand of Dominic himself received the
habit of the newly-founded Order. Upon returning to his native
land (1219), he established monasteries of his Order beyond the
Alps at Friesach, Prague, Olmütz, and Cracow.

From the Breviary we have this miracle. With three companions Hyacinth had arrived at the banks of the river Weichsel
during their journey to Vischegrad, where they were expected
to preach. But the waters had risen so high and had become so
violent that no ferryman dared to cross. The saint took his
mantle, spread it out before him, and with his companions rode
across the raging waters. After saying his Office for the day, he
died in 1257 with these words on his lips: "Into Your hands,
Lord, I rest my spirit!"

Application. The Church's night prayer, Compline, especially
the closing invocations, serves as a fitting preparation for death.
The two death scenes strike home with telling impact. Christ,
hanging on the Cross, is uttering His last word: "Father, into
Your hands I rest My spirit." Meditatively we repeat the words
and entrust our souls to the care of Christ in sleep, and if need
be, in death. For Hyacinth it actually was his dying invocation.
The second scene. The aged Simeon is singing: "Now You may
dismiss Your servant. . . ." How appropriate as one's last day
approaches! The Mass, *Os justi*, is from the Common of Confessors (explained on p. 402).

2. What does the liturgy see in a saint? The Church is the
architect of Christian character. And it is from the lives and the
feasts of saints that she procures much suitable material. *Words
instruct, but example moves*, says an old proverb. It is excellent
pedagogy to make use day by day of the precedents set by the
saints. The Mass formularies of the Common contain abundant
material because the Church has woven into them the ideals
realized by her heroes and heroines. Let us cull from the Mass
Os justi some practical points on how to live. The liturgy calls
the saints (martyrs as well as confessors) the "just ones," *justi*.
The just man practices the virtue of justice toward God, toward

his fellowmen, and toward himself; he gives to God the things
that are God's, and to his neighbor the things that are rightly his.
This same *Introit* reminds us that the just man masters his
tongue, since speech is the brook of which the heart is the spring.
The heart of the just man is filled with the wisdom and judgments of God. Recall how the apostle James put it: "If any man
does not offend in word, that person is perfect."

The *Reading* adds another point. The just man stands above
perishable goods, above earthly attractions. For him money and
material things are means to an end; and the end is God. This
is our great mistake: too often we stay with the means and
thereby make earthly objects our idols. The saint has the right
perspective — his gaze transcends earthly horizons. According to
the *Alleluia* verse, every just man must pass through the crucible
of suffering. That is the only way in which he can give proof of
his justice and win the crown of life. No sanctity without the
Cross.

Finally, the *Gospel* portrays the just man as an alert servant,
waiting, watching. Our Savior sees perfection in constant pre-
paredness. With burning lamp and girt loins, the saint keeps
continual watch till his Lord knocks. The lamp is the light of
baptismal grace; the girded loins, abstinence from sin. After
giving these instructions, the Church begins the Sacrifice proper.
Its Banquet is the parousia in preview; the Lord appears and
knocks and finds us watching. Thus each Mass resembles a test
drill for our Savior's final advent at death. What inspiration for
everyday morality lies open before us in the Common!

August 18

ST. AGAPITUS, Martyr

He who loves his life loses it

St. Agapitus. *Day of death*: August 18, about the year 257.
Grave: at Palestrina, Italy; later his relics were transferred to

Corneto. *Life*. The Office offers these legendary details: "Agapitus was only fifteen years old but already his heart was all aglow with the desire to die as a martyr. Upon orders from the Emperor Aurelian (*ca.* 257), he was mercilessly whipped with leaded scourges, then thrown into a vile basement to remain there four days without food. After further punishment under the lash, he was suspended head downwards over a smoldering fire so that he should die from the smoke; boiling water was dashed against him, and his jaws were battered. When wild beasts hesitated to harm him, he was beheaded with the sword."

Application. A boy of fifteen years a full-fledged hero! Has he any lesson for modern youth? Of you Christ is not demanding such suffering, neither blood nor death. But He is demanding a will that can say NO to the allurements of sin, a will that can bend itself humbly in obedience. In this you have opportunity to be a youthful hero.

August 19

ST. JOHN EUDES, Confessor

Help provide priests zealous for souls

1. **St. John Eudes.** *Day of death*: August 19, 1680. *Canonized*: 1925. *Grave*: at Caen, France. *Life*. He is known as the founder of a congregation of diocesan priests with the twofold aim of restoring the true Christian spirit among the laity through home missions and of training zealous clergy by means of well-regulated seminaries. Born in Normandy in 1601, he joined, while still young, the Congregation of the Oratory, was ordained priest in 1626, and soon began preaching missions throughout France. When he discovered, through his missionary work, how essential a clergy zealous for souls was for the maintenance of religion among the people, he organized a community known as the Congregation of Jesus and Mary. He was also the author of

HOW HAVE I DESERVED

THAT THE MOTHER OF MY LORD

SHOULD COME TO ME!

several books which served his work, e.g., *The Ideal Confessor* and *The Apostolic Preacher*. Against him the Jansenists directed unrestrained hatred and hostility. The Mass, *Os justi*, is from the Common of Confessors (explained on p. 402).

2. The Priesthood. The life-work of St. John Eudes consisted in raising the standards of the secular clergy. He knew well that the piety of the laity depends to a great extent upon the clergy. A striking interdependence may here be observed — a pious laity will produce many and good priests, and a good priesthood will keep the people pious and virtuous.

What is the significance of the priesthood in the Church? Christ is the true and only Priest, the eternal High Priest. His mission upon earth was a priestly one. The priest is the mediator between God and man. By the very fact of becoming man, Christ had joined man to God, but this union with God was only effected in a perfect manner through His death upon the Cross. For His followers, the members of the Catholic Church, He remains the one Mediator through the Eucharistic Sacrifice, through the sacraments, through prayer, which is always made *per Dominum Jesum Christum*.

Nevertheless, Christ shares His office of mediator, because the Body partakes in the honor and dignity of the Head. Therefore, all Christians share in the priesthood of Christ. St. Peter calls Christians "a royal priesthood." The Catholic Church is essentially a Church of priests. Because of their priestly character, all Christians have the right and the duty to take an active part in the liturgy.

There is, moreover, a special, a consecrated priesthood which has the duty to further the priesthood of Christ in a special manner. The special priesthood is the dispenser of the mysteries of God, it acts as mediator of divine life. Who begets life is a father. The priest is a spiritual father by conferring divine life through the administration of baptism, penance, the holy Eucharist, the sacraments in general. He is a second Christ because he works in the Name of Christ, takes His place. For the faithful he breaks a twofold bread, that of instruction and that of life; the word of God and the holy Eucharist are the greatest treasures over which he is steward and which he distributes to his children as a wise and faithful father in the family of the Lord. Hence the sublimity of the mission and work of a priest.

Let us pray that priests remain vividly conscious of their high duties. Let us pray for good priests, priests zealous for souls (at each Mass we may include priests too when praying in the Canon for all "who, cherishing true doctrine, guard the faith that is catholic and apostolic"). The laity likewise can do much to benefit the priestly state. Many a mother through example and prayer has reared a priest. And many promising young men need to be supported during seminary years. All honor to the priesthood!

A final word directly to priests. The liturgy is your special work. Today more than ever you must further liturgical worship. A priest who does not educate the people in the Scriptures and in the liturgy is ignorant of the demands of our century. Give the people the Bible, the Missal, the Breviary. That is your primary task today. Thereby you will best fulfill your sacred priestly office.

August 20

ST. BERNARD, Abbot and Doctor of the Church

The Mellifluous Doctor

1. **St. Bernard.** *Day of death*: August 20, 1153. *Canonized*: 1174. *Grave*: in the abbey church at Clairvaux (in front of the Blessed Virgin altar). *Life*. Bernard, the second founder of the Cistercians, the Mellifluous Doctor, the apostle of the Crusades, the miracle-worker, the reconciler of kings, the leader of peoples, the counsellor of popes! His sermons, from which there are many excerpts in the Breviary, are conspicuous for genuine emotion and spiritual unction. The celebrated *Memorare* is ascribed to him.

Bernard was born in 1090, the third son of an illustrious Burgundian family. At the age of twenty-two he entered the monastery of Citeaux (where the Cistercian Order had its beginning) and persuaded thirty other youths of noble rank to follow his example. Made abbot of Clairvaux (1115), he erected numerous abbeys where his spirit flourished. To his disciple, Bernard of Pisa, who later became Pope Eugene III, he dedicated his work *De Consideratione*. Bernard's influence upon the princes, the clergy, and the people of his age was most remarkable. By penitential practices he so exhausted his body that it could hardly sustain his soul, ever eager to praise and honor God. The Mass, *In medio*, is from the Common of Doctors (explained p. 400); a special *Lesson* stresses the contemplative, cloistral life of our saint. We watch Bernard praying through the night, holding vigil with his community. We see him guide his monks in wisdom; how anxious he is over the observance of monastic discipline! His memory continues in his Order and in the Church.

2. **Community Spirit.** St. Bernard, the illustrious abbot and founder of monasteries, understood well the value of community spirit. Today, therefore, we are more sensitive than usual to "community" allusions in the Mass formulary. Some examples. The *Introit* antiphon places our learned saint "in the midst of the Church." It is God Himself who "opens his mouth," and thereafter his voice no longer is silent. As in the past, so now too he is teacher; he is teaching today through the prayer texts of the Mass. The *Collect* develops the idea. God has commissioned St. Bernard to be His people's servant and guide unto eternal salvation, a service that he fulfills in a twofold manner — as *doctor vitae,* i.e., teacher of eternal life upon earth, and as *intercessor in coelis,* i.e., one who pleads for us in heaven. This prayer teaches us the benefits the doctor-saint renders to the Christian community.

Community allusions are not absent from the *Gospel.* Actually Christ is instructing us in our community duties by means of the four parables — salt, light of the world, city on the mountain, and lamp in the house. Let us examine these figures. Salt preserves meat from decaying; likewise the Christian, not so much by words nor even by his deeds, but rather by *being* Christ, counteracts the processes of moral decadence. More positive in nature is the second figure. The world's light is furnished by the sun. The Christian should resemble the sun; the sun gives light, warmth, growth, life, joy. The Christian is a city upon the mountain. Every true Christian should appear before men as Christ. Worthy of note, too, is the fourth comparison. You should be a lamp in the house, i.e., at home among the members of your family is the place to let the light of Christ shine.

And lastly the *Communion*. While the priest is active in the most exalted of all community acts, nourishing the family of God with Bread from heaven (Communion — community), the Church remembers how the holy abbot Bernard was appointed by the Lord to be steward and father over a monastic family, how he performed his office "faithfully and prudently," how he distributed the "measure of wheat," earthly food as well as the heavenly wheat of doctrine and the Eucharist. Indeed, in this sainted abbot the Church sees herself; she sees herself as a "faithful and prudent" mother who "at the proper time," i.e., day by day, measures out to us, her family, the wheat of heaven!

August 21

ST. JANE FRANCES FREMIOT DE CHANTAL, Widow

Fortiter et suaviter — Courageously, gently!

1. **St. Jane.** *Day of death*: December 13, 1641. *Canonized*: 1767. *Grave*: at Annecy, in the motherhouse of the Visitation nuns. *Life.* Jane Frances Fremiot de Chantal was the foundress of the Order of the Visitation of Mary. She came from a noble family (born 1572), was married by her father to the Baron von Chantal (1592). As mother she most zealously instructed her children in the ways of virtue and piety and in the observance of

every divine precept. With great generosity she supported the poor and took special joy in seeing how divine Providence often blesses and increases the smallest larder. Therefore she made a vow never to refuse anyone who asked for alms in the Name of Christ.

The death of her husband, who was accidently shot while on the chase (1601), she bore with Christ-like composure and with all her heart forgave the person who had killed him; then she acted as sponsor for one of his children in order to show her forgiveness openly. There was a holy friendship between her and her spiritual guide, Francis of Sales ; with his approval she left her father and children and founded the Visitation nuns.

The Mass, *Cognovi*, is from the Common of Holy Women (see p. 408). The three Orations are proper. The *Collect*, which departs from classic models in length and structure, puts before us our saint's spiritual courage and determination. The other two Orations allude to her ardent love of God, a spirit that should likewise inflame us. Schuster rightly observes that the *Secret* resembles a Postcommunion; it petitions God for that which is the effect and fruit of the Sacrifice-Banquet (*Liber Sacramentorum* VIII, p. 177).

2. Fortiter et Suaviter. In the Common of Holy Women there is frequent mention of the *mulier fortis,* i.e., the courageous woman (hymn, chapter, Epistle), an approach that may seem odd since we would rather stress tenderness and obedience. In the present instance, however, the liturgy's approach is particularly apt because Jane truly was a strong, courageous woman. Only through the meekness of St. Francis de Sales, her spiritual guide, did her energetic character become softened with strains of tenderness, valor's necessary complement.

Firm though tender, energetic though loving — such is the glorious tension between opposing virtues that makes the Christian character. These traits in their highest expression we see in Christ — firmness, tenderness. He could be astonishingly aggressive without ceasing to be meek and sympathetically indulgent. It may seem that we do not understand our Savior when we see

Him taking a scourge and driving the merchants from the temple, or when He says to Peter, to whom He promised the keys of the kingdom of heaven: "Get behind me, Satan; you are a scandal to Me." And soon so mild and condescending toward those who err, as for instance, Magdalen, the adulteress, the repentant thief, and Peter after his denial.

Thus, too, it should be with us — firm yet forgiving, and each at the proper place and in the proper measure. Our zeal must not make us hard, fanatic; neither may love degenerate into sentimentalism. In fundamentals, in faith, and in the commandments we must be firm, immovable, with no trace of tolerance; but in our contacts with men, patient, forgiving, tender, conciliatory. The Christian ought be firm and resolute as a father, mild and self-sacrificing as a mother. This tension between complementary virtues we find exemplified in a heroic degree in St. Jane Frances de Chantal.

3. A Page from Her Biography. Few days in St. Jane's life were more heartbreaking than that on which she said adieu to her family and entered the convent. "Her departure was set for the twenty-ninth of May, 1610. On that day all her relatives met at the Fremiot home. It was a large gathering, and all were in tears. Frances Chantal alone seemed to retain composure, but in her eyes too glistening tears betrayed how much strength of will was needed to keep her heart from breaking. She went from one to the other, and clasping each in turn, pleaded for forgiveness and commended herself to their prayers; but her attempts to dry their tears only resulted in fresh outbursts.

"When she came to her own children, she no longer was able to restrain herself. Her son Celsus Benignus clasped her tightly and tried with much affection to deter her from her purpose. With like emotion Jane Frances embraced her son, smothered him with a mother's kisses, and answered all his pleas and arguments without weakening in her firm resolve. This loving though painful dialog between mother and child touched every heart, even the least sensitive. Such expression of sympathetic tenderness could not, however, continue indefinitely; Jane Chantal sought to end a scene that moved her so profoundly and loosed herself from her son's embrace so as to be able to leave. Celsus Benignus now realized that his pleading had been ineffective; as a last attempt he threw himself down upon the threshold over which his mother was about to pass and said: 'O Mother, if it is impossible for me to keep you from leaving, then you must go by stepping over the body of your son.'

"At this the heart of that noble woman reached the breaking-point; she could hold back no longer, and fresh tears flowed in open streams. The pious Robert, who witnessed the event and feared that the Lady Chantal might possibly turn back at the last moment, said to her: 'Good woman, the tears of a child are not going to make you waver now?' 'No,' the saint answered, smiling tenderly, 'just remember that I am a mother.' Then lifting her eyes heavenwards like another Abraham, she stepped over the body of her son and departed" (from Bougand's *Life of St. Frances de Chantal,* published by Herder, Freiburg).

August 22

THE IMMACULATE HEART OF MARY

In me is all grace

1. **The Feast.** By a decree of the Sacred Congregation of Rites dated May 4, 1944, today's feast in honor of the Immaculate Heart of the Blessed Virgin Mary was introduced into the calendar of the universal Church. The final day of the former octave of the Assumption occasioned the choice of date.

Devotion to and veneration of Mary's Immaculate Heart began to spread during the seventeenth and eighteenth centuries. It was St. John Eudes (whose feast we observed a few days ago, August 19) who popularized the devotion. Recent Popes, beginning with Pius IX, furthered the cause by granting a proper Office and Mass formulary. Pius XII, whose personal devotion to our Blessed

Mother was most edifying, dedicated all mankind to the Immaculate Heart of Mary on December 8, 1942, in the midst of the second World War, hoping "that with the help of the holy Mother of God all nations would receive the gift of peace and the Church of Christ the blessing of freedom." Today's observance, therefore, is a kind of "votive feast" in memory of Mary's motherly protection during the great War. In Mary's immaculate and divinely privileged Heart man's noblest sentiments and emotions found expression; her sorrow-filled soul experienced all the suffering that can weigh upon mankind, while her compassionate and motherly Heart is able to comfort and strengthen her many children in the kingdom of her divine Son. The sixth Lesson at Matins summarizes this background as follows:

"Many saintly men and women had prepared the way for the liturgical cult which renders due honor to the Immaculate Heart of the Virgin Mary before the Apostolic See first gave its approval under Pope Pius VII at the beginning of the nineteenth century by instituting the Feast of the Most Pure Heart of the Virgin Mary. Upon request, dioceses or religious institutes that wished to observe the feast devoutly and religiously were accorded permission to introduce this feast; and somewhat later Pope Pius IX embellished it with a proper Mass and Office. But from the seventeenth century on, there had been a constantly growing desire and effort to keep such a feast with greater solemnity and throughout the universal Church. Listening to these ardent prayers, Pope Pius XII decreed that the Feast of the Immaculate Heart with its own Office and Mass be celebrated everywhere annually beginning with the year 1942, the year when the fiercest of wars was raging throughout nearly the whole world. For he was taking pity on the measureless misery of the people and in his piety and confidence in our heavenly Mother, dedicated the whole human race to her most loving heart by solemn and earnest prayer."

Because of the numerous feasts introduced and the emphasis given to Marian devotion in our century, one could be led to think that former ages lacked an appreciation and love of our Blessed Mother. Only a little patristic reading is needed to show

how superficial such a deduction would be. And new documents are being found that in magnificent phraseology sing the praises of Mary. One such is a fifth-century Greek manuscript from which the following excerpt is taken:

"Plunged into the depths of the mercies of God, and contemplating the salutary abyss of His love for men, I tremble, beloved brethren, and I am troubled in spirit. How, with a small raft, shall I dare to cross this virginal and incomprehensible sea? Now that the prophetic trumpets herald the conception not preceded by wedded love, and the first among the angels cries his greetings, I am divided between fear and joy, as I behold my Lord and my God become flesh, like myself and for my sake, according to His will. I shudder before this voluntary condescension, and, like a slave, I shun meddlesome inquiry.

"And if, summoning my courage, I make bold to inquire of the Mother of God herself: How is it that you became a mother without knowing man?, she will no doubt give this answer:

"Lately an angel stood before me and, with incorruptible converse, decked me with bridal robes. I heard his word, I conceived the Word, I brought forth the Word. I gave birth to the Light, I know not how. I have a child, I who know not man. I carry within me a fountain of milk, I who remain in unravished possession of the pasture of virginity. In my arms I bear an Infant, but how I became a mother I cannot say. As for the Infant, I acknowledge Him as my Son and as my Creator and my Demiurge, as a mere Child and as more ancient than the ages."

2. Holy Mass (Adeamus). In this formulary there occur a number of texts that are found in no other Marian Masses. The *Entrance Antiphon* rings true to context: "Confidently let us approach the throne of grace" (the altar, of course, is meant). As *Reading,* we hear lofty words from Jesus Sirach: "I am the mother of fair love. . . ." At the *Gospel* we "stand by the Cross of Jesus" and hear how He confided His Mother to the care of the Beloved Disciple. The passage is repeated as the *Communion* antiphon. Verses from the Magnificat are sung at the *Alleluia* and *Offertory.*

3. St. Timothy and Companions. *Day of death*: August 22. *Grave*: that of Timothy is shown at Rome near the tomb of St. Paul; that of Hippolytus, at Ostia; that of Symphorian, at Autun, France. *Life*. During the pontificate of Pope Melchiades (311–314), Timothy of Antioch came to Rome and preached the Gospel. The prefect of the city, Tarquin, placed him under arrest and after a period of imprisonment ordered that he be scourged three times because he refused to sacrifice to the gods. After further excruciating torments Timothy was beheaded. At Ostia, the bishop St. Hippolytus, a man of exceptional culture. Because he was an outstanding witness to the faith, he was bound hand and foot by Emperor Alexander and cast into a deep pit filled with water; thereby he obtained the crown. Not far away Christians buried his body. At Autun the youthful Symphorian was brought to judgment under Emperor Aurelian (270–275). His mother urged perseverance: "My son, think of eternal life. Raise your glance to heaven and behold your eternal King! Your life will not be taken from you, but transformed into a better one!" (*Martyrology*).

August 23

ST. PHILIP BENIZI, Confessor

Study the book of the Cross

St. Philip Benizi. *Day of death*: August 22, 1285. *Canonized*: 1671. *Feast*: 1690. *Grave*: at Todi, in Tuscany. *Life*. St. Philip had special talents for leadership and organization; he was the second founder of the Servites and a great missioner. Of him the Breviary says: "His love and sympathetic consideration for the poor was truly remarkable. On one occasion he gave his own clothing to a destitute leper at Camiliano, a village near Siena, and immediately the poor, sick beggar was healed. The report of the miracle spread far and wide, and many of the cardinals who had assembled at Viterbo after the death of Clement IV (1268) for the election of Christendom's chief shepherd were minded to choose Philip, whose angelic life and mature wisdom were universally acknowledged. But as soon as the saint became aware of this, he went into hiding upon a hill until Gregory X (1271–1276) had been elected; for he sought to be spared that burdensome dignity."

Philip died at Todi in Tuscany. During his last hours he requested the attending Brother to bring him his book. The Brother did not understand what he meant. "The crucifix," the saint added. That was the book the saint had studied all the days of his life. *Application.* In the Collect the Church focuses attention upon *humility* as our saint's most noteworthy virtue: "In the life of St. Philip You have provided for us a splendid example of humility." And we know the manual from which he learned this virtue, the Crucifix. — The Mass (*Justus*) is from the Common (see p. 403).

August 24

ST. BARTHOLOMEW, Apostle

Behold, an Israelite indeed in whom there is no guile

1. **St. Bartholomew.** The Church seeks to fill us with a "worthy and holy joy" today because we are celebrating the feast of an apostle, a "friend" of the Lord and a "prince" in God's kingdom, one who is enthroned with Christ, "judging the twelve tribes of Israel." We are thrilled with joy over the enthronement of St. Bartholomew because we are God's big family, because we are members of Christ's Body to which the apostle also belongs. While the members of this Body may have various offices, they nevertheless aid one another; and the glorification of one prefigures that of the others. Of this truth we are reminded by the Epistle: "You are the Body of Christ, and severally His members."

In St. John's Gospel, Bartholomew is known by the name Nathaniel (the liturgy does not always seem aware of this identity). He hailed from Cana in Galilee, was one of the first disciples called by the Lord. On that initial meeting Jesus uttered the glorious compliment: "Behold, an Israelite indeed in whom there is no guile!" After the resurrection he was favored by becoming one of the few apostles who witnessed the appearance of the risen Savior on the sea of Galilee (John 21:2). Following the ascension he is said to have preached in Greater Armenia and to have been martyred there. While still alive, his skin was torn from his body. The Armenians honor him as the apostle of their nation. Concerning the fate of his relics, the *Martyrology* says: "His holy body was first taken to the island of Lipari (north of Sicily), then to Benevento, and finally to Rome on an island in the Tiber; there it is honored by the faithful with pious devotion." Today is the anniversary of one of the many translations.

2. Holy Mass (Mihi autem). It will be easier to appreciate today's Mass texts if in spirit we worship in the presence of the ancient Church. In olden times the Christians celebrated the vigil during the entire preceding night, and at the rising of the sun the bishop with his clergy proceeded to the altar. The faithful would come from all sides to the church where the saint was buried and place their linens upon the grave, convinced that "power went forth" from the tomb. The sick too were brought. From this we may sense the mystery-action of the *Gospel*. The mystical Body of Christ, i.e., the parish (cf. *Epistle*), had "passed the whole night in prayer." That was the vigil.

Toward morning Christ calls his twelve apostles, and coming down to them, "He takes His stand on a level stretch," i.e., the holy Sacrifice; we see Christ enter with His "glorious choir of apostles" (*Allel.*). When the priest and his ministers proceed to the altar at the *Introit*, it is Christ we behold, and the apostles, the "friends and princes worthy of every honor." Assembled about the altar we are that "countless host" who "have come to hear Him" (*Lessons* and *homily*) "and to be healed of their diseases" (in the Sacrifice proper).

The *Communion* Banquet actualizes what the Gospel recounts: "And all the people sought to touch Him, because power went forth from Him and healed all" (in ancient times Christians received the holy Eucharist in their hands). Today the Bread from heaven has a double efficacy — as the Body of Christ and as power from the apostle's grave. It is the "pledge of eternal salvation" (*Postc.*). Today we are numbered among the "multitude" that with longing listened to the words coming from the Master's lips (Liturgy of the Word), that asked to be healed spiritually, that received the power emanating from His sacred Body. It is really the two Readings that make the Mass so inspirational and instructive.

3. Divine Office. St. Ambrose comments as follows on the Gospel: "And He passed the whole night in prayer to God. Here you have a precedent, a model that you ought zealously imitate. For should you not do everything possible for your own salvation, if Christ spent the whole night in prayer for you? At the beginning of some good work you decide to do, should you not resort to prayer, when Christ, before sending out His apostles, gave Himself so fully in prayer to God? Otherwise, too, if I remember correctly, you will never find Him praying in common with the apostles — He always prayed alone. For man with his multiple wants does not know the plans of God, and none, even His closest associates, can in this be a sharer with Christ.

"He called together His disciples, it reads, and selected twelve of them, to entrust them with the means for spreading man's salvation, planting the seeds of faith to the very ends of the earth. Note at once how heaven acts. For that mission He chooses fishermen and tax-gatherers — not the wealthy, not the intellectuals, not those with social prestige. For there should not even be the appearance of gaining an adherent through learning or through money or through making friends by means of human influence or status. Invincible truth, not fascinating speech, should win men's hearts."

4. Martyrology. "In Carthage, three hundred holy martyrs during the time of Valerian and Galienus. After they had endured various tortures, the judge ordered a lime-kiln to be heated. Incense and lighted charcoal were placed before it. Then he said to them: Now take your choice. Put incense on the coals in honor of Jupiter or be thrown into the molten lime. Once more they all professed faith in Christ and thereupon threw themselves straightway into the fire. So thoroughly were they burned in the smoking lime that only ashes remained. Accordingly this glorious army of saints received the honorable name *Massa Candida*, "The White Legion."

5. What Role Do the Apostles Have in the Liturgy? That the feasts of the apostles enjoy special significance in the liturgy is evident from their high rank; moreover, until 1955 they were introduced by a vigil, and in times past they had been holydays of obligation. The personal sanctity of the individual apostle commemorated, however, is not important; and ordinarily little is known of his life. Much more do we honor the office and dignity of apostleship and the apostolic college as such. For the apostles are the foundation stones of the Church. The liturgy distributes their feasts throughout the months of the year in order to indicate that they form the Church's foundation supports.

Today's Collect spells out how highly the Church esteems the apostolic office. First there is mention of the "venerable and holy joy" stemming from the feast. The liturgy never needs to exaggerate. These simple words cover much blessed festivity. May we experience it more fully. And our requests? That the Church "love what he believed and preach what he taught." To understand this petition, recall how the apostles were commissioned by Christ to bear witness to His work and to guard the Christian heritage. "You shall be witnesses unto Me in Jerusalem and in all Judea and Samaria, as well as to the very ends of the earth" (Acts 1:8). Those twelve men were indeed conscious of having assumed a most important mission. In the place of the traitor Judas, therefore, they chose another who had been "in our company all the time that the Lord Jesus came in and went out among us, from John's baptism until the day whereon He was taken up from us . . . a witness with us of His resurrection" (Acts 1:21-22).

Accordingly, the unique significance of the twelve apostles lies in this, that they faithfully delivered to the Church the treasury of faith and Christian morality. Without the apostles we should have no trustworthy source of revealed truth. Even the Bible derives its authority from apostolic testimony. These observations have provided a better understanding of today's Collect: (a) as members of the Church we ought *lovingly* embrace the heritage of faith (the text does not say "believe what he believed," but rather, "love what he believed," i.e., embrace with interior joy and affection the treasures of faith); (b) the Church continues the mission of teaching which the apostles began as a witness to Christ. For in addition to taking the place of God when teaching and preaching, she holds the office of teaching and preaching given to the apostles. Christ brought to earth the revelation of the will and wisdom of God and entrusted it to the apostles; from their hands the Church receives it, guards it carefully, and applies it now to us Christians. Without the apostles a needed link between us and our Savior would be lacking.

August 25

ST. LOUIS, King and Confessor

Make us co-heirs with the King of kings, Christ Jesus

1. **St. Louis.** *Day of death*: August 25, 1270, at Tunis. *Canonized*: 1297. *Grave*: at Paris, in the Church of St. Denis; his head is at Saint Chapelle in Paris. *Life*. Reigning from 1226 to 1270, Louis IX showed how a saint would act on the throne of France. A lovable personality, a kind husband, a father of eleven children, and at the same time a strict ascetic.

To an energetic and prudent rule Louis added love and zeal for the practice of piety and the reception of the holy sacraments. Brave in battle, polished at feasts, addicted to fasting and mortification. His politics were grounded upon strict justice, unshatterable fidelity, and untiring effort toward peace. Nevertheless, his was not a weakly rule but one that left its impress upon following generations. He was a great friend of religious Orders, a generous benefactor of the Church.

The Breviary says of him: "He had already been king for twenty years when he fell victim to a severe illness. That afforded the occasion for making a vow to undertake a crusade for the liberation of the Holy Land. Immediately upon recovery he received the crusader's cross from the hand of the bishop of Paris, and, followed by an immense army, he crossed the sea in 1248. On the field of battle Louis routed the Saracens; yet when the plague had taken large numbers of his soldiery, he was attacked and taken captive (1250). The king was forced to make peace with the Saracens; upon the payment of a huge ransom, he and his army were again set at liberty." While on a second crusade he died of the plague, with these words from the psalm upon his lips: "I will enter Thy house; I will worship in Thy holy temple and sing praises to Thy Name!" (Ps. 5).

2. The Common of Kings. The liturgy is very reluctant in granting titles and dignities. Mention is made of such only if the title in question is part of some eminent office and if a special consecration is given, e.g., bishop, pope. Kings, too, are sacred through consecration and anointing, and therefore the dignity of kingship among the saints is not overlooked. A nation's king shares in the sovereign ruling power of God and Christ. For this reason the Church since ancient times has honored kingship and has permitted special prayers to this end in the liturgy. Obedience to the king is not mere service of men, but a service rendered to God. The Church takes note if some saintly king, busy with the cares of state, does not forget "the one thing necessary," if amidst the "temptations of the world" he faithfully observes God's law (*Secr.*). His death is seen as a *translatio,* i.e., a transfer from an earthly kingdom to "the glory of the heavenly kingdom." And today we pray that all of us might become "co-heirs of the King of kings, Jesus Christ" (*Coll.*).

The chants of the Mass, it is true, are taken from the Common of Confessors (*Os justi*, p. 402). Nevertheless, the two proper Readings give ample grounds to entitle today's formulary "The Common of Kings." In its historical context the *Lesson* tells of Joseph, whom God liberated from prison in Egypt and gave "the sceptre of the kingdom." This can easily be accommodated to the life of St. Louis, for he was taken captive by the Saracens.

Recounting the parable of the gold pieces and the nobleman who went "to obtain for himself a kingdom," the *Gospel* is easily accommodated to our saint. (To grasp the historical allusions of this parable a knowledge of the political conditions at the time of Christ is needed. Palestine was then under the dominion of Rome, and whoever hoped to become king of any given Jewish province was obliged to go into "a far country," i.e., Rome, "to receive for himself that kingdom and to return." It would happen on occasion that the inhabitants of the province would send a delegation to Rome with the petition: "We do not wish this man to be king over us." If, nevertheless, the aspirant gained his end, it was taken for granted, according to the Oriental mind, that harsh treatment would be meted out to the objectors. Such the historical background of our parable.)

How does the liturgy apply it? The nobleman who "went into a far country to receive for himself a kingdom" is Christ, who since His ascension is sitting "at the right hand of the Father" but will return on the last day. To us His servants He consigns the care of His goods (various graces and natural abilities), and upon His return He will ask for an accounting.

The parable lists three types of Christians: first, those who make *perfect* use of the graces given, as, for instance, St. Louis; in reward he receives sovereignty over ten cities, by which is signified the heavenly reward (in which we may share by means of the Mass). The second group are those who put their gifts to *good* use; we try to be among these. The third group, those who do not cooperate with grace, are the bad Christians — a sobering warning to us.

The primary lesson of the parable is that men must cooperate with grace to obtain salvation. Christianity does not consist in attendance at Mass and in the reception of the sacraments; acting and living in a way pleasing to God is just as necessary. The Eucharist which we receive is a "gold piece" which the Lord entrusts to us throughout the day that we might work with it and "trade" with it. Tomorrow He will come again and give us the chance to show our gains at the Offertory.

A final thought on the Common of Kings. Just as there is a special priesthood and a priesthood common to all, so there is a special and a common kingship. For in varying degrees we all partake in the kingship of Christ. Our anointing with chrism at baptism and confirmation was our royal consecration. This anointing conferred upon us "the royal, the priestly, and the prophetic dignity." Here on earth, however, our royal dignity is hidden; only hereafter will it be evident how we, with Christ, are kings. This would be an excellent occasion to consider how we should exercise our common kingship here on earth. But we will content ourselves with citing a single passage from the Breviary (Matins on the twelfth Sunday after Pentecost): "In all truth the just are kings, great kings. The reason? Because they do not yield complacently to temptations but have learned how to triumph over them" (St. Bede).

3. **Martyrology.** "At Rome, St. Genesius. He had been a pagan, and an actor by profession. While mockingly imitating the Christian services before the Emperor Diocletian, a divine enlightenment flooded his mind; without delay he sought instruction and received baptism. It was not long till he was cruelly whipped by the emperor's order and put to the rack. His flesh was torn from his body with iron hooks, and his wounds burned with flaming torches. Still he remained loyal to the faith and said: There is but one King, and that is Christ. If I must suffer a martyr's death a thousand times, you shall never succeed in driving His praises from my lips or His love from my heart. Thereupon he was beheaded and thus received the well-earned palm of martyrdom."

August 26

ST. ZEPHYRIN, Pope and Martyr

Liturgy and priesthood

1. St. Zephyrin. *Day of death*: August 26, 217; he died a natural death and therefore is a martyr only in the wider sense. *Grave*: he is the first Pope who was buried in the papal chamber of the Callistine catacomb on the Appian Way (previous Popes were buried with St. Peter in the Vatican). His remains, together with those of St. Tarcisius, were translated to the Church of St. Sylvester (Marsfeld) during the ninth century. *Life.* The reign of the aged Pope was long (198 — 217) and notable. The Roman Church was passing through various phases of development and there were heresies to be overcome. The Breviary notes a number of liturgical modifications. Zephyrin decreed that ordinations take place on the Ember days in the presence of an assembly of clerics and lay people; and only learned and worthy men were to be chosen for the sacred offices. Furthermore, he ruled that all priests should attend the Mass offered by the bishop. He likewise ordained that a patriarch, primate, or metropolitan could proceed against a bishop only with apostolic approval. — The Mass, *Si diligis Me,* is from the Common of Sovereign Pontiffs (explained p. 378).

2. The Mass — a Community Sacrifice. That all priests should assist at the bishop's Mass was one of St. Zephyrin's ordinances. It may be doubted whether this particular Pope was actually responsible for the rule, but that the practice did exist in the ancient Church is certain. On one day in one church there was but one offering of the Mass, and all the priests celebrated it with the bishop. The Mass was regarded as a community Sacrifice. They understood well how the sequence and structure of the Mass are communal in character, how every *Dominus vobiscum,* every *Oremus,* every *Amen* calls for community.

The two principal divisions of the Mass presuppose two groups.

The Foremass, consisting of prayer and preaching, requires participants. The chants, the Kyrie, Gloria, Introit, the Collects are "group prayers." The reading of the Epistle and Gospel, and the homily, which belongs to the Liturgy of the Word, presuppose a gathering. The Sacrifice proper likewise is communal action; two of its constituent parts require group action, viz., the Offertory procession and the Communion procession. Twice the Canon uses words implying that priests and faithful are offering the Sacrifice in common. ("Here, then, is the offering that we, Your servants, and together with us Your whole household, present to You. . . . In memory, then, O God, of the sacred passion . . . do we Your ministers and with us Your holy people present to Your sovereign Majesty this offering").

Furthermore, the liturgy enables us to share in a higher community, for about the sacrificial table the universal Church is gathered, the community on earth, the community in heaven, the community in purgatory, yes, even the communities of angels! It is as if the liturgy would not re-enact Christ's exalted Sacrifice except in the presence of the entire Church.

And the implications for us? That we should be alert to furthering the basic work of active participation in the liturgy; that priests should foster community Mass-action in all its forms, while the laity, insofar as possible, should cooperate actively in the holy Sacrifice. They should pray along, sing along, read along; they should listen together, offer together, receive together. Oh, that in all parishes and churches the principal daily Mass would become a community Mass at which priest and people would be united in the offering! Oh, that priests would attribute less importance to private Masses and more willingly assist at a community Mass! May each in his own circle and with the means proper to his environment strive toward making the Mass a common act again, the Sacrifice of the Christian community in which all take active part.

ST. JOSEPH CALASANCTIUS, Priest, Confessor

Become a child, love children

1. **St. Joseph Calasanctius.** *Day of death*: August 25, 1648, at the age of ninety-two years. *Canonized*: 1767. *Feast*: 1769. *Grave*: at Rome, in the Church of St. Pantaleon; his heart and his tongue are preserved intact. *Life*. Our saint is the founder of the Poor Clerks Regular (Piarists), a community devoted to the task of educating youth. At an early age Joseph loved to care for children; he gathered them together, conducted religion classes in boyish fashion, and taught them how to pray. After a time of severe illness he was ordained priest. His zeal found expression as he organized the Order of the Poor Clerks Regular of the Mother of God of the Pious Schools and directed the members in the instruction and rearing of children from poor parents.

While residing in Rome, Joseph endeavored to visit the seven principal churches of that city almost every evening, as also to honor the graves of the Roman martyrs. During one of the city's repeated plagues a holy rivalry existed between him and St. Camillus (see July 18) in aiding the sick and in personally carrying away for burial the bodies of those who had been stricken. On account of his heroic patience and fortitude in the midst of trouble and persecution, he was called a marvel of Christian courage, a second Job. When eighty years old, he was led as a criminal through the streets of Rome by the Inquisition. His life is a consoling example of how God permits misunderstandings and opposition, even from ecclesiastics, to harass noble undertakings. At the time of his death his Order had almost been destroyed. Then, however, it again began to flourish.

2. **Holy Mass (Venite filii).** The Mass makes several allusions to the life of St. Joseph Calasanctius. Two virtues are emphasized, his love of children and his patience in suffering. To the former the *Introit* points: "Come, children, listen to me. I will teach you the fear of the Lord." The *Communion* likewise has a direct and

personal ring: "Let the little children come to me . . . for of
such is the kingdom of God." For at Communion time all of us,
like little ones, come to Christ. In the *Gospel* the divine Friend
of children admonishes us to become children, to love them.
"Amen, I say to you, unless you become as little children, you
shall not enter into the kingdom of heaven . . . he who receives
one such little child in My Name receives Me."

To Joseph's patience in suffering the *Lesson* refers: "God went
down with him into prison and did not forsake him in chains."
Our saint was actually imprisoned (the entire Lesson in its literal
sense treats of Joseph in Egypt — a unique coincidence of
names!). The *Alleluia*: "Blessed is the man who endures temptation, for when he has been tested, he will receive the crown of
life." Joseph received this crown, and today we may ask for a portion of its glory. Our prayers and offering are for his Congregation of Piarists and for the success of the work carried on by them.

3. The Child and the Liturgy. Christ ushered in an entirely
new concept of a child's dignity. The pagan attitude toward children at its best was quite negative; even the Old Testament takes
little cognizance of a child's status, although the blessing of having a family was highly cherished. It was Christ who first revealed
to the world the sanctity of childhood and its exalted state. He
sanctified childhood through His own childhood. His words concerning children were a true gospel to the world: "Suffer the little
children to come to Me, and forbid them not, for of such is the
kingdom of God" (Luke 18:16). "Whosoever shall receive this
child in My Name receives Me" (Luke 9:48). "Unless you be converted and become as little children, you shall not enter into the
kingdom of heaven" (Matt. 18:3-4). In these words Christ proclaimed two new concepts, viz., the child stands closest to the
kingdom of God, yes, it may be taken as a symbol of Christianity;
and we must direct it to Christ.

Mother Church has faithfully preserved this divine charge; she
bestows upon children her loving care and interest, as shown well
in the liturgy. She is at pains to confer upon the child as soon as
possible the first sacrament, baptism. She seeks to give the child

at an early age the sacraments of confirmation and holy Eucharist. Among the first decrees of the great liturgical reformer Pius X was that of the early reception of holy Communion.

The Church's care for the child is also shown in her numerous blessings for children, the blessing of the mother during pregnancy, the blessing immediately before childbirth, the blessing of the healthy and the sickly child, the blessing of a child in order that it obtain the mercy of God, the blessing of children when publicly presented in church. Priests should dispense these blessings more frequently, for these blessings are the answer to Christ's words: "Suffer the little ones to come unto Me."

How highly the Church treasures the child shows itself beautifully in the burial rites for infants. The body in the coffin is clad in a white garment; about are wreaths of blooming flowers and fragrant plants as signs of innocence. The burial liturgy is joyous, full of happy faith, because all are convinced that "God gives children who have been born again in the font of baptism eternal life immediately." Instead of a Requiem Mass there is a Mass of

praise, the Mass of the Angels. Also in other celebrations the liturgy bestows upon children a special place, e.g., the front pews at
Mass, the first place in processions and other services; and often
they appear in special dress. Children are the Church's treasure.

August 28

ST. AUGUSTINE, Bishop and Doctor of the Church

Our hearts are restless until they rest in Thee

1. St. Augustine. The *Martyrology* is unusually profuse today: "At Hippo Regius in the Roman province of Africa, the
death of the holy bishop Augustine, an illustrious doctor of the
Church. The holy bishop Ambrose gained him for the Christian
faith and baptized him. Immediately thereupon Augustine defended the Christian teaching against the Manicheans and other
heretics and showed himself a clear-sighted and penetrating
champion of orthodoxy. After a life of labor dedicated wholly
to the good of the Church, he entered heaven to receive an
eternal reward. For fear of the Vandals his remains were brought
to Sardinia from Hippo. Later Luitprand, king of the Lombards,
ordered his relics to be taken to Pavia, where they were enshrined with great honor."

Day of death: August 28, 430. *Grave*: since the eighth century
at Pavia in the Augustinian church of San Pietro in Ciel d'Oro.
Life. Augustine Aurelius was born on November 13, 354, in
Tagaste, North Africa. His father was a pagan, his mother St.
Monica. Still unbaptized and burning for knowledge, he came
under the influence of the Manicheans. As a rhetorician he went
to Rome, seeking that truth which he finally found at Milan
through the help of St. Ambrose. The tears of his mother, the
sanctity of Milan's bishop, the book of St. Anthony the hermit,
and the sacred Scriptures wrought his conversion, which was

sealed by baptism on Easter night 387. In 388 he returned to Tagaste, where he lived a common life with his friends. In 391 he was ordained priest at Hippo, in 394 made coadjutor to bishop Valerius, and then from 396 to 430 bishop of Hippo.

Augustine, numbered among the four great Doctors of the Western Church, possessed one of the most penetrating minds of ancient Christendom. He was the most important Platonist of patristic times, the Church's most influential theologian, especially with regard to clarifying the dogmas of the Trinity, grace, and the Church. A great speaker, a prolific writer, a saint with an inexhaustible spirituality. His *Confessions*, a book appreciated in every age, describes a notable portion of his life (until 400), his errors, his battles, his profound religious observations. Famous too is his work *The City of God*, a worthy memorial to his genius, a philosophy of history. Most edifying are his homilies, especially those on the psalms and on the Gospel of St. John.

Augustine's episcopal life was filled with mighty battles against heretics, over all of whom he triumphed. His most illustrious victory was that over Pelagius, who denied the necessity of grace; from this encounter he earned the surname "Doctor of grace." As an emblem Christian art accords him a burning heart to symbolize the ardent love of God which permeates all his writings. He is the founder of canonical life in common; therefore Augustinian monks and the Hermits of St. Augustine honor him as their spiritual father.

2. Holy Mass (In medio) from the Common of Doctors, p. 400. I see in the priest about to celebrate "in the midst of the Church" the great Doctor Augustine; for his spirit assuredly is living on. I see him in his "robe of glory"; I hear him preaching, "reproving, entreating, rebuking in all patience and wisdom." I behold him as the flame of love is effecting his "dissolution"; ready now to be sacrificed, he says: "I have fought the good fight, I have finished the course, I have kept the faith."

I see him as the Lord gives him "the crown of justice on that day" (of which today is part). I see him as the "salt of the earth," as the "light of the world," as the "candlestick" in the house of the Church which illumines all who are "in the house." He is the "city upon a mountain" which cannot be hidden away (*Gospel*). At the *Offertory* I accompany him to the Sacrifice, where he will be "multiplied" (*multiplicabitur*) in the assembled faithful. During the sacrificial Banquet he is the faithful steward who deals out to God's family the "measure of wheat," i.e., the wheat of instruction and the wheat of the holy Eucharist.

3. Augustine's importance may be studied from three view-points: as founder of a religious Order, as doctor of the Church, and as a man. Not as St. Benedict is Augustine the founder of a specific community; his ideal was a common life for clerics in imitation of community life in apostolic times. Yet his practice set a precedent which became a norm for cathedral chapters as also for the Order of Clerks Regular. The Rule of St. Augustine, which scientific research is placing closer and closer to the times of its nominal author, has been taken as the norm and guide for many Orders and Congregations. When we are gathered together celebrating the holy Sacrifice, there is present not only the individual saint but likewise all his children, those innumerable followers who have observed or are observing his rule of common life, whether already in glory or still upon earth. Augustine's is a mighty limb on the tree of the Church, and in its shade the Church is celebrating today's liturgy.

"In the midst of the Church the Lord opened his mouth" — these words apply to Augustine in their fullest sense, for he ranks among the very greatest of her doctors. Moreover, he is a teacher in the Church according to the liturgical sense, because God now is "opening his mouth in the midst of the Church" in many of his homilies and sermons. At Matins the Gospel according to St. John is explained almost exclusively by him, and most of the great feasts come with excerpts from his voluminous writings. His explanation of the psalms, perhaps the most popular of his works, reveals his profoundly liturgical spirit.

As a man, too, Augustine was unique. Few saints say and offer equally much to us moderns. Seldom among the saints can we so easily observe the working of divine grace. On current Sundays we have analyzed the two capital tendencies in the human heart; in Augustine's life both are easily detected. The son of a Christian mother and a pagan father, he was not baptized in infancy, being left free to make the choice as an adult. As the years passed, two tendencies sought mastery over him, the spirit of good and the spirit of evil. The good stood near him in the form of his virtuous and holy mother. The evil spirit, however, exercised greater influence and drove its victim farther and farther from virtue.

Augustine became a Manichean, which caused his mother intense sorrow. He left Africa for Rome, deceiving his mother, who was ever anxious to be near him. She prayed and wept. A bishop consoled her by observing that a son of so many tears would never be lost. Yet the evil spirit drove him constantly deeper into moral degeneracy, capitalizing on his leaning toward pride and stubbornness. Grace was playing a waiting game; there still was time, and the greater the depths into which the evil spirit plunged its fledgling, the stronger would be the reaction.

Augustine recognized this vacuum; he saw how the human heart is created with a great abyss; the earthly satisfactions that can be thrown into it are no more than a handful of stones that hardly cover the bottom. And in that moment grace was able to break through: *Restless is the heart until it rests in God*. Ambrose, the great bishop of Milan, was the instrument God employed. Augustine's mother went to Milan with joy and witnessed her son's baptism. It was what it should have been, the greatest event of his life, his conversion — *metanoia*. Grace had conquered. Augustine accompanied his mother to Ostia, where she died. She was eager to die, for now she had given birth to her son for the second time.

4. The Confessions of St. Augustine. Easily perceived in the opening paragraphs of Book One of the *Confessions* is the magnanimous heart of our saint, pouring itself out in praise and love of God:

"Greatness is Yours, Lord, and You are worthy of greatest praise. Great too is Your power, and Your wisdom limitless.

"And man indeed seeks to praise You! — man, a mere creature of Yours, man who ever bears about within himself death, a death witnessing both to his sin and to Your resistance of the proud. Still man seeks to praise You — man, a mere creature of Yours. It is your plan that pleasure comes from praising You, because You made us for Yourself and restless is the human heart until it rests in You.

"What, then, is Your nature, O God? Is it, may I ask, anything except Lord and God? For is there a lord besides the Lord? Is there a god besides our God?

"O most High, most Excellent, most Powerful, most Omnipotent, O most Merciful and most Just, infinitely Apart and intimately Present, Fairest and Strongest, beyond Fluctuation, beyond Comprehension. Immutable, You cause every change. Never new, never old — yet You are the source of all innovation. The proud You make senile — and they do not even know it! You are activity itself, You are the acme of rest. You gather while needing nothing; You sustain and fill up and protect, You bring into being and nourish and perfect and watch over — while all the time nothing is lacking to You. You love, but never with the heat of passion; You are zealous but never rash; when You regret, it is without grief. In anger You are tranquil. Procedures You may change, but never do You change Your providence. What You find You take, though never have You lost anything. Though never needy, You joy over gain; though never greedy, usurious are Your demands. Beyond what is due is given You that You may become a debtor — yet does anyone have anything that is not Yours? Debts You pay, while to no one are You a debtor; dues You cancel, without loss. Now what have we said, my God, my Life, my holy Sweetness? or what does anyone say when he speaks of You? Woe, woe, nonetheless, to the silent, to him who will not speak of You; for even we who babble are really mute.

"O, who can help me find repose in You! O, who can help me, so that You may enter my heart and inebriate it, making me forget my many lusts and embrace You, my one only good!"

If you have a copy of St. Augustine's *Confessions*, use it for meditation today, this week.

5. St. Hermes. St. Hermes was prefect of Rome. Along with Pope Alexander I (see May 4), he was put to death about the year 116. A cemetery on the Salerian Way bears his name. The *Roman Martyrology* reads: "At Rome the birthday of St. Hermes, a man of rank, who (as the Acts of the martyr-pope St. Alexander I narrate) was first cast into prison and then beheaded along with many others. He gained the martyr's crown under the judge Aurelian." His body rests in the Church of St. Mark, Rome.

August 29

BEHEADING OF ST. JOHN THE BAPTIST

I must decrease, He must increase

1. Beheading of St. John. In addition to the feast of the nativity of St. John the Baptist (see June 24), the Church, since the fourth century, commemorates the martyrdom of Christ's precursor. According to the *Roman Martyrology*, this day marks "the second finding of his most venerable head." The body of the saint was buried in Samaria. In the year 362 pagans desecrated the grave and burned his remains. Only a small portion of his relics were able to be saved by monks and sent to St. Athanasius at Alexandria. The head of the saint is venerated at various places. That in the Church of St. Sylvester in Rome belongs to a martyr-priest John. Also in the Dominican church at Breslau the Baptist's head is honored.

The narrative of the saint's death is among the most dramatic accounts in holy Writ. All three Synoptics refer to it: St. Mark goes into the greatest detail (6:14–29), from which the Gospel of the Mass is taken (cf. Matt. 14:1–12; and Luke, the briefest, 3:19–20; 9:7–9). Let us take today's Scripture Reading and reflect upon it.

Recall the historical setting. Herod Antipas, the vain, ambitious, weak ruler of several Palestinian sectors, was residing in his rocky fortress near the Dead Sea. He became passionately attached to the wife of his brother, Herodias by name, and took her to wife. It was an adulterous union and a great scandal to all the Jews. John the Baptist, who was preaching on the shores of the Jordan toward the Dead Sea, did not remain ignorant of developments. Fearing nothing, this man with hairy garments knocked at the palace door and with brief, earnest words stated his purpose: "It is not permissible for you to live with the wife of your brother; such conduct is evil, and a great scandal." John's judgment struck like a sword through Herod's heart and left its mark. The king trembled. The Baptist left.

Now Herodias was ambitious; she had determined to become queen and to remain queen. To silence the troublesome preacher of penance and to maintain her objectives became her primary occupation day and night. She pursued John with a woman's hate and with the aid of the Pharisees succeeded in having him imprisoned. It was the wicked woman's day of triumph. The Baptist lay chained in the dungeons below the citadel. But Herod had not yet made the ultimate decision. He was weak; at times he heard the voice of conscience. On these occasions he would call the Baptist and speak with him. Such action, however, Herodias must not permit. Herod vacillated; and the woman knew that as long as John lived, her throne would not be secure. John must die.

She sought to do away with him secretly. She tried to bribe the soldiers, but they were John's friends; they had heard him preach near the Jordan. Even at court there existed a party friendly to John, and now they appeared to be gaining greater favor. John's imprisonment was made easier; friends and disciples were permitted to visit him. And Herod was thinking of releasing him. Then the great feastday, Herod's birthday. Everything was prepared. On every road big names were coming to congratulate the king and eat his food. The sound of merriment echoed down into the Baptist's dark prison chamber. Would he too obtain a favor from the king on this day? Perhaps a special meal. No, today at least the executioner would not be on duty.

Herod has readied a festal board for his guests. Music, song, mirth. The feast was drawing to an end when a bevy of dancing girls entered — in their midst as queen, Salome, the daughter of Herodias. And she staged an exhibition that charmed and delighted everyone. Who was responsible? Her own mother, the king's wicked consort. She was preparing John's deathblow. Her project was proceeding well.

The king became emotionally overwrought as he watched the cavorting girl. A man with an iron will may struggle valiantly against passion, but the weak fall at first onslaught. Blinded by the concupiscence of the eyes, Herod hails the exotic dancer. "Ask whatever you want, half of my kingdom, and I will give it to you!" And he adds an oath in confirmation of his words. Do those about gasp? Half of his domain not worth that dance? And whose land was it? The Promised Land, the land where a Redeemer was traveling about and preaching penance, purity. To what extremes lust drives! How many barter away for the pleasure of sin the holy, "promised land" of their souls!

Salome finishes her number. She considers the words and the oath of the king. What should she ask for? Another costume, a pony, a palace for her future husband? She hastens to her mother who may offer good advice. "What should I pick?" she says hastily. Her mother need not delay her reply a moment; without reflection her answer is ready: "Demand the head of John." The adulterous woman knew her hour. For that moment she had been waiting. And her daughter, of like mind, does not hesitate; at once she returns to Herod: "I wish you would give me immediately upon a dish the head of John." Herod starts as from a trance; that kind of a request he had not anticipated. The Gospel says: "He was struck sad." The terrible surprise had rung a human note within. Before him stood the Baptist's pallid figure. Herod, however, was not the man who could profit by any noble sentiment. Someone reminds him of his promise, his oath; and he thinks of his guests, who rated the appearance of honor higher than conscience. And thus he lost the battle. A bodyguard is summoned and sent to the prisoner.

Let us visit the Baptist in his cell. Even there the strains of music, the laughter and cajolery of the feast penetrate. Of what is he thinking? Perhaps his thoughts have gone to Galilee, to the Redeemer. Is he conscious that his last hour is come? He hears footsteps. Is it a message of deliverance from imprisonment on the king's feastday? The bodyguard enters; what are his feelings? Had he perhaps been one of the soldiers who had heard the Baptist preach at the Jordan? The purpose of his presence is quickly stated. John's last moments. The thought of departure from this life did not come too hard for him. His work was ended. Certainly his thoughts turned to the Messiah. Like aged Simeon, he recites life's night prayer: "Now, Lord, You may dismiss Your servant, according to Your word in peace; because my eyes have seen Your salvation." And his head falls under the stroke of the executioner's axe.

The guard brings the bleeding head on the platter to the dining hall. Herod takes it. Would he dare look into those noble eyes? Did he sense the revulsion coming over the guests? He reaches it to his daughter, and she carries it to her mother. A revolting scene. Two monstrous women, mother and daughter gloating over the blood of a prophet, seemingly amused, victorious, as if the work of the prophet had fallen to the ground with his head. The Gospel tells nothing about a mishandling of the holy head, but rumors circulated that the adulteress was bent on keeping in her possession the tongue of him who did not spare her guilt.

2. Holy Mass (Loquebar). It is not a complex or abstruse formulary and its proper passages are few. The *Introit* and the *Lesson* describe John's fearless appearance before Herod, the beginning of his martyrdom: "I declared Your testimonies before the face of kings and did not spare myself" (rarely is the Introit psalm different from its antiphon — a sign that today's text is not very old. *Lesson*: "Speak to Judah all that I command you. Have no fear of them. . . . I shall make you a pillar of

iron . . . the kings of Judah and their princes, the priests and
people of the land will fight against you but will not prevail."

Our saint stands before us as the high cedar on Lebanon in the
Gradual, and as a pure and undefiled lily in the *Alleluia* verse.
For the *Offertory* and *Communion* we chant his beatitude, a
blessing we share in the sacrificial Banquet. Often in the Masses
of the sanctoral cycle the Foremass presents the saint in his passion, while the Sacrifice proper actualizes his glorified state. As
we unite ourselves in spirit with the former, so we participate
in his glory by the latter. The *Gospel* recounts the Baptist's martyrdom according to St. Mark, the most vivid and detailed of
the three New Testament narratives.

3. **St. Sabina.** *Day of death*: August 29, 126, at Terni or at
Rome. *Grave*: at Rome, in her basilica on the Aventine. *Life*.
According to legend, Sabina was born in Vindena, Umbria, and
became the wife of a notable person having the name Valentine.
She was converted to the faith by her maid Serapia, a Christian
virgin. When Serapia died a martyr's death (her feast occurs
on September 3 in the *Roman Martyrology*), Sabina gave her
servant's holy body an honorable burial. On that account she
was cast into prison by Emperor Hadrian and brought before
the judge Elpidius. "Are you Sabina, illustrious by family and
marriage?" he asked. "Yes, I am," came the reply, "but I thank
my Savior Jesus Christ that through His servant Serapia He has
freed me from the power of hell." Due to her contempt of the
gods, she was condemned to death. Christians buried her body
in the same grave as her teacher in the faith.

August 30

ST. ROSE, Virgin

Rose of My heart, you shall be My bride

1. **St. Rose.** *Day of death*: August 24, 1617. *Canonized*:
1671. *Feast*: since 1727. *Grave*: in the church of the Dominican

convent at Lima, Peru; her shrine is a highly popular place of pilgrimage. *Life.* Rose of Lima, a member of the Third Order of St. Dominic, was the "first blossom of sanctity that South America gave to the world." Hers was a life heroic in virtue and penance. The evils perpetrated by the conquerors of the land in their lust for gold, she expiated. For many her life was a silent sermon unto penance. Pope Clement X stated in the bull of canonization: "Since the discovery of Peru no missionary has arisen who effected a similar popular zeal for the practice of penance."

Already as a five-year-old child (born 1586), Rose vowed her innocence to God. While still a young girl, she practiced mortifications and fasts that exceeded ordinary discretion; during all of Lent she ate no bread, but subsisted on five citron seeds a day. In addition, she suffered repeated attacks from the devil, painful bodily ailments, and from her family, scoldings and calumnies. All this she accepted serenely, remarking that she was treated better than she deserved. For fifteen years she patiently endured severest spiritual abandonment and aridity. In reward came heavenly joys, the comforting companionship of her holy guardian angel and of the Blessed Virgin. August 24, 1617, proved to be the day "on which the paradise of her heavenly Bridegroom unlocked itself to her."

2. **Holy Mass (Dilexisti)** from the Common of Virgins (p. 406). On the feasts of saints the liturgy would have us (a) regard the saint as alive in our midst, an outstanding member of God's family; (b) consider the saint as a type and symbol of the Church, particularly women saints; (c) see the saint in individual Christian souls. In today's bridal Mass these points stand out prominently. (a) Before us as the God-Man's bride is the holy virgin Rose. We behold her entering heaven in a bridal procession (*Intr.* and *Off.*); we see Christ approach her (*Grad.*); she was indeed the wise virgin who with burning lamp awaited her Bridegroom; yes, through the Sacrifice-Banquet we are allowed a share in her divine nuptials. (b) In Rose we recognize the Church; for in every one of her members the Church celebrates and actualizes beforehand her own final glorification. How well the parable of the wise virgins applies to Mother Church, for during the night of earthly life she fills human lamps with the oil of her love (her prayer); further, her one desire is to await her Bridegroom's coming. Every Mass is a preview of His advent; with every Mass the nuptial day comes closer. (c) Because the individual soul is a cell of the Church, whatever Mother Church thinks and feels re-echoes in the Christian heart. Today, therefore, I go to Mass with bridal thoughts. My walk to church becomes a nuptial procession to the heavenly halls. During the *Offertory* I, the bride, adorned in royal fashion, stand next to the Bridegroom, and the Eucharistic Banquet anticipates the marriage feast of eternal union.

3. **Sts. Felix and Adauctus.** The priest Felix was martyred under Diocletian (*ca.* 305). On his way to judgment an unknown levite joined him. Observing how Felix suffered for the faith, he glowed with a holy desire for a similar good fortune

and cried out: "I confess the same teaching as this man; I adore the same Jesus Christ!" Thereupon he embraced Felix and the two were beheaded together on August 3. Because the Christians did not know his name, they called him Adauctus, that is, "joined to," since Felix by suffering martyrdom had joined himself to an eternal crown.

August 31

ST. RAYMOND NONNATUS, Confessor

From the slavery of Satan, deliver us

1. **St. Raymond.** *Day of death*: August 31, 1240. *Feast*: since 1681. *Grave*: after his death a dispute arose over the place for his burial. The coffin was therefore put upon a blind ass; the beast carried it to the chapel of St. Nicholas at Portbello (Spain), where the saint was then interred. *Life.* Raymond Nonnatus, that is, "the unborn," because he was taken from the womb of his dead mother (at Portbello in 1204), entered the Order of the Mercedarians. This community was devoted to the task of redeeming Christian slaves. Raymond went to Africa and, after his means for purchasing captives were exhausted, gave himself in ransom. When a number of Mohammedans had been converted to Christianity through his zeal for souls, he was cast into a dreadful prison. His lips were pierced and an iron lock inserted, a torture he bore with heroic patience.

Reports of Raymond's work and suffering reached Rome, and Pope Gregory IX created him a cardinal while he still wore the clothes of a slave. The saint died suddenly when only thirty-six years old, upon the return journey to Rome. As the priest who was to administer the last sacraments was slow in coming, angels, in the appearance of members of his Order, brought the holy Viaticum to him. Raymond ranks among those heroes who have given their life for their fellowmen. To him belongs the honorable title of confessor in its original sense.

2. Holy Mass (Os justi). Yesterday we regarded the day's saint (and ourselves) as a bride-virgin who with burning lamp awaited the Bridegroom through the night. Today we have a similar figure: the servant who, girded and a lamp in hand, watches through the night for the return of his lord; then as a reward he is served and nourished at his master's table. There are three points of similarity in these two parables: the burning lamp, awaiting the Bridegroom, and the reward.

How well these two parables depict Christian life! The burning lamp is the grace of filial adoption received in baptism. We must pass our lives with this lamp burning. Therefore sufficient oil must always be taken along; therefore, too, the light must be safeguarded against all the storms blown up by the devil. The early Christians were most careful to keep their baptismal light glowing until the day of death, that is, to die in the grace of baptism. To wait, to be prepared — such is the true Christian spirit. He will not let himself become engrossed with earthly interests or to be laden down with the cares and lusts of life. He will keep his eye steadily upon the future and his Lord's Second Coming. To "wait prepared" is the shortest expression of Gospel living according to the will of Jesus. The reward is lasting blessedness.

The Commons of the Saints

THE COMMONS OF THE SAINTS

See Volume 5, pp. 388–392, *for a discussion of the origin of the "Commons of the Saints," their nature, importance, and practical significance for developing a liturgical spirituality.*

1. COMMON OF THE BLESSED VIRGIN MARY

You are blessed, O Virgin Mother of God,
  for you have believed the Lord.
The things that were told you
  have been fulfilled in you.
Behold, you are exalted above the choirs of angels.
Intercede for us with the Lord our God.
  Hail Mary, full of grace, the Lord is with thee.
      — *Responsory on All Saints' Day*

In the celestial choirs of saints, Mary takes a first and unique position. Therefore there can be no question of a Common of Marian Masses in the same sense that the term applies to a group of saints. Mary's role is singular, she admits of no classification. Rather, she stands superior to all categories as Queen — Queen of apostles, Queen of martyrs, Queen of confessors, Queen of virgins, as we pray in her litany. Missal and breviary contain a Common only in the sense that Marian texts are brought together for common use, while her separate feasts emphasize one or the other specific grace or privilege. It is easily seen how important the Common becomes for the full appreciation of the different Marian Offices; we will gain a better understanding of the individual feasts if we assimilate the great underlying theology proper to the Common.

What are the ideas fundamental to the Marian Common? We could select the Invitatory at Matins as the briefest summary:

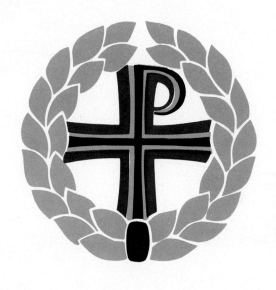

TO HIM BE THE GLORY
FROM WHOM COMES
OUR STRENGTH,
FROM WHOM COMES
OUR REWARD!

"Holy Mary, Virgin, Mother of God, plead our cause." These few words proclaim all Mary's greatness. (a) *Holy Mary* — her personal sanctity. (b) *Virgin* — it is with special predilection that the liturgy calls Mary Virgin; it is her unique title shared with no other, she who is both Virgin and Mother. (c) *Mother of God* — this prerogative is her most sublime privilege, the basic reason for all her other graces. (d) *Intercessor* — from this stems the boundless trust Christianity places in the "Help of Christians." These four truths are the fundamental points in the Marian Common; each separate prayer text can be related ultimately to one or the other.

The Common Office of the Blessed Virgin Mary in the breviary as well as the formularies for the separate Marian feasts are rich in metaphor; with colorful pictures and parables the liturgy brings our beloved Mother before us. Three of these figures deserve our special attention, viz., Bride, Wisdom, the holy City Jerusalem.

1. *The Bride of God*. Numerous passages from the Canticle of Canticles are found in the breviary's Marian Common. The Canticle of Canticles is one of the three Old Testament books ascribed to King Solomon; on first reading it might seem that its contents consisted simply of love poems between Solomon and a shepherdess. Topic headings would include: the longing of the two lovers for nuptial union; attempts to attain that objective; ditties and dialog betraying their inclinations and feelings; the obstacles preventing marriage. Actually, however, the message of the text when properly analyzed is God's love toward His people, a love that in turn prefigured the intimate bond between Christ and His Church, between Christ and the soul endowed with divine grace. The Bridegroom-Bride relationship is a very common one in the sacred books of the Old and New Testaments. God is "wedded" to the Chosen People; He calls Himself a "jealous" God; idol worship is equivalent to "adultery."

Christ, and later St. Paul, deepened the spiritual implications of the comparison; to his followers John the Baptist introduced

374 COMMON OF THE SAINTS

Christ as the Bridegroom, and Jesus referred to Himself as the Church's Spouse (John 3:29; Matt. 9:15). Christianity's chiefest blessings are indicated by the nuptial analogy — our oneness with God, the union of the soul with Christ, a union that attains its most perfect intimacy in the saints. This is why the Canticle of Canticles is used so often in the Marian Common; for with Mary the bond of divine love found the most intense expression imaginable; the holy Virgin was not only the most immaculate and most perfect of God's creatures, she was granted a most singular physical union with divinity in that for nine months she carried the Son of God in her womb.

2. *Wisdom*. Mary is meant when the term *wisdom* is used in her Offices. In the Old Testament Wisdom books God's attribute of wisdom is at times personified; a celebrated passage speaks of divine wisdom as a child that at the beginning played in Yahweh's presence and at His side during the work of creation; in another text wisdom is an instructress of God who teaches mankind wisdom and virtue, true religion. By wisdom the sacred writers often meant the divine attribute, the wisdom by which God created and arranged everything in the world, or the eternal divine ideas that God gives expression to more or less perfectly in creatures. The Fathers of the Church at times see the Son of God "through whom God created the world" in personified wisdom.

In the sacred books the word *wisdom* is also used of a type of created wisdom, the virtue of wisdom which God gave to His people through revealed religion. The concept of wisdom here becomes much more embracive than in modern languages; it is used to express morality, virtue, holiness, prudence. Somewhat similarly foolishness and sinfulness are correlative terms.

Wisdom texts are applied to Mary in the liturgy. Why? Creatures are reflections of God's wisdom; the more beautiful and perfect they are, the more do they mirror God's beauty, wisdom, holiness. Mary, God's most perfect creation, may then be equated with wisdom itself. Moreover, it was part of God's eternal plan and providence that His Son should become incarnate through her; with all the perfection of her beauty Mary stood in the divine presence from all eternity. And lastly, she possessed created wisdom, i.e., sanctity, the virtues, in the highest degree possible, another sense in which the term *wisdom* may rightly be used of her.

3. *Jerusalem.* In a goodly number of liturgical passages Mary is meant when the words *holy City Jerusalem* (or Sion) occur. Here is the reason. Among all the cities of the world, Jerusalem was unique. Jerusalem was the city where Yahweh set His throne. Jerusalem was His chosen city, His beloved city. Surely the application to Mary is not strained! In Jerusalem stood the temple, the dwelling-place of the Most High — Mary provided a living temple for God! Jerusalem was the "chosen city" of the great King — Mary, "blessed among women," Jerusalem, mother of nations, "whither all the tribes go up," Gentiles included — Mary, the Mother of Christendom. Jerusalem, besieged and smitten — Mary, Mother of sorrows. Jerusalem, prized and beloved by every Jew — Mary, most dear to every Christian.

MASS OF OUR LADY ON SATURDAY

Since ancient times the Roman Church has dedicated Saturday to the Blessed Virgin. A special Office and Mass in her honor are provided for all Saturdays on which no feast of some rank occurs. The psalms of the Office are those of the feria, Saturday; the remaining prayers are Marian from some aspect. Following the major divisions of the ecclesiastical year, five different formularies are given for the Mass of our Lady on Saturday, viz., (1) during Advent, the *Rorate* Mass; (2) during Christmastide; (3) from February 3 to Lent; (4) during Paschaltide; (5) after Pentecost. The formulary for the Pentecost season best reflects the spirit and tenor of the Marian Common; the following comment will help to understand its message.

The Mass *Salve Sancta Parens* is an ancient composition, profound in its simplicity. Two trends of thought are nicely interwoven: (a) the "Mother of God" theme runs like a golden thread through the formulary. Mary's greatest privilege and the reason for all her graces was her divine motherhood. (b) We Christians may and should take part in her dignity, through the medium of holy Mass. We may and should become "God's mother" — to use Christ's own words — in two ways: (1) by taking the "Word of God" into ourselves in a docile and obedient manner (the Foremass); (2) by receiving the living "Word of God" in the Eucharist and thus becoming in a still higher sense "mothers unto God." If we use this approach, a Marian feast with its Mass will always be a thrilling experience.

Upon entering the church we greet the "Holy Mother" who bore the King of heaven and earth, in the words of an ancient Christian poet, Sedulius (*ca.* 450); our salutation continues with the bridal-psalm, 44, which applies so perfectly to Mary. The two Readings proclaim the dignity of divine motherhood. In the *Lesson* divine Wisdom, i.e., Christ, comes to live in the holy City Sion and there takes root in the Chosen People, i.e., Christ enters the womb of the Virgin Mary, becomes man, and founds the Church, the new Sion.

Thus in the Lesson the physical and spiritual motherhood of Mary, of the Church, and of individual souls is expressed mystically. "My abode is in the full assembly of the saints" — how these words ring true now at Mass! For the assembled congregation represents the Church in miniature; to it divine Wisdom, Christ, descends full of grace in the holy Sacrifice; here the divine Vine "takes root." In the *Gospel* our Lord Himself reveals the beautiful doctrine of spiritual, divine motherhood. Alongside praise of His own Mother, He places praise for "all who hear the word of God and keep it." According to the spirit of the liturgy, the "word of God" in this passage is the Son of God.

Because of the Eucharistic banquet, the *Communion* text is easily applied to the Church and to souls: "Blessed the womb of the Virgin Mary that bore the Son of the eternal Father." Thus Mary is the model *par excellence* of holy Church and of our souls. The *Offertory*, culled from the *Rorate* Mass of Advent, repeats the "eternal greeting" of the angel Gabriel, the *Ave Maria* (the source of our "Hail, Mary"). The angel's greeting is directed to Mary and to all who now at Mass share her privilege of bearing Christ.

2. THE COMMON OF THE APOSTLES

Now we meet those who during their earthly lives
    planted the Church with their own blood.
They drank the chalice of the Lord and became
    God's friends.
Their voice resounds through all the world,
    their words to the very ends of the earth.

One can readily recognize a text from the Common of Apostles — its tone and character are so sharply defined. There are two major thought areas, viz., the apostles are *friends of Christ*, and they are *princes*, the Church's royal sons. Typical is the oft-repeated verse: "Your friends, O God, are very honorable to me; their rule is well established" (*Ps.* 138). Here is the reason why Psalm 138 is used at the Introit and for second Vespers (the psalm itself has little bearing on the office of the apostles; and even this very verse is a faulty translation of the original text). The antiphons of first Vespers give fine expression to the "friendship with Christ" theme; they are taken from the Gospel of what once was the vigil Mass: "You are My friends, if you do what I command you, says the Lord."

Besides the high dignity of the apostolic office, the Common reminds us of the call and the sufferings of the apostles. Their mission was to establish and spread Christ's kingdom on earth. They were, therefore, the first missionaries. To express this there is the text from Psalm 18, "Their voice resounds through all the world, their words to the very ends of the earth." In ancient times Psalm 18 was entitled "The Apostle," because the whole composition was commonly sung on feasts of the chosen

Twelve. In one of his homilies St. Augustine tells how "the apostles declared God's glory as other heavens" ("The heavens declare the glory of God" — the opening verse of Psalm 18).

Typical too is the so-called chapter at Vespers and Lauds: "Brethren, you are now no longer guests and strangers; you are citizens with the saints, members of God's household; you are built upon the foundation of the apostles and the prophets, with Christ Jesus Himself as the chief cornerstone." In the lofty edifice of the Church, Christ is the cornerstone; the apostles form the foundation, the members are the stones resting upon that foundation. Therefore the feasts of the apostles are not feasts of mere individual saints, rather they are redemption feasts, feasts of holy Church. During the Middle Ages churches often had twelve special pillars to represent the twelve apostles.

Union with Christ in love presupposes union with Christ in suffering. The apostles "drank the chalice of the Lord," and willingly embraced the pain of martyrdom. An apostle-feast should be a genuine religious solemnity.

3. THE COMMON OF SOVEREIGN PONTIFFS

On January 9, 1952, Pope Pius XII introduced a new Common, that of "One or Several Sovereign Pontiffs." The official bull gave the following reasons for the innovation:

"At all times holy Church has accorded a very special honor to those Roman Pontiffs who zealously defended the rights of the Apostolic See, who spread the truths of the Gospel through the world, and who by the holiness of their lives and by witnessing unto death were a glowing example to the faithful flock entrusted to them. In every age the gates of hell have struck out at the immovable rock of Peter through vain but ever more gruesome and bloody persecution, while at the present time the enemies of the Church endeavor to overwhelm the Popes with their venom and to disgrace them with diabolical calumnies. Now to counter these attacks and to increase the honor of the papacy —

an office conferred by God Himself — and also to celebrate with greater solemnity those Popes who were distinguished for holiness, Pope Pius XII introduced the new Common."

In the breviary this new Common consists merely of an Oration and a homily for the third nocturn; all the remaining prayers and texts are from the Common of a Martyr or the Common of a Confessor. The Mass, however, is a completely new formulary; from the opening words of the Introit it is referred to by the name *Si diligis me*. The dominant theme of this new Mass is our Savior's promise to Peter as it continues to be fulfilled and realized in the Apostle's successors, the Roman Pontiffs. Two of Christ's pronouncements to Peter dominate the text; the words, "If you love Me, Simon Peter, feed My sheep, feed My lambs," ring out in the Introit and continue to resound during the first part of the Mass as the "shepherd motif"; while the words, "You are Peter, and upon this rock I will build My Church," occur repeatedly from the Alleluia verse to the end of the sacred service.

The *Introit* departs from classical models by using a New Testament text as an antiphon. Enclosed in its frame, Psalm 29 comes from the lips of the day's pope-saint as an expression of gratitude for the call to shepherd the flock of Christ and for the protection from enemies accorded him in the task. We think of Christ's words, "The gates of hell shall not prevail." (There is no indication that the remaining verses of the psalm are alluded to.)

Reference to the Mass's double theme is easily seen in the two *Collects*. In the first God is addressed as "the eternal Shepherd" who should look mercifully upon His flock and protect it through the intercession of the day's saint and sovereign pontiff whom He appointed as shepherd over the whole Church. The second Oration, which is used very rarely, bases its petition upon the promise, "The gates of hell. . . ."

Appropriately the *Epistle*, a new selection, comes from the pen of Peter himself. The first supreme shepherd is admonishing his successors: "I exhort the presbyters among you — I, your fellow presbyter and witness to the sufferings of Christ (Peter was present on Olivet during Christ's agony and seizure), the partaker also of the glory that is to be revealed in time to come — tend the flock of God which is among you, governing not by constraint, but willingly, according to God; nor yet as lording it over your charges, but becoming from the heart a pattern to the flock. And when the Prince of shepherds appears, you will receive the unfading crown of glory. . . . The God of all grace, who has called us unto His eternal glory in Christ Jesus, will Himself, after we have suffered a little while, perfect, strengthen and establish us. To Him is the dominion forever and ever. Amen." There is no need to labor the point that this selection significantly enriches the treasury of missal readings.

The *Gradual*, which by nature should echo the Epistle, associates the words *seniores* and *consenior* with a verse from Psalm 106 and points to the elevation of the day's saint to the Chair of Peter. The *Alleluia* verse anticipates the Gospel, putting into relief its principal message: "You are Peter (the Rock), and upon this rock I will build My Church." Christ's words have been fulfilled in the papacy; for through the ages the popes have proven to be the immovable rock-foundation of holy Church. The *Gospel* presents Biblical proof that the primacy of Peter and of his successors was divinely willed and instituted. Through the centuries the popes have guided the Church with a sure and steady hand; they have held the keys to God's kingdom in heaven and on earth; and in them we see realized repeatedly our blessed Savior's prophecy that hell with all its powers will not triumph.

Today's *Offertory*, a passage from Jeremias, is usually applied to the Savior's precursor in the liturgy: "See, I am putting My words in your mouth. I am placing you over nations and kingdoms that you may destroy and tear down, that you may build and plant" (Jer. 1:9–10). The divine Shepherd is addressing Peter and his successors; to them He entrusts the work of teaching infallibly; upon them He places the threefold crown (tiara), and leaves with them the power to bind and to loose.

The *Secret* again touches upon the Introit motif: may God's pleasure rest upon flock and shepherd. While the faithful approach the Lord's table, we hear the familiar passage, "You are Peter, and upon this rock I will build My Church." It is a message that applies not only to the day's sainted pontiff, but to every one present before the altar. For each Christian must be a rock in faith and in grace and in love — a rock upon which Christ can build a spiritual Church. Holy Communion is part of His construction work.

Classic in form and content, the first *Postcommunion* is pointed less toward individual Christians than toward the Church now "nourished with holy refreshment" through the Eucharist; it petitions guidance, freedom, and purity of faith for the papacy. In the second Postcommunion the shepherd motif is met for the last time; note in particular the phrase parallelism: "The shepherd will not lack obedience from his flock, nor the flock lack the shepherd's protecting care." — All considered, a beautiful and instructive Mass formulary. One might, however, remark that its frequent occurrence (more than twenty-four times a year) could lessen devotion, while the previous arrangement did offer greater variety.

4. THE COMMON OF MARTYRS

You, My holy ones, bitter conflict was your lot
    in the days of your mortal life.
Now will I grant you reward for your sufferings.
Come, blessed of My Father,
    take possession of the kingdom.

How highly the Church esteems martyrs is indicated by the great number of Commons proper to them. Three series are distinguished: the Common of One Martyr, the Common of Several Martyrs, and a special Common of Martyrs during Paschaltide.

A. THE COMMON OF ONE MARTYR

This Common has four distinct formularies, two for martyr-bishops, two for martyrs who were not bishops.

1. Mass *Statuit*

This formulary blends together reflections on the priesthood as the extension of Christ's High Priesthood (*Allel.*) with martyrdom. In the priest ascending the altar we see represented the day's martyr-bishop; in him our saint is present before us. Of him the *Introit* says: "The Lord has confided to him the covenant of peace," i.e., the treasures of the Church. He is a prince in the kingdom of God; his priesthood is eternal because it is the priesthood of Jesus Christ. Psalm 131 follows. The reason for the choice lies in the psalm as such. David was chosen by a special act of God and therefore typified the call and consecration of our saint to the office of bishop. The psalm records a reciprocal oath; David swore to erect a temple for God, while God promised under oath to keep David's descendants upon the throne forever. David represents our sainted bishop who zealously safeguarded the interests of the Church, even to the point of shedding his blood. With his merits in mind we make our appeal: "Lord, think of David, and of his many services." *Collect*: our weakness crushes us down to the very ground; may our holy martyr-bishop come to our assistance by his intercession.

Ordinarily in the *Epistle* or *Lectio* the day's saint addresses us, or Mother Church speaks of him. Today it is the latter. The apostle James the Younger, himself an illustrious bishop (Jerusalem's first) and martyr, provides the script. Blessed is the martyr, he who stood the test. Martyrdom is God's norm for testing, His proving grounds. The prize for perseverance is the "(victor's) crown of eternal life, which God has promised to those who love Him." Eternal beatitude! Today, the anniversary of his death, our martyr received this crown from the hands of his divine King; and through the Eucharist we are enabled to share that glory. The remaining portion of the Epistle would have no relation to the feast, apart from the conclusion perhaps: eternal beatitude is that "best gift, that perfect gift coming from above, from the Father of lights." Thus does God love His children, the firstfruits of His creatures; we hope we are numbered among them.

In the *Gradual* God (or Christ) says: "I have found Myself a servant in David." Again David typifies God's chosen ones! Just as David, so too our bishop was anointed with holy oil; God's hand aided him, God's arm supported him in his every project (it may help to think of the scene on Lake Gennesareth, Christ and Peter walking hand in hand toward the little ship). Against such an alliance for defense and offense Satan can make no inroads. Upon these words of divine assurance do we rest our trust in our holy bishop.

The *Alleluia* signals the King's approach. Today He appears in priestly vestments; we greet Him with a verse from Psalm 109: "A priest You are forever, after the manner of Melchisedech!" Christ is our Eucharistic Priest forever; His priestly dignity finds an extension in our holy bishop and in the celebrant at the altar. It is the *Gospel,* and the divine High Priest stands in our midst. Next to Him is the day's saint, to whom He refers constantly. With serious and decisive words He says: You can be My followers on one condition, if you detach yourselves from "father, mother, wife, children, brothers, sisters — yes, and hate even your own life!"

All that pleases the natural man must be sacrificed, if God so asks; and even more, the cross of life with all its thorns must be borne patiently, perseveringly, after our cross-laden Savior. It is martyrdom by blood that He is alluding to. Christ, the King of martyrs, has a perfect right to enjoin so high an ideal, for He Himself set the example in every detail; and today's martyr imitated it perfectly. If we find it difficult to understand the Gospel's injunction about "hating" and "cross-carrying," relate it to the lives of Christ and His martyr; its implications will then be quickly seen. A tower is to be built — God's kingdom in my soul. A war is to be fought — Satan's hordes are ever lurking. Neither operation will be finished before death. Our bishop-saint has completed his.

The *Offertory* affords God (or Christ) another opportunity to speak of the day's martyr. Two "angel guardians" accompanied him through life, fidelity and mercy. Fidelity prompted him to meet all obligations, mercy poured redemption's graces lavishly into his soul; and thus came the day of death for him who "exalted his horn in God's Name." A last time God speaks of His beloved in the *Communion* refrain, again in terms of David. God swore to David that his descendants would occupy the throne forever, that his throne would continue glorious, like the sun and moon. In Christ Yahweh's solemn promise was fulfilled; and all His followers, the holy martyrs in particular, share in that eternal kingship. The holy Eucharist is the pledge and guarantee of its final, full realization.

2. Mass *Sacerdotes*

In this Mass more emphasis is placed on the eternal reward the holy martyrs receive than in the preceding one; it is also more joyous in tone and triumphant. The *Entrance Chant* challenges priest and people, the two great divisions of Christendom, to praise God (the laity are called the "holy and humble of heart"). Furthermore, all creation should praise God. By way of exception, a psalm is not used here, but the familiar "Canticle of the Three Youths." The reason for the joyous outburst of divine praise is the exaltation of our bishop-martyr whose anniversary we are celebrating (*Coll.*). In the *Epistle* the holy martyr uses words from St. Paul as he speaks to us. It is an exceptionally beautiful passage, and puts our celebration in a new light, viz., as a communion in suffering and consolation with the saint, and with Christ. We imagine the saint saying in our presence: Christ's "sufferings" abounded in me; therefore my "consolation" too is incomparably great in heaven; in both, you too may share, for "you ought be partakers in the passion and in the consolation, in Christ Jesus our Lord."

This is realized through the holy Sacrifice; for at the *Offertory* our martyr places his palm of martyrdom upon the altar and we follow his lead; by our oblation we merge ourselves into Christ's saving passion. Thus do the sufferings of Christ and those of the day's martyr become ours. In the sacrificial Banquet we share in his "consolation"; for the fruit of the Sacrifice is participation in his exaltation. So we sing at *Communion* time: "Lord, You have placed upon his head a crown of precious stones." Such is true of the martyr, it also holds true for us who are mystically one with him. The *Gradual* too crowns the day's saint "with glory and honor," while the *Alleluia* casts him in the role of a royal priest.

Presently Christ, the first among martyrs, appears (*Gosp.*). He repeats His homily on the necessity of shouldering the Cross. There is no other road leading to eternal good save the Way of Calvary. "He who wishes to follow Me must deny himself, embrace his cross, and walk in My footsteps." All through our earthly lives we must be "partakers in the suffering" of Christ and of His holy martyrs. For the sake of Christ we must "lose our earthly life." Our Lord closes His homily with a reference to the Last Day when He will return "with the angels in the glory of His Father," the day when we are destined to become partners and sharers of His consolation. This is typical of ancient Mass formularies — there must always be some allusion to the Second Coming. At the death of today's saint the Lord did return "to render him reward according to his works." In the Mass we experience this return of the glorified Savior with His angels and His martyr when at the consecration He appears under the veil of the sacred species. In the Offertory God says: "I have found Myself a servant in David." David represents the elect. Like David, our bishop was anointed with sacred oil; as a martyr he was anointed to fight; God's powerful hand assisted him in the mortal combat.

To sum up. The basic theme of this formulary is communion in suffering and communion in consolation. In the Foremass, communion in suffering dominates, in the Mass proper com-

munion in consolation. It is a theme underlying most Mass
formularies in honor of saints.

3. Mass *In virtute*

This, the first Mass of a martyr-not-a-bishop, likewise features
the joy and glory at the triumph over suffering. The day's saint
(*justus*) enters at the *Introit* (in the person of the celebrant)
resplendent with glory; he rejoices in the power of God and
exults in the salvation accorded him; his heart's desire has
been granted, he stands in our presence, the winner! (All of
Psalm 20 would be appropriate here; wherever the word *king*
occurs, simply substitute the name of the day's saint.) The psalm
was a thanksgiving prayer of one of Israel's kings after a telling
victory.

The *Collect* affords occasion to voice our plea that this martyr-
feast "make us strong in love toward God." A very special
fervor should mark our observance of ancient martyr-feasts, for
these fill us with the spirit of the early Church. In the *Reading*
the Church shows how our saint lived; how "the Lord conducted
him on the proper road and showed him the kingdom of God";
how He accompanied him in every struggle; how He did not
abandon him in time of distress but went down with him into
the pit of prison, in chains; then He favored him with the
"sceptre of the kingdom" and "everlasting glory" (in its original
context the passage describes the lot of Joseph in Egypt; it would
add depth to our use of the text if we placed it against the background of Joseph's experience, his suffering and exaltation in
the land of pharaoh). True to its nature the *Gradual* echoes our
reflections on the Lesson. Blessed is the person who fears God!
His children will be influential on earth. We are "his children,"
we who now associate ourselves with him at Mass.

Standing alongside Christ, we see our martyr wearing his
heavenly crown as the *Alleluia* is chanted. Then the Lord tells
how necessary it is to follow in the way of the Cross (as in the
two preceding formularies). His words help us realize the im-

plications of martyrdom, and how to make it part of our own lives. His message is no soft soap: "I have not come to bring peace but the sword!" Christianity is not a dollard's dream, no asylum for idlers — Christianity means struggle. Above all it is a struggle against flesh and blood; it presumes a willingness to take the cross upon oneself and to follow Christ. (Note that our Lord throws out the same challenge in all three Masses!) Jesus keeps His finger pointed at the martyr; he actually fulfilled His words most perfectly. We too, although an identical crisis may not confront us, may share with him the honor of "witnessing" to Christ by showing testimony in smaller ways, e.g., a cup of water handed to His poor.

Again in the *Offertory* we see our saint wearing the crown of victory, advancing toward the altar. During the Eucharistic Banquet we do not, as otherwise, sing a text reflecting the saint's (and our) transfiguration; rather, today's is a sobering message: "If you wish to follow Me, embrace your cross. . . ." Why these words at so sacred a meal? Perhaps Mother Church is reminding you that after Mass your "Way of the Cross" begins; and your source of strength is this holy Meal.

4. Mass *Laetabitur*

The second Mass for a martyr-not-a-bishop! We see the holy martyr (*justus*) in heavenly glory, and are very happy — such is the general content of today's text (*Intr.*). Read Psalm 63 as a description of the saint's martyrdom, listen to the *Epistle* as a sermon coming from the prison of our holy martyr who "for the Gospel of the Lord's resurrection labored even unto chains, as if he were an evildoer." He assures us that he suffers also for us, God's "elect," so that we "might attain salvation." He continues, exhorting us to a similar patience in trials and persecution. "All who live piously in Christ Jesus should be prepared for persecution." Yes, we are determined to walk in the footsteps of the martyrs, witnesses unto Christ.

The *Gradual,* a community meditation upon our saint, points out how the Lord sustained him when he fell, the victim of enemy hate; but now he stands erect, transfigured in glory. During life he dedicated himself to good deeds, therefore he now is blessed.

In the *Alleluia* Jesus speaks — through darkness to light. Such was the martyr's lot, such is ours. In the *Gospel* He urges us to a fearless profession of our faith. Now in the sacred precincts of church His holy words gladden us, but soon we must leave to "confess" Him before men fearlessly, for they can kill only the body. While our blessed Lord speaks He points to the day's martyr who puts His counsels into perfect practice. As an answer to His concluding exhortation comes the *Offertory* hymn; our saint stands "confessed" before the heavenly Father, "crowned with the crown of life." Again at the *Communion* Jesus whispers into our ear: Now you are with Me at a banquet, later be with Me through the cross and suffering.

B. COMMON OF SEVERAL MARTYRS

Because of the dramatic and mystery element in the liturgy, the saints commemorated on a given day are to be regarded as personally present. It is important therefore to note whether the prayer texts employed use the singular or plural, whether one or several of the blessed are in our midst. Here too we have the reason why distinct formularies are had for one or several martyrs. Three different Masses are found in the missal; there is no distinction between martyrs who were bishops and those who were not.

1. Mass *Intret*

There is a marked difference between this formulary and other martyr Masses, for in the present text it is not glory and triumph that receive attention, but torment, pain, and suffering. The Mass begins with a wrenching cry as Mother Church sees

her children languishing in prison chains. Picture yourself at
the scene of martyrdom. (At the night vigil the acts of the martyrs are read.) Our first reaction is spontaneous and natural, the
sentiments voiced in the *Entrance Chant*. For we hear the "cries
of the martyrs in chains," we see their blood flowing under
torture. Our sense of justice is roused, and we call out for
justice (*Intr.*).

Now Mother Church seeks to raise our sights (*Epistle*). It
is as if a consoling voice sounded from the heavens as we hear:
"The souls of the just are in God's hand. In the opinion of fools
they seemed to die, but they are in peace (i.e., transfigured by
glory). God tried them and found them worthy of His presence.
He accepted their sacrifice; now they shine and reign. The Lord
is their King forever." How beautifully the Church can spirit-
ualize and idealize suffering! And our own attitude begins to
change as we turn from lamentation to praise. At the Introit we
may not have understood God's seeming complacence, but now
we praise His majesty and His strong arm in our saint's heroic
passion. How differently the same act is viewed by nature and
by grace! The mystery of martyrdom is becoming intelligible:
"The bodies of the saints are buried in peace while their names
continue to live" (*Allel.*).

The *Gospel*: from the lips of Christ we hear the signs presag-
ing His Second Advent; among them are the trials of the
martyrs: "They will lay hands on you and persecute you . . .
dragging you before kings and civil officials on My account . . .
you will be hated by all." In the case of our saints these predic-
tions were fulfilled to the letter. United to them through the
bond of Christ's Mystical Body, we too must be witnesses unto
Christ. "By your perseverance you will save your souls." Today
we will take to the altar the little martyrdoms of life as our
Offertory gift. The Communion Banquet provides strength for
the conflict.

Do not fail to note the contrast between the opening and closing chants. The Introit approached martyrdom from the human
viewpoint; in the course of the Mass nobler insights are pre

sented; at the end the *Communion* antiphon enables us to see in a fully supernatural perspective — it is God who tries the martyrs. They are gold, and any slag must be removed; this is possible only through the fire of suffering. Martyrdom is an acceptable holocaust, which when united to Christ's, possesses an infinite value. This contrast between the initial and final chants is typical of the spirit of the entire formulary. Man comes to the sanctuary with his natural bents and inclinations, unredeemed, one might say; by means of the sacred Sacrifice he is sanctified, his work and suffering are consecrated. Oppressed he goes to Mass, relieved and consoled he returns home. God did not take away the cross from him, but He did transform and glorify it.

2. Mass *Sapientiam*

Originally this Mass was proper to the physician saints, Cosmas and Damian. Therefore it was quite fitting for the Gospel to begin with a reference to the Lord's work of healing; the Introit too praises the "wisdom" of these saints. At a later date the formulary was appropriated by the Common.

At the *Introit* "Christ's faithful" and the "nations" from afar (viz., ourselves) enter the burial church of our martyr-saints and admire their "wisdom." At the same time we invite them to "exult in the Lord." In the Readings it is the Church who sounds their praises: "The just will live forever and their reward is with the Lord . . . therefore will they receive a beauteous diadem and a splendid crown from the hand of the Lord." In the battle of spirit hosts that will rage about God's kingdom until the very end, the saints are well-equipped soldiers; they will provide protection for us too. In the *Gradual* we hear the martyrs say: we were like birds that a bird-catcher entices into his snare; now the snare is broken, God has freed us (so they represent their martyrdom).

The *Alleluia* chant gives a different view; we see the just above in the heavens, happy and merry at the celestial nuptial banquet. The *Gospel* is more easily understood if we recall the ancient practice of bringing the sick to the graves of the holy martyrs or of placing upon the sick linens that touched their tombs or relics. Christians were convinced that "a healing strength went out from them." The Gospel proposes a beautiful mystery-action, i.e., the episode recounted repeats itself spiritually in the holy Sacrifice; "much people," i.e., we the faithful about the altar, have come together to be healed of our spiritual ills. Jesus "descends from the (heavenly) mountain into the plain" (to us). And "all the people sought to touch Him (in ancient times the consecrated Host was placed in the hands of the communicants) for strength went out from Him (present in the holy Eucharist)." Immediately the good Lord pronounces our martyrs blessed, for in their lives they actualized His beatitudes, especially the fourth in St. Luke's series, "Blessed are you when men hate and persecute and calumniate you, and despoil you of your good name for the sake of the Son of Man; rejoice and be glad because your reward is great in heaven."

The *Offertory* affords us a glimpse into the heavens where we see Christ's promise fulfilled. There the saints are in their heavenly homes, in glory and peace, ever praising God. During the *Communion* banquet the Lord speaks to us. He calls us His friends: "Do not fear your persecutors." Implicitly He gives two reasons for His statement: look at today's martyrs; they did not fear, and now they are in glory; keep in mind, too, that I am with you; the Eucharist is your strength and power. The Communion chant should, of course, be sung during the distribution of the holy Eucharist.

3. Mass *Salus autem*

In this third Mass formulary the theology of our Savior's Second Advent is again strikingly prominent. For a summarizing picture imagine Christ appearing at the head of His "white-robed army of martyrs" in preview for the return on the last day (*Epist.* and *Gosp.*). The *Introit* directs our thoughts to the life of today's martyrs (the remaining verses of the psalm give further detail); evil persons were strong and fortunate, they oppressed the good, yes, tortured and put them to death, but God, the "salvation of the just," did not forsake them.

In the *Epistle* the martyrs speak to us. They recall the "former days" when Christians, after "being enlightened (baptized), endured great suffering." They languished in prisons, sustaining the loss of all earthly goods with joy. Will you join them? "You have need of patience that, doing the will of God, you may receive the promise: For yet a very little while, and He who is to come, will come" (Heb. 10:32–28). (Now at Mass we are witnessing a dress rehearsal of the parousia.)

The *Gradual* reflects the sentiments of the Epistle. The martyrs cried out in their need and God heard them. It will not be otherwise with us, "For the Lord is close to the broken-hearted; and those who are crushed in spirit He saves." In the *Gospel* Christ appears as the rewarder of martyrs (*Tract*), and seeks to instill the spirit of martyrdom in His followers; what we hear during the silent hour of worship must be preached aloud to the whole world.

We must not fear those who can "kill the body"; in fact, apart from everlasting death, we need not fear anything. Rather our efforts will be directed toward developing a lively sense of God's good providence, realizing that not even a hair goes lost without His knowledge. This attitude will aid us in becoming Christ's heralds upon earth, so that He "will confess us before the angels of God" at the Second Coming. Both Readings instill the spirit of martyrdom. In the first the martyrs speak to us, in the second, Christ Himself. Both have the same purpose, both come to a climax in the parousia theme.

In the *Offertory* hymn it is martyrdom again, but from a higher plane: "The souls of the just are in the hand of God . . . in the opinion of the unwise they seemed to die, but they are in peace" (Wis. 3:1–3), i.e., they are enjoying the beatific vision. The *Communion* reminds us of the dark catacombs from which these witnesses unto blood came forth. What the Lord in the nightly stillness whispered into their ears, they "preached from the housetops." This is our duty too. In the morning Mass Christ comes to us softly and, as it were, whispers in the darkness. Then we return to a hostile world as His confessors. In what does the secret of our strength lie? In an abiding love of Christ. May such love come to us through receiving His Body and imitating the example of the saints.

C. THE COMMON OF MARTYRS IN PASCHALTIDE

The high honor accorded martyrs by Mother Church finds its culmination in the special Common granted them during Easter time. This is to show that martyrdom is most intimately associated with Christ's own passion and triumph. The "white-robed company of martyrs" form the retinue for the Conqueror over death and hell. In celebrating the feasts of martyrs the liturgy seeks to dramatize in mystery St. Paul's dictum: "As you are partakers of His sufferings, so will you also be of the comfort." The two formularies, Common of One Martyr and Common of Several Martyrs, are classic in form and content, and breathe the triumphant martyr spirit of the ancient Church.

1. Mass for One Martyr *Protexisti*

The dramatic directness and freshness of the text, indications of its antiquity, impress us immediately. Without much ado the liturgy introduces the saint, has him speak, and projects a series of pictures descriptive of his life. In the *Introit* the martyr himself sings a hymn of thanksgiving; persecution merely heightened his triumph. On Good Friday and Holy Saturday, Psalm 63 (the whole composition must be considered) described the passion of Christ; today our martyr uses it to voice his own sufferings. We hear his cries and lamentations. We see his enemies whet "their tongues like a sword . . . and bend their bow to shoot down the righteous." We observe them devising their diabolical plans. Yet they never win, for their weapons "wound no more than children's arrows!" Enraged and humbled, they are forced to acknowledge God's good providence. But "the just man rejoices in the Lord, in Him glory all the upright of heart."

Equally dramatic is the *Lesson*. In spirit we are present at the last judgment and see both the martyrs and their persecutors. The latter now behold their victims in heavenly glory and cry out in agony and fear: "These are they whom we once derided. . . . Fools, we thought their life madness. . . . See, now they are numbered among the children of God."

The *Alleluia* song voices the reflections of the congregation; heaven and earth, i.e., the heavenly and earthly *ecclesia,* praise and confess God's wondrous designs as manifested in the martyrdom of the saints and in their heavenly reward. In Christian antiquity the word *confessio* or *confiteri* applied in a very special way to martyrs. The martyr was a "confessor" in the highest sense; he had "confessed" the Lord before men, and now the Lord and all the heavenly court "confess him crowned with glory."

At first glance the *Gospel* may disappoint us. As in other martyr Masses, we might have expected Christ's exhortation to take up our cross and follow Him; instead we find the allegory of the vine and the branches. But for what reason? It may be simply an historical coincidence. In ancient times the last part of St. John's Gospel was used as the *lectio continua* in paschal time. Today's Mass formulary undoubtedly dates to that period (see the Gospels for the Sundays after Easter and the feast of Sts. Philip and James).

A sensitive soul, however, will detect certain delicate relationships between martyrdom and this figure of the vine. Christ, the King of martyrs, is the Vine that entwined itself around a Cross; the martyrs are the ripe grapes hanging thereon. The Eucharistic wine, flowing from the wine-press of our Savior's passion, becomes the martyr's inebriating drink. In ancient Christian thinking the three concepts, Cross, Eucharist, and martyrdom, were so intimately related that one explained the other. In the Canon of the Mass, for instance, there are two lists of martyrs. Our Gospel provides pictorial explanation. Christ, the divine Vine clinging to the Cross, is likewise the Tree of life in the new paradise. The martyrs are the grapes hanging from the Vine; they have proven the Gospel true, for by remaining attached to Christ they have "brought forth much fruit," even the fruit of martyrdom.

We too are branches on the Vine, Christ. Now at Mass the life-giving sap of the Eucharist flows from the stem into the branches, so that we may "bring forth much fruit." The Vine unites us to the martyrs. And it is precisely in the Mass that this union is operative, for the Communion of Saints is a communion both of suffering and of consolation. See how the liturgy and patristics have made us understand the Gospel allegory.

At the *Offertory* God's great kingdom in heaven and on earth again praises, "confesses," and marvels at the wondrous work of the divine Vine. In the *Communion* we see our saint rejoicing at the heavenly banquet, while we, partaking of the Eucharistic Banquet, share his joy on earth. (Psalm 63 begins and concludes the Mass.) Note that most chants refer to the saint in the singular.

2. Mass for Several Martyrs *Sancti tui*

This second Mass is equally beautiful and edifying. With the *Introit* there rises a shout of praise from the "saints," (i.e., the martyrs, and we in union with them). This double choir proclaims the "glory of the kingdom" of Christ. Psalm 144 praises God (or Christ) for His goodness, greatness, fidelity. It is one of the finer psalms, although unfortunately it rarely occurs in the liturgy. What a beautiful picture the Introit sketches — Christ, the risen King, receiving the praises of His "confessors."

The theme continues in the *Epistle*. Through His resurrection Christ has procured for us an "incorruptible and unfading inheritance" in heaven. Toward this we are moving, even though it be through the dark valley of earthly trials and temptations; *modicum,* only a "little while," however, will these sorrows last. The gold must be purified by fire in preparation for the great day of "the revelation of Jesus Christ," a preview of which we experience with the martyrs at today's holy Mass. Again we see the holy martyrs in their lily-white garments; they are sweet like the odor of balsam, and their martyrdom precious in the sight of the Lord (*Allel.*).

The first three verses of the *Gospel* are identical with the final three verses of the preceding formulary. But taken as a whole, the emphasis is somewhat different. Christ is the divine Vine, and we the branches. It is a figure that touches the liturgy's very soul; there exists no consideration more profound. Both the saints and we enjoy organic union with Christ; from Him we draw the sap of divine life, the wine of the blessed Eucharist. From Him, the Vine, we receive strength to obey the commandments, and "to bring forth much fruit." (See comment on the previous Mass's Gospel.) Filled with Easter's joy, we proceed twice to the altar with the martyrs; once to die with Christ (*Off.*), and once to rise glorified with Him (*Comm.*).

In the Divine Office, too, martyrs receive special attention during Easter time; some of the shorter texts are particularly beautiful.

> His elect are gleaming white, alleluia;
> upon them shines God's glory, alleluia.
> They are white as milk, alleluia, alleluia.
> They are purer than snow, whiter than milk;
> they are more shimmering than old ivory,
> more beautiful than sapphire. (*Resp.*).

"Come forth, daughters of Jerusalem, and behold the martyrs and the crowns with which the Lord crowned them on this solemn, joyous day, alleluia, alleluia" (*Ben. Ant.*).

5. THE COMMON OF CONFESSORS

> Your loins should be girt,
> your hands should be holding lighted lamps.
> You should resemble servants
> who are awaiting their master
> as he returns from a wedding feast.

Be vigilant, for you do not know the hour
at which the Lord will return.

According to the Gospel ideal, a Christian is a confessor if
during the night of earthly life he "awaits the returning Lord
with girt loins and burning lamp in hand." This ideal is one
after which we are bound to strive.

The liturgy allows confessors four Commons, viz., the Common of Bishops, of Doctors of the Church, of Abbots, of other
Confessors.

A.   THE COMMON OF CONFESSOR-BISHOPS

There are two formularies in this Common. The first stresses
the gratuitous, divine election of the saint; the second emphasizes his priesthood.

1.   Mass *Statuit*

The bishop is the faithful "steward" of the divine fountain of
life in the Church, of God's revealed word, and of the sacraments.
In him Christ's priesthood finds its fullest extension. The celebrant of the Mass typifies or represents the bishop-saint commemorated. There is a mystic oneness between him, Christ, and the
priest at the altar. Repeatedly the Mass text correlates the priest's
actions and movements with the saint, and the saint with the
divine High Priest.

As the priest approaches the altar, it is our holy bishop whom
we see. The Church sings the praise of his divine election: "The
Lord entrusted to him the covenant of peace" (i.e., the treasures
of the Church); he is a prince in God's kingdom, a priest forever (*Intr.*). Psalm 131 follows, a reciprocal oath. David swears
to build a temple unto God, God swears to grant David the
throne forever. Of course, David here represents our saint-bishop
who zealously cared for the Church, and therefore receives an
eternal reward for himself and graces for the Church.

The *Lectio* praises the divinely wonderful selection of our sainted bishop. "See, before you there stands (in the person of the celebrant) the great high priest (our saint, and Christ too) who was pleasing to God during his life." He was the instrument of redemption unto many; his call is proclaimed in ringing words: "He gave him the crown of glory, He entered into an eternal covenant with him . . . that he should be His priest and praise His Name and present Him with a worthy incense offering, an agreeable and sweet-smelling odor." The message is re-echoed in the *Gradual*; in awesome wonder no new ideas are added, the text of the *Lectio* being simply repeated.

With the *Gospel* the divine High Priest stands before us, He who will consummate the offering "after the manner of Melchisedech." Typical of the *mysterium* character of ancient Mass formularies, the returning Lord calls for an accounting of talents entrusted to His followers. These talents are the graces of the priesthood; today, the day of his death, our bishop "enters into the joys of his Lord." We who have not received as many talents must still make good use of the two entrusted to us.

The Sacrifice proper now begins. At the altar table our sainted confessor is standing; as "David anointed with holy oil" he officiates in the Name of Christ; the "arm" of the divine High Priest supports him (*Off.*). Upon the altar we place all the hard-gained talents of our own efforts; then during the sacred offering "the Lord comes to His servants to demand an accounting as well as to confer the great reward." The pledge and earnest of that reward is the Eucharist; today our good bishop extends it to us during the Sacrifice-Banquet, for he is "the faithful steward whom the Lord placed over all His possessions and who now gives us our due measure of the divine wheat" (*Comm.*). Do not overlook the final Communion prayer. First we express our gratitude for the gifts received (rarely does the Postcommunion express thanksgiving) and then we ask for "greater blessings." Is there anything greater than the Eucharist? Only heavenly beatitude, the vision of God face to face!

2. Mass *Sacerdotes*

This formulary, which is used less frequently than the preceding one, shows more clearly how the priesthood is the extension of Christ's priestly dignity. Again today we see the saint commemorated approaching the altar in the person of the celebrant and offering the holy Sacrifice. There is an equation between the priest at the altar, the saint of the day, and our High Priest Christ. The Foremass is devoted to a consideration of the dignity of the priesthood. Our saint-bishop enters, clothed in the "garment of justice," the vestments of holy Mass. At his appearance we, "the saints," rejoice, for it is on his account that Christ Himself will now show His countenance. The oath in Psalm 131 involves mutual obligations; David, typifying our holy bishop, faithfully seeks the Church's welfare.

The *Epistle* teaches us the reason for a priest's high dignity; in him Christ, the eternal High Priest, manifests Himself. Through the priesthood "Christ lives on as a mediator for mankind." His sacrifice offered once — Himself as priest and sacrificial lamb — is reactualized in the Church through the priesthood. In a few words the Epistle tells the high significance of holy Mass and of the priestly office; also the strict duty of the priest to be "holy, innocent, undefiled, separated from sinners." Today's bishop-saint satisfactorily fulfilled this requirement; his salvation is indicated by the priestly vestments in which he is robed and over which we, "the saints," rejoice (*Grad.*).

In the *Gospel* the eternal High Priest appears; His entrance is greeted with a triple *Alleluia*. Again the Gospel sets the stage well for the Mass-mystery; our bishop is the "faithful and wise servant whom the Lord appoints over His family." "Until He comes" He gives us in type or proxy, i.e., through the priest who celebrates, the "meat" (doctrine and Eucharist) "in due season" (the present time). Today's holy bishop was found faithful at the Lord's advent, i.e., at his death; that advent we now commemorate by the anniversary Mass. Through participation we too become "watchful servants whom the Lord sets over all His possessions." The Eucharist is the pledge of these eternal possessions. Do not overlook how the *Communion* antiphon becomes intelligible only in context with the distribution of the holy Eucharist.

B.   THE COMMON OF DOCTORS

The formulary (*In medio*) from the Common of Doctors applies easily to the various types of saints who have been declared doctors of the Church. In the person of the celebrant the Church sees the particular saint-doctor commemorated today. As the priest (formerly the bishop) approaches the altar clothed in priestly vestments, we all sing: "In the midst of the Church God opens his mouth; the Lord fills him with wisdom and understanding; He clothes him with the garment of glory" (*Intr.*). Yes, today in our church a doctor of the Church speaks to us; he speaks to us through the voice of the celebrant. The priestly vestments symbolize the *stola gloriae,* the garment of his heavenly transfiguration. Using the words of Psalm 91 we praise God in His saint.

The *Collect* reminds us of the fact that our doctor-saint is a *doctor vitae* for us here upon earth — a teacher of life (i.e., how to live according to true wisdom, hence a physician of divine life), and at the same time an intercessor in heaven. In the *Epistle* we see the saint walking in the footsteps of St. Paul, a fearless, tireless soldier and herald of God's kingdom "in season and out of season." Today, the day of his death, is the Lord's parousia for him; today he might well say: "I have fought the good fight, I have finished my course . . . there is laid up for me a crown of justice which the Lord, the just Judge, will render to me in that day." With our saint we now relive "that day" in the holy Sacrifice. *Gospel*: the holy doctor is the salt of the earth, the city upon a mountain (we may think of the bishop enthroned in his cathedral), the lamp upon a candlestick in the Lord's house. Our little lamps must be lit from his. He is called "great" in the kingdom of heaven because he "does and teaches."

When we approach the altar carrying our gifts, our saint multiplies himself in us; he is the palm or cedar which is reproduced when we imitate him (*Off.*). While the *Communion* antiphon and psalm are sung, it is the doctor of the Church rather than the celebrant who distributes the Eucharist. With the eyes of the ancient Church we see the bishop performing his liturgical duties of preacher and priest; in the Foremass we hear him teaching; at the sacrificial Banquet he presides over the sacred meal; both, doctrine and Eucharist, are the divine wheat which the steward of God's family "wisely and faithfully" administers. This very day from the hands of the priest at the altar we receive that wheat according to the special spirit exemplified by the doctor-saint commemorated.

C.   THE COMMON OF ABBOTS

The Mass for the Common of Abbots (*Os justi*) borrows part from the Common of Bishops, part from the Common of Confessors; for abbots take a place midway between bishops and confessors. Among his own brethren the abbot is head and father; still he does not possess the full powers of jurisdiction and orders as bishops do. This is found expressed in the Mass; we see the abbot-saint as the faithful and wise steward who in due season administers the measure of wheat to his community (*Comm.*; the same verse occurs in the Common of Bishops and Doctors). The religious "leaves all things — home, brothers, sisters, father and mother and fields for the Lord's sake" and thereby complies most exactly with that evangelical counsel; he will accordingly share to a greater degree in the transfiguration of Christ's Second Coming (*Gosp.*). Today, the day of his death, he entered into glory; today he obtained "his heart's desire" upon receiving the "crown of precious stones" (*Grad., Off.*); it is a transfiguration in which we may share through the holy Sacrifice. The *Lesson* tells of our saint's elevation to the abbatial dignity in a mystery-enshrouded dialog between himself and God. The passage in the Bible refers to Moses; the comparison between Moses and an abbot has much to commend it.

D. THE COMMON OF CONFESSORS

This Common has two Mass formularies. The first seems to be more typical. Called the Mass of the "Vigilant Servant," it is more positive in content than the second, in which the ascetical aspect of Christian life, mortification, receives greater stress.

1. Mass *Os justi*

The Mass of the "Vigilant Servant" quite closely resembles the "Bridal Mass" in the Common of Virgins; both emphasize awaiting the Lord's return as essential to the Christian way of life. "The just man finds true wisdom in meditation" is the theme of the *Os justi* Mass (*Intr.*). The mysterium is that of the vigilant servant who "with girt loins and with burning lamp in hand awaits the Lord." Such was the life of the confessor-saint now honored; during the night of earthly life he was ever prepared for the journey home, the light of divine love always glowed brightly within him, his life was one long desire for the parousia. At death the Lord "knocked" and our saint "opened to Him immediately." "The Lord found him watching" and transported him to the heavenly banquet, there to "wait upon him" personally. Today at Mass we recall not only the day of the Lord's advent for our saint, but in the Eucharist his transfiguration assumes new glory, and we, united with him, meet the returning Lord. Thus we constitute the *dramatis personae* for the *Gospel*.

At the banquet table we witness the mystery unfolding itself further; the Lord knocks, we open to Him. He invites us to the wedding feast; *transiens ministrabit*, "passing by He ministers" to us. These words well describe the holy Eucharist — *passing by*, in contrast to the "eternal enjoyment of His divinity" in heaven. It is our task to "watch" as did our saint, with girt loins and burning lamp. Such response would be our guarantee to "stewardship over all His possessions." Here too one can see how expressive the *Communion* antiphon becomes when prayed in the perspective of the "Lord's Eucharistic coming."

The remaining texts of the Mass need no special explanation. Note, however, that the *Introit* text, "Do not envy evildoers," simply marks the beginning of the psalm (the passage itself has no connection with the feast). The *Lesson* describes the "Good Man" untouched by the lure of bribes or the enticement of money; now the *ecclesia sanctorum*, i.e., ourselves, praises his good works. The saint "flourishes like the palm" and "multiplies like the cedar of Lebanon" among those mystically united with him in the holy Sacrifice (*Grad.*). He was not spared the cross of suffering during life, and therefore at death and now again in the sacrifice of Calvary he receives the "crown of life" (*Allel.*).

2. Mass *Justus ut palma*

The two Masses in the Common of Confessors complement each other; the first emphasizes the positive, the second the negative requirements in professing the faith. The major theme in *Os justi* is that of the servant who with loins girt and burning lamp in hand awaits the returning Lord, i.e., preparation and longing for the parousia. In the second the primary notion is mortification and self-denial. The confessor commemorated detached himself from all the enticements of the world; he "left all to follow the Lord," a phrase from the Communion antiphon which could perhaps serve as title to the whole formulary. Text analysis is easy. Perhaps the walls of your church are decorated with palm trees; according to the *Introit* they would today represent our saint. In the *Epistle* he rises in our midst to speak; he makes a comparison between himself and us; it is a sad picture indeed, for we are yet so earthly-minded, ambitious, covetous, vain; while he, scorned as a fool, goes hungry, thirsty, the outcast of men. Yet the saint fears being too severe and exacting with us; he excuses himself, saying he only wanted to admonish us, his beloved children.

In the *Gospel* Christ says: "Fear not, My little flock. . . ." What consolation for us! They who want to follow the steep and narrow way after Christ will walk alone, because the great masses follow the broad highways of this world. The Gospel also counsels us: give up earthly goods; your treasure must be located in heaven. "Where your treasure is, there your heart will also be." While the faithful receive the Bread from heaven, Christ reveals the hundredfold reward reserved for those who have abandoned all to follow Him (*Comm.*). He is distributing to each the pledge and earnest of that reward.

6. THE COMMON OF VIRGINS

At midnight a cry was made:
See, the bridegroom comes!
Go out to meet him!
Wise virgins, trim your lamps.

This Common has four formularies, two for virgin-martyrs and two for virgins who were not martyrs.

1. Mass *Loquebar*

The first formulary tenders to the saint commemorated the double crown of martyrdom and virginity. Standing before us in the *Introit* our saint recounts her profession of faith: "Before kings I acknowledged Your testimony, I was not ashamed." Allusion is made also to the virgin's purity of heart: "I meditated upon Your commands, which I loved exceedingly," while the psalm verse praises her "immaculate way" of life. The *Lesson* is the martyr's prayer of thanks for her supreme victory over suffering: "I will glorify You, O Lord, O King; I will praise You, O God, my Savior . . . for You were my helper and protector. You preserved my body from destruction . . . from those who roared, ready to devour . . . from annihilation by the flames that surrounded me . . . therefore my soul will praise the Lord even unto death." It would seem that we were present in Rome's Colosseum watching the virgin consummate her martyrdom.

The *Gradual* and *Offertory* chants and the Gospel between them (on the wise virgins) feature the "bride theme." The

Church's bridal song, Psalm 44, tells the glories of Christ the Bridegroom and the Church His Bride; today's virgin-saint is one of the maidens in the royal retinue. The picture is embellished by the *Gospel*; here she becomes one of the five wise virgins who, having filled their lamps with the oil of virginal love, wait till the Bridegroom comes. He did come at her death; and at Mass we go to meet Him with lamps well filled under our virgin's leadership. At the *Offertory* we are the virgins who with today's saint (*post eam* . . . after her) are presented and offered (the old texts do not have *afferentur* but *offerentur*, hence a true offertory). With the *Communion* antiphon the liturgy again takes us to the scene of the martyrdom; again the saint speaks, giving testimony to God and professing her fidelity. In union with her and supported by Eucharistic strength, we try to make the same profession.

2. Mass *Me exspectaverunt*

The second formulary for a virgin-martyr differs from the first by giving greater prominence to the theme of martyrdom. In the *Introit* the day's martyr stands before us and we hear her pray: "The wicked waited for me . . . but I kept Your precepts in my heart." The *Lesson* is the saint's thanksgiving prayer upon triumphing over the ordeal: "O Lord, my God, You have exalted me to a dwelling high above the earth. I prayed that death should pass me by. I begged the Lord not to abandon me in my day of agony . . . I will praise Your Name forever . . . for You have snatched me from destruction."

In the *Gradual* the saint is compared to the city of Jerusalem besieged by enemies but still invincible: "The rush of the river means nought but joy to the city of God; for the Most High has sanctified His tabernacle." God who is in her soul will not permit her to waver. The "rush of the river" is her martyrdom, stirred up by hell. In the *Gospel* we follow the virgin as she seeks and finds the "hidden treasure" and the "pearl of great price." See, in exchange she gives all that earth can offer, even life itself. The bride-motif rings through the *Offertory*; we watch the holy virgin as she advances toward her Spouse in shining splendor (the altar is Christ; to it the faithful go with their Offertory gifts). The *Communion* antiphon affords the martyr a final opportunity to give witness to Christ; under her guidance and strengthened by the Eucharist, we too proclaim: "I hate all wicked ways."

3.   Mass *Dilexisti*

No other formulary in the Common betrays a prayer structure that so well develops a single theme. It is a genuine "bridal Mass." The Church, as the Lord's stainless Bride, appears in the person of the holy virgin whose feast we celebrate, who today stands in our midst in the *mysterium*. Moreover, she is a model for us, and more than a model — we enter into wondrous union with her, we become mystically one with her. This rapport may be detected in the various texts of today's Mass. The Gospel etches it in fine relief as it indicates the mystery; the saint (and we with her) are the virgin-spouses who during the night of this life remain ready with brightly burning lamps to meet the Bridegroom whenever He should come to the eternal wedding. The final reality takes place at the parousia (and at our death); but today at Mass it takes place by anticipation. Such are the implications of the text.

The route to church today is marked by a wedding procession; the saint leads, the faithful follow. Picture the festal march: the bishop, fully vested, proceeds to the altar; meanwhile Psalm 44, the Church's bridal song, is sung. Christ is the royal Bridegroom; the Church, the holy Virgin, myself, the royal bride. Yes, regard yourself as Christ's bride.

The *Epistle* continues the theme. We are again spoken of as brides of Christ. The divine Bridegroom is jealous of His bride. He will share His beloved treasure with no one; as an inviolate virgin must she be presented to her divine Spouse. Verses from Psalm 44 are to be found in all the chanted portions of the formulary. As the deacon in festal vestments proceeds with the Gospel book (i.e., Christ) to the ambo, we are again witnessing a wedding procession. There follows the *Gospel* with the beautiful parable of the five wise virgins (the five foolish ones do not form a part of the liturgical picture). It is we who are the virgins (the acolytes, holding lights while the Gospel is read, help us visualize this).

During the Sacrifice proper the Gospel becomes a reality; for at the *Offertory* procession we, virgin-brides, approach Christ (the altar is Christ). Our Offertory gifts are our oil-filled lamps, gifts to the Spouse. The bridal song is meanwhile chanted, occasioning new slants upon the familiar words; about the Queen richly appurtenanced we, the virgin-brides, are standing. At the consecration the Spouse makes His appearance; and at the Banquet we approach Him, *obviam Christo Domino* — Behold, the Bridegroom cometh! Open your hearts to Him! (Note the new turn in meaning the text receives after the consecration.) For the fourth time the bridal song is sung during the *Communion* procession.

4. Mass *Vultum tuum*

There is no essential difference between this formulary and the preceding ones. Here too the Church's bridal song, Psalm 44, is thematic. In the *Epistle* St. Paul shows the value of virginity in relation to the Second Advent: "The time is short." It will be virgins who will find it easier to give themselves wholly to the Lord. The *Gospel* may be either that of the wise virgins or the pearl of great price.

7. THE COMMON OF HOLY WOMEN

Holy women, too, viz., those who embraced the state of matrimony, particularly holy widows, have a special Common with two formularies, one for martyrs, another for non-martyrs.

1. Mass *Me exspectaverunt*

There is little difference between this formulary and those for virgin-martyrs; practically no text is wholly proper to it. The martyr leads us to the altar; we hear her pray: "The wicked have waited for me in order to destroy me . . . in my heart I have kept Your precepts." The *Lesson* is a beautiful prayer of gratitude sung by the martyr after her triumph over suffering: "I will glorify You, O Lord, O King . . . for You were my helper and protector. You preserved my body from destruction . . . from those who roared, ready to devour . . . from annihilation by the flames that surrounded me . . . therefore my soul will praise the Lord even unto death." Hearing these words we feel our-selves witnesses to the martyrdom.

The two following chants (*Grad*. and *Off*.) are culled from the Church's bridal song. In both we see the saint in the full attire of a bride worthy of God. The *Gospel* shows us how the martyr sought after and found the "hidden treasure," the "pearl of great price," i.e., the kingdom of God. To acquire this heav-enly treasure she divested herself of all earthly belongings, in-cluding life itself. Thus she paid the supreme price for it. In the *Communion* antiphon the saint again speaks. She tells how her enemies pursued her, while she feared God alone. Yes, she rejoiced over the kingdom of God as though she had found a great treasure. We too must feel these sentiments. The Eucharist gives us strength against the enemies of salvation; for us it is the one great treasure.

2. Mass *Cognovi*

This formulary for holy women expresses well two aspects of woman's nature, maidenly fervor and motherly foresight; vir-ginal love for Christ and courageous resolve; regard for material needs, yet ever rising above earthly attachments; carefree like Mary, yet careful about many things like Martha. The Mass begins, as is frequently the case, with a monolog by the day's saint. She glances back over her life; God had visited upon her many a sorrow, many a humiliation (widowhood, lack of ap-preciation for many sacrifices); now she acknowledges that all this was to her good and asks for an unbloody martyrdom.

The two Readings seem to stand in opposition to each other.

In the *Lesson* an ideal woman and wife is described, one who is wholly occupied with her manifold duties, one who provides for her husband, children, servants, and who has a kindly heart for the poor — a woman with both feet on the ground. The two parables of the *Gospel* (the hidden treasure and the pearl) show the woman whose heart is with Christ, the woman who surrenders all earthly things for the precious pearl of God's kingdom. It is our saint who understands how to combine harmoniously these seemingly contrary ideals, action and contemplation. The Lesson could serve as a good mirror for any woman. "A virtuous woman, where may she be found?" We have found her in today's saint. "Favor is deceitful, and beauty is vain; the woman who fears the Lord, she shall be praised."

The Gospel points out the reason for her greatness and her spiritual beauty; it is the "hidden treasure," i.e., her love for Christ. To us also does the Eucharist give direction and aid, both to find the treasure and zealously to perform our round of duties. The Eucharist keeps the fire of love for Christ aglow and it strengthens us to carry this fire abroad in the world. The Church's wedding hymn (Ps. 44) forms part of the three following chants; its theme, as we know, is the espousal of Christ to the Church. Does not our saint typify the Church, who is both Mother and Virgin? Do not the two Lessons reveal the nature of our Mother? Children should reflect their Mother's features.

THE DEDICATION OF A CHURCH

Annually the Church celebrates in a solemn manner the day commemorating the dedication of her churches in order to recall to the minds of the faithful the high dignity and sanctity and also the deep symbolism of the material edifice. She celebrates the dedication of the parish church, the cathedral church, and the four principal churches of Rome, the mother churches, we may call them, of Christendom.

Every parish church, then, celebrates two feastdays of its own each year, a namesday feast (patron saint) and a baptism feast (dedication). These two days should again be solemnized, using the means and inspiration provided in the liturgy. The house of God, the parish church, is dear to Christians for many reasons:

a) It is *the* house of prayer and *the* place of sacrifice for the whole congregation. Here the Triune God has set up His tent of grace and blessing. The altar signifies Christ and is to be considered the holiest spot in the structure. During the Sacrifice of Mass Christ personally enters this house and through His visitation our "salvation is again effected."

b) The parish church is the visible symbol of God's kingdom upon earth. Here Mother Church holds her official services; here her heart beats fastest for her Bridegroom Christ, as also for her children. The Church of Christ stands upon the foundation stones of the twelve apostles; of this fact the twelve crosses on the walls (the twelve places where the walls were anointed) are reminders. The parish priest should know the location of these holy crosses and have them marked by burning candles on the anniversary of the day of the dedication. The dignity and beauty of the material edifice should be a sign of the excellence and supreme importance of holy Mother Church.

c) The parish church is for us the gate of heaven, a foretaste of heaven, a preview of our heavenly home. The liturgy performed in the parish church continues the symbolism — much of its drama has its setting in heaven. The same holds true of the Office of Dedication, of many Masses during the ecclesiastical year, especially of the last Sundays after Pentecost. The entrance procession of priest and ministers to the altar is a figure of our journey heavenward (*Intr.* 18th, 23rd, 24th Sundays).

d) Lastly, the parish church symbolizes the individual Christian. This comparison was frequently used by the early Church Fathers to teach the sanctity of Christian life: "Do you not know that your body is the temple of the Holy Spirit, who lives in you?" Such symbolism is given beautiful expression in the dedication ceremonies of a church, for these rites in a very tangible way are modeled after the liturgy of baptism (exorcism, water specially consecrated, baptismal robes) and confirmation (anointing, invocation of the Holy Spirit, Mass with distribution of holy Communion). Here we find the reason for the imposition of a name and the celebration of the saint's day (titular); for if individual Christians celebrate their patronal feast, why not the parish body?

For understanding the Mass of Dedication two things must be kept in mind: (1) the liturgy identifies the anniversary and the actual day of consecration; (2) the material edifice as such represents the bride of Christ. Whenever we commemorate the consecration of a church, it is actually a feast *par excellence* of the Church that we are observing. The Dedication Mass is one of gratitude for all the favors and blessings that have come to us through the instrumentality of the Church. The text also stresses the rich symbolism of the house of God. Considered in itself, the edifice is most worthy of honor (*Grad.*) because (1) it has become the residence of God; and God has chosen it as the place for the distribution of His special graces (*Intr.*), as the place of sacrifice by the High Priest Jesus Christ (*Gosp.* and *Coll.*), and as the divinely appointed place of prayer (*Coll., Allel., Comm.*); (2) it represents the Catholic Church upon earth, Christ's immaculate Bride; (3) it is a symbol of the soul sanctified through baptism and the Eucharist (*Postc.*).

We enter the sacred edifice remembering that it has been solemnly consecrated by the bishop. Two seemingly contrary emotions well up within us, fear and joy. "How awe-inspiring is this place!" If we but realized that God has made this building the abode of His august presence! "Take off your shoes, for the place upon which you stand is holy ground," echoes in our ears, as from the burning bush. Psalm 83 in its entirety is most appropriate: "How lovely is Thy tabernacle, O Lord of hosts." What the temple was to the Jews, that and far more the church must be to us Christians (*Intr.*). Mother Church knows that here is the place for official, liturgical prayer; here God has promised to answer our petitions (*Coll., Comm.*).

Presently another picture unfolds before our eyes; we see Christ's bride magnificently adorned — the New Jerusalem —

descending from heaven (*Epist.*). Do not overlook the *mysterium* identity between the earthly and the heavenly: "*Today* has salvation come to this house!" This *today* must be taken literally. Not only on the occasion when the bishop first consecrated the church, *today* at the holy Sacrifice the Lord enters His tabernacle on earth, and we, poor publicans, are privileged to receive Him as guest. Remember that in spirit the Church repeats the day of consecration; that day's graces are reactivated today through the Mass mystery.

The awesome revelation of the Epistle echoes in the *Gradual*: This place is truly an unutterable mystery! The heart of Mother Church beats here! It is a temple peopled with choirs of angels! With them the faithful vie in the praise of the Lord their God (*Sanctus*).

With the *Alleluia* antiphon we turn and imagine the approach of Christ our King. Him we worship, Him we praise. The *Gospel* carries us back near the tax-gatherer's sycamore tree. With such joy, with such humility, with such a spirit of sacrifice as Zachaeus had, we too want to gaze upon the Lord. "See, half of all my goods do I give to the poor." In a like spirit let us come to the *Offertory*, and its antiphon will put our oblation into words. It is a prayer that David composed when he dedicated to God the funds and the materials he had gathered for the construction of the temple.

The *Secret* implies a "perfect oblation of body and soul." In the holy Sacrifice Christ comes into this building, the parish church, into this temple which is my soul, and says: "This day is salvation come to this house." In the *Communion* antiphon the Lord promises to answer all petitions made in "His house," while Mother Church straightway fulfills that promise and gives us the holy Eucharist as the guarantee of every needed gift and grace. The *Postcommunion* regards the material structure as a symbol of the spiritual edifice constructed from "living and predestined stones"; we petition that the excellence of the visible edifice may be signal of an ever-increasing invisible magnificence.